PERSON-CENTRED PSYCHOPATHOLOGY

a positive psychology of mental health

Edited by

Stephen Joseph and Richard Worsley

PCCS BOOKS
Ross-on-Wye

First published in 2005

PCCS BOOKS Ltd
3 Thomas Row
Alton Road
Ross-on-Wye
Herefordshire
HR9 5LB
UK
Tel +44 (0)1989 763 900
www.pccs-books.co.uk

**Person-Centred Psychopathology: A positive psychology of
mental health**

A CIP catalogue record for this book is available from the British Library

ISBN 1 898059 69 1

Cover design by Old Dog Graphics
Printed by Bath Press, Bath, UK

CONTENTS

To my parents, Clifford and Anne.

S.J.

To Chris, our children and our parents for their love and support.

R.W.

ACKNOWLEDGEMENTS

We would like to thank Pete Sanders for his guidance and suggestions along the way, and without whom this book would not have happened. We would also like to thank Sandy Green for her editorial work and attention to detail. Thank you. Our thanks also to our colleagues here at the University of Warwick in the counselling service and the psychology department for their support. Our thanks also to our students and trainees who have taught us so much, but most of all our thanks to all of our clients over the years from whom we have learned so much.

PREFACE

STEPHEN JOSEPH AND RICHARD WORSLEY

Person-centred theory is a meta-theoretical perspective to understanding the human condition. It is a radical and revolutionary perspective that is founded on the assumption that human beings have an inherent tendency towards growth, development and optimal functioning. But these do not happen automatically. For people to actualise their inherent optimal nature they require the right social environment. Without the right social environment the inherent tendency towards growth can become thwarted and usurped, leading instead to psychological distress and dysfunction. The assumption that human beings have an inherent tendency towards growth, development and optimal functioning serves as the guiding principle for client-centred therapeutic practice, even when working with people who are deeply distressed.

Person-centred theory is often misunderstood as superficial and naïve. But nothing could be further from the truth. It is a theory with real depth, which is able to confront both the dark side of the human condition as well as the positive aspects. Person-centred theory therefore promises to provide the foundation stone for a new positive psychology of mental health.

Stephen is a psychologist who embraces person-centred theory for grounding his practice and research, and building his theoretical perspectives. He believes that person-centred personality theory offers us the best psychological perspective we have yet of the human condition and a preferable alternative paradigm to the medical model for understanding human distress. Person-centred theory raises questions about our fundamental assumptions about human nature and about the values we hold as professional psychologists, counsellors, and psychotherapists. His purpose over the last few years has been to help begin to bring the ideas of the Person-Centred Approach back into mainstream psychological practice.

Richard's background is as a practitioner and a trainer. He has long been struck by the fact that even beginning counsellors have to make sense of the experiences of a wide range of clients, some of whom present with challenging issues. Both for trainee counsellors and for mature practitioners, the question hovers at the back of the mind: Is my approach adequate to the task? In multidisciplinary settings, the Person-Centred Approach can get a bad press in this respect. Richard has become keen to advocate the approach as a competent and humane way of being. He has learned much from his clients, but above all that the human spirit, rooted in the organism which is our embodied selves, has vast reserves with which to cope creatively in the face of seemingly overwhelming distress.

This book stands for both of us as a learning about, and an assertion of, the human capacity to grow in the face of adversity. We hope that practitioners, trainers, and those in training in the varied mental health professions will also find the learning and the wisdom in this book of value to them.

Stephen Joseph
Richard Worsley

Warwick, 1st March, 2005

CHAPTER 1

PSYCHOPATHOLOGY AND THE PERSON-CENTRED APPROACH: BUILDING BRIDGES BETWEEN DISCIPLINES

STEPHEN JOSEPH AND RICHARD WORSLEY

Over recent decades the Person-Centred Approach has become a major force in the world of counselling and psychotherapy. However, within the world of psychology and psychiatry, the Person-Centred Approach has become increasingly marginalised and often viewed by practitioners as a superficial approach to therapy that has little or no relevance to helping people with severe and chronic psychological problems. We believe however that the Person-Centred Approach has much to offer in how we work with people with a wide range of psychological problems, not just the so-called worried well, but also those with severe and chronic psychological problems.

The term 'psychopathology' refers to the study of unusual, distressing and dysfunctional psychological conditions. Most psychiatric and psychological texts on psychopathology make no mention of the Person-Centred Approach, and anyone training in psychiatry or psychology would be forgiven for assuming that the Person-Centred Approach could not help people with severe and chronic psychological problems. This is not a surprising state of affairs because the Person-Centred Approach does not adopt the medical model to understanding psychopathology and does not make the assumption that there are specific disorders requiring specific treatments. Insofar as practitioners in psychology and psychiatry do make this assumption and their textbooks are written around each of the different so-called disorders we can see why the Person-Centred Approach has become marginalised when it comes to understanding psychopathology. Some person-centred practitioners have indeed revelled in living on the edges, taking great satisfaction in the radical nature of the paradigm. However, this stance has also hampered communication and respect between different disciplines.

For too long in our view the person-centred community has isolated itself and allowed itself to become marginalised. By not speaking the language of psychiatry and psychology we cannot clearly articulate answers to those in the psychiatric and psychological profession about how the Person-Centred Approach can be used with people with severe and chronic psychological problems. Pete Sanders (2004) has also drawn attention to how the person-centred community has been largely unresponsive to calls from the National Institute for Clinical Excellence (NICE) to comment on the management of various so-called psychiatric disorders. NICE advises the government on who should be funded, and without the active engagement of the person-centred community in collecting and disseminating evidence for the effectiveness of person-centred approaches, we should expect the Person-Centred Approach to become further isolated.

We are not advocating adopting psychiatric or psychological techniques to practice. Even less are we condoning the medical model as a basis for understanding distress and dysfunction. What we are saying is that we think we have a duty to understand our psychological and psychiatric colleagues—what it is they do and why they do it, so that in turn we have the language to be able to articulate clearly to them what it is we do and why we do it. We realise that many counsellors and psychotherapists tend not to use psychiatric terms for ideological, social and political reasons. For sure, we agree that it is not a trivial issue how we label the phenomena that we are attempting to describe, but we also know that if you want to be understood sometimes you have to go to where the other person is and talk to them there. For this reason, we have asked our contributors to talk to us about the Person-Centred Approach in relation to the professions of psychology and psychiatry, the medical model and the various so-called psychiatric disorders, and issues of assessment and diagnosis.

The point is simply to illustrate that most of these 'psychiatric disorders' are terms used by psychologists and psychiatrists to give themselves a common language with which to communicate to each other about best practice as they see it. As counsellors and psychotherapists we can use the language of psychiatry and psychology to help us communicate to a wider audience, and to reach the new generation of psychologists and psychiatrists. This is particularly apposite at a time when the medical model is being questioned more widely, particularly in areas of clinical psychology (see, for example, Bentall, 2003; Maddux, Snyder and Lopez, 2004). We hope that those reading the book and who are unfamiliar with the psychiatric literature might become empowered by what our contributors have achieved.

Before we introduce the contributions themselves, let us first say a little more about the world of psychology and psychiatry, and the medical model. In the same way that psychologists and psychiatrists often misunderstand the Person-Centred Approach, person-centred practitioners often misunderstand psychological and psychiatric ways of thinking.

In an attempt to classify the different 'abnormal' psychological conditions, the American Psychiatric Association has produced what is called the *Diagnostic and Statistical Manual of Mental Disorders* (*DSM*). The roots of this system go back to the turn of the century and a German doctor called Kraepelin who in the late 19th century observed that some symptoms tended to occur together leading him to develop early classifications of mental disease. The DSM was first introduced in 1952 (*DSM-I*), followed by revised editions in 1968 (*DSM-II*), 1980 (*DSM-III*), 1987 (*DSM-III-R*), and is now in its fourth edition (*DSM-IV*) (American Psychiatric Association, 1994, 2000). The DSM is a voluminous work running to many hundreds of pages.

The DSM is the reference work used by psychiatrists as a basis for their diagnoses of psychiatric disorders. *DSM-IV* lists almost 300 separate disorders defined in terms of their observable symptoms. The disorders are further grouped into several major categories. It is beyond the scope of this book to go into detail on all of the separate so-called disorders.

In psychiatric terms, a disorder is something that people either have or don't have, and this serves various legal and medical purposes. Thus, a person who consults a psychiatrist or psychologist may be diagnosed as suffering from a psychiatric disorder. But we must be aware that although the legal and medical purposes might be served by the idea of a discontinuity between so-called normality and abnormality, in scientific terms whether there is a discontinuity or continuity between normality and abnormality is not always clear. In many instances, it is probably more accurate to conceptualise the experiences that constitute the so-called disorders as lying along a continuum, ranging from low levels of distress and dysfunction to high levels of distress and dysfunction. It is important to understand this because, despite DSM, most psychologists and psychiatrists are open to the view that psychopathology is often an extreme of normal behaviour, and the dividing line between the two is somewhat arbitrary (see, for example, Johnson, 1994, for a psychodynamically and psychiatrically informed exploration of the continuity between the normal and the non-normal). The truth is that we really don't understand that much about the nature of so-called 'psychiatric disorders', if some are continuous with normal behaviour while others are discontinuous, and what DSM provides is a common language which allows psychologists and psychiatrists to talk to each other and conduct research based on the assumption that there is a need for specific treatments for specific disorders. It is useful as a tool for communication but is by no means value-neutral.

This latter idea, that there are specific treatments for specific disorders, is the medical model. Psychiatrists and psychologists adopt the medical model to understand psychological problems. The idea is that in the same way that physical disorders can be classified, then so too can mental disorders. We recognise, for example, that a sore throat is a different condition from a skin rash. Both have different causes and consequently different treatments are applicable to each. So if a person goes to their doctor with a throat infection they might expect treatment with an antibiotic whereas if they had a skin rash they might expect treatment with hydrocortisone cream. If doctors did not distinguish between a throat infection and a skin rash and their different causes they would not be able to provide differential treatment. That's the basic idea behind the medical model. There is nothing wrong with the medical model per se, what we don't know is the extent to which it extends to understanding psychopathology.

In the medical model, psychological problems are seen as analogous to physical problems in terms of there being a need to identify the specific treatments for the specific conditions. Thus, in the same way that it is useful to distinguish a skin rash from a sore throat, it is useful to distinguish, say, depression from anxiety, and depression from post-traumatic stress, and anxiety from post-traumatic stress, and obsessive compulsive behaviour from depression, and so on. Therefore the point of the DSM is to facilitate communication between health professionals which in turn enables research programs to be carried out into the causes of these different conditions and which therapeutic interventions work with particular disorders. If different psychological problems are caused by different factors then it is important for researchers not to lump all psychological problems together but rather to look at separate psychological problems in relation to the different factors. The question is whether or not the various 'psychological disorders' are somehow different in the same way that you might say that a sore throat is different from a stomach upset, and thus require differential treatment. The client-centred school of thought says not. But to those outside the client-centred school such a stance is simply seen as unsophisticated and naïve. It is just not understood that person-centred theory provides an alternative paradigm to the medical model.

As already mentioned above, little has been written from the client-centred school of thought about the various so-called disorders. This is not surprising given that person-centred therapists have tended not to adopt the language of psychiatry, and do not make the assumption that specific conditions require specific treatments (see Bozarth, 1998; Bozarth and Motomasa, Chapter 19, this volume). Although the fact that writers in the person-centred tradition have been largely silent on the subject of psychiatric disorders is not surprising, it has meant that Client-Centred Therapy has become marginalised from mainstream psychological and psychiatric approaches. What has not been made explicit is how person-centred theory provides a conceptual underpinning to Client-Centred Therapy with people who would otherwise be considered as suffering from many of the 'psychiatric disorders'. We think it is important that any psychological therapy used to treat people suffering from a particular psychological condition is based on a clear theoretical conceptualisation of why the problem has developed and how the therapy works to alleviate the problem. Theory needs therefore to be able to account for: (1) the phenomenology associated with the concept of the disorder, i.e., does person-centred theory explain how the experiences characteristic of the disorder develop? and (2) reduction in symptoms through therapy.

Person-centred personality theory holds that psychological problems develop as a result of an internalisation of conditions of worth (Rogers, 1959). Through providing a social environment marked by unconditional acceptance, the conditions of worth dissolve, decline or are reconfigured. Rogers writes of how in his experience he found that whatever the client's problem was, whether it was to do with distressing feelings or troubling interpersonal relations, all were struggling with the same existential question: of how to be themselves. This is of course a very brief account of how psychopathology is usually conceptualised by person-centred theorists. To what extent can person-centred personality theory account for the range of psychopathology that is described in the DSM? We can't simply assume that person-centred theory can explain everything, and we certainly can't expect other health professionals who hold the medical-model view, to take us seriously when we don't provide theory and evidence.

CONTENT OF THE BOOK

In this book we have asked a range of internationally known authors who are able to cross the bridge and talk about their work in such a way as to show readers from the disciplines of psychology and psychiatry how the Person-Centred Approach deals with psychopathology, and which shows person-centred practitioners and trainees how the

Person-Centred Approach tackles some of the issues faced by psychologists and psychiatrists. We are left facing a number of questions. Are all psychiatric diagnoses explicable by the person-centred model or is there a boundary to what the person-centred model can explain? Is Person-Centred Therapy useful even if the theory is not able to explain the disorder? Are there some problems that are simply outside the scope of Person-Centred Therapy? Why is it exactly that the person-centred community does not adopt this language of psychology and psychiatry? Is person-centred theory an exclusive approach, or is it an inclusive approach? What are the implications of the person-centred model for assessment and diagnosis? What are the wider implications of the person-centred model to the community and to society in how we understand psychological suffering? What are the experiences of being a person-centred therapist in the context of mainstream psychology and psychiatry? These are the questions we challenged our contributors to tackle.

In the second chapter of this introduction section, Catherine Clarke shares with us her and her family's experiences of the mental health system. These are her and her family's experiences and although we would not want to claim that they are representative experiences of everyone who goes through the mental health system, they are a powerful testimony to the hurtful experiences of some and the need people have to feel valued and listened to within the healthcare system. In the third chapter, Pete Sanders raises some very interesting issues about the relationship we have with mainstream psychology and psychiatry; whether we ought to find ways to work collaboratively and alongside in the danger that we lose our values and identity, or whether we adopt a stance of principled opposition to the medicalisation of human distress even if it has negative consequences for us.

Moving into theory, Paul Wilkins addresses the major criticisms that have been made of the Person-Centred Approach, that it is not suitable for people with serious problems, and that it lacks a theory of personality development. Paul shows us that these criticisms are unfounded and that person-centred theory provides a substantial foundation for understanding psychopathology and its development. In Chapter 5, Mick Cooper presents his work on extending person-centred thinking to understand psychopathology drawing on recent developments in self-theory and his work as an existential therapist. Following on a similar theme in Chapter 6, Peter Schmid discusses the role of authenticity and alienation and how these concepts are at the core of the Person-Centred Approach to psychopathology. Margaret Warner then argues that person-centred theory offers a model of human functioning that is relevant to all of clinical psychology and the social sciences. It generates particular insights into the human qualities that should be central to all humane mental health practice.

Putting theory into practice, Lisbeth Sommerbeck discusses the conflict between the values of psychiatry and the Client-Centred Approach, and how she has been able to resolve the inevitable conflictual issues that arise for her as a client-centred therapist working in a psychiatric setting by drawing on complementarity theory. Paul Wilkins provides an overview of the role of diagnosis and assessment and in light of criticisms over their use, he discusses person-centred theory and what that offers us in thinking about assessment. Finally, Richard Worsley discusses the question of evil, and how we might think about this concept as a way into talking about the impact of client material upon practitioners.

The Person-Centred Approach has applicability in many clinical contexts, and the next set of chapters explores this. Dion Van Werde discusses his practical experience working in a residential psychiatric setting with people who have problems which might be described as psychotic. Leslie McCulloch discusses antisocial personality disorder, examining this category from a variety of perspectives, before turning to show how the Person-Centred Approach provides us with understanding and a way of working with these issues. Following this, Stephen Joseph discusses person-centred theory and how it is able to provide us with an understanding of post-traumatic stress, and how this resonates with other theories of post-traumatic stress. Elaine Catterall discusses maternal depression, the various theoretical perspectives and her personal experiences, before going on to show how Person-Centred Therapy can fit within a multidisciplinary way of working with women. Jan Hawkins reviews the literature on child abuse and its effects, showing how the effects can be wide-ranging and long-lasting, and then discusses the role person-centred practitioners can play in working with survivors of abuse. Marlis Pörtner discusses the important role that Person-Centred Therapy can have when working with people with special needs. It is important not to pathologise people with special needs, and we must also recognise and understand their impairments and limitations. Similarly, Jacky Knibbs and Heather Moran discuss their work with children and young people who are diagnosed with Asperger syndrome and autism. Drawing on first-hand accounts of living with these conditions, they point to the importance of understanding the child's world. Finally, Gillian Proctor discusses the historical roots of clinical psychology as a profession and how it relates to person-centred principles, going on to share her experience of working as a clinical psychologist who specialises in Client-Centred Therapy, and how she has been able to manage the conflict between the two hats she wears as a practitioner.

Turning to research, Jerold Bozarth and Noriko Motomasa summarise the psychotherapy research literature, strongly making the case for the role of the relationship rather than technique, and showing that the evidence is behind Person-Centred Therapy. Barbara Brodley asks us to think carefully about how we use research findings to bolster our practice reminding us that although research is important, what we do is also a value-based activity. Lisbeth Sommerbeck presents an evaluation of Client-Centred Therapy in psychiatric settings, paying attention to the famous Wisconsin project carried out by Rogers and his colleagues. Lisbeth shows us that although the findings from this project are often used by critics of the Person-Centred Approach to justify the claim that Person-Centred Therapy is not appropriate with certain client groups, the research itself was flawed in many respects, and thus although we have many lessons to learn from it, it is going beyond the data to claim that this is evidence against Client-Centred Therapy. Finally in this section, Richard Worsley discusses his own venture into the world of qualitative research and encourages us to look at research not only in terms of what we can learn professionally, but also personally.

We have aimed to bring together writers who, although all recognising the value of the Person-Centred Approach as a way of helping, have a variety of different perspectives. We have learned a great deal from reading their work and editing their chapters. Our hope is that the contributions in the book will serve to fuel debate and further research and writings on the topic of person-centred psychopathology. The Person-Centred Approach is an alternative to the medical-model approach, and we have no doubt ourselves that application of the Person-Centred Approach could be much wider than it currently is. But we also recognise that there are social, political and financial forces operating against the expansion of the Person-Centred Approach, and that the person-centred movement must make its voice heard if it is to continue to make inroads into new territories.

We also recognise that although applications of the Person-Centred Approach could be much wider, it is unlikely that the person-centred movement has the solutions to all of the problems experienced by all people all of the time. Some problems may have neuropsychological or biochemical deficits at their origin and require medical intervention. Nevertheless, even where person-centred personality theory may not be appropriate as an explanation for aetiology, Person-Centred Therapy may still be an effective way of helping the person live more fully with their problems.

We intend this book to be useful to person-centred practitioners and trainees in providing a source of understanding of how the Person-Centred Approach speaks to the more severe and chronic problems of living. These are the sorts of issues and problems we are told by the psychiatric and psychological establishment that are beyond the remit of Person-Centred Therapy. We also hope that practitioners and trainees of other disciplines will find the perspectives of our contributors thought-provoking. The full significance of the Client-Centred Approach is that it promotes a positive psychological understanding of how therapy is always focused equally on the facilitation of growth and development of human potential as well as the alleviation of distress and dysfunction.

The Person-Centred Approach to understanding psychopathology and therapeutic effectiveness in relation to the specific so-called 'disorders' has received little research attention. Person-centred therapists have not always valued the ideas underlying evidence-based practice and what they see as the inappropriate medicalisation of therapy. Theirs is a phenomenological stance where they are interested in the experience of the client as defined by the client. Thus, research questions from the person-centred perspective are not shaped around psychiatric disorders. However, if person-centred psychotherapy is not to continue to be marginalised within mainstream psychology, the onus must be on person-centred therapists to build stronger bridges with other approaches. It is hoped that this book will help to build bridges between practitioners of different approaches and that it will act as an encouragement to those phenomenologically-based person-centred practitioners to conduct research and theoretical work in this area.

REFERENCES

American Psychiatric Association (2000) *Diagnostic and Statistical Manual of Mental Disorders – text revision* (4th ed). Washington, DC: American Psychiatric Association.

American Psychiatric Association (1994) *Diagnostic and Statistical Manual of Mental Disorders* (4th ed). Washington, DC: American Psychiatric Association.

Bentall, R (2003) *Madness Explained: Psychosis and human nature*. London: Allen Lane.

Bozarth, JD (1998) *Person-Centred Therapy: A revolutionary paradigm*. Ross-on-Wye: PCCS Books.

Johnson, SM (1994) *Character Styles*. New York: WW Norton and Co.

Maddux, JE, Snyder, CR and Lopez, SJ (2004) Towards a positive clinical psychology: Deconstructing the illness ideology and constructing an ideology of human strengths and potential. In PA Linley and S Joseph (eds) (2004) *Positive Psychology in Practice* (pp. 320–34). Hoboken, NJ: John Wiley.

Rogers, CR (1959) A theory of therapy, personality and interpersonal relationships, as developed in the client-centered framework. In S Koch (ed), *Psychology: A Study of a Science, Vol. 3: Formulations of the person and the social context* (pp. 184–256). New York: McGraw Hill.

Sanders, P (2004) Panic now: Avoid the rush. *Person to Person*, January, 2004.

CHAPTER 2

A CARER'S EXPERIENCE OF THE MENTAL HEALTH SYSTEM

CATHERINE CLARKE

My experience of the mental health system started in the mid 80s, when I was concerned that my son was dyslexic and I requested a consultation with a specialist. The specialist informed me that he wasn't dyslexic—despite my son receiving no tests—and I was told that I was worrying unnecessarily which did not help my son or alleviate my growing concerns about my son.

My son was highly intelligent and exceptionally gifted in chemistry. His peers repeatedly teased him by calling him a 'boffin' and his discomfort was heightened when a teacher jibed at his intelligence. He had few friends and my son began to struggle with getting up to go to school. When I was at my wit's end to know how to help him, I requested an appointment with a psychiatrist.

Both my son and I were seen separately. He was acutely distressed after each appointment and refused to see the psychiatrist again. The situation at school continued in the same vein yet despite his distress he obtained nine GCSEs at top grades. Two years later, however, on the first day of his A-level exams, he told me that he had absconded and spent the day cycling in the country.

That autumn found him at an Adolescent Unit, diagnosed with depression and anxiety. With the help of the unit psychologist, he became less withdrawn and more interactive—making friends with a fellow patient. Because of his age[1] he was discharged, and returned home without any psychological support in the community. On challenging the GP about the absence of support, I angrily demanded, 'So, what do I do now? Bring him back when he is thirty?' There was no reply.

My husband and I encouraged our son to go to college and he passed three A-levels with high grades and was accepted at university to read chemistry. However, his levels of anxiety were so high in the presence of other people, that within a few weeks he withdrew from the course. Two years later on a second attempt, he withdrew again.

Meanwhile he was prescribed various antidepressants and was referred to a psychiatrist in another health authority who arranged a place at an anxiety management group. My son was unable to tolerate the stress he experienced in this situation and after a few sessions stopped attending. The NHS responded by letter, stating that since my

Note: All names have been changed and details modified so that no person is identifiable.

1. He was too old for the unit, having turned eighteen.

son was not bothering to attend the group, his place would be given to another patient who would be more appreciative. The underlying message was clear—because my son failed to attend appointments, they were shelving all their responsibility towards him. It was almost as if they had come to the end of the line of their expertise of help and care. No member of the psychiatric team had contacted my son to find his reason for non-attendance or taken any interest in how he experienced the anxiety management group. Yet again, my son was left to cope with his difficulties without professional help. I felt that the system had deserted both of us. I realised that the task of helping my son with his difficulties in functioning adequately within the adult world was once more on my shoulders.

In 1994, through my encouragement, he began to work on a voluntary basis, acting as an escort, taking the elderly to local clubs. Initially he found the work difficult. However the elderly people had a high regard for his thoughtfulness and care, which he instinctively showed towards each individual. His confidence grew and he increased his involvement in this line of work.

In 1997 he was employed as a trainee butcher, with the full assurance of being trained as a butcher. He worked hard to learn the ropes. As the days went by, he became aware that his position would be terminated when the head butcher, following chemotherapy treatment, returned to work. My son was dismissed on Christmas Eve, six weeks after commencing. Feeling deceived, his depression returned. As his depression deepened he was prescribed Prozac. As the Prozac dose was increased, he began to experience vivid nightmares and acted on them is if they were reality-based—giving a large sum of money to charity. I later read that nightmares are amongst the adverse effects of Prozac.

Another unwanted effect of Prozac is psychotic experiencing, and in the year 2000, my son's acute psychotic crisis experience led us both into the next stage—the inner world of the mental health system.

My husband had lain awake all night listening to my son having verbal conversations about religion in his bedroom. Our offer of help was angrily refused and fearing that this situation had the potential of becoming violent, I sent my youngest son down the road to a friend. I waited for the surgery to open to contact the GP. The receptionist told me I would have to wait until surgery finished—another three hours. In the interim period my son tore out of his bedroom, hurtled down the stairs, shrieking and screaming in terror. I was terrified and hid behind the sitting room door, dialling 999. My husband led my son into the kitchen and managed to reassure him. On our drive stood three police cars and an ambulance. I just shook from head to toe with shock as I went out to speak with the police.

When the GP arrived, she seemed more concerned about our impingement on her off-duty time than with our situation. She gave a prescription for Diazepam 2mg tablets and called out the crisis team. We tiptoed round the house, speaking in whispers and wondering if my son would explode again.

After four hours, the crisis team arrived. They seemed efficient and escorted us to the acute ward. A nurse took charge of my son and he was led away from us with her words ringing in my ears—'You may see your son provided he gives permission.' My heart sank. I had cared for my son for twenty-five years and here was this stranger who appeared to be severing my connection with my son. I thought she was callous and cold. I felt dismissed, bewildered and hurt. I asked for the ward phone number and we left.

That initial experience set the tone for me. I lay awake that night and resolved to be as fully involved as possible in the care of my vulnerable son. My son had entered this inner world of the mental health system. And so had I. My commitment to be alongside my son enabled me to learn and inwardly digest the intricate subtleties and nuances of the mental heath system.

Whilst he was an in-patient I telephoned frequently to enquire how he was doing and visited him daily. We discovered that the psychiatrist made all the decisions at the ward round, which my husband and I thereafter attended even though it disrupted our working commitments. In these meetings, it was often the case that the nurse presenting my son's psychiatric state had very little to do with my son and occasionally had not been in contact with him at all.

Within two weeks the Responsible Medical Officer (RMO) diagnosed schizophrenia. He discontinued Prozac abruptly and began treatment with an atypical neuroleptic. The pharmacologist stated that he would have to take medication for at least twelve months. We weren't informed about adverse effects—we learnt about these as the neuroleptics took a hold over my son.

My son was discharged after three weeks. I was relieved. He seemed all right and was pleased to return home and be back in his familiar surroundings. My complacency was short-lived, for three weeks later he experienced his second crisis. On walking to the ward my son suddenly surfaced into our shared reality and asked whether he was schizophrenic. I was distraught and avoided answering his question.

Initially I had trusted the mental health professionals with their knowledge of schizophrenia together with their psychiatric treatment, but in the following months as my son launched from one crisis to another I began to feel insecure and uneasy about the treatment he was receiving. His quality of life was poor and so was mine. What I couldn't understand was why on earth hadn't the medication been effective for him.

I began my own research into schizophrenia and neuroleptic treatment. The research I discovered contained information which professionals had failed to disclose to either my son or myself. On reading how the neuroleptics were impacting on my son's central nervous system, I felt a deep sense of revulsion. I could not believe what the treatment was doing to my son's brain tissue and it took me many weeks before I could fully take in all of this information. My trust in the mental health system plummeted to rock bottom.

The many crises my son was experiencing appeared to fit in with the academic literature about Super Sensitivity Psychosis (SSP). I realised that my son's extreme sensitivity to medication resulted in him being over-medicated and the neuroleptics were actually inducing and perpetuating his psychosis. The prevailing psychiatric belief that neuroleptics are *anti*-psychotics appeared not to be the case for my son.

11

When I took this factual research for my son's Multi Disciplinary Team (MDT) members to read, professional people would not give their opinion on it, despite it appearing extremely relevant to their neuroleptic treatment of my son. Invariably his SSP crisis resulted in the RMO attributing it to a 'relapse'—a worsening of his illness and further evidence of schizophrenia. His medication was either increased or changed to a different neuroleptic. It all seemed so random, rather like neuroleptic roulette.

When my son realised the neuroleptics were having a negative effect on his quality of life, he tried to withdraw from neuroleptics. My husband and I supported him. Due to our ignorance of neuroleptic withdrawal, he experienced a psychosis. The RMO regarded this psychosis as still further proof that my son needed to be medicated— giving the psychiatrist additional weight to his prescribing even more neuroleptic treatment. I perceived that this psychosis was connected with withdrawal and in line with my research into tardive psychosis. My son had basically gone 'cold turkey'.

On another occasion when the RMO withdrew my son's Lorazepam too abruptly, he began to experience psychotic symptoms within twelve hours. On a different occasion, six weeks after being admitted into a closed unit my son began to despair that he would ever see his home again. He became acutely distressed and experienced greater trauma through hallucinations. The MDT attributed my son's psychosis to his schizophrenic illness, to the exclusion of any other possible rationale.

In the same way that every psychotic episode was attributed to the presence of 'schizophrenic illness', the ward staff and professionals moulded my son's behaviour into the disease symptomatology. Negative symptoms[2] were also attributed to 'the disease'. For example, the RMO repeatedly stated that my son's deadpan expression was the negative mask of schizophrenia. Each time I would patiently point out that he had a facial paralysis resulting from an ear tumour. My son became overwhelmed during the ward rounds—his body shook violently and he became mute. The nurses believed that these were further negative symptoms of schizophrenia. I pointed out my son only shook in the presence of a group of people, because of his increased anxiety.

Another 'negative symptom' related to my son's lack of personal hygiene. I queried whether any MDT member had taken an interest in asking what difficulty my son was experiencing with his hygiene. On asking my son, I discovered he was reluctant to bath because the towels did not dry effectively and there was no change of clean clothing. These are all valid apsychotic reasons for not bathing and at that particular time had nothing at all to do with negative symptoms.

My son experiences difficulty in making 'small talk'. The MDT classified his withdrawn and antisocial behaviour as part of the negative symptomatology. I repeatedly emphasised that my son has Asperger syndrome and his preference to avoid socialising is an Asperger trait. My son spoke fluently and intelligently about Formula-One racing, and stocks and shares, when interest was shown in engaging with him about these topics. The emphasis on symptomatology seemed to distract the professionals from

---

2. Negative symptoms include apathy, lack of motivation, emotional flattening, withdrawn behaviour, difficulty in concentration and cognitive functioning and reduced curiosity.

taking an interest and seeing my son as a whole person in his own right. It seemed as though they couldn't see beyond the disease.

He was quizzed about voices and odd thoughts on a daily basis. This has posed problems since, having Asperger syndrome, my son interprets verbal communication literally and will respond concretely. He became increasingly confused with their questioning. For example, when another person speaks, he hears the voice of that person speaking and on subsequent questioning if he has heard voices, he would often reply affirmatively because he has just heard the voice of that person.

On most occasions when I spoke to the RMO and Care Trust Mangers about schizophrenia and neuroleptic treatment, I was looked at with incredulity, as though I had no right to comment. This was confirmed when I was told by the Mental Health Commission psychiatrist in no uncertain terms to leave such matters to them, the professionals. I got the message loud and clear. As a carer, they regarded the treatment of my son as none of my business. I disagree—this *is* my business when I see what my son has been made to suffer.

Within a few days of starting medication with a neuroleptic, he began to suffer Parkinsonian-induced shaking and the standard anti-cholinergic drug only gave him minimal relief. Akathesia,[3] yet another adverse effect, made my son pace up and down the corridor continuously. When he was at home he walked round and round the house and up and down the garden. Trying to settle down to watch television or read was an impossibility. His only relief was when he was asleep. This inner restlessness became so intolerable that my son said he would rather commit suicide than to suffer in this way for the rest of his life.

After one year my son began to develop involuntary facial movements. These included the blowing out of his cheeks, puffing though his lips and the protrusion of his tongue—his mouth looked full of tongue and eating became difficult. I recognised these as symptoms of tardive dyskinesia (TD). I had been dreading this, as I knew from my research that TD is potentially irreversible. Many older people develop these facial movements—it is a part of the aging process and results from the degeneration of the nerve endings in the brain. I was so concerned that I requested a referral to a neurologist for my son to be assessed. The RMO delayed this request indefinitely. A new RMO in the ward round placed emphasis on how 'the benefits outweigh the risks' regarding medication—as if acknowledging my son had TD but that this was acceptable because of the benefits of the drugs. We then received a letter from him which declared that in his opinion my son was not suffering from TD. This seemed to be an attempt to absolve himself from taking responsibility for the damage to my son's brain, brought about by his treatment.

Eventually two private neurologists diagnosed my son's TD and recommended that the neuroleptic drugs be discontinued, in accordance with pharmaceutical literature surrounding TD. Despite this, at a later date an NHS neurologist claimed that he did not know the reason for my son's facial movements. This NHS non-diagnosis was

---

3. Akathesia, an adverse effect of neuroleptic medication, is involuntary inner physical restlessness.

upheld for three years before one NHS psychiatrist finally acknowledged the diagnosis of TD.

I am aware that doctors in general medicine regard the deterioration of body organs as an important reason for discontinuing medication, in order to avoid further damage to the patient. I think this is caring practice. In psychiatry doctors seem to consider that physical signs of brain degeneration are trivial, irrelevant and unimportant. I do not consider this psychiatric practice to be caring—as far as I am concerned the 'risks *far* outweigh the benefits'. As the months and years have passed, my son has been admitted onto many different wards and units. He has experienced treatment from sixteen RMOs, every one of them being involved in sectioning situations in which the mental health professionals take absolute control over my son. The resulting professional relationship with my son is unbalanced and open to abuse.

I have found that coercive behaviour has been commonplace. A social worker, who I had entrusted to see my son alone in our home, told my son that he would extend his section for another year if he did not comply with attending group therapy. My son was left crying uncontrollably. One RMO stated that since my son had difficulty in expressing himself—she thought it appropriate that he should be sectioned and yet another RMO stated that he would extend the section until my son spoke about his problems. As a caring and responsible parent, I feel incensed when my vulnerable son is threatened and I am sure that threatening behaviour is not conducive to a trusting relationship.

In a closed unit, my son felt professionally badgered for six months, due to the pressure from the Multi Disciplinary Team (MDT) who wanted his agreement to increase medication. Browbeaten, he eventually succumbed in a Care Programme meeting. His statement was duly recorded and acted upon immediately by the RMO. In private my son told me his reason for finally agreeing —he just wanted to get them off his back. He also thought that if he was obedient and complied with their need to increase medication, he would be allowed to return home. This did not occur for many months since there were indications that the unit guidelines directed staff towards keeping my son locked up for a year, followed by another year locked up on a closed rehabilitation unit.

Not one MDT member showed any interest in why my son had suddenly succumbed to accepting an increase in medication, despite his repeated statements declaring his need to come off medication. I witnessed staff repeatedly ignore my son's plea to come off medication and to return home. When he stopped asking to return home, I asked him why. He replied, 'What is the point? They never listen to me.'

One RMO gave my son the option of not taking neuroleptic medication. On choosing not to take the medication, the psychiatrist then stated that if that were the case, she would have him sectioned so that he would have no alternative but to take medication. As my son and I left the ward round he said, 'She has trapped me.' I agreed with him. I thought her statement was manipulative and I felt intimidated by her threatening attitude.

As a routine, my son is *told* what neuroleptic to take and is *told* that if he stops taking the medication he will become ill. This emphasis on medication is further coercion intended to frighten him into submitting to treatment he does not want. Sometimes though, staff bypass any discussions, coercive or otherwise about treatment and instead simply use their ability to section him. My son and I have experienced the full weight of the legal sectioning power, which on one occasion enabled the RMO to medicate my son with nigh disastrous consequences.

The RMO in question embarked into a Section 3[4] without informing my husband, who is next of kin, in order to commence treatment with Acuphase. This treatment resulted in my son becoming so sedated that he was unable to stand or sit unsupported, he urinated on the floor and fell asleep with mouthfuls of food. As the medication wore off he became increasingly aggressive and psychotic. The psychiatrist, however, insisted that the course of treatment was completed and due to my son's uncontrollable physical aggression he was transferred to the Intensive Treatment Services (ITS).

I went to the Unit. The nurses had resorted to basic nursing care as my son had become as a little child. He showered with a teddy bear under his arm and took teddy to bed. My psychotic son refused an ECG when the staff were concerned about his fast heart rate. Despite their concern about his heart, this was a significant adverse effect they did not address. He looked terrible. Saliva dribbled constantly from his mouth, making his T-shirt sodden. He lost his hand-to-mouth coordination and lost a stone in weight over a period of one month as he was unable to feed himself. His speech was so slurred that even I wasn't able to understand him. My pleas to the nurses went in one ear and straight out through the other. When the RMO returned from holiday, he increased the routine neuroleptic. My son's reddened eyes began to protrude from his eye sockets. I thought he was going to die. I went to a friend and sobbed in despair with all this unwanted and needless suffering that both my son and I were being legally forced to endure. That afternoon a nurse from the previous ward made a routine visit to the unit. On seeing my son's physical deterioration she recommended that the neuroleptic be reduced.

Many of the signs and symptoms that my son experienced in that terrible time are described by Neuroleptic Malignant Syndrome, a potential life-threatening situation. It transpired that before the Acuphase treatment was started, half of the MDT had wanted this Section applied because it provided legal protection in the case of my son's death. Another RMO in a sectioning situation did declare that he was endangering my son's physical life but he would take full clinical responsibility.

I am absolutely appalled by these situations in which it is clear that psychiatrists can do anything they want to do with my son regardless of the consequences. I want my son alive not dead. I want a doctor who truly cares about my son.

Because of the medication, my son is more prone to having cardiovascular disease and I am aware that he could suffer from a neuroleptic induced heart attack or stroke, or die from a seizure or respiratory arrest. He will become sterile as well as impotent. As the medication continues I know my son's life span is being shortened as the medication accelerates his aging process and I know one day he will look more aged than his father, and TD is associated with dementia.

---

4. Section 3 is part of the Mental Health Act which enables a person to be detained in hospital for a six-month minimum period for treatment.

My son was getting worse, not better. He was receiving all sorts of different medication treatments, but only medication. He had not received any psychological help at all. I was told that psychological treatment was not included as part of treatment on the acute ward. My husband and I worked hard to persuade one RMO along these lines by influencing the Trust managers to allowing a special provision for 'talking treatment' for my son. Part of this 'talking treatment' necessitated my son writing down his hallucinations and delusions, together with the potential triggering factor with the date and time. Although he attempted to write a few of his experiences, this exercise posed him some difficulties. His concentration was impeded due to the sedation effect of medication at that point in time. Another side effect impaired his cognitive functioning making it harder for him to work things out. It transpired that the psychologist's input was primarily designed to correct my son's behaviour in order to ease the nurses' management of my son. When he was acutely psychotic on a closed unit, a PSI (Psychosocial Intervention) psychologist stated he was too psychotic for therapy. Neither psychologist made progress and both gave up, my son being classified as unsuitable for therapy.

My distress at seeing my son constantly psychotic propelled me to pluck up courage to try to link with him by trying Garry Prouty's Pre-Therapy contact method. I felt greatly encouraged when I found that I was able to decrease his distress by grounding him back into our shared reality. As I developed an interest in this approach, I also became more aware that some of his body language and fragmented words were connected with situations from his past. I realised that his hallucinations had some meaning for him. This seemed to be an alien concept to professionals who saw his psychotic expressions as unimportant and needing to be stamped out at all costs; no one considered his psychotic experiencing to have any potential value in helping my son in the long term.

My son eventually realised I was able to help him in this way and would frequently ring me at home pleading with me to come and ground him saying that the nurses did not know what to do.

On discovering I was able to help my son, I made contact with Professor Prouty, who invited me to a Pre-Therapy International Network meeting and I eventually attended workshops by Professor Prouty and Dion Van Werde, the Lead Psychologist at the St-Camillus Hospital, in Ghent, Belgium. I realised Pre-Therapy provides the vital link which is essential for all professionals to be able connect with people experiencing psychosis—enabling them to have meaningful conversations. I began to share this knowledge with various Care Trust personnel. CBT (Cognitive Behavioural Therapy) and Psychosocial Intervention (PSI) psychologists were uninterested, preferring to focus on their particular approach. One nurse seemed to find my knowledge threatening and became defensive, claiming she had nursed and managed patients for over twenty years. Only one nurse who was present when I was working with my son realised that I was able to link in with him.

Because of the minimal interest shown, I decided to search further afield and made contact with universities and Care Trusts. A Reader in Mental Health at the University of Central England recognised the importance of Prouty's work and supported me in several Pre-Therapy taster workshops. Many people showed interest and I received positive feedback on several occasions although following one presentation, the presiding nursing tutor told her students that if they used this skill they would be struck off from the course. During a telephone conversation, a psychiatrist from a high-secure hospital said, 'You might as well teach your grandmother to suck eggs.' I felt insulted.

Some of my lowest ebbs occurred when my son was detained on the ITS and the low-secure unit. Both of these situations are closed wards, where access to see my son was through three sets of locked doors and I had to make arrangements with staff prior to visiting. On many occasions I was not able to visit my son because of 'clinical activity' in these units. On one unit I was not allowed into his room—visiting took place in a tiny open communal area or in the dining room. There was always a nurse within earshot and despite reassurances that we were not being overheard, a nurse would frequently interrupt our conversation. This was a gross and completely unwarranted invasion of our privacy.

On one occasion when my son began to get annoyed with the staff, the nurse in charge suddenly grabbed hold of my son and physically forced him into the isolation room. When the nurse finally came out I asked to speak with him in private. My husband joined me as I confronted this nurse's 'manhandling' of my son in a situation where my son's annoyance could have been resolved less aggressively. After half an hour of tussling with this nurse's denial of his aggressive physical behaviour towards my son, he apologised, realising that he had been heavy-handed. I respected him for his apology and my son was treated with more respect in my presence. In my experience, apologies for inappropriate behaviour have been exceedingly rare.

During my son's tardive psychosis resulting from Lorazepam withdrawal, he became increasingly delusional eventually refusing our requests for visits. He told the MDT members that he did not want either my husband or myself to know anything about his treatment or progress. Each time I rang I got the same answer from every nurse. They told me they had to respect my son's wishes and confidentiality and refused to tell me anything. This went on every day for two weeks. I had no idea how my son was faring and we were not able to give him support at the ward rounds. I began to despair as my connection with him appeared to be severed and feared that this was the final cutting-off point in the care of my son. I was worried that this would be only a small step away from him disappearing forever into a succession of medium- and high-secure units without me having any knowledge whatsoever regarding his whereabouts.

I knew I had to do something. The one connection I still had was with the nurses. I rang the ward once again to see how he was, saying I felt totally cut off from my son— I was his Mum after all and I needed to know how he was doing. The ward manager gave me the same response about respecting my son's confidentiality. I told her that my son was delusional and did not have an informed choice about our support and involvement in his care. She continued to listen. I went on to say that if, in my son's delusional state he wanted to have oral sex with the male staff nurse, would all the MDT members respect his delusion? To my enormous relief, she then proceeded to tell me how he was. My challenge to the nurse regarding his delusional state slowly filtered through to the staff, who eventually encouraged my son to see us both again.

In this inner world of the mental health system, I experienced professionals acting like gods, who reign supreme within their 'received medical wisdom'. I experienced professionals' rigid compliance with treatment in relation to national and local policies. When I introduced them to published research, I met their resistance, arrogance and superiority. I have felt powerless to help my son in sectioning situations and vulnerable in the face of their power and control of my son. I am affected considerably by these 'professional attitudes' and how their behaviour impacts upon their relationship with my son. Needless to say my son is also affected.

On one closed unit I realised how scared he was of interacting with MTD members. When he was apsychotic I used to encourage him to stand his own ground in relation to the nurses. He would reply, 'I must never upset the nurses'. This situation, where my son had to spend twenty-four-hours-a-day minding his Ps and Qs, is asking something practically impossible of *any* person. It is as though in being careful to stay on the 'right side' of the MDT members, he was actually protecting the staff from their own difficulties in their relationship with him. Furthermore, whenever my son was given extra medication, it always seemed to be the same nurses on duty. It was as though my son appeared to be more distressed in the presence of some nurses rather than others.

My ultimate frustration and exasperation was when on a closed unit, the MDT members made a united stance in refusing to help my son with Prouty's contact work. Seeing my son being needlessly distressed at the expense of this collective decision, I began to confront their psychiatric practice together with professional attitudes and behaviour. The MDT reacted defensively by involving the Trust managers, who summoned myself and my husband to a meeting. Their issues included, disproportionate amount of time spent dealing with us as relatives; attitudes, behaviour and manner directed at staff; and difficulties arising from differences of opinion regarding treatment and its consequences. Initially I felt threatened. Then I realised that I was receiving all the blame for these issues. There was no indication of professionals' accountability for their behaviour in our relationship. It was as though all their behaviour was impeccable and unquestionable. I certainly didn't feel understood in my distress.

Similarly there were many occasions when no attempt was made to understand my son when he was distressed. For example the nurses used CBT reasoning techniques to modify my son's physical aggressive behaviour, such as 'When you stop hitting out I will let go of your arm'. When the nurse let go of his arm, my son lashed out again. In these times of emotional distress, *he* always had to understand what the nurses wanted from him. For their part, the nurses made little or no attempt to understand the reason for his anger or what it was like to be in his shoes. Not being understood only served to heighten his distress.

On another similar occasion he was refused home leave. The nurse abruptly left him without seeing what effect this damning news would have on him. My son reacted once more by lashing out. He was pounced upon, manhandled and frogmarched down to the isolation room. When the door opened for him to be given extra sedation I could hear him shrieking in anger and indignation. I offered to sit with him. Sitting beside him, he began to sob profusely. We returned to his room, where he verbally let out his vengeance towards the nurses. I reflected what I thought was going on for him. 'You're angry and all you want to do is to hurt the nurses.' He nodded. 'You want to come home. I want you to come home. I am not sure how we are going to manage this, but we will work on this together.' I watched my son's face as my understanding of his dilemma began to seep into the core of his being. He felt understood and became calmer.

Many times during my interactions with professional staff, I experienced their cool, polite indifference and silence. Sometimes I had difficulty knowing whether they had understood the gist of my communication. I felt I was trying in vain to relate with people who had turned into stone, and yet when I heard laughter and lively conversations with drug representatives, I knew they had a warmer quality, with more openness in their relationships with other people. It seemed to me that in their professional relationships, their ability to be more human was stifled. I decided that there must be a way of reaching through to this important part of them, so I began to search for some of their humanity. The following are examples of what happened when I tried to relate to the staff as *people*.

When one nurse informed me that medication had not been discussed at the ward round because my son had failed to attend (stressing it was my son's responsibility to attend at the ward round) I explained that my son experienced high levels of anxiety in group situations and found the ward round difficult. I asked the nurse whether he had been in a similar position of being the subject of discussion surrounded by a group of people. He said that this was personal and it was his prerogative not to answer. His refusal or inability to be upfront with me ended our interaction.

Because of my dissatisfaction, I approached the staff nurse and asked him the same question. Slightly hesitantly he answered that he had been involved in similar situations and had felt most uncomfortable. He said he was able to understand how my son felt. Although he was probably taking a risk with his response, he was open and authentic. He did not hide behind his professional façade—we were able to talk on the same level as equals, and were able to continue our conversation.

On another occasion I told a nurse how upset I felt at seeing my son suffer with TD and EPS. I asked her opinion about the drugs. Her response was automatic, telling me that her role as the nurse was to dispense the medication. Recognising her aloofness, I gently pointed out that she was talking from behind her professional position. 'I want to know from you, Agitha, what you think.' Eventually her face and her tone of voice changed, becoming softer as she slowly said that she would not like to be in my position, as a mother seeing her son suffering with the results of medication. My heart warmed to her. I had reached through to her as another member of humanity.

In these latter interactions, when I have managed to find others' humanity, I have felt deeply respected and validated as a person of worth and value.

On all of the occasions when the RMOs have denigrated my son by saying he will need care for all his life because he is schizophrenic, I doubt they were aware of the negative impact their words have had on him. The result was that my son basically gave up striving to make a living—he could survive on handouts from the Department of Health and Social Security for the rest of his life. The diagnosis compounded his belief that he would never, ever, achieve anything in life. It was terrible to see my son hammered into the ground in this way. I need professionals to validate my son's intrinsic worth and value, so that he will gain confidence and move forward in life and achieve his full potential. However, overall he has experienced relationships where support is virtually non-existent. It has only been on rare occasions that he has felt respected and supported.

One staff nurse told me that my son appeared to respect him more than the other nurses. It transpired that this nurse set boundaries, gave clear communication and was genuine when interacting with my son. In a nutshell, by having a strong personal boundary, this nurse respected his own person and therefore was able to respect and support my son. My son, in his sensitiveness, perceived the nurse's genuineness, returning the respect in kind.

One support worker inadvertently referred to her strong personal boundary as she accompanied my husband and myself though locked doors—she suddenly turned around and told us how she could understand our concerns over the treatment of our son. Sensing her genuineness, I asked her why she, as a support worker, was able to understand when the professionals weren't. She replied that she had 'broad shoulders'. She gave me a hug and my whole being filled with her warmth. For once, my faith in humanity returned.

Before my son entered the inner world of the mental health system he had difficulties. Five years later those original difficulties are still there and are now compounded with problems arising from by NHS treatment and the professionals' ways of relating, which I think are tantamount to physical and emotional abuse.

My son did not ask for this; he does not need this. And I feel betrayed.

By hanging on to my son by the merest thread, he is now back home. Over the months within our supportive and caring environment, he is becoming more secure.

In public he is still incredibly vulnerable. His facial and body movements make him look odd, so losing credibility in society. His life has been directed, controlled and dominated to such an extent that any vestige of self-empowerment has been scuppered. It is as though his very being does not belong to himself any more. Any feelings of trust have long since disappeared. He is like an empty shell. I wish with all my heart that this was not so. Beneath my anger is my ocean of sadness. When my sadness washes over me, it is replaced by my love for my son, which provides me with an inner strength to carry on.

If I can hang on to my deep-seated belief that in every person there is the potential for a change of heart, then I do have a glimmer of hope. I believe that the key lies with those professionals who are committed to their own personal development towards strong personal boundaries. Only in an environment where professionals embrace others by being open, upfront and genuine in caring for others as members of humanity, do I believe my son would be in receipt of a healing relationship. Within his shell there remains a hidden pearl, which can be reached, touched and revealed as the person he truly is.

20

PRINCIPLED AND STRATEGIC OPPOSITION TO THE MEDICALISATION OF DISTRESS AND ALL OF ITS APPARATUS

PETE SANDERS

These schools of thought will not be abolished by wishful thinking
Carl Rogers, 1951: 8

The field of counselling and psychotherapy in the UK is, at the time of writing, considering its next move towards the statutory registration of therapists. It has been a depressingly familiar journey thus far—professional interests and political expediency have taken precedence over ethical and theoretical debate and the interests of the people we serve: our clients. In a recent article in *Ipnosis* Douglas McFazdean catalogued his correspondence with various government agencies. He explained that the consultation process lacked 'hard statistical evidence' and comprised discussions with 'primarily self-interested professional organisations whose members have never been proven to practise more effectively or ethically than non-members!' (McFazdean, 2004: 29). One relevant dynamic in this process is the position taken by counsellors and psychotherapists regarding the medicalisation of human distress and the subsequent issues of psychopathology and psychodiagnosis. This chapter asks why counsellors have abdicated the radical position occupied by Client-Centred Therapy (CCT) in the 1950s, and become tacit supporters of the medical psychiatric system.

In this chapter, I am presenting only one of many ways that client-centred therapists might choose to position themselves and act in regard to human distress. I am promoting a particular approach, but I am not arguing that it is the only approach. Furthermore, I do not intend my critical position to be totalising or dismissive of other positions, however strongly I state it. If our shared aim is to improve the treatment of people suffering from everyday distress and chronic distress ('neurosis' and 'psychosis'), then we should debate the various options vigorously. One option, frequently dismissed as impracticable, irresponsible and self-defeating, is one of rejection and principled opposition (but not disengagement). This is the position described in this chapter. This position, however, must not become entangled with discussion about safety, risk or dangerousness of distressed and distressing people. These important, but separate issues are frequently conflated with an anti-medical stance as a tactic by those wishing to defend the status quo.

If the development of theory and practice is a matter of *evolution* rather than *progress*, then it is vital that diversity is at least preserved, and at best promoted. The aim of this chapter is to breathe life into the radical tradition and revolutionary elements of client-centred theory and practice. My intention is to remind client-centred therapists that it is honourable, constructive and ethical to *refuse*, even if the personal consequences might sometimes be very uncomfortable. I also wish to give support to those client-centred therapists who continue to explain the radical, ethical, humane principles of this approach against all the fashions that deny them.

METAPHORS FOR DISTRESS

Many writers (e.g. Boyle, 1990, 2003) have clearly documented the assumption, even amongst some of those presenting 'progressive' views, that human distress is an illness. Arguments about the role of psychiatry frequently take the illness metaphor as the starting point. The observation that illness might be a *metaphor* for distress, rather than a *fact* determined by 'scientific' analysis, is met in some circles with incomprehension. Although writers and practitioners from Szasz (1961) to Parker, et al. (1995) have questioned the assumption, it still is taken as given by the general public and the vast majority working in the helping professions.[1] However many people use the metaphor,

Table 3.1 (Abridged from Blackburn and Yates, 2004: 32.)

	Traditional mental health services	Learning disability services
Metaphor used	Illness	Communication
Professional discourses privileged	Psychiatrists	Speech and language therapists, social workers, psychologists, carers, parents
Method of defining	Diagnosis	Client's experience. Description as created in the conversation between client, carers, family, professionals, etc.
Beliefs about how change is brought about	Providing the right treatment to enable client change	By the system understanding and addressing the client's needs
Aims of intervention	To recover previous state of being	Development to new state of being
Professional relationship to client	Therapist	Advocate

---

1. It is essential continuously to remind ourselves that this 'medical model of mental illness' is a list of 'illnesses' based entirely on similarity of symptoms, not (as is the case with somatic illness) on aetiology.

it cannot be rescued from being a metaphor and therefore a representation of reality, not reality itself. It is a way of thinking that is intended to be helpful. The key questions are (1) is *illness* still a useful, helpful metaphor? (2) how can we evaluate the usefulness/helpfulness of the metaphor? (3) what metaphors might be more useful? and (4) how do we shift cultural thinking to a more useful metaphor?

I will argue that illness is not a helpful metaphor, and is certainly discordant with the core values of CCT. Further, it was installed as the dominant cultural metaphor for professional and political reasons and so will resist both evaluation by science and replacement by more culturally appropriate metaphors—those that have a perceived better fit to contemporary professional experience.

CCT suggests an *organismic growth* metaphor for human distress and person-centred/client-centred theorists and practitioners should declare this in juxtaposition to the dominant illness metaphor at every *appropriate* opportunity. There is, as Blackburn and Yates (2004) point out, a contemporary model for challenging the illness metaphor which has met with considerable success. They compare present-day traditional mental health services with learning disability services[2] as shown in Table 3.1. A similar protocol can be adapted to compare traditional mental health services and CCT, shown in Table 3.2.

Table 3.2

	Traditional mental health services	Client-Centred Therapy
Metaphor used	Illness	Organismic growth (adaptation) and/or client's own metaphor
Professional discourses privileged	Psychiatrists	No professional discourse privileged above client's experience
Method of defining client's experience	Diagnosis	Client experience/empathy
Beliefs about how change is brought about	Providing the right treatment to enable client change	Actualising tendency of client released by therapist-provided conditions
Aims of intervention	To recover previous state of being	Fulfilment of inherent potential
Professional relationship to client	Expert therapist	Therapist/companion

2. Thirty years ago, in the UK, learning disability services used an illness metaphor but since the advent of a social model of disability, this is no longer the case. A further example of 'metaphor-reassignment' is the wresting of pregnancy from the illness metaphor, see Catterall, 2005, Chapter 14 this volume.

I am not suggesting metaphors are bad *per se*, however much a rationalist and literalist I might be. Metaphors and myths serve important functions in the understanding and management of our social world, but only in so far as they are useful and consensual rather than harmful and unchallengeable. It is, however, increasingly difficult to keep the medical metaphor of distress within challengeable range—so that challenges to it are not seen as fatally heretical or irresponsible.

METAPHORS, PRACTICE AND SERVICES TO CLIENTS

A social model of learning disability has supplanted the medical model in professional circles and this was achieved in a number of ways. One strategy has been to challenge the medical model, its hierarchical structure, potential for abuse and sheer lack of fitness for purpose at every possible turn. Another strategy has been to support, and align with, the groups of users of disability services. Whether or not such strategies would be suitable to challenge the illness metaphor in mental health remains to be debated in client-centred circles—in fact the notion of *organised* opposition to the medical model has never been contemplated. What cannot be in doubt, however, is that any alternative argument is weakened every time academics, writers and practitioners whose logical position is set against it, make reference to, or accept the medical model and diagnosis without comment. The progress of alternative practice is hindered, and its character damaged, every time practitioners silently accept the authority of psychiatrists over user groups and carers.

Counsellors and therapists, both individually and, more importantly as a group, have valuable contributions to make to this debate. I do not favour arguments which have counsellors and psychotherapists as acontextual, apolitical servants of individual clients. Rather, as Sanders and Tudor (2001) insist,

> Psychotherapists should be concerned with change, not adjustment; should be explicit about their values and should be intentional—socially and culturally ... Psychotherapists and counsellors [must] base their practice on a thorough and critical understanding of psychiatry and psychotherapy *in context* ... Psychotherapists' practice should reflect the awareness that the struggle for mental health involves changing society ... Psychotherapists should organise and challenge oppressive institutions ... in the organisation of mental health services, and professional monopoly in the control of service provision and direction, and the colonization of the voluntary sector in mental health. (p. 157)

One key step is to organise collegial groups and professional associations better to represent the alternatives held at the centre of CCT.

HISTORY

The history of Client-Centred Therapy is a history of radical theory and practice.

Carl Rogers and his colleagues in the Client-Centred Therapy[3] movement were the first to give an account of what really happened in a psychotherapy session by using wax-disc recordings of sessions and publishing transcripts—revealing the arcane practices of psychotherapy and presenting them for public scrutiny (Kirschenbaum, 1979). Rogers trained lay people (non-medically qualified psychologists and socialworkers),[4] causing further controversy. As CCT developed, it made the client the centre of the healing process and effectively factored-out the medical expert—the client was assisted by another, equal, person. Psychiatrists forbade him to use the term 'psychotherapy' for this work, in order to protect their status, so he appropriated the word 'counselling'. On moving to Chicago in 1945, Rogers initiated research into psychotherapy, and in so doing turned the emerging CCT into the first evidence-based psychological (as opposed to medical) treatment programme—it became a *human science*. Understandably, none of this went down well in the professional circles of the day.

When news of the success of the Chicago Counseling Center spread, CCT was criticised for only being applicable to middle-class, articulate, worried-well clients. Rogers' research was criticized for being small-scale and only using clients whose symptoms were not severe. In response he moved to the University of Wisconsin, where, as the first joint professor in psychology and psychiatry, he conducted research in a hostile environment (a State Mental Hospital where patients were kept in locked wards (Rogers, Gendlin, Kiesler and Truax, 1967)) with people who had the least hope of recovery (those with diagnoses of 'schizophrenia'). In its heyday CCT was *the* radical, vibrant, anti-medical establishment, system-threatening, research-based psychological practice—and at its core it was non-invasive, non-medical, mindfully humane and just.

When I first read Rogers in the early 1970s, he was, to me, radical psychology made flesh. It was his speaking out against the medicalisation of distress and professional expertism, whilst formulating a coherent theory and workable practice embodying these principles, which attracted me to CCT.

Meanwhile, those supporting the medicalisation of distress have continued to entrench their position; the anti-psychiatry movement in the '60s and '70s, and the work of Szasz (1961) and Laing (e.g. 1965) hardly caused the medical model to break

---

3. Rogers initially termed his therapy method 'Non-directive therapy', changing it to 'Client-Centered Therapy' around 1950. He introduced the term 'Person-Centered Approach' in the late 1970s to signify applications of his approach beyond therapy, although in the UK, the term 'Person-Centred Therapy' (which Rogers never used) became popular. This chapter is founded in the radical roots of classical Client-Centred Therapy, and so I shall use this term throughout.

4. In the US in the late 1930s only medically-qualified doctors, in particular psychiatrists, were permitted to offer psychotherapy. Rogers' clinical work and writing had already blurred the accepted boundaries between psychology, sociology and social work so it was no surprise that the Rochester Council of Social Agencies insisted that the new community guidance centre (proposed by Rogers) be headed by a psychiatrist. After a year-long battle with the authorities, Rogers (not medically qualified) was made the director.

its stride as it became not only the dominant ideology of distress, but the *only* ideology of distress. It has become a 'given' to be taken for granted—that which we think *from*, rather than are able to think *about*. The thought that human distress might not be an 'illness' is not merely radical, it is inconceivable. This status quo,[5] to which we were all socialised from birth can be summarised thus:

1. The best way of thinking and talking about human mental distress is to medicalise it—to think and talk in terms of 'illness' and 'health', or if we prefer, 'normality' and 'abnormality'.
2. Severe and enduring mental illness has a biological base.
3. Since mental distress is a medical condition, we need a psychopathology and system for classifying symptoms and, by association, treatments (diagnosis).
4. Psychosis is discontinuous with ordinary mental functioning and so it requires special treatment by experts.
5. Psychotherapy and counselling are ineffective treatments for severe and enduring mental illness. Worse than that, they are actually dangerous.
6. Psychiatry is scientific, deals with the facts of the world, is based on evidence, is rational and therefore responsible.
7. Criticisms of psychiatry are unevidenced, subjective, politically motivated, rhetorical, and therefore irresponsible. Further, they appeal to and hold false hope for, impressionable, vulnerable people.

How such ideas came to be installed as the status quo is another story of professional interests and political expediency. Space does not permit even a summary of the history here, so readers are directed to accessible accounts by Pilgrim (1990), Newnes (1999), Bentall (2003), Boyle (2003) or Read (2004).

CRITICAL PSYCHOLOGY

In recent years a growing number of psychology academics, authors and practitioners have taken up the reins of the anti-psychiatry movement of the 1960s and '70s to present a critique of the medicalisation of distress. The position presented by this group[6] advocates thorough reform of the psychiatric system based on the fundamental question regarding the nature of human distress and how it should be viewed. That some people

---

5. Referred to by some sociologists as 'doxa' (Bourdieu and Wacquant, 1992) and described by Charlesworth (2000) as 'constituted by those systems of classification which establish limits to what we contemplate in discursive consciousness, thus producing an inability to see the arbitrariness on which the classification and the structures have been established' (p. 31).
6. Although I refer to these persons as a 'group' this is just convenient shorthand. Worldwide, many work completely independently and only a few could be considered to be professional associates. What unites the group is their general critical position vis-à-vis mainstream psychiatric practice and the medical model of mental illness, and the critique itself is not entirely unitary and cohesive.

suffer many manifestations of disabling distress everyday of their lives is not in question. What is it, however, that makes us think that they are the symptoms of an *illness*?

The following extracts capture many of the defining sentiments of these critics:

> The heightened sensitivity, unusual experiences, distress, despair, confusion and disorganisation that are currently labelled 'schizophrenic' are *not* symptoms of a mental illness. The notion that 'mental illness is an illness like any other', promulgated by biological psychiatry and the pharmaceutical industry, is not supported by research and is extremely damaging to those with this most stigmatising of psychiatric labels. The 'medical model' of schizophrenia has dominated efforts to understand and assist distressed and distressing people for far too long. It is responsible for unwarranted and destructive pessimism about the chances of 'recovery' and has ignored—or even actively discouraged discussion of—what is actually going on in these people's lives, in their families and in the societies in which they live. Simplistic and reductionistic genetic and biological theories have led, despite the high risks involved and the paucity of sound research proving effectiveness, to the lobotomizing, electroshocking or drugging of millions of people. (Read, Mosher and Bentall, 2004: 3)

Dorothy Rowe implicates the medical *profession*, thus:

> If such illnesses exist, then they can be treated by one profession only—psychiatry. But if such illnesses do not exist, if 'illness' is simply a metaphor for the various ways we can feel despair and alienation, then psychiatrists have nothing unique to offer. Anyone who has the necessary wisdom, sympathy and patience—a psychologist, a counsellor, a good friend—could give the help the sufferer needs. Psychiatry would vanish, just as the profession of hangman vanished from Britain once the death penalty was abolished. (Rowe, 1993: xx)

And Peter Breggin is blunt:

> Dozens of mass-marketed books misinform the public that a 'broken brain' or 'biochemical imbalance' is responsible for personal unhappiness.
>
> Yet the only biochemical imbalances that we can identify with certainty in the brains of psychiatric patients are the ones produced by psychiatric treatment itself. (Breggin, 1993: 14)

An enduring criticism of the earlier anti-psychiatry movement was that it gave the impression of being *anti*-psychiatry, but not *pro*- very much—there seemed to be little systematic promoting of alternative treatments—the exception being the work of Laing and his associates (e.g. Laing and Esterson, 1964). Whilst presenting a persuasive array of arguments pointing to the doxic[7] nature of psychiatry, more recent objectors offer a much more rounded critique, tending to be research-based, proposing tentative

---

7. Doxic — referring to 'doxa' — see footnote 5.

psychological explanations and non-medical treatment regimes. Some of these treatments originate in a broad cognitive approach and are evidence-based[8] (see, for example, Birchwood, Fowler and Jackson, 2000). However, others, based on practitioners' clinical experience (a different kind of 'evidence'), provide an interesting story for us to contemplate.

In 1983, the Soteria programme was closed after 22 years.[9] Well researched and reported in many journals (see Mosher 1999; Mosher and Burti 1994) the programme was a residential acute psychiatric unit in California specialising in mainly drug-free treatment. It achieved good results with what psychiatrist Loren Mosher described as ' … 24 hour a day application of interpersonal phenomenologic interventions by a non-professional staff' (Mosher 1999: 37). The project was initially part-funded by the US NIMH[10] and the evidence showed that disturbed and disturbing persons were best helped by relationships with people, not by drugs. It showed that the best help for the majority of people was provided in a supportive, growth-oriented community, not in a hospital. It showed that helping improve mental life included improving the environment (micro and macro)—interventions are better if they are psychosocial. Their experience also showed that diagnosis was anti-therapeutic, as were helping interventions that put a theory or ideology before the needs of the person being helped. Definitions of 'health' and disturbance were found to be better if they were functional (rather than normative); so people were best served by being supported to live fulfilling lives, not by trying to change them to fit society's ideas of normality. I urge all readers to study Mosher's work.

Although Mosher and others replicated the results in other facilities, the human contact oriented, drug-free approach never caught on. What kind of 'treatment' do you imagine it could have been that Mosher described as '24 hour a day application of *interpersonal phenomenologic* interventions' (my italics)?

In 1987 Dutch psychiatrist Marius Romme was inspired by his work with a patient, Patsy Hague, who heard voices. His conclusion was that rather than to instruct patients to ignore and suppress the voices or eliminate them with medication, the better treatment was to encourage patients to talk about their voices and understand meaning implicit in the experience (see Romme and Escher, 1993). This led to (amongst other things) the formation of Hearing Voices Network in the UK. Self-help work in which voice-hearers listen to each other's experiences and swap ideas is now well-established.

In 1993, Peter Breggin, an American psychiatrist, published *Toxic Psychiatry*—a

---

8. Many readers may lodge objections to this claim, but the purpose of this chapter is not to challenge the nature of the evidence base of different therapeutic approaches.

9. Funding was withdrawn. When asked why, (if it was so successful), at a recent lecture in Birmingham, England, Mosher explained that since the project had offended drug companies (by recommending an initial medication-free period on admission), psychiatrists (by using non-medically qualified staff) and hospital administrators (by locating in a residential neighbourhood), the funding *had to be withdrawn*. The dominant medical ideology gets what it wants when the evidence might go against it, through alleged fraud (see, e.g. Lynch, 2004) and alleged corruption (see the account of the affair regarding the [non]appointment of psychopharmacologist David Healy at the University of Toronto at www.pharmapolitics.com).

10. National Institute for Mental Health.

coruscating attack on the mental health system. He described the importance of seeking and finding meaning in the worlds of frightened, disturbed people; he realised that these people and their worlds have value; he treated patients with respect, rather than forcing dehumanising physical treatments on them; he understood that therapists must relate to clients as people, not distant, powerful experts.

Richard Bentall, in his tour-de-force *Madness Explained* (Bentall, 2003) concluded: 'If people can sometimes live healthy, productive lives while experiencing some degree of psychosis … if the boundaries between madness and normality are open to negotiation … and if … our psychiatric services are imperfect and sometimes damaging to patients, why not help some psychotic people just to *accept* that they are different from the rest of us?' (Bentall, 2003: 511). Bentall demonstrated that there is no dividing line between psychological health and disturbance; that diagnosis is largely an irrelevance and the medicalisation of human distress is at best a diversion. He then invited understanding *and* explanation of the experiences of people who receive diagnoses of psychosis. Both of these elements—*understanding* and *explanation*—are key to his thesis. Third, he linked the experience of madness to events in the everyday lives of people—the foundation of a truly *psychosocial* approach. Such an approach builds a psychology of the ordinary—a theory of you and me, of our lives and experiences—a theory of mental life in the round.

Wherever evidence is reviewed, similar stories emerge: most recently Houghton (2005) commented on the Cochrane Review which concluded that Cognitive Behavioural Therapy (CBT) had no better effect on improved mental states or relapse and readmission rates for schizophrenia compared with 'supportive psychotherapy' (a term which is used to describe a control group that includes CCT/PCT). And in the same publication, commenting on similar evidence, Stickley explains:

> CBT expands on the unique meaning the person attaches to their experience … encourages dialogue about the person's experiences … stresses collaboration … [and] an understanding of their goals … expanding on the personal significance and meaning of their experiences. (2005: 25)

He goes on to say, 'I believe such factors are central to helping people with distressing psychotic experiences' (p. 25).

So, a significant group of critical psychologists, academics and psychiatrists have discovered that the best way to help chronically distressed people is to offer them:

1. Relationships …
2. that are characterised by interpersonal, phenomenologic interventions,
3. offered by non-professional staff (not medically qualified),
4. who relate to the client as a person, not a distant and powerful expert,
5. where the staff help clients understand implicit meaning in their experiences and
6. value clients' experiences, treating them with respect
7. in growth-oriented, supportive communities, not hospital/medical settings.

They further discovered that diagnosis is anti-therapeutic; that help should include a focus on the *context* of client's experiences (family, social context, class, race, etc.) and all of these treatments are often best done in the absence of prescribed psychotropic drugs.

They are describing counselling in all but name and in particular they seem to be re-inventing CCT from their own clinical experience—replicating Rogers' work of the 1940s and '50s, who similarly distilled a series of principles for effective practice from his clinical experience. Many of the same commentators hold CCT/PCT in negative regard, using untrained practitioners in control groups and calling the activity 'supportive counselling' or 'supportive psychotherapy'. This is a state of affairs which the community of person-centred therapists should not accept without individual and collective comment. The critical psychologists and psychiatrists have some things to learn from our seventy years of theory and practice development on 'such factors' that are 'central to helping people with distressing … experiences'. We will be wasting our time if we wait for them to come knocking on our door.

CLASSICAL CLIENT-CENTRED THERAPY, THE MEDICALISATION OF DISTRESS, PSYCHOPATHOLOGY AND DIAGNOSIS

Earlier in this chapter I stated that CCT circa 1950 was the radical option in psychology. This radical nature has its foundation in the theory of CCT and in how the theory demands practice with integrity, that is, practice congruent with, in harmony with, the values and principles lying at the core of the approach. These core principles are all in opposition to the medicalisation of distress.

ACTUALISING TENDENCY

At the heart of any therapy theory is a view of human nature. One core debate on the constitution of human nature relates to our fundamental disposition. Does fulfilment come through release of potential or regulation of destructive impulses? Rogers' basic humanist declaration of the actualising tendency was, according to Merry (2003) a biological view which can be summarised as a directional tendency towards greater differentiation and fulfilment of the organism's constructive potential. Specifically Rogers defined it as follows in 1959:

> This is the inherent tendency of the organism to develop all its capacities in ways which serve to maintain or enhance the organism. It involves not only the tendency to meet what Maslow terms 'deficiency needs' for air, food, water, and the like, but also more generalized activities. It involves development toward the differentiation of organs and of functions, expansion in terms of growth, expansion of effectiveness through the use of tools, expansion and enhancement through reproduction. It is development toward autonomy and away from heteronomy, or control by external forces. (Rogers, 1959: 196)

Rogers was wise to accusations of naïveté which the idea attracted:

> Some have thought of the client-centered therapist as an optimist. Others have felt that this line of thought follows Rousseau. Neither criticism seems to me to be true. The hypothesis in regard to the capacity of the individual is, rather, distilled out of an accumulated experience with many mildly and deeply disturbed individuals, who often display destructive or self destructive tendencies. Contrary to those therapists who see depravity at men's [sic] core, who see men's deepest instincts as destructive, I have found that when man is truly free to become what he most deeply is, free to actualize his nature as an organism capable of awareness, then he clearly appears to move toward wholeness and integration. (Rogers, 1959, in Kirschenbaum and Henderson, 1990: 27)

To unilaterally contain or categorise such a general, positive tendency would, in practice, be illogical, unhealthy and anti-life. Practice in harmony with the actualising tendency construct would be cooperative and phenomenological, dedicated to removing obstacles to actualisation within the personality and the environment.

NON-DIRECTIVITY

In Barry Grant's recent article, he wrote 'Client-Centered Therapy is the practice of simply respecting the right to self-determination of others' (Grant, 2004). This is achieved by principled (rather than instrumental) non-directivity, a distinction made by Grant in 1990. He (Grant, 1990) outlined the difference between *using* non-directivity as an instrument or tool (as do integrationists, for example) rather than holding it as a fundamental quality or core value of human living. The principle of non-directivity or non-interference only makes sense as a way of living with the actualising tendency. If human nature has such a basic tendency to self and other destruction, then such a principle would be obviously naïve. However, since a core element of CCT *is* the actualising tendency, the principle of non-directivity as a core value and attitude follows logically. Non-directivity has a historical line through twentieth century anarchy back at least to 600 BC and the *Tao te ching*. This principle has many names—non-interference, non-action or the principle of *wu-wei*; where wu means 'not' and wei means 'artificial, contrived activity that interferes with natural and spontaneous development' (Ames, cited in Marshall, 1992: 55). None of these terms are indicative of idleness or inertia or the *laissez-faire*. They are the *mindful* application of actions which follow, rather than act contrary to, nature.

To have such a principle actively informing practice helps determine the whole attitudinal framework of the practitioner towards the client as a member of the human race. It points towards an organismic appreciation of humanness (the person as an organism in process), with *growth* (or adaptation) and *flourishing* as metaphors for change. It militates against an instrumental appreciation of humanness (the person as machine), with *manualised repair* and *adjustment* as metaphors for change. It points towards ethical human relational *healing* and militates against invasive, disrespectful, quasi-medical *treatment.* In short such an irreducible principle determines our entire perception of what therapy is for and how to do it.

HOLISM

Classical CCT is intrinsically holistic. From Rogers' (1951) writings onward, the idea that the organism is an 'organised whole' (p. 486) and should be viewed as such and responded to as such is paramount in theory and practice. In terms of the present discussion, any theory or treatment paradigm which is partial in its regard to the person would be antagonistic to CCT. In particular, the reductionist medical model of distress, with its almost exclusive focus on the physical dimension of the human being, is clearly out of step with CCT.[11] The physical, somatic, cognitive, affective and spiritual domains of human existence are given equal opportunity for expression in CCT, depending upon the client's own biases and partialities with regard to their experience of themselves.

AN ANTI-DIAGNOSTIC STANCE

A logical progression from the actualising tendency, non-directivity and holism is the classical client-centred position on diagnosis. There are two related senses of the term 'diagnosis' as used in the fields of counselling, psychotherapy and mental 'health'. First is the founding medicalised definition: diagnosis as the centrepiece of the medical model. Second is the evolving definition developed by the social/psychological sciences: the use of the faux-medical methodology of diagnosis, but using psychological descriptors and symptoms rather than out-and-out medical signs and symptoms. These two senses are hopelessly conflated and have been since their inception, as the history of social science is largely one of attempting to mimic the physical and/or medical sciences to gain credibility and professional status. It would be convenient if the term *psychodiagnosis* described diagnosis within *psychological* models of distress, and the term *diagnosis* described *medical* models of distress, but both terms are used interchangeably, and I will not try to discriminate between usages in this chapter.

Classical CCT has strong complaints with both senses of the term as I will outline below, but the main thrust of this chapter is to protest against the medicalisation of distress and the inappropriate diagnosis that inevitably comes in its wake.

Psychodiagnosis is clearly concerned with the political domain as well as the clinical, due to its association with the social control of people who are distressing (or inconvenient) to us or society. Such issues have been comprehensively dealt with recently by such

---

11. I concede that with successive editions of diagnostic manuals, such as the *Diagnostic and Statistical Manual of Mental Disorders* (DSM), there has been an increasing lean towards psychological symptoms/ descriptors and diagnostic categories and away from physical disease analogues. However, the medical model is still just that, medical. It uses reductionist medical protocols of diagnosis and treatment—an illness metaphor methodology where *symptom similarity* is used to identify a 'disease category' which leads to a differentially applied 'treatment', *as though it had been arrived at aetiologically.*

writers as Mary Boyle (1999) and Ian Parker and his associates (Parker et al., 1995). However, few writers in the client-centred tradition critique the fundamental problem, i.e. the medicalisation of human distress. Rogers himself rejected diagnosis from the start for both clinical reasons and the ethical reasons detailed above. He despaired whenever a client was treated as a collection of symptoms rather than as a *person*. In the introduction to a new edition of *A Way of Being* Irving Yalom recalled Rogers:

> At an academic symposium on Ellen West, a heavily studied patient who committed suicide several decades before, Rogers startled the audience by the depth and intensity of his reaction. He spoke about Ellen West as though he knew her well, as though it were only yesterday that she had poisoned herself. Not only did Rogers express his sorrow about her tragically wasted life, but also his anger at her physicians and psychiatrists who, *through their impersonality and preoccupation with precise diagnosis*, had transformed her into an object. (Yalom, 1995: viii, my emphasis)

Rogers addressed the issue of 'The Problem of Diagnosis', (1951: 219) in which he described the distinction between a model of pathology for organic disease and a model for psychopathology. His argument for a client-centred rationale for diagnosis was made when it was still possible to hope for a future where psychological therapies were not forced to practise under the shadow cast by the medical model. Even within this psychological domain, Rogers did not address the inherent redundancy of detailed diagnosis given the phenomenological nature of client-centred theory. Shlien (1989) is critical of Rogers:

> Rogers did not really develop a 'rationale for diagnosis.' He made one of his many mistakes of a particular academic sort: he paid momentary lip service to the positivistic logic he felt stuck with at that period. The mistake was to call his own statement (quoted by Boy) as a 'rationale for diagnosis' (Rogers, 1951: 223). On the same page Rogers says it is really a rationale for psychotherapy *without* (not built upon) external diagnosis. It does not pay to make even temporary concessions to logic you believe to be false, or professional conventions you believe unworthy. They haunt one forever. (p. 160)

Psychodiagnosis was left in a rather uneasy limbo until it was addressed in 1989 by Angelo Boy who headed the most extensive CCT exploration of psychodiagnosis to date[12] in the 'Symposium on Psychodiagnosis' published in *Person-Centered Review*. Boy's purpose was to 'review some historic questions about the usefulness of psychodiagnosis' and he acknowledged that 'They still need to be raised today, however, before psychodiagnosis becomes so routinized that its adherents cease to accept "questions from the floor" regarding its purpose and accuracy' (p. 132). He located and then accepted

12. Notwithstanding a whole conference, held in Egmond aan Zee in 2003, which mostly deftly danced around the whole subject of psychodiagnosis and the medical model (without using those words): 6th World Conference of Person-Centered and Experiential Psychotherapy and Counseling, *Process Differentiation and Person-Centeredness*. 6–11 July.

the rationale for diagnosis in the medicalisation of distress without much of a challenge. Again, the largely unquestioned starting point for the debate was acceptance of the logic of a medical model of mental distress. His conclusion was one which has become more familiar in recent years, suggesting that client-centred therapists either help revise and improve the medical model, or provide an alternative diagnostic tool. Again Shlien is robust in his criticism:

> For the 'psychodynamic' therapist whose theory is based on pathology, or for the eclectic who thinks he has many different methods in his armory of equipment, diagnosis makes some sense.
>
> But client-centered therapy has only *one* treatment for *all* cases. That fact makes diagnosis entirely useless. If you have no specific treatment to relate to it, what possible purpose could there be to specific diagnosis? Nothing remains but the detrimental effects.
>
> Then, diagnosis is not good, not even neutral, but bad. Let's be straightforward and flat out about it. The facts might be friendly, but what are the facts? Diagnosis comes not just from a medical model, but from a theory of psychotherapy that is different from ours, antagonistic to ours. It is not only that its diagnostic predictions are flawed, faulty, and detrimental to the relationship and the client's self-determination, they are simply a form of evil. That is, they label and subjugate people in ways that are difficult to contradict or escape. There is no value in being 'reasonable' about that, in wanting to participate in reformulation of the psychodiagnostic endeavor that will generate a universally agreed-upon answer. Why petition to be a partner to reformulation when it is wrong from the beginning? (Shlien, 1989: 160–1)

I cannot state strongly enough my belief that therapists dedicated to emancipation, freedom, self-determination, growth, fulfilment, and empowerment, are in poor company with diagnosticians. Furthermore, an important dynamic of the healing process is highlighted here. The journey through emancipation, empowerment, self-determination and growth to fulfilment represents the very heart of the process of healing identified by Rogers (1951, 1959, 1978) and is increasingly implicated in psychological health by others (e.g. Bentall, 2003). Diagnosis requires an already vulnerable person to submit to the arbitraty, damaging 'authority' of the expert diagnostician. Moreover it is an unscientific, amoral authority borne out of historical precedent, political expediency, and maintained by professional interests. Client-Centred Therapy is the only approach which enshrines the client's right to access healing without sacrificing their personal power. They are the expert, and the client-centred therapist goes 'back to the client' for authority (Schmid, 2004). For a full discussion of the fundamental phenomenological and anti-expert positions of CCT, see Schmid, 2005, Chapter 6 this volume.

This right must be re-established by repeated re-presentation of these views in a hostile medically-dominated system. This situation is not new. Rogers (1957) wrote of his ' fear and trembling', because of a 'heavy weight of clinical opinion to the contrary' (p. 230 in Kirschenbaum and Henderson, 1990). In the same paper he asserted that diagnosis was 'for the most part, a colossal waste of time … There is only one useful purpose … Some therapists cannot feel secure in the realtionship with the client unless they possess such diagnostic knowledge' (*ibid*: 232). There is still good reason for us to be afraid and tremble, but Shlien speaks for me when he writes: 'There is no advantage in cooperating with the dominant clique. The lion and the lamb may lie down together, but if it is in the lion's den, the lion is probably quite relaxed, looking forward to breakfast in bed' (*ibid*: 161).

A CLIENT-CENTRED PSYCHOPATHOLOGY?

The main theme of this chapter is the invalidity, unevidenced and damaging nature of psychodiagnosis and that this argument derives from the doxic idea that human distress is an 'illness'. Therefore, if there is no reasonable evidence that human distress constitutes an 'illness' then applying a medical model and its associated elements is at least inappropriate. Between the medicalisation of distress and diagnosis lies the apparatus of psychopathology—the very term 'pathology' indicates its medical origin. I could then argue that if the cause (medicalisation of distress) and the effect (diagnosis and damaging inappropriate treatment) are invalid, we need spend no time dismantling the material in-between.

In addition I have also briefly drawn attention to a faux-medical diagnosis method developed by social scientists for use with psychological models of distress wherein adherents to this position argue for a humanistic or client-centred, or process-experiential formulation of psychopathology. Humanistic psychology is generally critical of the medicalisation of distress, since it contravenes one of the foundation stones of humanistic psychology—holism. Humanistic alternative diagnostic formulations mainly consist of replacing one set of labels with another, again failing to address the inherent redundancy of detailed diagnosis and the iatrogenic nature of categorisation.

Of course, CCT does have a system of understanding and, to some extent, categorising distress (Rogers, 1959). This could, in the strictest sense, be considered to constitute a psychopathology, since it describes the cause of psychological tension and in very general terms outlines sets of symptoms as examples. Elke Lambers (2003) and Paul Wilkins (2003) both outline how PCT/CCT theory is, if treated as a static *system*, more than adequate as a system of explanation for medical model categories of 'illness'.

However, CCT parts company with the usual symptom-driven diagnostic system when the theory makes it clear that even though there may be a unitary source of tension, the ways in which this may be made manifest are unique to each individual. Understanding the individual characteristics of each person's experiences can only be achieved through empathy. A further departure from medically-orientated psychopathologies arises when CCT theory proposes that the experience of resolution of the distress may not be due to the *instrumental* effects of the *techniques* of empathy, unconditional positive regard (UPR) and congruence, but rather as a result of the totality of the relationship—a unique, co-created healing moment where complex human contact is the curative factor.

Amongst person-centred theorists, Margaret Warner presents an alternative psychopathology, not merely a diagnostic framework, based on client-centred and experiential theory. She accepts the primacy of diagnostic methodology, with its ancestry a direct line to the medical model—Warner's position is founded on the pragmatism of compromise and revision. Her alternative psychopathology[13] is clearly outlined and explained in Chapter 7 of this volume (Warner, 2005). She aims to provide PCT/CCT with some of the apparatus valued, if not required, by insurance companies, government agencies and others holding the purse strings. Along the way she manages to humanise the brutal medical model diagnostic terminology.[14]

Some promote a holistic framework, incorporating elements of the organic, social, psychological and ethereal, declaring that labelling is fine as long as it isn't partial. Yet others, originally antagonistic to diagnosis, have mellowed or done an about-turn. A recent example of such a change in attitude can be found in process-experiential psychotherapy literature. Elliott et al. admit:

> Diagnosis based on [the *DSM-IV*] is an expert-based, nonempathic approach to working with clients. Thus it is inconsistent with the kind of therapeutic relationship desired in PE [process-experiential] therapy. Does this mean that client diagnosis should be ignored in PE therapy? Although this was our position 20 years ago ... in the meantime we have found that knowing something about the patterns of difficulty their clients experience can help therapists to work with them more effectively. (2004: 275)

So it would appear that a principled position is set aside on the basis of evidence. However, on the same page Elliott et al. state: 'At the same time, PE [process-experiential] therapists attempt as much as possible to bracket the client's diagnosis, setting it to one side. The client is not the diagnosis.' Here we have the worst of both worlds—hinting that although diagnosis is bad in principle, the therapist will do it anyway. And, although not made explicit, another factor may be at work here, namely the requirement for research evidence. It is understandable—when therapeutic approaches vie for funding based on 'evidence', and when that evidence is only deemed trustworthy when presented in terms of diagnostic categories—that theorists and practitioners might be persuaded to be pragmatic, swallow their objections and play the game.

Elke Lambers gives a good account of the context of a person-centred perspective on psychodiagnosis (Lambers, 2003). She also offers a person-centred framework for psychodiagnosis built upon theoretical constructs and gives examples of working in a

---

13. Alternative to the medical model, and also attempting to present a new and unifying 'person-centred psychopathology' as a development and extension of Rogers' work.

14. Changing language is an important project, since language is intimately connected with thinking. Change the way we *talk* about distress and a change in the way we *think* is brought one step closer. It could be argued that, e.g. 'fragile process' is a less alienating label than 'borderline personality disorder' (see Margaret Warner's Chapter 7, this volume). Lisbeth Sommerbeck pointed out in a private communication that the *intention* with which words are used in vitally important, e.g. the term 'depression', can be prescriptive (as used by the medical model) or descriptive (as used by an individual client).

client-centred way with people who have received diagnoses of differing severity. She develops all of this in a scenario predicated upon the pragmatic need to articulate with the medical model in order to better serve our clients. This is helpful for those who are not familiar with medical-model methodology and reassuring for the many practitioners who lack the confidence to work with disturbed and disturbing clients.

Finally (although this is not a comprehensive roll call) Lisbeth Sommerbeck's work is testimony to the success that is possible when compromise is relentlessly pursued whilst standing one's ground in terms of theory. In common with Lambers, she insists that client-centred therapists become familiar with the medical model and diagnostic categories in order better to integrate into the system. Sommerbeck introduces a novel way of approaching the discrepancies between CCT and the psychiatric medical model. She suggests that 'understanding (in the theory of client-centred therapy) and explaining (in the medical model theory of psychiatry), are complementary, not contradictory, activities' (Sommerbeck 2003: 5). She argues for a very different strategy from the options presented in this chapter—one in which psychiatrists will be persuaded of the complementarity of the approaches by the experience of working with a dedicated, *congruent* client-centred therapist. (In her own practice she voices her critical view of psychiatry at every appropriate opportunity, at a general level, being careful not to compromise her relationship with individual clients.) CCT will then sit comfortably in the range of possible treatment options. Sommerbeck (2005) outlines her position in Chapter 8, this volume and in her book (Sommerbeck, 2003).

By and large, however, all of the above arguments are, in Shlien's colourful analogy, already lying down with the lion (with no guarantee that they will not be on the breakfast menu)—their starting-point is an acceptance (however obviously compliant, reluctant and pragmatic) of the precursive medical model of distress and its diagnostic methodology.

I agree with Lambers' and Sommerbeck's calls for therapists to become familiar with the language and procedures of psychodiagnosticians, but for me it is more a case of 'if you want to defeat your enemy, sing his song'. I am also all for articulation, but I fear it means that we, and the users of mental health services, will be the tail that articulates with the dog, and will be wagged without consideration by the psychiatric profession.

CONCLUSION AND STRATEGIES

Whilst critical psychologists and psychiatrists have been developing their arguments in favour of dismantling the medical model, psychopathology and psychodiagnosis, client-centred therapists have been treading water. As the professionalisation of psychological therapies gathered pace, practitioners were required to be inducted into the lower echelons of the medical model as diagnosticians. Diagnosis became, as John Shlien put it, 'their security blanket as well as their entering wedge'. Client-centred therapists briefly wrestled with the issues and evolved three basic ways of dealing with the growing requirement to diagnose. Some simply reject the medical model and diagnosis for the reasons outlined in this chapter. Others just as simply accept the primacy of the medical model and either renounce or 'work around' their person-centred principles. In between these poles of behaviour are others who try to forge a variety of compromises.

There are those who take a pragmatic position, knowing that if we reject the medical model and diagnosis, person-centred therapists would effectively disenfranchise themselves, becoming unemployable in the majority of services which accept the medical model and require assessment and diagnosis as routine.[15] Those taking this route effectively comply whilst resisting the ideology. With disenfranchisement comes disempowerment and to avoid this, the argument that articulation as the realistic alternative to retreat or conformity, has been eloquently and passionately developed by Mearns (2003, 2004). Mearns' 2003 paper is the antidote to this chapter and Lambers (2003), Warner (2005, Chapter 7 this volume) and Sommerbeck (2003 and 2005, Chapter 8, this volume) take similar, but crucially different, lines. Indeed my guess is that the majority of academics and practitioners take one of many middle-routes.

Nevertheless, I seek to keep the option of refusal and principled opposition on the table not only for those in a position to use it in practice (although this would be reason enough), but also because the evolution of ideas requires diversity in the pool of ideas. To keep the poles of the argument struck firmly into the ground provides the tension required for vibrant and creative exchange to prevent the middle ground in the debate becoming a well-trodden, comfortable bog.[16] My final reason is that the metaphor for distress that we as therapists carry with us into our work influences *every aspect* of our relationship with our clients. If we think sick we will see sick, and nothing in that resonates with my understanding of CCT.

A further criticism of my position is that it will needlessly antagonise the lion that others are trying to make peace with. However, I do not believe that the position of opposition and refusal is necessarily self-defeating, disenfranchising and irresponsible. It sits constructively alongside articulation, compromise and complementarity in the range of possibilities which comprise the PCA responses to the medicalisation of distress which offends our theory. In private correspondence, Margaret Warner correctly pointed out to me that something must be done *today* to help bring the PCT tribe back into the mix of funded treatment options wherever it has been excluded. Her work is, in part, an attempt to address such exclusion where it is based on the idea that PCT has no recognisable, unified psychopathology,[17] before my utopian medical-model-free order is installed. Client choice and emancipation is our shared aim—a humanising revision from Warner for the moment, whilst we all plan and organise a future where to be frightened, confused and overwhelmed is not considered to be an 'illness'.

---

15. See Wilkins, Chapter 9 (Wilkins, 2005), this volume, for more on this.
16. Of course, I understand that *practice* in this middle ground is anything but comfortable, for the practitioner committed to reforming the system from within whilst sticking to their CCT principles.
17. Although this point will be contested by those who argue that there is a perfectly adequate CCT psychopathology, my own view is that it runs out of both steam and detail when human distress is severe and enduring, and is also light on developmental theory (see Paul Wilkins' Chapter 4, this volume for the alternative view, Wilkins, 2005).

Opposition to the medicalisation of distress is shared by a number of academics and practitioners critical of the psychiatric system. Scrutiny of their manifesto reveals that they are discovering not only that relationships are important for healing but also that the active qualities are what CCT practitioners would call empathy, UPR and congruence. An exchange of ideas at least, if not a strategic alliance, is indicated. Attempts actively to change the centrality in our culture of the illness metaphor of distress is not a lost cause. That it has happened in other fields, most notably learning disability, is a cause for optimism only if those dedicated to oppose the medicalisation of mental distress are prepared to stand up and organise, locally and within professional associations and to actively, and publicly, align themselves with users of psychiatric services. Opportunities to organise in this way have always been overlooked by client-centred therapists, possibly because our gaze has been unerringly on the potential of the individual. It is time to change. An individual therapist working in isolation will never change the culture of mental health services, but a special interest group in a professional organisation might. Again, John Shlien (2003) speaks for me when he recalls a conversation with a therapist working with analysts in Vienna:

> ... he said, 'I like the person-centered people because they don't fight so much.' Probably that is true. I think that we are a nation of sheep. I think that we may stand quietly, watching our own disintegration with the silence of lambs. I think it would be better to fight more openly, and to know why. I believe that many people here do not say what they think. I *know* it. (pp. 220–1)

If enough of us start making a noise, what democracy remains in therapists' professional bodies can be called upon to produce a challenge to medicalisation. Read, Mosher and Bentall (2004: 5) reflect on 'the sterility and futility of trying to explain and treat "madness" with the crude concepts and tools of biological psychology ...' They conclude the introduction to their book with the words: 'It [the book] is ... a straightforward, unashamed wake-up call. Everyone involved should act, in whatever way your circumstances allow to end this madness' (*ibid*: 5). And that is the essence of the message of this chapter.

CCT/PCA practitioners hold congruence in high esteem. Whatever your definition of it, one meaning is that human flourishing is achieved, at least in part, when we live in harmony with our beliefs. Failing clearly to oppose that which we are in opposition to in our professional field perpetuates an ideology and sanctions practice which damages our clients, ourselves and society as a whole. And, as John Shlien declared: 'There is a special debating tactic in such challenges: take one step not in keeping with your philosophy and you lose the whole of it' (1984: 8).

REFERENCES

Bentall, RP (ed) (1990) *Reconstructing Schizophrenia*. London: Routledge.
Bentall, RP (2003) *Madness Explained: Psychosis and human nature*. London: Allen Lane/Penguin.

Birchwood, M, Fowler, D and Jackson, C (2000) *Early Intervention in Psychosis: A guide to concepts, evidence and interventions.* Chichester: John Wiley.

Blackburn, P and Yates, C (2004) Same Story—Different Tale. *Mental Health Today.* December/January, 2004–5: 31–3.

Bourdieu, P and Wacquant, L (1992) *Invitation to Reflexive Sociology.* Cambridge: Polity Press.

Boyle, M (1990) The Non-discovery of Schizophrenia. In RP Bentall (ed) *Reconstructing Schizophrenia.* London: Routledge.

Boyle, M (1999) Diagnosis. In C Newnes, G Holmes and C Dunn (eds) *This is Madness* (pp. 75–90). Ross on-Wye: PCCS Books.

Boyle, M (2003) *Schizophrenia: A scientific delusion?* London: Routledge.

Boy, A, Seeman, J, Shlien, J, Fischer, C and Cain, DJ (1989/2002) Symposium on Psychodiagnosis. *Person-Centered Review, 4,* 132–82. Reprinted in Cain, DJ (ed)(2002) *Classics in the Person-Centered Approach* (pp. 385–414). Ross-on-Wye: PCCS Books.

Breggin, P (1993) *Toxic Psychiatry.* London: HarperCollins.

Catterall, E (2005) Working with maternal depression: Client-centred therapy as part of a multidisciplinary approach. Chapter 14 (pp. 202–25) this volume.

Charlesworth, SJ (2000) *A Phenomenology of Working Class Experience.* Cambridge: Cambridge University Press.

Elliott, R, Watson, JC, Goldman, RN and Greenberg, LS (2004) *Learning Emotion-Focused Therapy: The process-experiential approach to change.* Washington DC: APA.

Grant, B (1990) Principled and Instrumental Non-Directiveness in Person-Centered and Client-Centered Therapy. *Person-Centred Review, 5,* 77–88. Reprinted in DJ Cain (2002)(ed) *Classics in the Person-Centered Approach* (pp. 371–7). Ross-on-Wye: PCCS Books.

Grant, B (2004) The Imperative of Ethical Justification in Psychotherapy: The special case of client-centered therapy. *Person-Centered and Experiential Psychotherapies, 3,* 152–65.

Houghton, P (2005) Stop the juggernaught. *Mental Health Today.* February: 22–3.

Kirschenbaum, H (1979) *On Becoming Carl Rogers.* New York: Delacorte.

Kirschenbaum, H and Henderson, VL (1990) *The Carl Rogers Dialogues.* London: Constable.

Laing, RD (1965) *The Divided Self.* Harmondsworth: Penguin.

Laing, RD and Esterson, A (1964) *Sanity, Madness and the Family: Families of schizophrenics.* London: Tavistock.

Lambers, E (2003) The person-centred perspective on psychopathology. In D Mearns, *Developing Person-Centred Counselling* (pp. 103–19). London: Sage.

Lynch, T (2004) *Beyond Prozac: Healing mental suffering without drugs.* Ross-on-Wye: PCCS Books.

Marshall, P (1992) *Demanding the Impossible: A history of anarchism.* London: HarperCollins.

McFazdean, D (2004) Regulation: Who is being or will be consulted? *Ipnosis 16, Winter,* p. 29.

Mearns, D (2003) The humanistic agenda: Articulation. *Journal of Humanistic Psychology, 43,* 53–65.

Mearns, D (2004) Problem-Centered is not Person-Centered. *Person-Centered and Experiential Psychotherapies, 3,* 88–101.

Merry, T (2003) The actualisation conundrum. *Person-Centred Practice, 11,* 83–91.

Mosher, LR and Burti, L (1994) *Community Mental Health: A practical guide.* New York: Norton.

Mosher, LR (1999) Soteria and other alternatives to acute psychiatric hospitalization: A personal and professional view. *Changes 17,* 35–51.

Newnes, C (1999) Histories of Psychiatry. In C Newnes, G Holmes, and C Dunn (eds) *This is*

Madness (pp. 7–27). Ross-on-Wye: PCCS Books.

Newnes, C, Holmes, G and Dunn, C (1999) (eds) *This is Madness.* Ross-on-Wye: PCCS Books.

Newnes, C, Holmes, G and Dunn, C (2001) (eds) *This is Madness Too.* Ross-on-Wye: PCCS Books.

Parker, I, Georgaca, E, Harper, D, McLaughlin, T and Stowell-Smith, M (1995) *Deconstructing Psychopathology.* London: Sage.

Patterson, CH (1948/2000) Is psychotherapy dependent upon diagnosis? In CH Patterson (2000) *Understanding Psychotherapy: Fifty years of client-centred theory and practice* (pp. 3–9). Ross-on-Wye: PCCS Books.

Pilgrim, D (1990) Competing Histories of Madness. In RP Bentall (ed) *Reconstructing Schizophrenia.* London: Routledge.

Read, J (2004) A History of Madness. In J Read, LR Mosher, and RP Bentall (eds) *Models of Madness.* London: Brunner-Routledge.

Read, J, Mosher, LR and Bentall, RP (2004) (eds) *Models of Madness.* London: Brunner-Routledge.

Rogers, CR (1951) *Client-Centered Therapy.* Boston: Houghton Mifflin.

Rogers, CR (1957) The necessary and sufficient conditions of therapeutic personality change. *Journal of Consulting Psychology, 21,* 95–103. In H Kirscenbaum and V Henderson (eds) (1990) *The Carl Rogers Reader* (pp. 219–35). London: Constable.

Rogers, CR (1959) A theory of therapy, personality and interpersonal relationships, as developed in the client-centred framework. In S Koch (ed) *Psychology: A study of science, Vol. 3: Formulation of the person and the social context* (pp. 184–256). New York: McGraw-Hill.

Rogers, CR, Gendlin, ET, Kiesler, DJ and Truax, CB (1967) *The Therapeutic Relationship and its Impact: A study of psychotherapy with schizophrenics.* Madison: University of Wisconsin Press.

Rogers, CR (1978) *Carl Rogers on Personal Power: Inner strength and its revolutionary impact.* London: Constable.

Romme, M and Escher, S (1993) *Accepting Voices.* London: Mind Publications.

Rowe, D (1993) Foreword. In P Breggin, *Toxic Psychiatry. Drugs and Electroconvulsive Therapy: The truth and the better alternatives* (pp. xvii–xxix). London: HarperCollins.

Sanders, P and Tudor, K (2001) This is Therapy. In C Newnes, G Holmes and C Dunn (eds) *This is Madness Too* (pp. 147–60). Ross on-Wye: PCCS Books.

Schmid, PF (2004) Back to the Client: A phenomenological approach to the process of understanding and diagnosis. *Person-Centered and Experiential Psychotherapies, 3,* 36–52.

Schmid, PF (2005) Authenticity and alienation: Towards an understanding of the person beyond the categories of order and disorder. Chapter 6 (pp. 75–90) this volume.

Shlien, JM (1984) Introduction. In RF Levant and JM Shlien (eds) *Client-Centered Therapy and the Person-Centered Approach: New directions in theory, research and practice.* New York: Praeger. Reprinted in JM Shlien (2003) *To Lead an Honorable Life: Invitations to think about client-centered-therapy and the person-centered approach.* Ross-on-Wye: PCCS Books.

Shlien, JM (1989/2001) Response to Boy's Symposium on Psychodiagnosis. In DJ Cain (ed) *Classics in the Person-Centered Approach.* Ross-on-Wye: PCCS Books.

Shlien, JM (2003) *To Lead an Honorable Life: Invitations to think about client-centered therapy and the person-centered approach.* Ross-on-Wye: PCCS Books.

Sommerbeck, L (2003) *The Client-Centred Therapist in Psychiatric Settings: A therapists' guide to the psychiatric landscape and its inhabitants.* Ross-on-Wye: PCCS Books.

Sommerbeck, L (2005) The complementarity between client-centred therapy and psychiatry: The theory and the practice. Chapter 8 (pp. 110–27) this volume.

Stickley, T (2005) Learn to listen. *Mental Health Today.* February: 24–5.

Szasz, T (1961) *The Myth of Mental Illness.* New York: Harper and Row.

Warner, MS (2005) A person-centered view of human nature, wellness, and psychopathology. Chapter 7 (pp. 91–109) this volume.

Wilkins, P (2003) An Absent Psychopathology: A therapy for the worried well? In P Wilkins *Person-Centred Therapy in Focus* (pp. 99–107). London: Sage.

Wilkins, P (2005) Assessment and diagnosis in person-centred therapy. Chapter 9 (pp. 128–45) this volume.

Yalom, I (1995) Introduction. In CR Rogers, *A Way of Being* (new edn). Boston: Houghton Mifflin.

Author's note

I thank Margaret Warner and Mick Cooper for their feedback on an earlier draft of this chapter. I especially appreciate Lisbeth Sommerbeck for her enthusiastic engagement with the issues, thorough reading of my work and lively debate. Her input has sharpened my thinking and improved this chapter.

Chapter 4

PERSON-CENTRED THEORY
AND 'MENTAL ILLNESS'

Paul Wilkins

Person-Centred Therapy has been criticised for its perceived lack of a theory of psychopathology and therefore of differentiating the needs of clients experiencing mental ill-health. In this chapter, the validity of this criticism is explored and rebutted with both reference to early theoretical statements and research and to the views of current practitioner/researchers. Differences within the person-centred family of therapies are indicated by briefly examining (for example) the situations in the UK and in continental Europe.

Four major contemporary positions to mental ill-health within the person-centred tradition are explored. These are those based on:

1. (Psychological) contact
2. Incongruence
3. Styles of processing
4. Issues of power

CASES FOR AND AGAINST: A MULTIPLICITY OF VIEWS

A THERAPY FOR THE WORRIED WELL?

One of the widespread beliefs therapists of other orientations have about Person-Centred Therapy is that it is 'psychotherapy lite'; that it may be perfect for those who are mildly and acutely disturbed but it lacks the teeth necessary to get to grips with people experiencing real, chronic distress. On the other hand, Person-Centred Therapy is also seen as useful for people who are so deeply disturbed or dysfunctional as to be 'unsuitable' for psychotherapy (see Kovel 1976: 116). In other words, Person-Centred Therapy is not going to do anything for 'psychologically minded' people with real problems. Also, practitioners of Person-Centred Therapy are seen as naïvely clinging to an optimistic (and outmoded) model of the person, a commitment to a non-directive approach that prevents effective intervention and an antipathy to assessment and diagnosis. Thus Person-Centred Therapy is criticised as lacking a theory of personality and, in particular, of child development. This leads to an inadequate view of how (for example) neuroses and psychoses may arise and thus how they may be addressed. These factors are seen to preclude any notion of 'psychopathology'. This is why Wheeler (in Wheeler and McLeod, 1995: 286) has two 'serious reservations' about Person-Centred Therapy. Firstly, she is concerned that there is an assumption of human goodness which does not hold water. Her second reservation is that there 'is a lack of theory of human growth and development to underpin the practice, and [a] subsequent disregard for assessment'.

The first of these doubts is easily dealt with. Person-centred theory makes no claim as to the inherent 'goodness' of people (see Wilkins, 2003: 60–3). The belief that it does seems to stem from a misunderstanding of the concepts of the actualising tendency and what it means to be 'fully functioning'. These terms imply direction, not an end point and the actualising tendency is a biological force, common to all living things. In incorporating these concepts into theory, no moral judgement is made or implied.

Wheeler's second point presupposes that emotional distress and psychopathology can only be understood in the context of a theory of child development. This is a belief, not a proven fact. An alternative belief, perhaps more in keeping with a person-centred philosophy, is that mental distress is rooted in inequality and 'based on internalised oppression' (see Proctor, 2002: 84). This leads to a need to consider the power relationships and social position of the individual experiencing distress. However, Wheeler's assertion that there is no person-centred theory of child development is an error. Rogers (1959: 222) postulated that:

> the individual, during the period of infancy, has at least these attributes:
>
> 1. He perceives his *experience* as reality. His *experience* is his reality.
>
> *a.* As a consequence he has greater potential *awareness* of what reality is for him than does anyone else, since no one else can completely assume his *internal frame of reference.*
>
> 2. He has an inherent tendency toward *actualizing* his organism.
>
> 3. He interacts with his reality in terms of his basic *actualizing* tendency. Thus his behavior is the goal-directed attempt of the organism to satisfy the experienced needs for *actualization* in the reality as *perceived.*
>
> 4. In this interaction he behaves as an organized whole, as a gestalt.
>
> 5. He engages in an *organismic valuing process*, valuing *experience* with reference to the *actualizing tendency* as a criterion. *Experiences* which are *perceived* as maintaining or enhancing the organism are valued positively. Those which are *perceived* as negating such maintenance or enhancement are valued negatively.
>
> 6. He behaves with adience toward positively valued *experiences* and with avoidance toward those negatively valued.

In the same chapter, Rogers (pp. 224–6) explains the development of conditions of worth and (pp. 226–30) the development of incongruence and its consequences. Indeed, Rogers (1959) includes comprehensive theoretical statements about the human organism. He traces both 'healthy' development and 'dysfunctional' development and shows how there may be movement from ill-health to health. In this way, Rogers' chapter can be seen as the bedrock on which person-centred theories of psychopathology may be built.

Other person-centred theorists have modelled child development. Biermann-Ratjen (1996: 13), drawing on Rogers' necessary and sufficient conditions, offers necessary conditions for self-development in early childhood. These are:

1. That the baby is in *contact* with a significant other.
2. That the baby is preoccupied with *evaluating experience* which might possibly arouse *anxiety*.
3. That the *significant other person* is *congruent in the relationship* to the baby, does not experience anything inconsistent with her self concept while in contact with the baby when it is preoccupied with evaluating [its] experience.
4. That the significant other is *experiencing unconditional positive regard* toward the baby's processes of evaluating his experience.
5. That the significant other is *experiencing an empathic understanding* of the baby's experiencing within his *internal frame of reference*.
6. That the baby gradually *perceives* both the unconditional positive regard of the significant other person for him and the empathic understanding so that in the baby's *awareness* there is gradually a *belief or prognosis* that the unconditionally positively regarding and empathically understanding object would when reacting to other experiences of the baby also exhibit positive regard and empathic understanding.

Biermann-Ratjen (p. 14) goes on to state 'positive regard is the precondition for self development'. Rogers (1959: 223) wrote that the need for positive regard is 'universal in human beings, and in the individual, is pervasive and persistent'. In person-centred theory, it is the pursuit of positive regard at the expense of the organismic valuing process that underlies mental ill-health. Put another way, if there is sufficient disharmony between the organism and the self (-concept), the resulting incongruence is likely to manifest as one or more of the complexes of thinking, behaviour and processing which in other models may be called neuroses and psychoses, mental illness or disease. Holdstock and Rogers (1977: 136) describe the acquisition of psychological disturbance thus:

the continuing estrangement between self-concept and experience leads to increasingly rigid perceptions and behavior. If experiences are extremely incongruent with the self-concept, the defence system will be inadequate to prevent the experiences from overwhelming the self-concept. When this happens the self-concept will break down, resulting in disorganization of behavior. This is conventionally classed as psychosis when the disorganization is considerable.

From the early days of Person-Centred Therapy, there have been theoretical explanations of the acquisition and development of psychopathological ways of being and these have continued to be refined and expanded (see, for example, Cooper, 2000: 87–94). As well as the theoretical structures mentioned above (and those below), in the simplest terms 'disorder' can be understood with reference to the necessary and sufficient conditions. Thus difficulties with 'communication' (including autism, and some other 'special needs') relate to 'contact' and 'perception' (conditions 1 and 6) while emotional distress and thought disorder are to do with incongruence (condition 2). Of course, there is often overlap between the two areas but the theories and practices of Person-Centred Therapy have evolved to take account of each. In fact, work with 'disturbed' populations has been a feature of person-centred practice from at least the 1950s. It may be that practitioners of other orientations disagree with these theories and practices but that is a very different position from being critical of their supposed absence.

AN HISTORICAL PERSPECTIVE

Perhaps the best known and best documented early instance of person-centred practice with people considered to be 'mentally ill' is the so-called 'Wisconsin Project'. Barrett-Lennard (1998: 68–9, 267–70) writes of this 'massive study of psychotherapy with hospitalized schizophrenic patients' which lasted for much of the time Rogers worked at the University of Wisconsin (1957–1963) and led ultimately to the publication of a massive report (see Rogers et al., 1967). Besides Rogers, the project team comprised Eugene Gendlin, Donald Kiesler and Charles Truax, with contributions from many others. Although it was a difficult time for those concerned, riven with personal differences, leading to partings of the ways of colleagues and erstwhile friends and added little to knowledge of Person-Centred Therapy, Barrett-Lennard (1998: 68) records that:

> The work is more of a milestone in respect to the conduct and reporting of research in its complex sphere, and in the development of strategies and instrumentation, than in terms of clear-cut findings from fully tested hypotheses.

Also, although Shlien (2003: 125) argues that the project as a whole 'became a failure' because the staff team was 'not prepared to provide Client-Centered Therapy that was adequate to test the hypotheses' and the research methods employed are now seen as flawed (see, for example, Prouty, 2001: 583–4), it did offer evidence that high levels of congruence and empathy correlated with client improvement. Significant publications other than that of Rogers et al. (1967) resulted from this study. Chief among these are Shlien's 1961 paper 'A client-centered approach to schizophrenia: first approximation' on his work with a deeply disturbed client (see Shlien, 2003: 30–59), Gendlin (1963) and Rogers (1961a) both of which 'include direct and sensitive portrayals of the human condition of the schizophrenic person' (Barrett-Lennard, 1998: 68). Also important in terms of the historical perspective on psychopathology in Person-Centred Therapy is the symposium on psychodiagnosis published in *Person-Centered Review* printed in 1989 and reprinted in Cain (2002). This is dealt with more thoroughly in the chapter on assessment (Wilkins, Chapter 9, this volume).

From the 1960s until the 1990s, as in so many other areas, research into Person-Centred Therapy with schizophrenics and reports of case studies are largely absent from the (English language) literature. Following a conference for client-centred and experiential psychotherapies in Leuven, Belgium, the published proceedings contain two significant papers about working with schizophrenic people; Prouty (1990) and Teusch (1990). This trend continued in the following international conferences on client-centered and experiential counselling and psychotherapy. For example, Berghofer (1996) reports on her work with long-term patients and (p. 492) concludes that '[t]he most important element in psychotherapy with schizophrenic patients is the active establishment and maintenance of a reliable interpersonal relationship'. Milsch (2000) too stresses the importance of the relationship in working with this client group while Warner (2002a) emphasises not only the quality of the relationship but also the importance of allowing this client group (and others experiencing 'thought disorders') to express themselves in their own voices. She (p. 471) writes:

> I suspect that the common psychiatric practice of ignoring or actively discouraging expressions that sound psychotic may actually stop clients from processing experiences in ways that could allow them to gain a more integrated sense of their own reactions and preferences.

Until the last decade of the 20th century, there does not seem to be much written about Person-Centred Therapy with specific 'disorders' other than schizophrenia. The research effort in the 1960s and 1970s was largely directed towards establishing the efficacy of the therapist conditions of congruence, empathy and unconditional regard. Although this research yielded some interesting results, as a way of testing Rogers' hypothesis as to the necessity and sufficiency of the six conditions, because the therapist conditions were usually separated from the other three and often attempts were made to consider them separately, it is flawed. Another main area for research throughout this time and henceforward was into the comparative effectiveness of Person-Centred Therapy with respect to other approaches. This too is suspect because, as Elliott (2001: 67–8) confirms in his meta-analysis, 'researcher allegiance' (i.e. the approach to therapy to which the researcher is predisposed) tends to influence findings. It is also true that, in terms of classic Client-Centred Therapy, because there is only one 'treatment' regardless of the client's difficulty (see Wilkins and Gill, 2003: 177), there was little impetus to research the hows and whys of Person-Centred Therapy with different issues and different client groups. However, Lambers (1994: 106–20) did make an important, accessible statement about 'person-centred psychopathology' setting out in straightforward terms how the major psychiatric categories of:

- neurotic disorders
- borderline personality disorders
- psychotic disorders
- personality disorders

may be understood in a person-centred way. She (p. 109) makes the 'key point' that although person-centred theoreticians and practitioners are resistant to diagnostic labels, 'it is possible to understand, for example, neurosis in terms of person-centred theory. Such an analysis may help the counsellor to understand her own responses to the neurotic client.'

Lambers (1994: 106–7) understands neuroses in terms psychosomatic symptoms, anxiety and incongruent communication. She (p. 107) advances the idea that neurosis develops from strong conditions of worth, the punishment for not conforming to which 'took the form of *withdrawal of affection and acceptance*' [original italics]. There is a resulting externalisation of the locus of evaluation, a negative self-concept, feelings may be denied or distorted; in every way, neurosis equates with incongruence. Lambers (p. 110) describes borderline personality disorder as characterised by a wide variety of symptoms and states that the life of a person experiencing it 'may appear chaotic'. She (pp. 110–11) sees the development of borderline personality disorder as possibly developing from an inconsistency in conditions of worth and experiences leading to an inability to develop a self-concept informed by experience. She (p. 111) writes that the self-concept of a person experiencing borderline personality disorder 'lacks boundaries, consistency, continuity and protection; it is constantly under threat as it has no effective means of evaluating and integrating new experiences'. Borderline personality disorder is further characterised by episodes of adequate functioning interspersed with times of chaos and disturbance. Lambers (p. 111) takes the view that the defensive responses manifesting as disturbed behaviour 'only occur in situations where the self is threatened by new experiences'. Of psychosis, she (p. 113) reminds her readers that this is not a diagnostic category but a description of a mental state characterised by withdrawal from normal contact both with reality and with other people. She (pp. 113–14) goes on to reiterate Rogers' view that psychosis is 'a state of disintegration, involving the breakdown of the neurotic defences of denial and distortion and the development of extreme forms of defence such as paranoid and catatonic behaviour'. The need for such an extreme reaction Lambers (p. 114) understands in terms of an enormous threat to the self. Personality disorder she (p. 116–17) describes in terms of 'subjective distress or significant impairment of the person's ability to function as a social being' and as characterised by a sense that the causes of misfortune and threat are located in others and outside the control of the sufferer. Lambers (p. 117) writes that personality disorder arises from early significant relationships 'characterised by neglect or persistent abuse of power' in which 'conditions of worth have been linked with satisfying the needs of those with the power'. Because of the unpredictable nature of such relationships, people with personality disorders have learned to live only in the moment and have not been able to learn from experience. This results in a profound negation of self and a deep-seated sense of worthlessness. Lambers (p. 118) states that 'to bring this core sense of worthlessness into awareness would be very dangerous'.

COMING UP TO DATE

In the later years of the 20th century and into the 21st century, this situation changed radically. This change may be partly because of the need to demonstrate the effectiveness and applicability of the person-centred family of therapies to funders (healthcare providers, medical insurers and the like) but it also reflects a zeitgeist. Whatever the reason, the person-centred community has turned its attention once more to 'psychopathology'.

This is evident, for example, from the review of research in the German language region produced by Eckert et al., (2003) where (p. 5) they indicate that the focus of research has become 'increasingly disorder-specific' listing studies addressing:

- agoraphobia
- panic disorder
- borderline personality disorder
- depression
- psychosomatic disorders

More recently, there has also been a debate 'person-centred versus problem-centred' (see Takens and Lietaer, 2004: 79–80). At one extreme, Sachse (2004: 24) argues:

> [Client-Centered Therapy] urgently needs disorder-specific concepts ... Therapists must act in a more disorder-specific fashion. To do this, they must first identify the disorder—they must make a diagnosis. To do this they must have disorder-specific knowledge.

Sachse sees diagnosis as leading to a conclusion as to which therapeutic approaches a client will respond. Mearns (2004: 89–90) casts doubt on the validity of a 'problem-centred' approach to mental illness pointing out that there has been little serious, mainstream questioning of the appropriateness of the medical model as a way of understanding mental health and demonstrating that individuals respond differently to the same or similar stimuli. Because individuals who share a diagnosis (the example Mearns uses is alcoholism) almost certainly will not share (p. 90) 'the constellation of [their] symbolizing of their past, their present processing and their future vision for their self' so disorder-specific treatment is a nonsense. Schmid (2004: 46) takes a similar view stating:

> Different ways of relating by the client in-form [sic] the therapist to relate and answer differently. This is crucial, because the relationship is unique. Each client deserves to get the answer and relationship they need and ... not some preset 'type of intervention'.

For Mearns (2004: 94), the effective way of being with someone experiencing emotional distress or mental ill-health is to work at relational depth; that is to engage with the client in a fully empathic, accepting and congruent way (see also Mearns, 1996). In his final paragraph. Mearns (2004: 99) points out that clients' difficult processes (see below) are not problems in themselves but 'both barriers and *gateways*' to engaging at relational depth. In conclusion, Mearns writes: 'We do not need to be *more than* person-centered therapists; we just need to be *good* person-centered therapists.'

As the title of his 2004 paper suggests, Sachse is probably seen by himself (and certainly others) to have deviated from the basic tenets of Client-Centred Therapy. Mearns on the other hand remains close to classic Client-Centred Therapy although he places more emphasis on the centrality of the relationship. Throughout their paper, Takens and Lietaer (2004) make it clear that others are positioned differently within this spectrum. They (p. 85) emphasise that between the extremes there are those who experience the two models as in tension rather than in conflict. This is their position and it is a tension they believe to be fruitful.

MODELS OF PSYCHOPATHOLOGY IN PERSON-CENTRED THEORY AND PRACTICE

Treatment of people who are disturbed, suffering mental and/or emotional ill-health or what you will has, in the West, been dominated by practitioners who adhere to a medical model whether they are medically trained or not. So, an epistemology developed for the diagnosis and treatment of physical ailments has been applied wholesale to maladies of mind and spirit without rigorous empirical testing. Barbara Douglas, counselling psychologist and historian of the treatment of people experiencing mental ill-health (personal communication, 2004) points out that early success in treating 'general paralysis of the insane' (late stage syphilis) with a drug and some subsequent success in the drug treatment of neurological disorders reinforced the notion of the applicability of a '(symptoms)–diagnosis–treatment–cure–(lack of symptoms)' model to people whose disorder of thought and feeling is of other origins. This has not been established in the same way. A second influence on psychotherapy has been psychoanalysis (which, to at least some extent, can in itself be consider an offshoot of medicine). It is from this source that some of the labelling language arises—'borderline personality', 'narcissism', etc. Historically, both these ways of thinking about people have been opposed by person-centred practitioners (although latterly there has been some move towards a common language especially by those who practice in medical settings). There are person-centred alternatives, person-centred theories and practices amounting to ways of working with the mentally and emotionally disturbed and distressed; some of them are described below.

PSYCHOLOGICAL CONTACT AND PSYCHOPATHOLOGY

One of the most important contributions to person-centred understanding and practice in the last years of the 20th century was made as a result of Garry Prouty questioning what happens if the first of Rogers' necessary and sufficient conditions for constructive, therapeutic change (that there be contact between client and therapist) is not met. For me, the importance of this lies not only in the subsequent development of theory and action (Pre-Therapy: see Prouty 2002a, b and c) but in the very raising of the difficulty. As Sanders and Wyatt (2002: viii) indicate, over the years little attention has been paid to 'contact/psychological contact' and there is not really a definition of this concept—Rogers (1959: 207) is vague suggesting that two people are in contact 'when each makes a perceived or subceived difference in the experiential field of the other' and this looseness leads to a lack of agreement persisting to this day. Wyatt and Sanders (2002) offer the first comprehensive exploration of contact (with perception, condition 6).

Prouty (2002b: 55) defines pre-therapy as 'a theory of psychological contact ... rooted in Rogers' conception of psychological contact as the first condition of a therapeutic relationship'. This theory 'was developed in the context of treating mentally retarded or psychotic populations' (Krietemeyer and Prouty, 2003: 152) because, in Prouty's experience, such people are 'contact-impaired' and have difficulty forming interpersonal connections. Prouty (2002b: 56–60) describes contact in terms of three levels: contact reflections, contact functions and contact behaviours. These are summarised in Tudor and Merry (2002: 31–2). The theory led to a set of practices by which psychological contact could be established (see, for example, the case studies presented by Van Werde (1994: 125–8) and Krietemeyer and Prouty (2003: 154–60)) and for which Prouty (2001: 595–6) summarises research evidence noting that (p. 596) '[p]ilot studies with clients with severely limited mental abilities provide suggestive evidence for further empirical exploration'.

Warner (2002b: 89–91) also pays attention to the role of contact in 'difficult process' (see below for an explanation of Warner's models of processing). She points out that (p. 89) 'being blocked from psychological contact is almost always experienced as an affliction' and briefly describes the contact-impairment likely or possible in people experiencing fragile, dissociated and psychotic process.

THEORIES OF INCONGRUENCE

In person-centred theory, it is explicit that extreme incongruence is what leads to mental ill-health or, if you prefer, it is the conditions of worth leading to incongruence that are the roots of psychological disturbance. As stated in the fourteenth of Rogers (1951: 483–522) nineteen propositions:

> Psychological maladjustment exists when the organism denies to awareness significant sensory and visceral experiences, which consequently are not symbolized and organized into the gestalt of the self-structure. When this situation exists, there is a basic or potential psychological tension.

This Merry (2002: 36) helpfully rephrases as 'When we experience something that doesn't fit in with our picture of ourselves and we cannot fit it in with that picture, we feel tense, anxious, frightened or confused.' When a person has a poor self-concept which is out of touch with the organism, she or he is disturbed. In extreme cases, this manifests as 'madness'. Since incongruence is central to mental/emotional distress, it follows that person-centred practitioner/theoreticians base models of psychopathology around it. Thus, Van Kalmthout (2002, 134, 135–6) asserts that avoiding experiencing 'what there really is' and the resulting lack of contact between inner and outer reality 'can lead to problems and even psychopathology'. Speierer (1996: 300) goes so far as to state 'client-centered therapy is ... the treatment of incongruence' and (1990, 1996) proposes a 'differential incongruence model' which (1996: 299) offers 'a specific illness concept for client-centered psychotherapy'. Speierer's contention is that incongruence is the root of emotional distress and that it has three main causes. These are (1996: 299):

- 'well-known client-centered social communicative factors' by which Speierer means the acquisition of conditions of worth and a 'form of incompatibility between societal and organismic values'
- 'a non-socially caused bio-neuropsychological inability to reach congruence'
- 'social and non-social life-changing events'

Speierer's model goes far beyond the concepts of classic Client-Centred Therapy not least because he is suggesting that different 'disorders' are the result of differences in incongruence and then he draws the conclusion that (1996: 307) 'different therapy options can be offered according to the individual's needs and his disorder'.

Biermann-Ratjen (1998) also writes about incongruence and psychopathology. She devotes sections to 'post-traumatic stress disorder', 'psychogenic illnesses' and 'neurosis' as manifestations of incongruence. For example, she (p. 126–7) writes:

> Any symptom of psychogenic illness is the expression of experiencing incongruence:
> 1. The person may be unable to symbolize completely and communicate verbally certain experiences.
> 2. The person may be unable to understand and/or accept certain experiences as self-experiences.
> 3. The person may experience certain ways of defending against experience (stress reactions, acute incongruence) or different forms of stagnation in self-development (chronic incongruence).
> 4. In any case experiencing incongruence will include experiencing physical tension.

For Biermann-Ratjen, it is at what stage self-development is interrupted that determines the nature of distress.

STYLES OF PROCESSING

Rogers (1961b: 27) refers to life as 'a flowing, changing process in which nothing is fixed'. He also (p. 126, p. 171) refers to an acceptance of the fluid nature of existence as an outcome of therapy and (p. 186) characterises the 'good life' as 'a process, not a state of being'. He also (pp. 132–55) described the seven stages of process in therapy by which an individual changes from fixedness to a fluid way of being. From this, it is clear that people are defined as 'in process' rather than as of a particular 'personality type'. A person's process is their way of experiencing and encountering the world, a way of making sense of all the stimuli and information to which they are exposed. Process is cognitive, behavioural, emotional and (arguably at least) spiritual. Worsley (2002: 21) points out that process is both in and out of awareness and may be either reflexive or spontaneous. Also, a person's process may flow in the easy way Rogers described as desirable or it may be 'difficult' (and, of course all stages between). The notion of difficult process forms the basis of the theory and practice of Warner (1998, 2000, 2002a, 2002b).

Warner describes three kinds of difficult process (summarised briefly in Warner, 2001: 182–3). These are:

Fragile process: 'Clients who have a fragile style of processing tend to experience core issues at very low or very high levels of intensity. They tend to have difficulty starting and stopping experiences that are personally significant or emotionally connected. In addition, they are likely to have difficulty taking the point of view of another person while remaining in contact with such experiences' (Warner, 2000: 150).

Dissociated process: 'Clients who experience "dissociated process" go through periods of time when they quite convincingly experience themselves as having selves that are not integrated with each other. Sometimes, they experience a disunity of self that feels "crazy" to themselves and to others. At other times they may have periods of forgetfulness for the minutes or hours when alternate personality parts have been dominant. They may go for years without being aware of such parts by keeping very busy and leading quite restricted lives, only to have past experiences return in times of crisis' (Warner, 2001: 183).

Psychotic process: 'When clients have a psychotic style of processing, they have difficulty forming narratives about their experience that make sense within the culture, or which offer a predictive value in relation to their environment. Clients experiencing psychotic process ... (have) impaired contact with 'self', 'world' and 'other'. Such clients often experience voices, hallucinations or delusions that are neither culturally accepted nor are easy to process' (Warner, 2001: 183).

In her various papers, Warner describes the possible origins of these styles of processing and effective ways of working with each group of clients in a person-centred way.

Mearns (2004: 99) indicates that he, with Mick Cooper, is investigating a fourth style of processing which they are currently calling *disconnected process*. In this style of processing, the actualising tendency and an inferred balancing process of social mediation (see Mearns and Thorne, 2000: 178–86) 'are separating and creating disjunctions between the self and the phenomenological context'.

Although these styles of processing may be identified with traditional psychiatric/ psychoanalytic categories, they are conceived of in a very different way and the methods of working with people experiencing difficult process are firmly rooted in person-centred practice.

POWER AND MENTAL AND EMOTIONAL DISTRESS

Another view of the aetiology of mental and emotional distress which is compatible with person-centred theory and practice but which moves away from the notion that such difficulties are intrinsic, intra-personal and a response to relationships with significant others is that their origin is social and/or environmental. Proctor (2002: 3) is clear that 'there is much evidence to associate the likelihood of suffering from psychological distress with the individual's position in society with respect to structural power'. She (pp. 3–4) shows how women are more likely than men to be diagnosed with a range of disorders and that working class people as a whole are over-represented in the mental illness statistics.

It is argued that psychiatric systems are inherently systems of control and power. It follows that if distress flows from an experience of inequality and an encounter with psychiatric services is disempowering, then psychiatry may be making people worse rather than better. In a much more sophisticated way, this is the case made by the anti-psychiatry movement (proponents of which include Szasz and Laing) and, currently, by those involved in critical psychology (see, for example, Newnes et al., 1999 and 2001). As articulated by Holmes and Dunn (1999: 2), critical psychology 'lays down a challenge to the idea that the psychiatric system is largely benign'. In the same book, Newnes and Holmes (1999: 281–2) offer a view as to the role of 'talking therapies' in the future of mental health services. Although they (p. 281) are wary of 'the dangers and limits of talking therapies', they see value in 'collaborative conversation' in which therapist and client meet with the intention 'to understand each other and work together on the [client's] goals'. They (p. 282) also emphasise the importance of 'empathy through personal disclosure' as a 'powerful way of relating to and helping people'. Proctor (2002: 90) refers to the demystification of therapy as a way of addressing the imbalance of power in the therapy relationship and states 'the demystification of my therapist as a person was a strong factor in my not feeling disempowered in the relationship'. In Person-Centred Therapy, the relationship is seen to be at the centre and, in respect of it, there is a case to be made for 'willingness to be known' on the part of the therapist so perhaps it can go some way to meeting the needs seen by Newnes and Holmes. Certainly, Pete Sanders (speaking at the 2nd Conference held by the British Association for the Person-Centred Approach) and Gillian Proctor (2002: 103) both emphasise the potential for Person-Centred Therapy to offer a radical alternative to orthodox psychiatry (and medicalised psychotherapy) and (Proctor, 2002: 103) 'to emphasise the autonomy and trustworthiness of the client'. However, Proctor (2002: 137) warns that although Person-Centred Therapy 'addresses all aspects of power in the therapy relationship' there is a danger that 'the focus on the therapist as a person' may obscure 'the power inherent in the role of therapist'. She also sees that within Person-Centred Therapy, 'there is the potential for therapists to miss levels of oppression resulting from structural positions unless the socially positioned person is acknowledged'. This is something to be addressed if the criticisms of the critical psychology movement are to be rebutted. A person-centred model to address power issues would involve working at 'relational depth' but it would also take account of inequalities of structural power both within and without the therapy relationship.

The position of Person-Centred Therapy with respect to the contemporary psychiatric system is explored and explicated by Sanders and Tudor (2001). They (p. 148) declare 'we are proponents of the Person-Centred Approach precisely because it offers a radical view of psychology and psychotherapy and a critical contribution to contemporary concerns about mental health.' They are equally clear that they are not uncritical of Person-Centred

Therapy. For example, throughout their chapter, they argue that to consider individuals separately from the social and political milieus in which they live is a shortcoming of psychotherapy and one by which Person-Centred Therapy is not untainted. Using Rogers' notion of process as an inspiration, Sanders and Tudor (pp. 156–7) characterise:

> a [r]evolutionary effect on psychiatry and mental health services, based on movement towards:
>
> • A non-defensive openness in all interpersonal relationships—throughout the psychiatric system, regardless of status.
>
> • A holistic approach and attitude to the individual—for example, complementary health practitioners working in psychiatric services.
>
> • Human-sized, rather than institutional-sized, groupings—reflected in an emphasis on small units at all levels of the psychiatric system (i.e. primary, secondary and tertiary).
>
> • Attention to the quality of personal living—both in the community and in the asylum (crisis house, hospital, etc.).
>
> • A more genuine and *inclusive* caring concern for those who need help—which would require a radical shift of thinking and practice on community care ... and an openness to creative, therapeutic alternatives to institutional care.

Behind all the views presented in this section is an assumption that 'madness' is socially defined and that social and political circumstances at the very least contribute to mental ill-health and are possibly causal. There is also a belief that the imbalance and abuse of power relate to mental ill-health and that it is only if power in all its aspects is openly addressed can therapy be successful. In this model of mental disturbance, although there is a challenge to person-centred theory and practice, it is one that it may meet more easily than many other approaches.

CONCLUSION

It is clear that, although the term may have been resisted, from its earliest days Person-Centred Therapy has been concerned with the issue of 'psychopathology'. Rogers and his collaborators went to great pains to present theories of development and explanations for maladjustment which they then attempted to test in a variety of therapeutic situations. More recently, early client-centred theoretical statements have been reinterpreted to offer (for example) theories of child development and support for different conceptions of working with people experiencing more extreme forms of emotional and mental distress. For the most part, these different conceptions of 'psychopathology' draw on the original six necessary and sufficient conditions for constructive personality change, the different emphases resulting from the originators' experience and allegiance (for example, whether closer to client-centred or experiential traditions). Presumably in the interests of dialogue and mutual understanding, these models also tend to draw to some extent on the language of psychiatry and psychoanalysis (although most usually to point out person-centred conceptions of phenomena recognised in these ways of thinking). An exception is the idea that the Person-Centred Approach could (and should?) offer a radical alternative to existing philosophies and practices in the mental health system. Adherents of this view are inclined to the belief that by being true to its roots and by drawing on its strengths with respect to the exercise of power and as a socio-political model as much as an intra- and interpersonal one, the Person-Centred Approach can become a natural ally to the critical psychology movement in developing real and effective alternatives to current mental health practices.

REFERENCES

Barrett-Lennard, GT (1998) *Carl Rogers' Helping System: Journey and substance*. London: Sage.

Berghofer, G (1996) Dealing with schizophrenia—a person-centered approach providing care to long-term patients in a supported residential service in Vienna. In R Hutterer, G Pawlowsky, PF Schmid and R Stipsits (eds) *Client-Centered and Experiential Psychotherapy: A paradigm in motion*. Frankfurt-am-Main: Peter Lang.

Biermann-Ratjen, E-M (1996) On the way to a client-centred psychopathology. In R Hutterer, G Pawlowsky, PF Schmid and R Stipsits (eds) *Client-Centered and Experiential Psychotherapy: A paradigm in motion*. Frankfurt-am-Main: Peter Lang.

Biermann-Ratjen, E-M (1998) Incongruence and psychopathology. In B Thorne and E Lambers (eds) *Person-Centred Therapy: A European perspective*. London: Sage.

Cain, DJ (ed) (2002) *Classics in the Person-Centered Approach*. Ross-on-Wye: PCCS Books.

Cooper, M (2000) Person-centred development theory: reflections and revisions. *Person-Centred Practice 8*, 87–94.

Eckert, J, Höger, D and Schwab, R (2003) Development and current state of the research on client-centered therapy in the German language region. *Person-Centered and Experiential Psychotherapies 2*, 3–18.

Elliott, R (2001) The effectiveness of humanistic therapies: a meta-analysis. In DJ Cain, (ed) *Humanistic Therapies: Handbook of research and practice*. Washington, DC: American Psychological Association.

Gendlin, ET (1963) Subverbal communication and therapist expressivity: trends in client-centered therapy with schizophrenics. *Journal of Existential Psychiatry 4*, 105ff.

Holdstock, TL and Rogers, CR (1977) Person-centered theory. In RJ Corsini (ed) *Current Personality Theories*. Itasca, IL: Peacock.

Holmes, G and Dunn, C (1999) Introduction. In C Newnes, G Holmes and C Dunn (eds) *This is Madness: A critical look at psychiatry and the future of mental health services*. Ross-on-Wye: PCCS Books.

Kovel, J (1976) *A Complete Guide to Therapy: From psychotherapy to behavior modification*. New York: Pantheon Books.

Krietemeyer, B and Prouty, G (2003) The art of psychological contact: the psychotherapy of a mentally retarded psychotic client. *Person-Centered and Experiential Psychotherapies 2*, 151–61.

Lambers, E (1994) Person-centred psychopathology. In D Mearns *Developing Person-Centred Counselling*. London: Sage.

Mearns, D (1996) Working at relational depth with clients in Person-Centred Therapy. *Counselling* 7, 306–11.

Mearns, D (2004) Problem-centered is not person-centered. *Person-Centered and Experiential Psychotherapies 3*, 88–101.

Mearns, D and Thorne, B (2000) *Person-Centred Therapy Today: New frontiers in theory and practice.* London: Sage.

Merry, T (2002) *Learning and Being in Person-Centred Counselling* (2nd edn). Ross-on-Wye: PCCS Books.

Milsch, G (2000) Client-centered psychotherapy with schizophrenic patients. Personal experiences and formulation of a helpful setting. In J Marques-Teixeira and S Antunes (eds) *Client-Centered and Experiential Psychotherapy.* Linda a Velha: Vale and Vale.

Newnes, C and Holmes, G (1999) The future of mental health services. In C Newnes, G Holmes, and C Dunn (eds) *This is Madness: A critical look at psychiatry and the future of mental health services.* Ross-on-Wye: PCCS Books.

Newnes, C, Holmes, G and Dunn, C (eds) (2001) *This is Madness Too: Critical perspectives on mental health services.* Ross-on-Wye: PCCS Books.

Proctor, G (2002) *The Dynamics of Power in Counselling and Psychotherapy: Ethics, politics and practice.* Ross-on-Wye: PCCS Books.

Prouty, G (1990) Pre-therapy: a theoretical evolution in the person-centered/experiential psychotherapy of schizophrenia and retardation. In G Lietaer, J Rombauts and R Van Balen (eds) *Client-Centered and Experiential Psychotherapy in the Nineties.* Leuven: Leuven University Press.

Prouty, G (2001) Humanistic therapy for people with schizophrenia. In DJ Cain, (ed) *Humanistic Therapies: Handbook of research and practice.* Washington, DC: American Psychological Association.

Prouty, G (2002a) Pre-therapy: an essay in philosophical psychology. In G Wyatt and P Sanders (eds) *Rogers' Therapeutic Conditions: Evolution, theory and practice. Vol. 4: Contact and Perception.* Ross-on-Wye: PCCS Books.

Prouty, G (2002b) Pre-therapy as a theoretical system. In G Wyatt and P Sanders (eds) *Rogers' Therapeutic Conditions: Evolution, theory and practice. Vol. 4: Contact and Perception.* Ross-on-Wye: PCCS Books.

Prouty, G (2002c) The practice of pre-therapy. In G Wyatt and P Sanders (eds) *Rogers' Therapeutic Conditions: Evolution, theory and practice. Vol. 4: Contact and Perception.* Ross-on-Wye: PCCS Books.

Rogers, CR (1951) *Client-Centered Therapy: Its current practice, implications and theory.* Boston: Houghton Mifflin.

Rogers, CR (1959) A theory of therapy, personality and interpersonal relationships, as developed in the client-centered framework. In S Koch (ed) *Psychology: A study of science, Vol. 3: Formulation of the Person and the Social Context.* New York: McGraw-Hill.

Rogers, CR (1961a) A theory of psychotherapy with schizophrenics and a proposal for its empirical investigation. In JG Dawson, HK Stone and NP Dellis (eds) *Psychotherapy with Schizophrenics.* Baton Rouge: Louisiana State University Press.

Rogers, CR (1961b) *On Becoming a Person: A therapist's view of psychotherapy.* London: Constable.

Rogers, CR, with Gendlin, ET, Kiesler, DJ and Truax, CB (eds) (1967) *The Therapeutic Relationship and its Impact: A study of psychotherapy with schizophrenics.* Madison: University of Wisconsin Press.

Sachse, R (2004) From client-centered to clarification-oriented psychotherapy. *Person-Centered and Experiential Psychotherapies 3*, 19–35.

Sanders, P and Tudor, K (2001) This is therapy: a person-centred critique of the contemporary psychiatric system. In C Newnes, G Holmes and C Dunn (eds) *This is Madness Too: Critical perspectives on mental health services*. Ross-on-Wye: PCCS Books.

Sanders, P and Wyatt, G (2002) Introduction. In G Wyatt and P Sanders (eds) *Rogers' Therapeutic Conditions: Evolution, theory and practice. Volume 4: Contact and Perception*. Ross-on-Wye: PCCS Books.

Schmid, PF (2004) Back to the client: a phenomenological approach to the process of understanding and diagnosis. *Person-Centered and Experiential Psychotherapies 3*, 36–51.

Shlien, JM (2003) *To Lead an Honorable Life: Invitations to think about Client-Centered Therapy and the Person-Centered Approach*. A collection of the work of John M Shlien (P Sanders, ed). Ross-on-Wye: PCCS Books.

Speierer, G-W (1990) Toward a specific illness concept of client-centered therapy. In G Lietaer, J Rombauts and R Van Balen (eds) *Client-Centered and Experiential Psychotherapy in the Nineties*. Leuven: Leuven University Press.

Speierer, G-W (1996) Client-centered therapy according to the Differential Incongruence Model (DIM). In R Hutterer, G Pawlowsky, PF Schmid and R Stipsits (eds) *Client-Centered and Experiential Psychotherapy: A paradigm in motion*. Frankfurt-am-Main: Peter Lang.

Takens, RJ and Lietaer, G (2004) Process differentiation and person-centeredness: a contradiction? *Person-Centered and Experiential Psychotherapies 3*, 77–87.

Teusch, L (1990) Positive effects and limitations of client-centered therapy with schizophrenic patients. In G Lietaer, J Rombauts and R Van Balen (eds) *Client-Centered and Experiential Psychotherapy in the Nineties*. Leuven: Leuven University Press.

Tudor, K and Merry, T (2002) *Dictionary of Person-Centred Psychology*. London: Whurr.

Van Kalmthout, M (2002) The farthest reaches of person-centered psychotherapy. In JC Watson, RN Goldman and MS Warner (eds) *Client-Centered and Experiential Psychotherapy in the 21st Century: Advances in theory, research and practice*. Ross-on-Wye: PCCS Books.

Van Werde, D (1994) Dealing with the possibility of psychotic content in a seemingly congruent communication. In D Mearns *Developing Person-Centred Counselling*. London: Sage.

Warner, MS (1998) A client-centered approach to working with dissociated and fragile process. In L Greenberg, J Watson and G Lietaer (eds) *Foundations of Experiential Theory and Practice: Differential treatment approaches*. New York: Guilford Press.

Warner, MS (2000) Person-Centred Therapy at the difficult edge: A developmentally based model of fragile and dissociated process. In D Mearns and B Thorne *Person-Centred Therapy Today: New frontiers in theory and practice*. London: Sage.

Warner, MS (2001) Empathy, relational depth and difficult client process. In S Haugh and T Merry (eds) *Rogers' Therapeutic Conditions: Evolution, theory and practice. Volume 2: Empathy*. Ross-on-Wye: PCCS Books.

Warner, MS (2002a) Luke's dilemmas: a client-centered/experiential model of processing with a schizophrenic thought disorder. In JC Watson, RN Goldman and MS Warner (eds) *Client-Centered and Experiential Psychotherapy in the 21st Century: Advances in theory, research and practice*. Ross-on-Wye: PCCS Books.

Warner, MS (2002b) Psychological contact, meaningful process and human nature. A reformulation of person-centred theory. In G Wyatt and P Sanders (eds) *Rogers' Therapeutic Conditions: Evolution, theory and practice. Volume 4: Contact and Perception*. Ross-on-Wye: PCCS Books.

Wheeler, S and McLeod, J (1995) Person-centred and psychodynamic counselling: a dialogue. *Counselling 6*, 283–7.

Wilkins, P (2003) *Person-Centred Therapy in Focus*. London: Sage.

Wilkins, P and Gill, M (2003) Assessment in Person-Centered Therapy. *Person-Centered and Experiential Psychotherapies 2*, 172–87.

Worsley, R (2002) *Process Work in Person-Centred Therapy*. Basingstoke: Palgrave.

Wyatt, G and Sanders, P (2002) *Rogers' Therapeutic Conditions: Evolution, theory and practice. Volume 4: Contact and Perception*. Ross-on-Wye: PCCS Books.

CHAPTER 5

FROM SELF-OBJECTIFICATION TO SELF-AFFIRMATION: THE 'I-ME' AND 'I-SELF' RELATION STANCES[1]

MICK COOPER

At the heart of Rogers' (1959) model of psychological distress is the assertion that an individual may come to deny or distort self-experiences, such that an incongruence develops between self-experiences and self-concept, with anxiety and breakdown possible outcomes. In contrast to other models of psychological defence, however (for instance, the psychodynamic model), Rogers' understanding of these processes is relatively undeveloped. Moreover, in recent years, many theorists and practitioners within the person-centred field—as well as in the wider therapeutic and psychological community— have argued that human beings do not have just one self-concept, self, or mode of experiencing (e.g. Cooper, 1999; Cooper, Mearns, Stiles, Warner and Elliott, 2004; Elliott and Greenberg, 1997; Mearns and Thorne, 2000; Stiles et al., 1990) but a plurality of different 'I-positions' (Hermans and Kempen, 1993), and therefore a multitude of different ways in which they may defend—and construct—themselves. There is a need, therefore, to develop person-centred understandings of how people defend themselves against their own experiences, and the implications that this might have for an understanding of psychological distress and health.

My own thoughts in this area arose following some work with a young woman who had experienced many years of sexual and physical abuse as a child.[2] She came to therapy deeply unhappy about her life and would spend most of her days pacing around her flat: frustrated, angry, but feeling incapable of venturing further outside or forging meaningful friendships. As she spoke about herself and how she was, I was struck by the parallels that her attitude towards herself seemed to have with Buber's (1958) notion of an 'I-It attitude'. For instance, she talked about her 'self-who-paced-around-the-room' as if it was an object without volition and choice, and she seemed to have no empathy with this way of being: no ability to enter into 'its' frame of mind. She also accounted for her present experiences in entirely deterministic terms: as something that was *caused*

---

1. This chapter is an edited, revised and updated version of: Cooper, M (2003) 'I-I' And 'I-Me': Transposing Buber's interpersonal attitudes to the intrapersonal plane. *Journal of Constructivist Psychology, 16*, 131–53. ©2003 from *Journal of Constructivist Psychology* by Mick Cooper. Reproduced by permission of Taylor and Francis.

2. To ensure complete confidentiality, some details in the case-examples used in this paper have been changed.

by her past, and something over which she had no control. It occurred to me, then, that if I-It modes of interpersonal relating were a major source of interpersonal discord, perhaps I-It modes of *intra*personal relating were closely related to *intra*personal discord and subsequent psychological distress. This led me to suggest that we can talk about an 'I-Me' mode of self-relating, which is like an I-It attitude towards an other, except that it is towards ourselves or between different 'parts' of ourselves (Cooper, 2003, 2004). Concomitantly I suggested that we could talk about an 'I-I' form of self-relating, which is like the I-Thou form of relating, except, again, to ourselves or within ourselves rather than to others. Such an extrapolation from the interpersonal level to the intrapersonal level makes particular sense if we follow the argument of the Russian psychologist Vygotsky (1962) that our internal dialogue and thinking processes are essentially an internalisation of those modes of communication that have existed on the interpersonal plane.

This 'I-Me' mode of self-relating is, in many respects, akin to Rogers' (1959) notions of distortion and denial; but by drawing on Buber's (1958) distinction between the I-Thou and the I-It attitudes, it becomes possible to broaden and deepen an understanding of these processes. The aim of this chapter, then, is to develop a person-centred model of 'defensive' psychological processes, as well as to further our understanding of how such processes may lead to psychological difficulties. In doing so, however, this chapter also aims to advance a fundamentally humanistic model of psychological distress. That is, one in which psychological difficulties are seen as arising, not from a person's primary, pre-reflective responses to their world, but from their secondary, reflective experiences. Put differently, what is being proposed here is a model of psychological distress which starts from the assumption that human beings have an inherent tendency to experience, and act towards, their world in self-maintaining and self-enhancing ways—Rogers' (1959) actualising tendency—and that psychological distress emerges when people distrust, devalue and/or deny these experiences. Such a model may be of particular interest to psychologists, psychiatrists and other clinicians who are keen to retain some notion of human intelligibility and meaningfulness as part of their understanding of human psychological distress.

The chapter begins by outlining Buber's distinction between the I-Thou and I-It attitudes, and then goes on to show how this can be transposed to an intrapersonal level. It then explores ways in which the I-It mode of self-relating might lead to psychological distress, before discussing implications for therapeutic practice.

I-THOU AND I-IT

There are a number of elements to Buber's (1958) distinction between the I-Thou and the I-It attitude. It should be borne in mind, however, that Buber's philosophy was fundamentally holistic. Hence, these elements cannot be understood in isolation: each is fundamentally interrelated to, and implied by, the others. The differences outlined below, then, need to be understood as facets of a difference-as-a-whole, rather than as independent dimensions.

EXPERIENCING VERSUS RELATING

One of the first distinctions that Buber (1958) makes between the I-It attitude and the I-Thou attitude is that, in the former, an other person is *experienced*, whilst in the latter, the other is *related to*. That is, in the I-It attitude, I distance myself from the other and survey, study, measure and observe him or her—practices that tend to be quite common in the psychological and psychiatric fields. The other becomes something apart from me, something to which I direct my attention and from which I extract knowledge. By contrast, 'When *Thou* is spoken, the speaker has no *thing*; he has indeed nothing. But he takes his stand in relation' (p. 17). Here, I do not face the other, but stand alongside him or her. He or she is not the object of my experiencing, but an intrinsic part of my being-in-relation. 'I do not experience the man to whom I say *Thou*' writes Buber, 'But I take my stand in relation to him, in the sanctity of the primary word. Only when I step out of it do I experience him once more' (p. 22).

This I-Thou attitude also differs from an I-It attitude in that I have an immediate and direct encounter with the other. There is nothing that mediates the meeting: I do not meet my *idea* of the other, but confront him or her directly (Levinas, 1967). Furthermore, for Buber (1958) there are no 'aims', 'anticipations' or 'lusts' that intervene between I and Thou. In this relationship, I am not encountering the other for some purpose or some need. I do not want anything from him or her—or, at least, those needs have been put to one side. 'Only when every means has collapsed', writes Buber, 'does the meeting come about' (p. 25).

'IT-IFYING' VERSUS HUMANISING

In this objectifying, I-It attitude, the other is also experienced as a 'thing': an object, an entity, an 'it' (Buber, 1958). 'He is then thought of as a being of size, surface area, weight, function, desire, consciousness, characteristics and capability of all sorts', writes von Weizsäcker (1964: 407). Such a way of experiencing others, again, tends to be quite common in the psychological and psychiatric fields, where others may be construed in such objectifying terms as 'a neurotic' or 'a borderline personality'. This 'it-ification' of the other has parallels with Sartre's (1958) notion of 'the look', in which the gaze of one human being constantly threatens to objectify—or to use Laing's (1965) term 'petrify'—the being of the other. Whilst for Sartre, however, this objectification is the primary mode of human relatedness; for Buber, 'If I face my human being as my *Thou*, and say the primary word *I-Thou* to him, he is not a thing among things' (p. 21). That is, I also have the possibility of encountering the other as a vibrant, dynamic humanity: a 'psychic stream' (1988: 70) that can not be objectified or labelled, but which I can only relate to in its fluidity and spontaneity. In Bakhtinian (1973) terms, I have the capacity to affirm someone else's 'I', not as an object, but as another subject.

FRAGMENTING VERSUS RELATING TO WHOLENESS

For Buber (1958), a further distinction between the I-It and the I-Thou attitude is that the former fragments what it experiences, whilst the latter relates to the other in its wholeness. In the I-It attitude, things are divided into sub-things: objects or people are analysed, reduced, broken down into essences, laws, psychometric scores, or such parts as 'id', 'ego' and 'superego' (Freud, 1923). By contrast, in the I-Thou attitude, the other is beheld and revered in its totality. Buber gives the example of relating to a tree, in which 'everything, picture and movement, species and type, law and number, [is] indivisibly united in the event. Everything belonging to the tree is in this: its form and structure, its colours a chemical composition, its intercourse with the elements and with the stars, are all present in a single whole' (1958: 20).

CONSTRUING AS DETERMINED VERSUS ACKNOWLEDGING FREEDOM

Buber (1958) also describes the I-It attitude as one in which the other is construed in determined, mechanistic terms, rather than as an other that is freely choosing and deciding its way of being. He, she or it is seen as something that is caused to be, that is driven by forces and mechanisms, rather than being encountered in his, her or its freedom and spontaneity. Again, such a form of it-ification can be common in the psychiatric, psychological and psychotherapeutic fields. For instance, a therapist may construe their client's anger towards them as a consequence of his or her relationship with his or her father, rather than a choice that the client is making towards the therapist's immediate presence. 'Causality' writes Buber, 'has an unlimited reign in the world of It' (p. 71).

EXPERIENCING IN THE PAST OR FUTURE VERSUS ENCOUNTERING IN THE PRESENT

This leads on to a further distinction between the I-It and I-Thou attitudes. In the I-It attitude, the other is experienced in terms of pre-defined schemata: in terms of what has previously been experienced and known. In addition, as discussed above, in the I-It attitude, the other may be experienced in terms of future projects and needs: the other becomes an instrument for the actualisation of the I's possibilities. In the I-It attitude, then, the I is not really experiencing an other at all. Rather, it is experiencing a 'mirror' of its own schemata and interests (Woods, 1969)—the other only exists in as much as it is an object for the self. By contrast, in the I-Thou relationship, the other is met in the immediate present. Hence, there is a breaking-through of a true otherness into the I's world: a movement beyond a solipsistic engagement with the I's own past or future.

GENERALISING VERSUS INDIVIDUATING

'Every real relationship in the world is exclusive', writes Buber (1958), it 'rests on individuation, this is its joy—for only in this way is mutual knowledge of different beings won' (p. 128). By this, Buber means that the I-Thou attitude takes the other as unique, distinctive, and inexchangeable. It is an encounter with *a* particular being at *a* particular 'now', which can not be replicated or repeated. By contrast, the experiencing of an It—an entity that is stripped of its complexity and individuality and experienced as a we-remember-it or as a I'll-do-this-with-it—can be repeated over and over again.

NON-CONFIRMING VERSUS CONFIRMING

For Buber (1958), an I-Thou attitude also involves a fundamental *confirmation* of the other. Friedman (1985) defined this as 'an act of love through which one acknowledges the other as one who exists in his own peculiar form and has the right to do so' (p. 134). There are clear parallels here with Rogers' (1957) notion of ' 'unconditional positive regard'—particularly the emphasis on the acceptance of the other in his or her whole-ness. However, Buber emphasises the way that confirmation involves an acceptance of the other in his or her 'own peculiar form'. In other words, it is an acceptance of the other in his or her otherness, and is clearly distinct from both absorbing the other into one's own schemata, and being absorbed by the other such that one's own position and uniqueness is lost. Indeed, as Buber (1958) points out, to fuse or merge with another person is not to encounter him or her: one can not encounter something that one is.

RELATING IN FRAGMENTS VERSUS RELATING AS WHOLENESS

As we have seen, Buber (1958) states that an I-Thou attitude is one in which an individual relates to the whole of the other. For Buber, however, such an I-Thou attitude also requires the I to bring his or her totality into the encounter. '[T]he primary word [I-Thou] can only be spoken with the whole being' writes Buber, 'He who gives himself to it may withhold nothing of himself' (p. 23). The person who adopts an I-Thou attitude to the other, then, engages with the other in a transparent and open way, in which nothing is deliberately held back or obscured (though this does not necessarily entail a 'universal un-reserve' (Buber, 1947)). Furthermore, such a relationship requires the I to transcend a purely cognitive mode of relating, and to encounter the other as a cognitive-affective-embodied whole (Cooper, 2001). This contrasts with the I-It attitude, in which an individual engages with another in only a partial, non-transparent, or superficial way.

PROTECTIVENESS VERSUS WILLINGNESS TO TAKE RISKS

As we have seen, for Buber (1958), an I-Thou attitude requires an I to engage with a Thou in an immediate and spontaneous way—in a way that is open to the other's freedom, uniqueness and otherness. For Buber, then, an I-Thou meeting is a 'perilous' and 'unreliable' encounter, in which 'the well-tried context' is 'loosened' and one's 'security shattered'. Furthermore, because the I is engaging with the other with the whole of his or her being, he or she has no firm foothold from which to control or determine the encounter—no external position of certainty or safety. Everything he or she is is thrown into the relationship, and this means that he or she may be changed by the encounter in ways that he or she cannot predict or control. As Buber writes: 'The human being who emerges from the act of pure relation that so involves his being has now in his being something more that has grown in him, of which he did not know before and whose origin he is not rightly able to indicate' (p. 140). This contrasts with the I-It relationship, in which the other is experienced in a predictable and controllable—i.e. safe—way; in which a part of the self is always held back, such that there is never a full commitment to, or involvement with, the other.

MONOLOGUE VERSUS DIALOGUE

One of the most useful ways, perhaps, of drawing together the distinctions that Buber makes between the I-It and I-Thou attitudes is by relating them—as Buber does—to monologue and dialogue. In his 1929 essay *Dialogue* (published in 1947), Buber distinguishes between three realms of communication: 'genuine dialogue', 'technical dialogue' and 'monologue disguised as dialogue'. The first of these realms, genuine dialogue, corresponds most closely to Buber's (1958) notion of the I-Thou attitude. For Buber (1947, 1988), genuine dialogue involves a turning towards the other: an openness to being addressed by the other in his, her or its present and particular otherness, and a confirmation of the otherness of the other. This is similar to the model of dialogue outlined by Linell and Marková (1993), in which a person's position or formulation is modified in and through the dialogic exchange. For Buber, such genuine dialogue requires each respondent to bring what is really in his or her head to the dialogue, without artifice, seeming or pretence. However, as Buber emphasises, such dialogue does not require all of those involved to necessarily speak. For Buber, true dialogue and exchange can take place in silence.

In contrast to Linell and Marková (1993) however, Buber (1947) does not consider all forms of discursive interaction to be based on a dialogic form. Rather, he argues that the kind of dialogue in which interactants genuinely respond to each other's utterances are becomingly increasingly rare. Instead, he suggests, much modern communication takes the form of 'technical dialogue', 'which is prompted solely by the need of objective understanding' (p. 37). This is utilitarian, goal-focused communication, but communication in which real dialogue remains hidden away in 'odd corners', occasionally breaking through to the surface: 'as in the tone of a railway guard's voice, in the glance of an old newspaper vendor, in the smile of the chimney-sweeper' (p. 37).

It is the third form of communication, 'monologue disguised as dialogue', however, that Buber (1947) seems to consider most prevalent in the contemporary world. By this, Buber means a form of communication that has a semblance of interpersonal openness and receptivity, but is essentially a turning towards, and concern with, oneself: a 'reflexivity', rather than a reaching out to an other. Here, 'two or more men, meeting in space, speak each with himself in strangely torturous and circuitous ways and yet imagine they have escaped the torment of being thrown back on their own resources' (p. 37). In this form of communication, each individual's concerns are not with learning from the other, but with self-presentation and self-enhancement. Hence, spontaneity and transparency are replaced with artifice, phoniness and manipulation. Buber describes a number of forms of communication that make up this 'underworld of faceless spectres of dialogue' (p. 38). In *debate*, for instance, points are not made as they exist in the protagonist's mind, but are designed to strike home as sharply as possible—a 'word duel' that is far more about self-aggrandisement than any genuine learning. In *speechifying*, on the other hand, 'people do not really speak to one another, but each, although turned to the other, really speaks to a fictitious court of appeal whose life consists of nothing but listening to him' (Buber, 1988: 69).

MOMENTS OF I-THOU AND DIALOGUE

In concluding this section, two important points need to be noted. First, in drawing this distinction between I-Thou and I-It modes of relating, Buber (1958) is not suggesting that we can consistently relate to others in an I-Thou, dialogic way. 'It is not possible to live in the bare present' (p. 51) he writes. For Buber, then, it is inevitable that we will sometimes relate to others and the world in an I-It manner. In this respect, the I-Thou attitude is best understood as something that we can experience moments of, rather than as something that we can experience on an ongoing basis (Anderson and Cissna, 1997). Furthermore, Buber does not see the I-It attitude as inherently negative. For him, it is through objectifying, and separating from, entities and people that human beings can progress from an undifferentiated state of connectivity towards a deeper and more profound encounter (Woods, 1969). The I-Thou and I-It attitudes, then, are seen as dialectically related. Hence, as with Heidegger (1966), Buber's concern is not that we should consistently maintain an attitude of *Gelassenheit* (openness) towards the world. Rather, it is that we should not become so seduced by a technical and manipulative way of experiencing the world that we forget a more contemplative and relational possibility. As Buber writes: 'without *It* man cannot live. But he who lives with *It* alone is not a man' (p. 52).

FROM EXTERNAL DIALOGUE TO INTERNAL DIALOGUE

The basic premise of this chapter, then, is that we can usefully transpose this interpersonal distinction to the intrapersonal plane. That is, that we can meaningfully distinguish between two particular modes of relating to ourselves. In the first of these, we—or a particular 'part' of ourselves—relates to another part of ourselves in an it-ifying, fragmenting, generalised, non-confirming, fragmentary, protective and monologic way—construing the other part as determined, and on the basis of past experiences or future desires. In the second form of intrapersonal relating, by contrast, we relate to ourselves in a humanising, individualising, confirming, holistic, risk-taking, dialogic manner: in a way that takes us, or a part of ourselves, as a present, choice-making whole. This former mode of intrapersonal relating I have termed an 'I-Me' self-relational stance, whilst the latter mode I have termed an 'I-I' self-relational stance (Cooper, 2003, 2004). In other words, in the I-I self-relational stance, the I relates to itself as an *I*: as an active, phenomenologically-experiencing, meaning-orientated being. By contrast, in the I-Me self-relational stance, the I relates to the I as a *me*: as an empirical, object-like entity (cf. Mead's (1934) distinction between the 'I' as self-as-subject, and the 'Me' as self-as-object). As with the I-Thou attitude, the suggestion here is not that human beings can, or should, consistently relate to themselves in an I-I manner. Rather, the suggestion is that people may be able to experience moments of I-I relating to themselves, and that, as will be argued later, these moments of I-I encounter are of crucial importance in determining their psychological well-being.

An example may help to illustrate this distinction between I-I and I-Me forms of self-relating, and how the various differences between an I-Thou and I-It attitude, as outlined above, can be transposed to the intrapersonal plane. Martha was a twenty-five-year-old female client who experienced intense and terrifying panic attacks, often in social situations where she felt an enormous pressure 'not to put a foot wrong'. Martha's relationship to this panicking, vulnerable I-position—from the adult, rational I-position that she tended to inhabit during the psychotherapy sessions—is a good example of an I-Me mode of intrapersonal relating.

First, from her adult I-position, she tended to talk *about* her experiences of panic and terror, rather than relating to these experiences in an immediate and direct way. There was a sense of her surveying and studying this mode of experience from a distance—from the position of an 'objective', disconnected observer—rather than standing alongside her terrors and fears and allowing herself to fully connect with them. Second, from her adult I-position, there was a tendency to 'it-ify' her vulnerable I-position. She described it as something that took her over, something that came from outside, rather than a fluid, meaning-orientated phenomenological stream of experiencing. Third, then, her adult I-position did not relate to the totality of her vulnerable I-position, but focused primarily on its behavioural and physical manifestations, to the exclusion of its intentional, meaning-orientated facets. Fourth, from her adult I-position, Martha had a great tendency to look for explanations as to *why* she was experiencing such panic and terror, rather than considering the possibility that, in the midst of that vulnerable mode of being, she might be experiencing freedom and choice. Fifth, as touched on earlier, Martha, from her adult I-position, did not invoke a meeting with her vulnerable I-position in the present. Rather, it was something that she talked about in the past: how she *had* panicked, *had* felt afraid; and also something that she experienced in terms of her future: specifically, as a 'block' to becoming the person she wanted to be. Sixth, from her adult I-position, her experiences of panic were construed in generalised terms: her panic attacks were manifestations of a trans-personal disorder, rather than *a* particular mode by which she, as the individual she was, encountered her world. Seventh, from her adult I-position, Martha was entirely disconfirming of her vulnerable I-position. It was something she hated, detested, and was desperate to get rid of—in no way did she confirm or validate her vulnerability and fear. Eighth, Martha's relationship to her vulnerable I-position, from her adult I-position, was an exclusively cognitive one. She analysed and deconstructed it, but did not allow herself to also engage with it in an emotional and embodied way. Ninth, from her adult I-position, Martha had no intention of allowing herself to open up to her fears and vulnerabilities, and letting herself be touched or affected by this way of being. In summary, then, we can say that Martha, from her adult I-position, was in no way willing to enter into a dialogue with her vulnerable I-position. She was willing to 'speechify' to it: to tell her fears that they were 'stupid' and 'unfounded', but she was not willing to engage with them in a mutual and symmetrical way.

As the therapy progressed, however, Martha was increasingly able to experience moments of I-I encounter between her adult and vulnerable I-positions. Here, Martha, from her adult I-position, was able to temporarily stand in the shoes of her vulnerable self, and to remind herself of just how terrifying those moments of social anxiety were. She also became increasingly able to acknowledge that she was not 'stupid' or 'cowardly' for running away from social situations at these times, but that, from this I-position, this action seemed like the best way of dealing with her immediate situation. In this I-I mode of relating, then, Martha became increasingly able to confirm her vulnerable I-position, and to accept its legitimacy within her intrapersonal world, rather than seeing it as a foe to be eliminated at all costs.

In the case of Martha, it is interesting to note how her relationship to her feelings of panic and anxiety seemed to mirror those that others in her family had held towards them. Her parents, for instance, were generally warm and loving to her, but saw Martha as an outgoing and self-confident person (in contrast to her highly anxious brother), and virtually refused to acknowledge that she ever felt particularly vulnerable or afraid. Such a mirroring, however, is quite comprehensible if we follow the Vygotskian (1962) line of reasoning that psychological ways of being exist first on the interpersonal plane, before becoming internalised on the intrapersonal plane. In other words, I-Me intrapersonal attitudes towards oneself may be the result of experiencing I-It attitudes from others. This raises the possibility, then, that clients who have experienced particularly severe forms of it-ification by others—for example, through sexual or physical abuse— may come to develop particularly objectifying self-relational stances, as in the example at the beginning of this chapter.

THE I-ME SELF-RELATIONAL STANCE AND PSYCHOLOGICAL DISTRESS

As a working hypothesis, it is suggested that an individual's levels of psychological distress is related to the extent to which they relate to themselves in an I-Me way. In other words, the more they it-ify themselves, the more they may tend to experience psychological difficulties. Put conversely, it suggests that psychological well-being can be defined as the ability to relate to oneself—as well as others—in a thou-ifying way. Such a proposition can be seen as an extension, and encompassment, of Rogers' (1959) assertion that psychological difficulties are related to high levels of negative self-regard. It also encompasses, extends and brings together many other models of psychological distress:

for instance, the existential idea that psychological problems are related to perceiving oneself in an inauthentic way, or the feminist idea that psychological well-being requires an ability to develop a 'self-empathic' capacity (Jordan, 1991). As with the I-It relationship, however, this is not to suggest that all moments of I-Me relating are necessarily distress-related; indeed, at times they may be of positive benefit. Richard Worsley (personal communication, 2004), for instance, gives the example of a young man who was bullied, and learnt to reduce the pain of the verbal threats by 'standing off to one side of the character who was being attacked'. Nevertheless, as with the I-Thou and I-It relationship, it is proposed that, when a person experiences themselves predominantly or wholly in an I-It way, then he or she is likely to experience high levels of psychological distress. This is for a number of reasons.

First, if a person can communicate with other parts of their being and acknowledge that part's needs, then they are more likely to be able to work 'together' as a coherent, functioning whole. If, on the other hand, the person, in one I-position, refuses to confirm another way that they have of being, then the resulting conflict is likely to absorb much of the individual's attention, making them less able to fulfil their in-the-world projects. Cooper and Rowan (1999) sum this up by writing:

> Where there is a lack of communication, where selves disown each other or where one self dominates to the exclusion of all others, then the result tends toward a cacophony of monologues—a discordant wail which will always be less than the sum of the individual parts. But where selves talk to selves, where there is an acceptance and understanding between the different voices and an appreciation of diversity and difference, then there is the potential for working together and co-operation—an interwoven harmony of voices which may transcend the sum of the parts alone. (p. 8)

Second, an I-I self-relational stance is associated with the experiencing of positive feelings towards oneself: such as acceptance, confirmation, openness, harmony, and a belief in one's uniqueness, wholeness and humanity. By contrast, an I-Me self-relational stance is associated with derogatory, objectifying, rejecting, dis-confirming feelings towards one self. An I-I self-relational stance, then, is more likely to be associated with a positive mood state than an I-Me self-relational stance.

Third, the existence of I-Me self-relational stances is likely to be closely associated with the creation and maintenance of 'subjugated' (Hermans and Kempen, 1993)—or what have also been termed 'disowned' (Stone and Winkelman, 1989), 'shadow' (Cooper, 1999), 'neglected', 'subdued' and 'suppressed' (Hermans, 2001; Hermans and Kempen, 1993)—I-positions. These are the voices that are banished, ignored and rejected within the intrapersonal community (Satir, 1978): the I-positions that are consistently it-ified, dis-confirmed, and talked at, rather than with. As in the case of Martha, Stone and Winkelman suggest that the 'vulnerable child' is one of the voices that is most consistently disowned, alongside other voices that an individual may have been taught were unacceptable, such as the 'daimons' (May, 1969) of rage and sexuality.

Such subjugation of internal voices is likely to lead to a number of psychological difficulties. First, from a humanistic perspective (e.g. Rogers, 1959), each aspect of a person's being is seen as having a positive potentiality. This means that, in subjugating certain aspects of his or her being, an individual locks up part of his or her full potentiality: losing touch with 'some very beautiful, useful qualities' (Vargiu, 1974: 54). A young woman, for instance, who silences her angry voice, then surrenders her ability to stand up for her own needs and demands. Moreover, the positive potentiality of each voice consists, not only in what it can contribute alone, but what it can contribute in dialogue with other voices. Hence, where particular voices are subjugated, the person's ability to think creatively and innovatively through open intrapersonal communication is also likely to be attenuated.

Furthermore, because these I-positions are expressions of vital elements of our being, they will not simply go away if attempts are made to silence them. Rather, like a young child, the more they are told to shut up, the more they are likely to shout and demand repatriation. This will inevitably lead to an increase in anxiety in the person: a constant sense of being threatened by something alien and undesirable. Moreover, because the individual, from the position of the dominant voices, refuses to dialogue with the subjugated voices, he or she then has little ability to mediate or control their expression. Martha, for instance, does not look her fears and anxieties in the face. She hopes that they will go away. In a social situation, then, she does little more than cling to the desperate hope that, this time, she will somehow, magically, not start to feel anxious. When the voice of terror does begin to emerge, therefore, she feels completely helpless in the face of it. She has no way of engaging with it, of retaining some sense of being in control.

This leads on to a further reason why the existence of I-Me intrapersonal relationships—and the creation and maintenance of subjugated I-positions—may be closely associated with psychological distress. Because the subjugated I-positions are vital elements of an individual's being, it is inevitable that, at certain times, a process of 'dominance reversal' (Hermans, 1996) will take place. Here, 'a hidden or suppressed position can (without therapy) become, quite suddenly, more dominant than the position that corresponds with the trait the person considers as a prevalent and stable part of his or her personality' (Hermans, 1996: 46). The question, then, is what happens when an it-ified 'me' becomes a dominant 'I'? One answer may be that, because the usually dominant I-positions have not established a dialogical relationship with this I-position, then the subjugated I-position has no way of dialoguing back. In other words, no *bridge* has been created between the usually dominant I-positions and the usually subjugated I-position; such that, when the person comes to inhabit the latter, she or he has no way of connecting with the former. When Martha experiences extreme social anxiety, for instance, she is unable to connect with the adult, rational voice that 'knows' that not everyone is staring at her. And because she is unable to connect with other voices, she is unable to stand back from her vulnerable I-position and regain some perspective on her situation.

THERAPEUTIC IMPLICATIONS

Based on this analysis, it can be proposed that one of the central aims of therapy should be to help clients develop the ability to relate to themselves in an I-I manner. Not only will such a development allow clients to experience more productive intrapersonal relationships, feel better about themselves, and more fully actualise their potential, but it will help them to establish a dialogue with their subjugated selves such that, when they do become immersed in those ways of being, they have the capacity to take a step back and connect with other voices.

In the process-experiential therapeutic and gestalt therapy fields (e.g. Greenberg and Elliott, 1997; Greenberg, Rice and Elliott, 1993), specific techniques have been developed—most notable two-chair work—to facilitate more open and effective communication between the person and their different parts, or between the parts themselves. From the psychotherapeutic literature, it would seem that such techniques can be an effective means of facilitating the emergence of I-I relationships (Cooper and Cruthers, 1999; Elliott, 2002). There are a number of reasons, however, why such techniques may also be counter-therapeutic at times: reducing the prevalence of I-I relating rather than increasing it. First, these techniques, through encouraging clients to identify and define certain I-positions, may lead them to experience these I-positions in a more objectifying, fixed and detached way. The I-position becomes a definite *thing*, rather than a vague and ill-defined voice that is simply encountered; and, whilst it may be important for clients to go through a dialectical process of objectifying different voices, separating from them, and then re-encountering them at a deeper level, there is always the danger that the voices will remain isolated and objectified. Second, and closely related to this, as a client starts to identify and define certain voices, so there is the danger that these voices are taken out of the context of the dialogic whole, such that the client develops an increasingly fragmented view of his or her own being. In other words, at the level of the person-as-a-whole, these techniques may lead to an increasing it-ification. Third, such strategies may require the therapist to relate to his or her client in a relatively technical, if not mechanistic, way. And if intrapersonal relationships emerge as the internalisation of interpersonal relationships, then the establishment of an I-It dialogue between therapist and client may ultimately increase the prevalence of I-Me relating; as might many other commonplace psychological practices, such as conducting psychological tests on clients or providing clients with specific psychiatric diagnoses and formulations.

More significantly, then, the analysis presented in this chapter may point towards—and provide a rationale for—the importance of establishing an I-Thou, relationally-deep encounter (Mearns and Cooper, in press) with clients. Here, through a process of internalisation, clients may come to develop a confirming, 'thou-ifiying' voice towards themselves: a mode of self-relating which is willing to witness and confirm the otherness within. Certainly, I have witnessed this process in my own therapeutic work, where several clients have reported 'hearing' my voice in their day-to-day activities, telling them that it is 'OK' to feel scared or angry.

However, as I have argued previously (Cooper, 1996), it may often be the case that clients tend to inhabit a relatively constant I-position within the therapeutic relationship: and generally the one of the rational, observing adult. Hence, whilst a client may experience confirmation of—and learn to confirm for themselves—their rational, adult I-position, there is the danger that their more subjugated I-positions—those that do not emerge within the therapeutic relationship—may fail to experience confirmation. If this is the case, it would seem important that, from a person-centred standpoint, we think about ways in which we can help clients to bring their more subjugated ways of being into the therapeutic environment. Creating safety, warmth and unconditional acceptance are no doubt key means of achieving this, but perhaps it also means that, at times, we need to take a somewhat more process-directive stance: inviting the subjugated voices in to the room (see Mearns, in Cooper et al., 2004), and helping clients to 'unpack' those experiences that are usually it-ified.

CONCLUSION

The argument presented in this chapter is an attempt to examine, expand, and clarify a person-centred understanding of how people relate to—or within—themselves, and the particular forms that problematic self-relational stances might take. The I-Me mode of self-relating outlined here has many parallels with Rogers' (1959) notions of distortion and denial, but it also serves to develop our understanding of the form(s) that such defensive responses might take. Furthermore, by drawing on a model of interpersonal attitudes and relating, the notion of 'I-Me' and 'I-I' self-relational stances provides a means whereby we can understand both interpersonal discord and intrapersonal discord on one continuum: *as the tendency to 'it-ify'*—whether self, others or world.

The analysis presented in this chapter also provides psychologists, psychiatrists and other clinicians with one means of understanding psychological distress that is rooted in a fundamental respect for human beings. Its starting point is that human beings experience their world in inherently intelligible and meaningful ways, but come to grief when they start to distrust, deny or objectify these experiences. This is not to suggest that all forms of psychological distress are reducible to such I-Me modes of relating—problems like autism, for instance, would seem to have a significant biological component (Comer, 1998, Knibbs and Moran Chapter 17 this volume)—but even with such conditions, how a person relates to this 'given' way of being may have a significant impact on their overall levels of well-being. It has also been suggested in this chapter that problematic I-Me self-relational stances may be particularly prevalent in clients who have experienced severe objectification by others.

Finally, the discussion presented in this chapter lends strong support to a person-centred way of working, and highlights the dangers of adopting therapeutic techniques, which, if internalised, can serve to further objectify and alienate the self. Through engaging with others in a relationally-deep manner (Mearns and Cooper, in print), therapists can help clients to develop the capacity to heal themselves at the deepest possible level. Through a humanising interpersonal relationship, they can come to witness, value and honour their own fundamental humanity.

REFERENCES

Anderson, R and Cissna, KN (1997) *The Martin Buber–Carl Rogers Dialogue: A new transcript with commentary*. Albany, NY: State University of New York Press.

Bakhtin, M (1973) *Problems of Dostoevsky's Poetics* (RW Rostel, trans, 2nd ed). Ann Arbor, MI: Ardis.

Buber, M (1947) *Between Man and Man* (RG Smith, trans). London: Fontana.

Buber, M (1958) *I and Thou* (RG Smith, trans, 2nd ed). Edinburgh: T and T Clark Ltd.

Buber, M (1988) *The Knowledge of Man: Selected essays* (M Friedman and RG Smith, trans). Atlantic Highlands, NJ: Humanities Press International Inc.

Comer, RJ (1998) *Abnormal Psychology* (3rd ed). New York: WH Freeman.

Cooper, M (1996) Modes of existence: towards a phenomenological polypsychism. *Journal of the Society for Existential Analysis, 7*, 50–6.

Cooper, M (1999) If you can't be Jekyll be Hyde: An existential-phenomenological exploration on lived-plurality. In J Rowan and M Cooper (eds), *The Plural Self: Multiplicity in everyday life* (pp. 51–70). London: Sage.

Cooper, M (2001) Embodied empathy. In S Haugh and T Merry (eds), *Rogers' Therapeutic Conditions: Evolution, theory and practice, Vol 2, Empathy* (pp. 218–29). Ross-on-Wye: PCCS Books.

Cooper, M (2003) 'I-I' And 'I-Me': Transposing Buber's interpersonal attitudes to the intrapersonal plane. *Journal of Constructivist Psychology, 16*, 131–53.

Cooper, M (2004) Encountering self-otherness: 'I-I' and 'I-Me' modes of self-relating. In HJM Hermans and G Dimaggio (eds), *Dialogical Self in Psychotherapy* (pp. 60–73). Hove: Brunner-Routledge.

Cooper, M and Cruthers, H (1999) Facilitating the expression of subpersonalities: A review and analysis of techniques. In J Rowan and M Cooper (eds), *The Plural Self: Multiplicty in Everyday Life* (pp. 198–212). London: Sage.

Cooper, M, Mearns, D, Stiles, WB, Warner, MS and Elliott, R (2004) Developing self-pluralistic perspectives within the person-centered and experiential approaches: A round table dialogue. *Person-Centered and Experiential Psychotherapies, 3*, 176–191.

Cooper, M and Rowan, J (1999) Introduction: Self-plurality—the one and the many. In J Rowan and M Cooper (eds), *The Plural Self: Multiplicty in everyday life* (pp. 1–9). London: Sage.

Elliott, R (2002) The effectiveness of humanistic therapies: a meta-analysis. In DJ Cain and J Seeman (eds), *Humanistic Psychotherapies: Handbook of research and practice*. Washington, DC: American Psychological Association.

Elliott, R and Greenberg, LS (1997) Multiple voices in process-experiential therapy: dialogue between aspects of the self. *Journal of Psychotherapy Integration, 7*, 225–39.

Freud, S (1923) The ego and the id (J Strachey, trans) in *The Standard Edition of the Complete Psychological Works of Sigmund Freud* (Vol. 19, pp. 12–59). London: Hogarth Press.

Friedman, M (1985) *The Healing Dialogue in Psychotherapy*. New York: Jason Aronson, Inc.

Greenberg, LS and Elliott, R (1997) Varieties of empathic responding. In AC Bohart and LS Greenberg (eds), *Empathy Reconsidered: New directions in psychotherapy* (pp. 167–186). Washington, DC: American Psychological Association.

Greenberg, LS, Rice, LN and Elliott, R (1993) *Facilitating Emotional Change: The moment-by-moment process*. New York: Guilford Press.

Heidegger, M (1966) *Discourse on Thinking* (JM Anderson and EH Freund, trans). London:

Harper Colophon Books.

Hermans, HJM (1996) Voicing the self: From information processing to dialogical interchange. *Psychological Bulletin, 119*, 31–50.

Hermans, HJM (2001) The dialogical self: towards a theory of personal and cultural positioning. *Culture and Psychology, 7*, 243–281.

Hermans, HJM and Kempen, HJG (1993) *The Dialogical Self: Meaning as movement*. San Diego, CA: Academic Press.

Jordan, JV(1991) Empathy and self-boundaries. In JV Jordan, AG Kaplan, JB Miller, IP Stiver and JL Surrey (eds), *Women's Growth in Connection: Writings from the Stone Center* (pp. 67–80). New York: The Guilford Press.

Laing, RD (1965) *The Divided Self: An Existential study in sanity and madness*. Harmondsworth: Penguin.

Levinas, E (1967) Martin Buber and the theory of knowledge. In PA Schlipp and M Friedman (eds), *The Philosophy of Martin Buber* (pp. 133–150). London: Cambridge University Press.

Linell, P and Marková, I (1993) Acts in Discourse—from monological speech acts to dialogical inter-acts. *Journal for the Theory of Social Behaviour, 23*, 173–195.

May, R (1969) *Love and Will*. New York: WW Norton and Co, Inc.

Mead, GH (1934) *Mind, Self and Society*. Chicago: University of Chicago Press.

Mearns, D and Cooper, M (in press) *Working at Relational Depth: The heart of Person-Centred and Existential Therapies*. London: Sage.

Mearns, D and Thorne, B (2000) *Person-Centred Therapy Today: New frontiers in theory and practice*. London: Sage.

Rogers, CR (1957) The necessary and sufficient conditions of therapeutic personality change. *Journal of Consulting Psychology, 21*, 95–103.

Rogers, CR (1959) A theory of therapy, personality and interpersonal relationships as developed in the client-centred framework. In S Koch (ed), *Psychology: A study of science, Vol. 3*, (pp. 184–256). New York: McGraw-Hill.

Sartre, J-P (1958) *Being and Nothingness: An essay on phenomenological ontology* (H Barnes, trans). London: Routledge.

Satir, V (1978) *Your Many Faces*. Berkeley, CA: Celestial Arts.

Stiles, WB, Elliott, R, Firthcozens, JA, Llewelyn, SP, Margison, FR, Shapiro, DA, et al. (1990) Assimilation of problematic experiences by clients in psychotherapy. *Psychotherapy, 27*, 411–20.

Stone, H and Winkelman, S (1989) *Embracing Our Selves: The voice dialogue manual*. Mill Valley, CA: Nataraj Publishing.

Vargiu, JG (1974) Psychosynthesis workbook: Subpersonalities. *Synthesis, 1*, 52–90.

Von Weizsacker, V (1964) Selected readings. In M Friedman (ed), *The Worlds of Existentialism: A critical reader*. Chicago: University of Chicago Press.

Vygotsky, LS (1962) *Thought and Language*. Cambridge, MA: MIT Press.

Woods, RE (1969) *Martin Buber's Ontology: An analysis of I and Thou*. Evanston, IL: Northwestern University Press.

CHAPTER 6

AUTHENTICITY AND ALIENATION: TOWARDS AN UNDERSTANDING OF THE PERSON BEYOND THE CATEGORIES OF ORDER AND DISORDER[1]

PETER F. SCHMID

Don't ask the doctor, ask the patient
Jewish proverb

If we take the Person-Centered Approach (PCA) seriously as a *client*-centered approach, we have to go back to our clients in order to engage them in an individualized, shared process of encounter and reflection. Following Rogers it is argued that the essential conditions of psychotherapy exist in a single configuration, even though they occur uniquely with each client. From a dialogical point of view, therapists and clients are not only seen as being *in* relationships; as persons they *are* relationships, which makes them different in each therapeutic contact. Furthermore, the traditional concepts of psychological health and disorder are rejected, seeing symptoms as a specific cry for help that has to be understood in a process of a personal encounter between therapist and client. Following this concept it is appropriate to speak about clients as persons who are suffering from inauthentic or alienated forms of being in the world. The value of concepts and conceptions for helping us understand different types of clients are acknowledged and emphasized. However, the existing concepts for, and descriptions of, our clients still exist only at a primitive, unsystematic stage of development and thus we need the development of a genuinely human science of Person-Centered Therapy.

PERSONAL ANTHROPOLOGY: AUTHENTICITY AND ALIENATION

Carl Rogers' approach to mental health was humanistic, not medical. Taking the point of view of the social sciences, not the natural sciences, his holistic standpoint on human beings encompassed not only the biological and individual nature but also the relational and social nature of the person. From the very outset, Rogers' psychology was a social psychology (Schmid, 1994, 1996). In trying to understand the human being within his

---

1. Slightly revised version of a paper first printed in Person-Centered and Experiential Psychotherapies, *3*, (2004) 36–51.

or her respective frame of reference Rogers came to view every individual as a unique being. Therefore, as opposed to an observational and analytical approach, he stood in the tradition of phenomenology, existentialism, hermeneutics and constructivism (Zurhorst, 1993).

THE SUBSTANTIAL-RELATIONAL NOTION OF THE PERSON AS A SOCIAL CRITICISM

But Rogers' personality theory is not only a social psychological theory; it is also implicitly social criticism, a critical theory of socialization. Central to his understanding of the person is the process of authenticity, the perpetually striven for congruence between the 'experiencing organism' and the self concept. For a long time this was misunderstood individualistically, as referring only to isolated individuals. On the contrary, Rogers (1965: 20) clearly stated that the nature of the human being itself is 'incurably social'. From a personal, dialogical viewpoint we are not only *in* relationships; as persons we *are* relationships. Therefore the human person must be understood at one and the same time from both an individual or substantial view (which points to autonomy and sovereignty) *and* from a relational view (highlighting interconnectedness and solidarity) (Schmid 2001, 2002a, 2003). Self-determination *and* interrelatedness refer essentially to one and the same human nature; we only view and experience these as different dimensions. To regard the human as a substantial-relational being is what is meant by designating him/her as a person. Therefore any *person*-centered consideration on what 'healthy' or 'fully functioning' means, must include a theory of social criticism.

'PSYCHOLOGICAL HEALTH': A THEORY OF AUTHENTICITY INSTEAD OF A 'HEALTH' CONCEPT

Authenticity as the process of balancing individuality and interrelatedness
To be a person means to be truly living the process of authenticity, developing one's potential in a constructive way. To live authentically means to be able to keep the balance, or better, to gain always anew the synthesis between the substantial and the relational task of living. A man or woman is authentic if they maintain this balance in the process of realizing their own values and needs, their individuality and uniqueness, while *at the same time* living together with their others and the world, meeting the needs and challenges of these relationships in interdependence and solidarity. Who is fully him-/herself is fully social, and vice versa. Self-realization and solidarity coincide. This is how Rogers viewed what he called the 'fully functioning person'. It was not by coincidence that Rogers referred to the biblical notion of 'agape', which embraces both dimensions: 'You shall love your neighbor as yourself.' (Leviticus 19:18; Matthew 22: 39)

From a superficial point of view, a person who lives this process of authenticity is called 'healthy' (etymologically connected with 'whole'), 'sane' or even 'normal' or 'in order'—whence the term 'dis-order' derives. This is in line with the meaning of 'infirmity' or 'dis-ease'. But authenticity has nothing to do with being firm or at ease. These common terms are not only misleading, but completely wrong (see Sanders 2005, Chapter 3 this volume), because a severely ill person can live very authentically. This includes pain, fear, grief, struggle, sorrow, agony, transience, and stages of inauthenticity in which there is a new striving towards balance. It also means that each person is different in their way of being authentic.

Rogers always thought about the fully functioning person in terms of the *process* of becoming, never about a state or an end product. The significant meaning of authenticity is to live to become more and more authentic, that is, to become the author of one's own life (Schmid, 2001).

In summary: The image of the human being in person-centered anthropology differs qualitatively from the respective image in the natural sciences. It is human science, not natural science. Thus person-centered thinking sets out from a process theory of authenticity, not from a theory of failure or disorder. The person is understood as an existential process, a process of striving towards authenticity in every given moment of his/her existence, a joint process of self-development and relationship development. Therefore person-centered in itself is process-centered (which is clearly different from process-directive). In the view of a genuinely personal anthropology it makes no sense to separate the process from the person and it is impossible to separate content and process: in a very significant sense the process is the content is the meaning. (Therefore it also seems to be artificial to separate between relationship-, content- and process-experts.)

ALIENATION: THE SUFFERING PERSON INSTEAD OF A CONCEPT OF 'DIS-ORDERS'

Trouble with the ongoing process of becoming authentic can be caused by the development of an inauthentic self-concept or by the lack of the development of some parts of the organismic experiencing capabilities (Spielhofer, 2003). In both cases, inauthentic or missing relationships play a crucial role, because a person becomes, and is, the relationship they have, as stated above. A person becomes inauthentic, if they are alienated from self and Others, i.e., from the experiencing organism and the necessary genuine relationships. Psychological suffering is usually the result. Such a process must be understood as a fundamental self-contradictoriness (*Selbstwidersprochenheit*; Zurhorst, 1993) between the capabilities and the natural process of experiencing, on the one hand, and the rigid and in itself torn structure of the self and resulting rigid relationships, on the other hand.

Inauthenticity and maladjustment
Consequently, for a critical theory of socialization, diagnosing and repairing a deviation from a norm is not an appropriate guideline. In trying to understand how far a person is alienated from self, the prevailing and ruling cultural norm cannot be a constant, although it must be taken into account. This notion of 'inauthenticity' differs qualitatively from the common meaning of illness or disorder. What is experienced from an internal

frame of reference as 'psychological suffering', from an external point of view is seen as alienation or maladjustment. If it is called 'disorder', one must *permanently* keep in mind that the 'order' always is also a cultural norm.

The 'deviation' can appear to be more on the substantial side, inasmuch as there are problems with a person's individuality and being all wrapped up in the social roles, e.g., what is called melancholy, or it can look as if the difficulties are more relational, when a person refuses to engage in their social tasks, e.g., with schizophrenia (see Zurhorst, 1993). No matter whether it is a deficit of substantial authenticity in the sense of 'not being who you are' or a deficit of relational authenticity in the sense of maladjustment, in either case the *person* is suffering. The 'maladjusted person' (see Rogers, 1959)—a term matching with the 'fully functioning person'—who has not succeeded in gaining the authentic balance always suffers from both sides: they lack self-confidence due to an incongruence between self and experience (autonomy deficit) *and* lack trust in the world and others due to an incongruence between the others as perceived by the self and the others as really being Others (relationship deficit). So, suffering due to alienation is a signal of a deficiency or a loss of authenticity. A psychological symptom therefore is a cry for help. (Schmid, 1992)

The symptom as a specific call for help to overcome inauthenticity
The Greek word 'symptom' originally meant 'coincidence, temporary peculiarity'; only later came to mean 'sign, warning, distinguishing mark'; and finally took on the medical sense of a 'characteristic sign of a specific disease'. A symptom is a phenomenon, something that is shown by the person. As everyone familiar with the psychiatric field knows, symptoms often appear to be accidental, they can be subject to fashion; e.g., think of co-morbidity and the intercorrelation of symptoms. One and the same client is quite often given a variety of diagnoses, frequently even contradictory ones.

In the light of a philosophy of the person, a symptom is always a specific cry, coming out of the attempt to be seen and receive help. It is an expression of being severely out of balance in the process of striving for authenticity and the request for support, an attempt to deal with a situation by notifying oneself and others of the balance problem. In the specific cry lies the key to the understanding of the suffering person. It might often be a compromise between the problem and the request for help, but in any case it is, on psychological, mental, physical levels, a *unique* expression of this particular person in this particular situation, an expression of the wish to be understood and to understand oneself. It is a call to others, to overcome the vicious circle and to get the process of authentic personalization restarted. Thus it always creates a unique situation of relationship. In this the key for therapy is to be found.

Symptoms are as manifold as persons and situations are manifold. Many authors who regard differential treatment as necessary, reproach the Person-Centered Approach for adhering to a uniformity myth. What a gross misunderstanding! According to personal anthropology, each suffering person is not viewed uniformly but is seen as entirely different. And so the therapeutic answer is: not uniform but unique (Schmid, 1992).

In summary: Inauthentic persons are alienated from themselves and others. Suffering persons are communicating to themselves and others by symptoms that their process of striving towards authenticity in a given moment of their existence has severely failed or got stuck, that they need help in their processes of self and relationship development. Since the person is their existential process, the task is to understand the particular process, which is the same as understanding the particular person. The challenge is not so much what has gone wrong, but where the possibilities are to facilitate the process of life, i.e., the self-healing capacities.

THERAPY: PERSONALITY DEVELOPMENT THROUGH ENCOUNTER

If it is correct that the reason for alienation and suffering is inauthenticity and therefore relationship, then it is also relationship that helps. Aptly, the kind of relationship that can reconcile the alienated person with self and the world was called 'encounter' by Rogers (1962).

Person-Centered Therapy is such a relationship: the facilitation of personalization (i.e., becoming a person) as a process of becoming independent and of co-creating relationships. Thus, therapy overcomes the stagnation (Pfeiffer, 1993). From a relational point of view, therapy is personal encounter; while from a substantial point of view it is personality development (which, by the way, sets the person-centered stance clearly apart from a merely systemic view as well as from other ahistoric therapies). That is, personalization occurs through encounter, personality development by working at relational depth (Mearns, 1996).

Thus, although symptoms are manifold, the answer is always of the same kind: a certain relationship. Despite symptom specificity, the answer is a special kind of relationship. The same relational conditions that are crucial for the development of the infant and child are necessary and sufficient for psychotherapy. Psychotherapy is a special chapter of developmental psychology.

Therefore the relationship is always the same and always different: the same, because it is always the presence (unfolded as the core conditions; Schmid, 2002b, 2003; Geller, Schmid and Wyatt, 2003) of the therapist that is needed and constitutes the answer to the cry expressed by symptoms. It is unique, because it is the special relationship of the persons involved at any given moment of the process that is needed, co-created in the encounter process.

Does this mean 'intervention homogeneity' (Heinerth, 2002)? Yes and no. Yes, because therapy is independent of symptoms and circumstances, insofar as it is always the same 'type' of relationship that is needed: encounter. No, it is specific because two or more unique persons are involved in unique moments of encounter. Differentiated answers are necessary according to differential cries and different perspectives that the client expresses. They require differential empathy for the moment-by-moment process of the client's self-exploration and the forms of relationships that are offered.

In summary: Person-specific is not symptom-specific, or problem-specific (Mearns, 2003), or disorder-specific, and not at all disorder-oriented, but instead is uniquely process-specific.

Consequently, disorder-oriented or goal-oriented is not person-oriented or process-oriented. Since it is the relationship that facilitates the process of personalization, differentiated relationships are needed: each person-to-person relationship is different, otherwise it would not be a personal *relationship. But the kind of relationship is always the same: an encounter, although in very different ways. The client is seen as an active self healer 'using' the therapist for support in this 'co-created interpersonal process' (Bohart, 2003). As a part of the relationship, the therapist is different, if the client is different.*

PHENOMENOLOGICAL EPISTEMOLOGY: ACKNOWLEDGEMENT AND KNOWLEDGE

If we were fully functioning persons we could always, with all persons and moment by moment, be the person the client needs in the given moment and provide the answers the client needs, thus creating the optimal relationship at any given instant. But we are not fully functioning persons, we are all more or less maladjusted persons. This raises the question, What we do 'have' that can be of help and that can allow us to enter encounter processes in difficult relationships, in spite of our being restricted by our own fears and security needs?

The answer is: we have our ability to reflect. We have our intellect.

THE RELEVANCE OF KNOWLEDGE AND CONCEPTIONS IN PCT

Acknowledgment: the art of not-knowing

In immediately encountering another person I do not think about what I could know about him/her; rather I am ready to accept what they are going to disclose. This is a change of epistemological paradigms of tremendous importance for psychotherapy. It expresses acknowledgement as an active and proactive way of deliberately saying yes to the Other as a person. Specifically, this portrays psychotherapy as the art of not-knowing (Schmid, 2002a), the art of being curious, open to being surprised—a kind of sophisticated naïvety towards the client, where the challenging part is the unknown (see Takens, 2001) and not-yet-understood, the openness to wonderment, surprise and what the client has to disclose. 'Each experience, which deserves this name, thwarts an expectation' (Gadamer, 1999: 362). Thus back to the client! For a new, truly human image of the human being we need what Mearns (2003) calls a new epistemology.

Reflection: the human capability of dealing with experience

But life is not only surprise. We are able to think about our experiences and create expectations. We form specific concepts and theories. We inevitably do so and should be aware of this instead of ignoring it: we cheat ourselves if we think we do not think, expect and categorize. For a personal encounter relationship, both are necessary: acknowledgement *and* knowledge; experience *and* reflection.

Experiences lead to reflection. In order to be a personal encounter, therapy needs reflection both within and outside the therapeutic relationship. Reflection is necessary for a personal relationship not only *after* or *outside* therapy (e.g., in supervision, theory building or scientific work), reflection is also needed *within* the relationship, together with the client. A therapeutic encounter relationship is not only co-experiencing; it also is 'co-thinking' (Bohart, 2003). First, there is the immediate presence of persons, and then there is the co-reflection by the involved persons about the meaning of their encounter experience. The experience needs a second view, a critical view from 'outside' of the immediate encounter but within the relationship. The experience needs to be looked at, thus objectifying it. Only after this does the 'initial encounter' become a 'personal encounter' relationship.

As encounter philosophy has discerned, all en-*counter* processes start by being affected by the essence of the Other, of the unexpected as something or somebody that I experience as *counter* to me. Encounter means to face the other person, thus appreciating them as somebody independent, as an autonomous individual, different from me, and worthy of being dealt with (Schmid, 1994, 1998, 2002a). What at first is always an 'initial encounter', a naïve encounter as experienced by an unaffected child, becomes a 'personal encounter' by the passage through reflection. It needs the potential to make oneself, Others and relationships into objects of reflected awareness, thus overcoming the mere naïvety and unity which lie before freedom and responsibility. Distance is necessary for reflection. In this way, analyzing and evaluating become feasible, and with them so do the freedom and responsibility that characterize a mature encounter relationship. This free and responsible way of relating is the pre-condition for understanding what the call of the Other means and for the ability to answer adequately.

Immediate encounter and reflection modes

In the *process of immediate encounter* the epistemological road goes from client to therapist, so that the therapist asks, 'What does this person show, reveal, indicate?' (Not: 'What do I see over there?') Or: 'What can we understand, comprehend, empathize?' The movement goes from the Thou to the I, constituting a Thou-I-relationship (Schmid, 2002a). In this way we need to go 'back to the client' as our starting point, to a truly *client*-centered approach.

In the *process of reflecting*, however, the epistemological movement is the opposite, and so we ask, 'What do we perceive?' This requires that we look at the experiences and reflect on them (though sometimes or initially it might be only the therapist who starts reflecting).

Both epistemological movements are necessary; we need the subjective and the objective. In good moments of therapy they alternate, often quickly oscillating between both modes. The more reflecting follows experiencing and is connected with it, the more it feels like a holistic process, as 'one whole step'. (If the order is reversed or if encounter is missing at all, it is no longer *person*-centered therapy. If the critical reflection is missing, the therapist would no longer be the counter-part in the en-counter.)

In the *'immediate encounter mode'* it is impossible to do anything different from experiencing (otherwise one quits the encounter mode). Categorization is impossible: clients do not show categories, they show themselves (or parts of them)—even if they use categories to describe themselves. Rogers (1962:186–7) was very clear on this

> ... the existential encounter is important ... in the immediate moment of the therapeutic relationship, consciousness of theory has no helpful place ... we become spectators, not players—and it is as players that we are effective ... at some other time we may find it rewarding to develop theories. In the moment of relationship, such theory is irrelevant or detrimental ... theory should be tentatively, lightly, flexibly, in a way which is freely open to change, and should be laid aside in the moment of encounter itself.

While in the encounter mode categorization is impossible, in the *'reflection mode'*, the—whenever possible shared—enterprise is to understand the meaning of what was just experienced, and so we must use categories. We may feel reminded of an earlier situation with this person or of somebody similar, or an experience we have had ourselves that we use as comparison. We recognize that a feeling was stirred up that we had in another situation: although it was somewhat different, it feels similar. And so we create and use categories, concepts and conceptions. We cannot not think. We cannot not categorize: we cannot (and shouldn't) ignore that a certain behavior reminds us, let's say, of puberty. If we use this concept after the respective encounter experience, it can help us to better understand what the client wants to have understood and how they stage and direct the relationship. Categories and concepts may not be systematically reflected upon or hardly reflected on at all, but they always rule our acting.

Conceptions and categories

It is important, however, not to think that the self-created categories are given by nature. We need to be aware that the concepts and conceptions are our own constructs. We have to avoid reifying or ontologizing the categories created by ourselves. In the immediate encounter mode we experience, while in the reflection mode we perceive, which means 'to take'. But if we think that we just take what is there, we are wrong. We are construing what we think we see. We cannot perceive without pre-*inform*-ation. We do not look at the client with eyes that have never seen a client before. We are ourselves no *tabulae rasae*, but are biased by our experiences and the concepts derived from them.

Therefore we must be aware that *we* are the ones who determine what we hear and see, and how we arrange what clients tell and show. We decide about the frame of reference of our perceptions out of a pre-understanding and pre-interpretation (Spielhofer, 2003). Thus we need to be aware that a person does not 'have' a disorder, she 'is' not 'out of order' (Fehringer, 2003). A phenomenological approach rather requires the question: In which situation does he/she *show* something? On the basis of personal anthropology it is not possible to say what a symptom or a cluster of symptoms means, i.e., what the client wants to say, merely from an external frame of reference—without taking the relationship and thus ourselves and the cultural context into consideration.

Though it is impossible to think without concepts, we must keep in mind that they are likely to be more wrong than right (e.g., they always oversimplify). Therefore clients must have a chance to upset our concepts. To do this, we need first of all to disclose our concepts and to keep them as transparent as possible. Implicit conceptions must become explicit in order to be falsifiable. Clients must have a chance (even more: must feel invited) to falsify the therapists' concepts and conceptions. These need not only to be open for correction, they must invite correction. They must be ready to be upset and exploded. The last word for the therapist always has to be the Socratic 'I know that I know nothing'.

Existential knowledge: Context-, experience- and relationship-based

We have the choice either to use randomly what pops up in our mind, coincidental intuition or whatever, biased by ourselves, or we can reflect on the conceptions we have and investigate them in a scientific way systematically, that is, methodically and in dialogue with others, which will reduce the probability of systematic errors or biases. Responsibility requires reflecting on our conceptions.

This means: in the reflection mode we work with knowledge. From a personal point of view, this needs to be existential knowledge—knowledge that can provide a basis for our decisions to act. It must come out of experience and must remain bound to it and open to be changed by it. Reflected conceptions have to be process conceeptions, which do not pin down but open up. Such knowledge means to be in-form-ed, to be brought 'in form' by experience and reflection on experience. Experience-based knowledge does not ask whether something is *absolutely* (i.e., detached from the context) right or wrong, it can only be 'right' or 'wrong' within the *relation*-ship. Relevant knowledge is not only relationship-based, it is necessarily context-based and dependent on culture and social norms. (Many people were instantly 'cured' when homosexuality was removed from the list of diseases by the American Psychiatric Association (APA); now the 'Association of Gay and Lesbian Psychiatrists' is an affiliated organisation of the APA! (Fehringer, 2003).)

So, for knowledge the same applies as for empathy: back to the client! Clients are the ones who in-form us about the next steps in therapy. They bring us 'in form'. Knowledge serves understanding, empathy and acknowledging (i.e. unconditional positive regard; see Schmid 2002a). Empathy is always knowledge-based. Existential knowledge 'in-forms' empathy, 'in-forms' understanding, and thus can be of help, just as theory 'in-forms' practice (Iossifides, 2001). Knowledge fosters therapeutic understanding: Ute Binder (1994: 17–18) is convinced that, at least in the clinical field, we stay far below the possible and necessary level of the realization of the core conditions if we do not try to understand specific phenomena, the respective ways in which they are experienced and the conditions under which they develop. Binder and Binder (1991) emphasize that empathy needs knowledge about disorder-based specific peculiarities, or at least is furthered very much by it. This does not mean that the therapeutic conditions are not sufficient and need supplementation or addition by knowledge; rather it means that knowledge is an intrinsic part of the realization of the conditions. (Only barely enlightened, allegedly person-centered people play knowledge off against relationship and emotion.)

In summary: Epistemologically, the person-centered process of understanding is a process of personal encounter. This includes the process of experiencing, acknowledging the Other and empathy and the process of reflecting on the co-experiences. Both modes require each other. The task is to personally and professionally handle the resulting dichotomy of not-knowing and knowing, acknowledgement and knowledge. To be truly a personal encounter there needs to be reflection within and outside of therapy. Reflection is based upon knowledge and leads to new knowledge. Although knowledge must not get in the way of the immediacy of encounter, it must be seen as an essential dimension of a personal encounter relationship. A personal use of concepts, conceptions and theories does not hinder experience but fosters it.

DO WE NEED DISORDER-SPECIFIC CONCEPTIONS AND DIAGNOSTICS?

Therefore the crucial question or decision is which theories we use. On which conceptions do we base our therapeutic endeavor? Which knowledge do we choose to determine what we do? On the basis of a personal understanding, presence and reflection belong to each other and require each other as stated above. We need to offer the client the best conceptions available, the best to foster presence and personalization. The phrase 'to the best of one's knowledge and belief' shows clearly that this is an ethical task, just as doing psychotherapy itself is an ethical enterprise (Schmid, 2002a, c).

Disorder-specific?

Since we need reflection, concepts and knowledge to help us understand the processes in and with our clients and in ourselves as well as possible, it becomes clear that it is useful and necessary to have knowledge about specific processes in the person (which is different from the misleading term 'disorder'-specific knowledge). Rogers himself acted differently in different situations; he further developed his way of doing therapy and modified it (e.g., after the Wisconsin project and encounter groups experiences), even though he did not systematize and classify this. He clearly stated, 'with some fear and trembling', because of a 'heavy weight of clinical opinion to the contrary' that 'the essential conditions of psychotherapy exist in a single configuration, *even though the client or patient may use them very differently*' (1957: 101; italics mine). The second clause of the sentence is often overlooked, though it is essential and marks the task: to understand how clients use the relationship differently. Again: back to the client! Different ways of relating by the client in-form the therapist to relate and respond differently. This is crucial, because the relationship is unique. Each client deserves to get the answer and the relationship they need, and—this seems self-evident from the relationship conditions—not some preset 'type of intervention'.

At the same, we need concepts that help us to reflect on our therapeutic experiences, because it is better to act on the basis of critically reflected knowledge and scientifically investigated conceptions than on coincidental and randomly acquired knowledge. Thus it is essential to develop carefully grounded and considered, genuinely developed systems of concepts. In this sense, process-differentiation makes sense, as do specific concepts when they help us to better understand different authentic and inauthentic processes.

On the other hand, *disorder*-centered conceptions are not *person*-centered (see Mearns (2003): 'Person-centered is not problem-centered').

Quite a lot of person-centered 'disorder'-specific knowledge exists. There have been many attempts to describe and better understand characteristic processes. In recent years many theoreticians and researchers have made much effort, and there is quite a body of literature. Out of different motivations—to be recognized by the authorities, to communicate with colleagues, to further develop understandings of PCT—numerous conceptions were developed. The experiential movement deserves credit for strongly emphasizing the necessity of conceptions. The work of Hans Swildens (1988), Ute and Johannes Binder (1994), Margaret Warner (1998) and Garry Prouty (Prouty, Van Werde and Pörtner, 2002), for example, have contributed substantially to our understanding of person-centered processes and to the development of PCT theory.

Furthermore, much time has been spent on finding a way of dealing with the prevailing conceptions of medicine and psychiatry, the other therapeutic orientations, and the requirements of the public health system. It seems clear that simply to adopt one of these other systems of thought will hardly correspond with person-centeredness. As a result quite a few attempts have been made to translate traditional models into person-centered categories. Although we cannot ignore these traditional conceptions and therefore must understand them, and although we are often forced to use them in order to communicate with colleagues and institutions or simply in order to get access to social security money, I am convinced that they are not at all consistent with the image of the human being as a person. (In the same way, in training lack of self-assurance and competence should not be replaced by rules and techniques; instead, training should support personalization and further trust in one's own capabilities and a proper reflection on them just as therapy does.)

It is now my turn to state 'with some fear and trembling' (because of 'a heavy weight of opinion to the contrary' and because the result may be disappointing) that, according to the preceding considerations, it is obvious that there is not yet a genuinely person-centered taxonomy (systematic classification), one that meets the criteria of person-centered anthropology and epistemology described earlier in this paper. Even more: I am not convinced that all the knowledge we have gathered about processes in clients allows us to state that we already know enough about their experiences to elaborate systematic conceptualizations about specific processes.

Diagnosis?
Intrinsically connected with concept-specificity is the question of diagnostics. In the field of medicine rational treatment cannot be planned and executed without an accurate diagnosis, which also means prognosis of likely progress and possible cures and thus prescription of treatment. Such diagnoses are typically stated in terms of symptoms or etiology. For psychotherapy, however, Rogers (1951: 223–5) was convinced that psychological diagnoses are not only unnecessary, but also detrimental and unwise, because they place the locus of evaluation and responsibility in the therapist as the sole expert, which also has long-range social implications for the social control of the many

by the self-selected few. (Again an indication of the social criticism included in his theory and practice.)

Rogers' alternative view sees the client as the expert on their life, because they are the one with the experience: 'Therapy *is* diagnosis, and this diagnosis is a process which goes on in the experience of the client, rather than in the intellect of the clinician.' (Rogers, 1951: 223; see also his process description of therapy). This shows that the basic problem of diagnosis is the question of who is to be regarded as the experienced one. In a *person*-centered perspective, both are experts, yet in a different sense: the therapist is the expert on not being an expert of the life of another person.

The Greek word 'dia-gnosis' means 'distinguishing judgment'. Diagnosis is the hard work of the client, who works on the process of distinguishing: the client is constantly trying to find out—by experiencing and reflecting—which development is on the agenda next, what they need in the process of personalization. Thus there must be diagnosis, although in a person-centered sense this is differently understood from the common meaning. And though it runs completely counter to the traditional and widespread understanding, from a *person*-centered point of view psychological diagnosis can only be a phenomenological process diagnosis, step by step unfolding through the joint process of experiencing and reflecting by both client and therapist. Just like therapy, diagnosis needs both modes and requires both persons involved in the relationship, thus making it a *co-diagnostic process*.

In summary: Although quite a lot of person-centered 'disorder'-specific knowledge exists and there are phenomenological descriptions that provide a very valuable contribution to person-centered personality and therapy theory, a genuinely person-centered systematic description of inauthentic processes is only rudimentary and a genuinely person-centered taxonomy of process-specificity does not exist at all.

PHILOSOPHY OF SCIENCE:
TOWARDS A TRULY HUMAN SCIENCE

So there still is a lot of work ahead. We are not yet able to set up a genuinely person-centered system. Thus the only thing I can provide at this stage in the development of the paradigm is to name criteria such a systematic conceptualization would require. Thus, I state some tentative theses as criteria for a genuinely person-centered conceptualization of different processes of personality development.

1. Conceptions (that is, systems of concepts) must be created on the basis of *personal anthropology*, i.e., on the basis of dialogical or encounter philosophy. Among others this means that conceptions must include thinking in relationship categories as well as in substantial categories. It necessarily includes thinking in processes. The matrix is a conception of personal authenticity, not a concept of dis-*order*, dis-*ease* or the like. Such a conception must be based on growth, a conception that rests on potential

and actualization. Since it will embrace the past and future of the person as well as the present, thus thinking in life-long categories, it will also be of etiological value.

2. Conceptions must be *phenomenological*, i.e., they must go back to the client as a person. Such an approach keeps in mind that what the person shows is relevant and not just what can be analyzed or explained. Person-centered conceptions must be as close to experience as possible, in keeping with the phenomenological radicalism of Rogers.

3. Hence it must be possible to *falsify* the conceptions or parts thereof. Conceptions are useful when they stimulate a process that leads to their being overcome by better ones. It must constantly be possible to revise specific concepts through experience. It is this sort of '*orthopractice*' that always challenges orthodoxy.

4. Conceptions must be *hermeneutic*. The original meaning of hermeneutics applies here: reconstruing the meaning the author of a damaged text had in mind. It also has to be clear that this understanding is ultimately for the client's sake, not for the therapist's; that understanding is impossible without knowledge of the cultural context; and that it is impossible to get rid of all prejudices. The task of existential hermeneutics rather is to become aware of the prejudices and pre-understandings of one's own existence and to make them transparent (see 3).

5. Person-centered conceptions need to be *existential*, i.e., they must have a relation to the whole existence of a person as well as to human existence in general.

6. Conceptions must include *social criticism*. They must have a critical eye on power and control, on interests and expertism; and they have to be emancipatory in nature. Therefore such conceptions must make transparent whose interests they serve and who will benefit from them.

7. Conceptions must trigger *research that is genuinely humanistic* (Rogers, 1964). It goes without saying that person-centered conceptions must allow the influence of empirical research, even if the results are disconfirming. But more important is that person-centered researchers overcome empiricism and positivism and are able to initiate truly person-oriented approaches to research, e.g., intensive case studies or creative types of research such as Elliott's (2002) Hermeneutic Single Case Efficacy Design (HSCED).

CONCLUSION

'Back to the client' means back to the human being. We need a human science to understand what goes on in human beings. If the movement goes from the client to the therapist, then in a client-centered approach we need to go back to the client as the primary source of knowledge and understanding. Therapy is more than a matter of therapist variables, it is a matter of the client's self-healing capacities. This implies an epistemological paradigm change resulting in a fundamental counter-position to traditional diagnosis and classification: it is the client who defines their life and the meaning of their experiencing and thus 'in-forms' the therapist. The therapist is truly challenged to open up and to risk *the co-creation of becoming (part of) a unique relationship and also*—no less a risk—*to co-reflect on it.*

Why do we have all these discussions and debates about disorder-specific treatment? One main reason is that we want to reply to those who reproach us for not meeting their criteria for scientific work and research, criteria developed by people who start from a completely different view of the human being—if they have a view of the human being at all and not only of some parts or aspects of behavior. If we try to adapt ourselves to those criteria we will lose our identity and abandon the radical paradigm change to the person in the center. We might temporarily gain some applause, but we would lose the reason for being an independent approach, because we would lose our unique stance, the unique offer and ethical challenge of person-centeredness. We would vanish into a general psychology.

The alternative, however, is not an easy task. We face the enterprise of encountering—in the sense of making steps counter to—the mainstream by responding in new categories. We face the job of working hard to develop a human, truly *person-*centered understanding of science, knowledge and research, including genuinely person-centered conceptions of what are called psychological disorders. *We face the challenge of creating an understanding of ourselves beyond the categories of order and disorder*—no less than an uncompromising continuation of the social criticism Carl Rogers pursued with his personality and therapy theory.

REFERENCES

Binder, U (1994) *Empathienentwicklung und Pathogenese in der Klientenzentrierten Psychotherapie.* Eschborn: Klotz.

Binder, U and Binder, J (1991) *Studien zu einer störungsspezifischen klientenzentrierten Psychotherapie: Schizophrene Ordnung—Psychosomatisches Erleben—Depressives Leiden.* Eschborn: Klotz.

Binder, U and Binder H-J (1994) (eds) *Klientenzentrierte Psychotherapie bei schweren psychischen Störungen.* Frankfurt: Fachbuchhandlung für Psychologie.

Bohart, AC (2003) How does empathy facilitate? Paper, 6th PCE Conference, Egmond aan Zee.

Elliott, R (2002) Hermeneutic single case efficacy design. *Psychotherapy Research, 12,*1–20.

Fehringer, C (2003) Brauchen wir Störungswissen, um personzentriert arbeiten zu können? Unpublished paper. PCA, Vienna.

Gadamer, H-G (1999) *Wahrheit und Methode: Grundzüge einer philosophischen Hermeneutik. Vol. 1.* Tübingen: Mohr.

Geller, S, Schmid, PF and Wyatt, G (2003) A dialogue on therapeutic presence: A precondition, a meta-condition or fourth condition in Person-Centered Therapy? 6th PCE Conference,

Egmond aan Zee.

Heinerth, K (2002) Symptomspezifität und Interventionshomogenität. *Gesprächspsychotherapie und Personzentrierte Beratung 1*, 23–26.

Iossifides, P (2001) Understanding the actualizing tendency through the recent events. Unpublished paper, International Colloquium on the 100th Anniversary of Carl Rogers, Vienna.

Mearns, D (1996) Working at relational depth with clients in person-centred therapy. *Counselling, 7*, 306–11.

Mearns, D (2003) Person-centered is not problem-centered. Unpublished keynote lecture, 6th PCE Conference, Egmond aan Zee.

Pfeiffer, WM (1993) Die Bedeutung der Beziehung bei der Entstehung und der Therapie psychischer Störungen. In L Teusch and J Finke (eds) *Die Krankheitslehre der Gesprächspsychotherapie* (pp. 19–40). Heidelberg: Asanger.

Prouty, G, Van Werde, D and Pörtner, M (2002) *Pre-therapy*. Ross-on-Wye: PCCS Books.

Rogers, CR (1951) *Client-Centered Therapy: Its current practice, implications, and theory*. Boston: Houghton Mifflin.

Rogers, CR (1957) The necessary and sufficient conditions of therapeutic personality change. *Journal of Consulting Psychology, 21*, 95–103.

Rogers, CR (1959) A theory of therapy, personality, and interpersonal relationships, as developed in the client-centered framework. In S Koch (ed), *Psychology: A study of science. Vol III.* (pp. 184–256). New York: McGraw Hill.

Rogers, CR (1962) The interpersonal relationship: The core of guidance. In CR Rogers and B Stevens. *Person to Person. The problem of being human* (pp. 89–104). Moab: Real People.

Rogers, CR (1964) Towards a science of the person. In TW Wann (ed) *Behaviorism and Phenomenology* (pp. 109–140). Chicago: University of Chicago Press.

Rogers, CR (1965) 'A humanistic conception of man'. In R Farson (ed) *Science and Human Affairs* (pp. 18–31). Palo Alto: Science and Behavior Books.

Sanders, P (2005) Principled and strategic opposition to the medicalisation of distress and all of its apparatus. Chapter 3 (pp. 21–42) this volume.

Schmid, PF (1992) „Herr Doktor, bin ich verrückt?": Eine Theorie der leidenden Person statt einer Krankheitslehre. In P Frenzel, PF Schmid, M Winkler (eds) *Handbuch der Personzentrierten Psychotherapie* (pp. 83–125). Cologne: EHP.

Schmid, PF (1994) *Personzentrierte Gruppenpsychotherapie: Ein Handbuch, vol. I.: Solidarität und Autonomie*. Cologne: EHP.

Schmid, PF (1996) *Personzentrierte Gruppenpsychotherapie in der Praxis: Ein Handbuch, vol. II.: Die Kunst der Begegnung*. Paderborn: Junfermann.

Schmid, PF (1998) 'Face to face': The art of encounter. In B Thorne and E Lambers (eds) *Person-Centred Therapy* (pp. 74–90). London: Sage.

Schmid, PF (2001) Authenticity: the person as his or her own author. Dialogical and ethical perspectives on therapy as an encounter relationship. And beyond. In G Wyatt (ed) *Rogers' Therapeutic Conditions: Evolution, theory and practice. Vol. 1: Congruence* (pp. 217–32). Ross-on-Wye: PCCS Books.

Schmid, PF (2002a) Knowledge or acknowledgement? Psychotherapy as 'the art of not-knowing'— Prospects on further developments of a radical paradigm. *Person-Centered and Experiential Psychotherapies, 1*, 56–70.

Schmid, PF (2002b) Presence: Im-media-te co-experiencing and co-responding.

Phenomenological, dialogical and ethical perspectives on contact and perception in person-centred therapy and beyond. In G Wyatt and P Sanders (eds) *Rogers' Therapeutic Series: Evolution, theory and practice. Vol 4: Contact and Perception* (pp. 182–203). Ross-on-Wye: PCCS Books.

Schmid, PF (2002c) 'The necessary and sufficient conditions of being person-centered': On identity, integrity, integration and differentiation of the paradigm. In J Watson, RN Goldman and MS Warner (eds) *Client-Centered and Experiential Psychotherapy in the 21st Century* (pp. 36–51). Ross-on-Wye: PCCS Books.

Schmid, PF (2003) The characteristics of a person-centered approach to therapy and counseling: Criteria for identity and coherence. *Person-Centered and Experiential Psychotherapies, 2,* 104–20.

Spielhofer, H (2003) Störungsspezifische Konzepte in der Personzentrierten Psychotherapie. Unpublished paper. PCA, Vienna.

Swildens, H (1988) *Procesgerichte gesprekstherapie.* Leuven/Amersfoort: Acco/de Horstink.

Takens, RJ (2001) *Een vreemde nabij: Enkele aspecten van de psychotherapeutische relatie onderzocht.* Lisse: Swets and Zeitlinger.

Warner, MS (1998) A client-centered approach to therapeutic work with dissociated and fragile process. In LS Greenberg, JC Watson and G Lietaer (eds) *Handbook of Experiential Psychotherapy* (pp. 368–87). New York: Guilford.

Zurhorst, G (1993) Eine gesprächspsychotherapeutische Störungs–/Krankheitstheorie in biographischer Perspektive. In L Teusch and J Finke (eds) *Die Krankheitslehre der Gesprächspsychotherapie* (pp. 71–87). Heidelberg: Asanger.

CHAPTER 7

A PERSON-CENTERED VIEW OF HUMAN NATURE, WELLNESS, AND PSYCHOPATHOLOGY

MARGARET S. WARNER

Most person-centered writings focus on health and actualization rather than on illness and psychopathology. This tendency results in large part because person-centered theorists are acutely aware of a number of problems that emerge when one tries to equate human psychological distress with physical illness as it has been construed within the traditions of Western medicine.

Several issues are central for person-centered theorists. Western medicine tends to relate specific diseases to specific cures, rather than focusing on the operation of the organism as a whole. As a result, it requires expert diagnosis of specific disease syndromes in order to specify and implement the right treatments. Given this overall approach, psychological practices based on traditional medical models tend to assume that the person's own judgment should not be trusted in making sense of his or her life or in deciding the personally best ways to solve problems. And these tendencies are accentuated when clients have more severe emotional disturbance or life difficulties, since such clients are seen as even less able to make judgments on their own behalf.

This sort of medical-model framework is highly problematic to person-centered practitioners. Person-centered theory is grounded in the hypothesis that human beings have a deeply rooted organismic tendency toward making a very personal sense of life and toward constructive problem-solving, particularly when supported by genuine, empathic, prizing relationships. Reliance on expert diagnosis and externally determined, symptom-specific interventions runs contrary to the practices supported by this theory.

Yet, despite its various conceptual problems, the illness metaphor is difficult to ignore entirely, since it has such a central role in organizing the distribution of resources to people in need within modern industrial societies. And, clients who suffer from extreme psychological distress have strong needs for emotional and physical support. Given this ideological tension, I think that it is worth struggling to find a way of relating actualization and psychopathology that is consistent with the person-centered view of human nature. And, if, as person-centered theorists, we are able to clarify such an overall model of health and pathology, we may also be able to increase our effectiveness in critiquing and offering constructive alternatives to current systems of mental health services.

I believe that a version of psychopathology can be developed from within person-centered theory which avoids many of the pitfalls of the traditional medical model and which is truer to the functioning of human beings as understood within the best of contemporary social sciences. In brief, I suggest that the ability to process meaning—both intra-psychically and within human relationships—is so central to human nature that any inability to do so is likely to be experienced as affliction and to cause profound life disturbances. This ability to process meaning is embedded in relationships and culture and is fundamental to the particular ways that human beings are able to connect with other human beings.

This distinctively human way of making sense actualizes some broad purposes that are universal to human beings. Yet the particular ways of making sense are open to a significant degree of existential freedom within individuals as they live in the context of traditions of meaning current in their own social groups and cultures. This view allows us to consider that a particular person's innate abilities to actualize can be challenged in such a way that that person needs and deserves societal support. Yet it makes sense of a person-centered approach to psychopathology which approaches the individual as a whole, and addresses most challenges to actualization by offering facilitative conditions rather than disease-specific interventions.

To explore this sort of framework for psychopathology, I will first present a brief version of the development of processing capacities and of several forms of 'difficult process' I have experienced within Client-Centered Therapy. In my experience, clients experiencing each of these forms of difficult process work very well within a client-centered approach to therapy. Yet, the experience of difficult process offers severe challenges to the human capacity to make sense of experience and to make personally meaningful life-choices. Then, I will combine recent work in contemporary social sciences and philosophy with the work of person-centered theorists to create a distinctively person-centered view of health and dysfunction as it relates to the processing of meaning. Using this framework, I will consider implications for person-centered contributions to and critique of current mental health practice. While I am placing particular emphasis on individual process in this initial formulation, I believe that the overall model that I am presenting is equally relevant to the understanding of human relationships and cultural phenomena.

THE DEVELOPMENT OF PROCESSING CAPACITIES

Initially, infants are almost totally dependent on their relationship with adults to manage their experiencing. They need the attentive presence of care-giving adults to avoid falling into either distracted boredom or states of physical and emotional trauma (Stern, 1985). This sort of child-adult attachment relationship provides the 'environment of evolutionary adaptedness' that is essential for normal human development (Warner 2000, 2002a). This attachment relationship seems to require physical care in combination with Rogers' core conditions—empathy, genuineness and prizing. Much the way that the organization of lungs in an unborn child anticipates and requires oxygen after birth to come into full functioning, infants anticipate and require a sustained benign caregiving to develop into functioning adults. Both adults and infants are strongly oriented to forming this sort of attachment relationship, and in the context of this sort of attachment relationship the child's abilities to process experience follow a natural path of development.

I propose that several particular aspects of processing initially require a strong partnership with a caregiving adult in an attachment relationship in order to develop fully (Warner, 2000). Infants are initially almost totally dependent on adults to hold experience in any sort of sustained attention, to modulate the intensity of experience, and to name experience. With a benign attachment relationship, young children naturally acquire increasing abilities to perform these functions in a more or less autonomous fashion. With these abilities and with increasing complexity of cognitive capacities, young children begin to be able to form an understanding of other people's experience without totally losing a sense of their own experience.

COMMON FORMS OF DIFFICULT PROCESS

While the human organism is strongly oriented toward developing processing capacities, a good-enough early childhood attachment relationship—as well as the normative development of the biological structures and processes that support processing—is required for this development to unfold optimally. Individuals (and those in relationships with them) are likely to experience their processing as difficult when such biologically and psychologically developed processing capacities are impaired. Likewise, physical or psychological damage that occurs later in life may disrupt the person's capacities to process experience in normative ways.

I have found that three kinds of difficult process emerge most often in my practice as a client-centered therapist—fragile process, dissociated process and psychotic process. The three styles of process are described at length elsewhere. (Warner, 1991, 1998, 2000, 2001; Prouty, 1994). I will offer a somewhat brief description here and then consider some general aspects of difficult process that I have found important in therapeutic work.

Clients seem to develop a fragile style of processing experience when the sort of empathic caregiving needed to develop processing capacities in early childhood has been lacking. Clients who experience 'fragile process' (Warner, 1991, 1997, 2000) have difficulty holding experience in attention at moderate levels of intensity. As a result they tend to have difficulty starting and stopping experiences that are personally significant or emotionally connected, and often feel discomfort or shame in the process. Given this difficulty holding onto their own experience, they often have difficulty taking in the point of view of another person without feeling that their own experience has been annihilated. As an example, a client might talk in a way that seems quite circumstantial for most of a session and suddenly feel a sense of connection to her experience that is intensely vulnerable. She may express this vulnerability quite indirectly and yet feel annihilated if the therapist doesn't sense the importance of vulnerability and receive it in a welcoming way. Yet, if the therapist attempts to understand in a way that doesn't catch her feelings in exactly the right words, or if the therapist offers advice or interpretations she may well lose her ability to stay with the experience, feeling enraged or ashamed in the process. Or, she may feel flooded by emotion and feel that it could go on forever, doing damage to herself and the therapist. Afterwards she may feel exposed and ashamed at having lost control.

In personal relationships clients with fragile process are likely to feel violated and misunderstood a lot of the time. Other people often experience them as being unreasonably angry, touchy and stubborn, since they often feel the need to defend their experience to avoid feeling that it is annihilated. Others often become angry and rejecting in return, intensifying the clients' sense that there is something fundamentally wrong with their experience. If, on the other hand, people who experience fragile process give up on connecting or expressing their personal reactions, they are likely to feel empty inside. Many people alternate, holding in their reactions while feeling increasingly uncomfortable and then exploding with rage at those around them. A number of client-centered and experiential psychotherapists have described valuable ways of working with clients experiencing fragile or other closely related sorts of process. (Bohart, 1990; Eckert and Biermann-Ratjen, 1998; Eckert and Wuchner, 1996; Lambers, 1994; Leijssen, 1993, 1996; Roelens, 1996; Santen, 1990; Swildens, 1990).

Clients who experience 'dissociated process' quite convincingly experience themselves as having selves that are not integrated with each other for periods of time (Warner, 1998, 2000; Roy, 1991; Coffeng, 1995). They may experience a disunity, alternating between different autonomous experiences of self that feels 'crazy' to themselves and to others. When alternate personality parts have been dominant, they experience periods of forgetfulness lasting for minutes or hours. Or, they may live for years keeping very busy while leading quite restricted lives, only to have the experience of parts emerge in times of crisis. Yet when such parts do emerge, the parts themselves express their experience of having been present all along, but having been separate from the awareness of the client in her everyday self.

In my experience, dissociated process of this sort virtually always results from severe early childhood trauma. Before they are seven or eight years old, children lack the cognitive and emotional capacities that would let them understand or moderate the intensity of traumatic experiences. As a result, they rely almost totally on the comfort and protection of parenting figures to mitigate any experiences of emotional flooding. When traumatic experiences occur in the absence of such comfort and protection, young children are likely to stumble on an ability to move into trance-like states in response. These trance-like states have a particular tendency to separate into clusters of experience that have independent, person-like qualities. Such 'parts' tend to develop a variety of opposing strategies for responding to emotional pain of traumatic experiences, revolving around a core belief that traumatic experiences could destroy the client if allowed to emerge. In adulthood, separate parts tend to emerge when for one reason or another, trauma memories threaten to return.

Clients who have a psychotic style of processing have difficulty forming narratives about their experience that make sense within the culture, or which offer a predictive validity in relation to their environment. Prouty (1990, 1994) describes clients experiencing psychotic process as having impaired contact with 'self', 'world' and 'other.' Often, such clients experience voices, hallucinations or delusions that are neither culturally accepted nor are easy to process (Prouty, 1977, 1983, 1986). Still, various client-centered therapists who have worked with psychotic process have found that psychotic experiences tend to be meaningful and have the potential to process into more reality-oriented forms (Rogers, 1967; Prouty, Van Werde and Pörtner, 2002; Prouty, 1994; Raskin, 1996; Van Werde, 1998; 1990; Binder, 1998; Warner, 2002b). Prouty (1994) suggests that therapists use 'contact reflections' that stay close to clients' concrete expressions as a way of restoring more reality-based connection.

Research suggests that a complex interaction between genetic propensities, disruptions of perinatal development and life stress are involved in the development of schizophrenic disorders. Other psychotic disorders can develop as a result of later physical trauma or organic degeneration (Green, 1998).

I suspect that numerous other forms of difficult process exist. Certainly, any significant impairment of physiological or biochemical processes in the brain is likely to make the ordinary processing of experience difficult. Yet, the human organism is deeply oriented toward trying to make sense of experience and has numerous alternative ways of processing available to it. I believe that therapeutic relationships characterized by Rogers' core conditions will tend to foster processing utilizing any biological capacities that are available to the person.

Virtually all clients and therapists have experiences of 'difficult' process at certain moments. Yet, for some clients, experiences of difficult process are so intense and create such a feeling of vulnerability that they have problems working within standard psychotherapy formats. Often, these clients get labeled with serious and stigmatizing diagnoses—such as borderline or narcissistic personality disorders, dissociative identity disorders or schizophrenia.

These categories can have some descriptive validity, but they often oversimplify and distort the actual situation of the client. Difficult styles of process can exist in varying combinations with each other, while clients tend to be diagnosed as having a single disorder. Difficult process can operate at differing levels of intensity or may apply to some aspects of a person's experience, but not others. Traditional schools of thought in psychology often suggest that non-normative forms of experience characteristic of severe disorders should be ignored or responded to with external interpretation and structuring. The central life dilemmas of clients diagnosed with severe psychopathology tend to be experienced in the form of difficult process. I believe that a lack of empathic responding—particularly when combined with structured, interpretive sorts of interventions—is likely to discourage clients from the sort of processing that is essential if they are to develop a personally authentic sense of self or understanding of their life situations.

STRATEGIES FOR WORKING WITH DIFFICULT PROCESS AS EXPERIENCED BY INDIVIDUAL CLIENTS

Person-centered therapists have found that the same relational conditions that facilitate process in high functioning clients—empathy, congruence and unconditional positive regard—are helpful to clients engaging with such difficult process experiences (Warner, 1991; Prouty, 1994; Rogers, 1967). The human impulse to make sense of experience is so central to human survival that human beings continue to try to process, even when more ordinary ways of processing are compromised. To the extent that any organismic capacities exist, relationships that embody Rogers' core conditions will tend to provide support for the person's processing.

Clients often alternate between impulses to remain safe and impulses to engage with crucial though troubling aspects of experience and relationship. Person-centered therapists are committed to supporting the person's existential freedom in deciding whether, when, and how to process their own experience. Yet, the human impulse to make sense of experience and to connect with others in relationship is so fundamental that clients are very likely to move in the direction of processing when in the presence of a genuine, empathic and prizing therapeutic relationship. As they process, clients are likely to develop more personally grounded, coherent, reality-based ways of experiencing themselves and their life situations.

Even if such processing has biological limits, any progress in the direction of having a sense of self and of making sense of experience—particularly when it occurs in a context that allows the person to feel genuine, accepting contact with other human beings—has intense benefits for the individual. Indeed, such experiences often allow clients to move from feeling lost in states of alienation, confusion, emptiness and panic to having a sense of themselves as authentic human beings in relationship to other human beings.

A number of theorists have noted that work with difficult process makes particular demands on therapists' empathy and on their ability to communicate that empathy to clients. Therapists may have intense personal reactions to client experiences that are foreign to them or if familiar to them, are similar to difficult experiences in their own lives that have not been fully resolved (Warner, 2000, 2001). As a result, they may find it difficult to stay empathic and prizing to the client's actual experience. Therapists can easily distort their understanding of unfamiliar client experiences to fit more normalized experiences from their own lives. Given the vulnerability and shame that tend to accompany difficult process, clients may express their most important experiences indirectly or tentatively. As a result, clients may not find it easy to correct the therapist's understanding of difficult process. And, when experiences of difficult process aren't received, clients can easily give up on possibilities of genuine contact with the therapist. I believe that the therapy process is likely to feel safer to clients and they are more likely to take the risk of exploring more vulnerable aspects of their lives as therapists increase their empathic attunement to difficult process.

Clients in the midst of difficult process may also have difficulty receiving complexly formulated expressions of empathy from others without becoming confused or disconnected from their own experiences. Client's experiencing fragile process (or the very fragile experiences of dissociated parts) may only be able to receive silence or expressions of understanding that stay extremely close to their own words without feeling that their experience has been annihilated (Warner, 2000, 2001). Prouty (1994) notes that personally meaningful, reality-based contact with self, world and others tends to be fostered by 'contact reflections,' empathic responses that are very concrete and close to the clients' actual words and facial and body gestures.

ACTUALIZATION, PROCESSING AND THE NATURE OF HUMAN NATURE

Rogers (1957) makes a strong claim about human nature when he declares that human contact embodying broad human relational qualities—empathy, congruence and unconditional positive regard—is 'necessary and sufficient' to generate constructive personality change across diagnostic categories. While Rogers (1959, 1961) grounds his theory in the human 'actualizing tendency,' and makes many observations about process, he offers relatively little elaboration as to how human beings are organized such that they would have such a strong tendency to process in these ways. On the one hand, Rogers makes his claims for the actualization tendency on pragmatic grounds. He has experienced that psychotherapy grounded in these principles works. On the other hand, he supports his opinions with broad research results of the 'if-then' variety. If the core conditions are offered, one will find increases in inner-directed, pro-social behaviors and decreases in symptoms and antisocial behaviors. And, indeed strong research results continue to validate the claims for effectiveness for person-centered psychotherapies (Cain and Seeman, 2002). While both of these approaches to validation are relevant, I believe that a more detailed analysis of human nature is warranted.

Recent work in ecological psychology combined with the work of person-centered theorists allow us to consider why human beings would respond to these core relational conditions in such a significant way and what this says about psychopathology in general. Tooby and Cosmides (1992) suggest that a series of adaptations in the Pleistocene era formed the basis of the relatively rapid human leap into culture. These combined adaptations offered an adaptive advantage that was strong enough that it has remained relatively stable in the millennia since. Human universality is not seen as contradicting the variability of human personalities and cultures. Rather, it is the basis of it.

> Culture and social behavior is complexly variable, but not because the human mind is a social product, a blank slate, or an externally programmed general-purpose computer lacking richly defined evolved structure. Instead, human culture and behavior is richly variable because it is generated by an incredibly intricate, contingent set of functional programs that use and process information from the world ... (p. 24)

97

Tooby and Cosmides (1992) suggest that the consistency of these evolved structures for processing information can be easily masked by the sheer variety of manifest behaviors and cultural forms. Yet, these more subtle, deep structures are likely to remain constant—since they are essential to human adaptive success—while many more obvious and compelling aspects of human living will undergo constant change. Much of social science, they suggest, has looked for constancy in the wrong places.

> Mainstream sociocultural anthropology has arrived at a situation resembling some nightmarish short story Borges might have written, where their scientists are condemned by their unexamined assumptions to study the nature of mirrors only by cataloguing and investigating everything that mirrors can reflect. It is an endless process that never makes progress, that never reaches closure ... whose enduring product is voluminous descriptions of particular phenomena. (p. 42)

On the one hand, ecological psychologists suggest that many specific adaptations form a taken-for-granted backdrop for human living.

> By adding together a face recognition module, a spacial relations module, ... a fear module ... and emotion perception module ... a friendship module, a grammar acquisition module, a theory of mind module, and so on an architecture gains a breadth of competencies that allows it to solve a wider and wider range of problems. (p. 113)

Yet, they propose that such specific capacities of mind necessitate more function-general capacities.

> ... the more alternative content-specialized mechanisms an architecture contains, the more easily domain-general mechanisms can be applied to the problem spaces they create without being paralyzed by combinatorial explosion. (p. 113)

I propose that 'processing'—a particular sort of self-directed, individual way of making sense of life experience in the context of human relationships—is a central aspect of the way human beings are adapted to function as human beings. As such it is a core aspect of the universal human architecture outlined by Tooby and Cosmides (1992), and constitutes one of the common modes of functioning that undergirds the vast variety of more particular individual and group modes of living and experiencing life.[1] Because such processing is central to the adaptive advantage acquired in the human leap into culture, one can expect it to be universal and to be over-determined. One would expect

---

1. While the results of process research are consistent with this hypothesis, ecological psychologists would require a detailed analysis of ways that each alteration in capacities offered significant adaptive advantages in the Pleistocene era to offer definitive support for this sort of ecological hypothesis. Detailed ecological analysis of this kind would be a worthwhile project, but is beyond the scope of this paper.

people to keep trying to process, even under conditions of severe challenge. Any significant inability to process would tend to be experienced as affliction and to cause severe dysfunction in a person's ability to live effectively among other human beings.

All of the above qualities resonate deeply with the accumulated theory, experience and research in person-centered therapies. If this proposition is accurate, one would expect processing to emerge with a constancy that is less ephemeral and changeable than most social science phenomena. Extending the metaphor of Tooby and Cosmides (1992), one could say that in analyzing processing one is working with the mirror that is human nature itself rather than the images reflected in the mirror, that make up much of the day-to-day content of life. With this in mind, let me propose the nature of such universal modes of processing, blending insights from Rogers, Gendlin and other person-centered process theorists, as well as various philosophers of meaning.

A PERSON-CENTERED MODEL OF PROCESSING

Human beings make sense of life using what I call 'soft meanings' (Warner, 1983). These are versions of life experience that don't have a hard existence which is likely to stay constant across observers, across time and space, or even within a particular person over time. Soft phenomena include individual phenomena such as wanting, desiring, having emotions, or thinking, as well as a variety of social qualities such as responsibility, justice or freedom. Whether a wedding occurred or not is a 'hard' phenomenon—since the various participants can agree that it happened and are likely to hold to that observation in the future. Whether the bride and groom were 'really in love' is a soft phenomenon. Various participants at a wedding are likely to disagree, even the bride and groom may offer quite different versions a few years later.

One major aspect of this human tendency to operate with soft meanings comes from what Dennett (1987) calls the 'intentional stance'—the idea that the behavior of other people is guided by invisible internal entities such as beliefs or desires In a similar vein, Baron-Cohen (2001) notes that human beings cannot construe the simplest daily situations without recourse to a sort of 'mind-reading' that involves soft phenomena. It is virtually impossible to understand a simple set of behaviors such as 'John walked into the bedroom, walked around and walked out' without recourse to intentions, wishes, beliefs, emotional states and the like. For example, one might propose that 'Maybe John was looking for something he wanted to find and he thought it was in the bedroom.' Or, 'Maybe John heard something in the bedroom and wanted to know what had made the noise' (p. 1).

While the processing of such soft phenomena occurs within individuals, the phenomena themselves are about the totality of lived experience within human contexts. I suspect that the very softness of these phenomena—the fact that they have no hard existence and are subject to ongoing interpretation and re-interpretation—allows a bridge between individual consciousness and the culturally embedded life of human beings in relationships and communities. This particularly human capacity of individuals living

99

within cultural groups to make sense of experience is what developed in the evolutionary leap into humanness. It seems likely that this flexible ability to make sense is responsible for much of the adaptive success and dominance of human beings over other species.

But, a significant question arises as to how human beings form and reform such constructions of soft phenomena in relation to themselves, or in their understanding of the actions of others. This cannot be a simple matching of constructs with data, since the phenomena themselves don't have concrete existence and are subject to varying interpretations. Yet, despite their variability and openness to interpretation, soft phenomena have as much or more impact on a person's life as any more concrete and stable hard phenomena. For example, whether a person is sentenced to death may rest on the question of whether he 'intended' to pull the trigger of a gun.

Gendlin (1964, 1968, 1997) suggests that rather than any machine-like computation, human organisms have 'implicit' within them a kind of seeking that is 'carried forward' as the organism finds something that at least partially completes that which is implicit and, in the process changes the nature of the seeking. Meaning is a particular sort of carrying forward that is characteristic of human beings. One metaphor for carrying forward into meaning is the completion of a poem (Gendlin, 1995). If a poet has written three lines and is looking for a final fourth line, she may try on any number of lines before finding one that 'works'. Once she has written the final line, it may well feel like the only line that could have been written. Yet, if she had waited until a week later she might have come up with a different last line, one that also worked. Meaning, in Gendlin's philosophy, is like the last line of the poem in that it is neither totally constrained nor is it totally arbitrary.

Gendlin (1964, 1968) also emphasizes that making sense (or carrying forward into meaning) is a whole body process. There is no mind-body split. Following Gendlin's theory, I would place human experiencing on a continuum from that which is implicit to that which is articulated as follows:

Physiological Processes (e.g. blood pressure)	*Physiological Body Sensing* (e.g. pain in muscle)	*Vague Sense a Situation* (e.g. images scenes, gestures or body sensing giving a feel of a life situation)	*Partially Articulated Version of a Situation* (e.g. 'Something about X is getting to me' or, 'I have a vague feeling of Y'	*Articulated Version* (e.g. 'I feel X about Y for Z reason)

At every point on this continuum, the body offers a lived way of responding to the person's whole situation. Under some circumstances, physiological processes are carried forward into subjective experience. And, human beings can take action in response to such subjective experience at any further point in this continuum without further articulation of their experience. Yet, human beings have a tendency, especially when an organismic process is blocked from carrying forward, to attend to their experience and to try to carry it forward into meaning. So, for example, if a person is breathing effortlessly, he may pay very little attention to his breath. But if suddenly he is unable to breathe, he is likely to start looking for causes and explanations in the hope of finding a remedy. If a person is feeling content in an activity, she may continue without special attention to her experience. But if she is feeling bored or frustrated or lonely or frightened, she is likely to try to make sense of what is going on and try to change the situation in some way. Sometimes this sort of attending occurs spontaneously, sometimes with conscious intentionality.

However it occurs, attending to experience tends to create a shift in the quality of experiencing and to bring related experiencing into play in ways that can easily carry forward into increasing articulation of meaning. If a person attends to a tightness in the shoulders, he may come to sense a feeling of dread. If he attends to the feeling of dread, life scenes or thoughts relating to this sense may to come to mind. For example, he may picture the scene of a recent fight with his boss. If he pictures that scene he may picture other times that he felt helpless and humiliated. From there he may articulate a version of what happened and why. For example, 'It wasn't fair to expect me to know what he wanted when he never told me. That's just the way my stepfather always was.' In each step of such carrying forward into meaning, the whole body changes—heart-rate, breathing, blood pressure, immune response and the like.

I suspect that the broad purposes of such carrying forward into meaning are universal. Human beings try to make sense in ways that are personal—that carry forward their particular lived experience in a way that feels authentic. They try to make predictive sense of life experience—so that they will know why things happened and what is likely to happen next. They try to make cultural sense—so that their version of life experience isn't seen as crazy by those around them. And, they try to make hopeful sense, to find a version of their experience that lets them live into the future without total despair.

As part of making sense, human beings tend to look for narratives or stories, and try to pull these together to form a coherent whole. In the process, they do something that I call 'selfing'. They tend to experience an 'I' at the center of clusters of feelings, motives, beliefs, personal qualities, experiences (and the like) within themselves and they experience clusters of such 'I' experiences as being part of somewhat coherent 'self'. Likewise, they are likely to postulate a 'self' or personality as organizing the actions of others. Yet, if contrary experiences emerge, the person may well experience a dual self or selves that operate in various ways on other selves (Cooper et al., 2004). They can experience themselves as being a self at one moment, and experience themselves as standing outside and watching various self experiences at another moment. For example, a person can sensibly say 'I have to pull myself together because this lazy person that I have been for the last week is just not who I really am.'

These self-experiences operate like many other soft phenomena in the sense that human beings often experience them as if they had as much concrete reality as any hard phenomenon. A person may say 'I am a Fitzgerald through and through. Everything about me is like my family.' Yet, such articulated self-experiences are a carrying forward to the totality of the person's lived experience in ways that are neither totally arbitrary nor totally pre-determined.

Experience could have been carried forward into an experience of self in more than one way, yet not just any self-experience will resonate with the person's lived experience. And, in a literal sense, there is no concrete existence to 'self', only an articulation of lived experience that carries forward more or less fully. And there certainly isn't a single 'real' self that already exists someplace 'under the surface'.

This experience of self is so humanly universal that I suspect that it is integrally related to human processing. Processing meaning allows a person to integrate clusters of experience in ways that carry forward the whole organism. This allows him or her to form a sense of 'I-ness' in relation to feelings, beliefs, life narratives and the like. Yet, however much organismic experience has been articulated, there is always more that could be articulated in addition or in different ways. On the one hand a sense of self offers a coherence that allows the person to organize life projects. On the other hand, articulating an 'I' experience and holding that in attention allows the person to sense what in his or her experience is not carried forward by the articulation of experience that the person has come to thus far.

Different versions of self and of experience may work better in serving the purposes of the individual person, much the way that some last lines of a poem work better. Yet the person always has a range of existential freedom in choosing how to make sense, and even has the existential freedom to go against aspects of human nature. For example, a person may choose to tolerate being seen as crazy by everyone around him.

Rogers (1959), in his 'Theory of Personality' notes a tension between 'self-actualization' and the actualization of the whole organism. On the one hand human beings have a wish for 'congruence'—a way of making sense of life that fits with the totality of organismic experiencing. On the other hand, human beings have a need to maintain some sense of coherence and stability in their sense of self. I would suggest that, while some level of processing is essential for human beings to function as human beings, processing, by its very nature is morphogenic. As a person processes experience, experiential change occurs which can never be fully controlled or predicted. As such, processing is essential to human functioning, yet it exists in tension with a need to maintain the coherence and functional effectiveness of one's more personally and culturally established strategies and ways of viewing life.

And, while a sense of self seems to be a human universal that is essential to processing, particular ways of experiencing or holding onto self are often seen as problematic in human living. For, example, many of the world's religions, in one way or another, suggest that letting go of a rigid or excessively individualist sense of self is essential to spiritual advancement.

PROCESSING AND RELATIONSHIP

Given the inherent role of processing in bridging between individuals and communities, it makes sense that relationships are so central in developing and fostering human abilities to make sense of their lived situations. The relational qualities posited by Rogers—empathy, congruence (or realness) and unconditional positive regard (or prizing) seem likely to be human universals relating to this particularly human way of remaining individual while connecting deeply to the experience of others.

Empathy, in which people use various mental, emotional and intuitive capacities to create within themselves an experience of what it is like to be another person, seems essential to the human ability to take the intentional stance that Dennett (1987) and others see central to the ways that human beings construe situations. Given this, it makes sense that empathy is a crucial aspect of the attachment relationships in which processing capacities are initially developed. And, it makes sense that empathic understanding relationships tend to facilitate processing in adults. Rogers (1959) notes that empathic understanding within a real and prizing relationship tends to lower the sense of fear that an individual feels in the face of incongruent experiences. I suspect that this lowering of fear tends to shift the balance toward the wish to make sense of that which is not yet clear in experiencing (Warner, 1997).

The sort of processing that I have been describing allows human beings to develop congruence—a coherent version of who they are that carries forward their whole body sense of themselves. This sort of congruence allows human beings to operate within relationships in a reliable and comprehensible way. Notably, Mary Main (1991) found that mothers who could present a coherent version of their life histories tended to have infants who were more securely attached. And children who had been securely attached tended to be able to offer a coherent life history in their early teens.

The sort of prizing described by Rogers involves a human valuing of another in a way that is empathic and genuine at the same time. It is also a quality that is notably present in optimal infant attachment relationships. I suspect that a high-level combination of the three qualities, which Dave Mearns (1997) calls 'relational depth', is a universally valued aspect of intimate human relationships.

PROCESSING AND CULTURE

While processing meaning is a human universal, societies vary considerably in the emphasis placed on elaborated individual understanding of life situations. A parallel can be drawn with language. While all known cultures use language, some emphasize talking a great deal and have elaborated literary languages, while others place much more emphasis on silence or action.

I suspect that individual processing has particular importance in modern societies as individuals become less constrained by hierarchical power relationships and as a result have broader scope for personal choice. And, as societies become more diverse, individuals have a greater need to differentiate their understandings of themselves in relation to others who approach life differently.

If it is correct that processing is fundamental to human nature, one would expect processing capacities to be central to human well-being and functioning in all cultures. But, processing might be used quite differently within different cultural traditions. For example, in many cultures, decisions made at the level of the family or group are given greater weight than individual personal inclinations. The best ways to support individuals and groups in their processing may be quite different and may need to be developed within particular contexts.

A PERSON-CENTERED VIEW OF PSYCHOPATHOLOGY

This view of processing as central to human nature, gives us the groundwork to formulate a person-centered view of psychological dysfunction. In day-to-day living, individuals often meet the press of life with actions grounded in familiar understandings using well-established strategies for living that allow the person to proceed without processing the situation freshly. Ordinarily, the ability to process freshly is available, useful and personally satisfying to human beings. But, it becomes crucial whenever pre-established understandings and strategies don't work to meet the implicit needs of the organism. Psychological distress, then, can be expected to result when pre-existing understandings and strategies don't work to meet the needs of the organism and the person (or the group of people) is unable to use processing capacities to generate new more workable alternatives. Person-centered theory suggests that Rogers' 'necessary and sufficient' relationship conditions of empathy, genuineness and prizing offer a support for the processing capacities of individuals (and of dyads and groups) that is deeply grounded in human nature.

One can, then, form a three-sided model that will let us consider various sources of psychological distress.

Press of life
(unresolved by pre-existing
understandings and
strategies)

Processing capacities
–grounded in early childhood
physical and psychological
development of the organism

*Relational support of
processing*
via empathy,
genuineness and
unconditional positive
regard

A continuum of psychological wellness and dysfunction, applying to families and groups as well as individuals, can then be developed as follows:

1. Well-developed processing capacities used effectively (with or without the relational support of psychotherapy) to develop or enhance life possibilities in the absence of distress caused by an overwhelming press of life;
2. Well-developed processing capacities temporarily stressed or overwhelmed by the press of life, benefiting from the relational support for processing capacities offered in psychotherapy;
3. Difficult process, resulting from deficits in the early-childhood caregiving (necessary for the development of processing capacities), deficits in the organic structures and processes that support processing and/or deficits that result from trauma to or degeneration of the organism which occurs later in life. In situations in which individuals (or people in relationships) are suffering from difficult process, psychotherapy offers both relational support of currently functioning processing capacities and it tends to foster the development or reconstitution of impaired processing capacities.

A PERSON-CENTERED MODEL AS IT RELATES TO TRADITIONAL CATEGORIES OF PSYCHOPATHOLOGY

Traditional categories of psychopathology offer descriptions of characteristic states of distress to the person (such as anxiety or depression) or to others (as in conduct disorders) that may be useful to professionals communicating to each other about the superficial characteristics of client difficulties. But, a person-centered view of dysfunction suggests that such states can result from such infinitely varied, personally unique problems in living that the categories themselves don't offer much guidance to the therapy. Yet, person-centered theory suggests that, if a person is able to process the uniqueness of his or her life situation, this is likely to bring experiential changes that ameliorate anxiety and depression, to enable the person to alter beliefs that are not serving him or her well or to alter behaviors that are creating problems.

This person-centered view does not rule out the possibility of biological dysfunction or genetic predisposition to particular sorts of emotional distress. But it would suggest that the human organism is so deeply oriented to processing that human beings will continue attempts at making sense, even when some aspects of ordinary processing capacities are impaired. As with many capacities which are central to human functioning, multiple alternate ways of accomplishing the same ends are available within the organism. When particular ways of processing are impaired, clients who have therapeutic support continue expressive efforts and, ultimately, are likely to develop alternate ways of processing their experience.

This person-centered view of psychopathology doesn't rule out the use of medications, but it does raise serious concerns. Given the side effects of medications and the possibilities of long-term organic damage, the risks and benefits of medication should be weighed carefully. And, it makes sense that more process-oriented approaches should be used whenever possible, whether as a substitute to medication or as an adjunctive treatment. Processing and making sense are so central to human existence that medication should be carefully calibrated to protect and foster the clients' abilities to be aware of moment-to-moment experiencing. And, the ability to form one's own opinions and choices is so central to human nature that support for the client's own ability to make choices about medication and therapy should be a central priority.

IMPLICATIONS FOR MENTAL HEALTH SERVICES

This view of processing as central to human nature offers a particular understanding of what it is to live fully as a human being. To be a human being is to experience oneself as a person able to make sense of one's own situation and to choose one's own right next steps in living. And, it is to live in relationships in which one can understand and be understood, value and be valued. This view has ethical, compassionate and pragmatic implications for mental health services.

Ethically, this would suggest a need to intervene in ways that support the qualities that are fundamental to human nature and to avoid interventions that impede the full functioning of core human qualities. In terms of human compassion, it emphasizes the need to recognize the depth of human affliction that is experienced when one is unable to process and make sense of lived experience in these ways—suffering often experienced as organismic panic, personal emptiness, fragmentation or existential despair.

Such a view of human nature opens a critique of common societal responses to psychological dysfunction. Medical systems often respond to physical illness while ignoring psychological dysfunction. When a person is unable to process experience, the sense of affliction is likely to be as damaging to core well-being and as threatening to prospects of physical survival as almost any physical illness.

Yet, when mental health services are offered, they often seem determined to shape clients' behaviors to be like those that are fully human without considering the human qualities of the client's actual experience. Thus, clients are often taught to behave in culturally appropriate ways whether or not this behavior is grounded in any of their own feelings, wants or intentions. They may be required to participate in social activities whether or not these activities correspond to any sociable feelings. They may be taught to speak in ways that don't sound 'crazy' whether or not this cuts them off from any sort of personally grounded experience. Medication is sometimes prescribed in ways that shut down negative emotions and culturally 'crazy' expressions, without considering the need to foster the person's ability to make sense of her own life and to make choices in the light of those understandings. Pragmatically, this view points to the effectiveness of Rogers' core conditions in fostering and re-constituting abilities to process experience. Therapy grounded in these conditions allows clients suffering from severe forms of disturbance to begin to form a sense of self that is personally authentic and to make personally meaningful sense of their lived experience.

106

CONCLUSION

A person-centered process stays attuned to the client's own rhythm, remaining open to the exactness and existential freedom of the person's own choices. Given the client-directed quality of such therapy, it is less likely to trigger or re-evoke experiences of abusive authority from the client's past than more confrontational or interpretive forms of therapy. Person-centered theory, understood in this way, offers a model of human functioning that is relevant to all of clinical psychology and the social sciences. It generates particular insights into the human qualities that should be central to all humane mental health practice. It strengthens the rationale for Person-Centered Therapy as an effective and compassionate approach to psychotherapy with clients at all levels of psychological dysfunction. It makes a particularly strong case for the humane value of the Person-Centered Approach to work with clients experiencing the difficult process characteristic of the most severe psychological disorders.

REFERENCES

Baron-Cohen, S (1995) *Mindblindness: An essay on autism and theory of mind.* Cambridge, MA: MIT Press.

Binder, U (1998) Empathy and empathy development in psychotic clients. In B Thorne and E Lambers (eds), *Person-Centred Therapy: A European perspective.* London: Sage Publications.

Bohart, AC (1990) A cognitive client-centered perspective on borderline personality development. In G Lietaer, J Rombauts and R Van Balen (eds), *Client-Centered and Experiential Psychotherapy in the Nineties.* Leuven, Belgium: Leuven University Press.

Cain, D and Seeman, J (eds) (2002) *Humanistic Psychotherapies: Handbook of research and practice.* Washington, DC: APA Press.

Coffeng, T (1995) Experiential and pre-experiential therapy for multiple trauma. In R Hutterer, G Pawlowsky, PF Schmid, and R Stipsits (eds) *Client-Centered and Experiential Psychotherapy: A paradigm in motion* (pp. 499–511). Frankfurt am Main: Peter Lang.

Cooper, M, Mearns, D, Stiles, W, Warner, M and Elliott, R (2004) Developing self-pluralistic perspectives within the person-centered and experiential approaches: A roundtable dialogue. *Person-Centered and Experiential Psychotherapies, 3*, 176–91.

Dennett, D (1987) *The Intentional Stance.* Cambridge, Mass: The MIT Press.

Eckert, J and Biermann-Ratjen, E (1998) The treatment of borderline personality disorder. In L Greenberg, J Watson and G Lietaer (eds) *Handbook of Experiential Psychology.* New York: The Guilford Press.

Eckert, J and Wuchner, M (1996) Long-term development of borderline personality disorder. In R Hutterer, G Pawlowsky, PF Schmid, and R Stipsits (eds) *Client-Centered and Experiential Psychotherapy: A paradigm in motion.* Frankfurt am Main: Peter Lang.

Gendlin, ET (1997) How philosophy cannot appeal to experience, and how it can. In DM Levin, (ed) *Language Beyond Postmodernism: Saying and thinking in Gendlin's philosophy.* Evanston, IL: Northwestern University Press.

Gendlin, ET (1995) Crossing and dipping: Some terms for approaching the interface between natural understanding and logical formulation. *Minds and Machines, 5*, 547–60.

Gendlin, ET (1968) The experiential response. In E Hammer (ed) *The Use of Interpretation in Treatment* (pp. 208–27). New York: Grune and Stratton.

Gendlin, ET (1964) A theory of personality change. In P Worchel and D Byrne (eds) *Personality Change* (pp. 100–48). New York: John Wiley and Sons, Inc.

Green, MF (1998) *Schizophrenia from a Neurocognitive Perspective*. Boston: Allyn and Bacon.

Lambers, E (1994) Borderline personality disorder. In D Mearns (ed) *Developing Person-Centered Counseling* (pp. 110–12). London: Sage Publications.

Leijssen, M (1993) Creating a workable distance to overwhelming images: Comments on a session transcript. In D Brazier (ed) *Beyond Carl Rogers*. London: Constable.

Leijssen, M (1996) Characteristics of a healing inner relationship. In R Hutterer, G Pawlowsky, PF Schmid and R Stipsits (eds) *Client-Centered and Experiential Psychotherapy: A paradigm in motion*. Frankfurt am Main: Lang.

Main, M (1991) Metacognitive knowledge, metacognitive monitoring, and singular (coherent) use multiple model of attachment. In CM Parkes, JS Hinde and D Marris (eds) *Attachment Across the Life Cycle*, (pp. 127–59). London: Tavistock/Routledge.

Mearns, D (1997) *Person-Centred Counselling Training*. London: Sage.

Prouty, G (1977) Protosymbolic method: A phenomenological treatment of schizophrenic hallucinations. *Journal of Mental Imagery, 1,* 2 (Fall).

Prouty, G (1983) Hallucinatory contact: A phenomenological treatment of schizophrenics. *Journal of Communication Therapy, 2,* 1.

Prouty, G (1986) The pre-symbolic structure and therapeutic transformation of hallucinations. In M Wolpin, J Schorr and L Krueger (eds) *Imagery, Vol 4*. New York: Plenum Press.

Prouty, G (1990) Pre-therapy: A theoretical evolution in the person-centered/experiential psychotherapy of schizophrenia and retardation. In G Lietaer, J Rombauts and R Van Balen (eds) *Client-Centered and Experiential Psychotherapy in the Nineties* (pp. 645–58). Leuven, Belgium: Leuven University Press.

Prouty, G (1994) *Theoretical Evolutions in Person-Centered/Experiential Therapy*. Westport, CT: Praeger.

Prouty, G, Van Werde, D and Pörtner, M (2002) *Pre-Therapy: Reaching contact-impaired clients*. Ross-on Wye: PCCS Books.

Raskin, NJ (1996) Client-centered therapy with very disturbed clients. In R Hutterer, G Pawlowsky, PF Schmid, and R Stipsits (eds) *Client-Centered and Experiential Psychotherapy: A paradigm in motion*. Frankfurt am Main: Peter Lang.

Roelens, L (1996) Accommodating psychotherapy to information-processing constraints: A person-centered psychiatric case description. In R Hutterer, G Pawlowsky, PF Schmid and R Stipsits (eds) *Client-Centered and Experiential Psychotherapy: A paradigm in motion* (pp. 533–43). Frankfurt am Main: Peter Lang.

Rogers, CR (1957) The necessary and sufficient conditions of personality change. *Journal of Consulting Psychology, 21,* 2.

Rogers, CR (1959) A theory of therapy, personality and interpersonal relationships, as developed in the client-centered framework. In S Koch (ed) *Psychology: A Study of Science, Vol 3. Formulations of the person and the social context*. New York: McGraw-Hill.

Rogers, CR (1961) *On Becoming a Person: A therapist's view of psychotherapy*. New York: Houghton Mifflin.

Rogers, CR (ed) (1967) *The Therapeutic Relationship and its Impact: A study of psychotherapy with schizophrenics*. Madison, WI: University of Wisconsin Press.

Roy, B (1991) A client-centered approach to multiple personality and dissociative process. In L Fusek (ed) *New Directions in Client-Centered Therapy: Practice with difficult client populations* (Monograph Series 1). Chicago: Chicago Counseling and Psychotherapy Center.

Santen, B (1990) Beyond good and evil: Focusing with early traumatized children and adolescents. In G Lietaer, J Rombauts and R Van Balen (eds) *Client-Centered and Experiential Psychotherapy in the Nineties* (pp. 779–96). Leuven, Belgium: Leuven University Press.

Stern, DN (1985) *The Interpersonal World of the Infant.* New York: Basic Books.

Swildens, JCAG (1990) Client-centered psychotherapy for patients with borderline symptoms. In G Lietaer, J Rombauts and R Van Balen (eds) *Client-Centered and Experiential Psychotherapy in the Nineties* (pp. 623–35). Leuven, Belgium: Leuven University Press.

Tooby, J and Cosmides, L (1992) The psychological foundations of culture. In J Barkow, L Cosmides and J Tooby, (eds) *The Adapted Mind: Evolutionary psychology and the generation of culture,* (pp. 19–136). New York: Oxford University Press.

Van Werde, D (1990) Psychotherapy with a retarded schizo-affective woman: An application of Prouty's pre-therapy. In A Dosen, A Van Gennep, and G Zwanikken (eds) *Treatment of Mental Illness and Behavioral Disorder in the Mentally Retarded: Proceedings of international congress, May 3rd and 4th, Amsterdam, The Netherlands.* Leiden, The Netherlands: Logon Publications.

Van Werde, D (1998) Anchorage as a core concept in working with psychotic people. In B Thorne and E Lambers (eds) *Person-Centred Therapy: A European perspective.* London: Sage Publications.

Warner, MS (1983) Soft meaning and sincerity in the family system, *Family Process, 22.*

Warner, MS (1991) Fragile process. In L Fusek (ed) *New Directions in Client-Centered Therapy: Practice with difficult client populations* (Monograph Series 1). Chicago: Chicago Counseling and Psychotherapy Center.

Warner, MS (1997) Does empathy cure? A theoretical consideration of empathy, processing and personal narrative. In AC Bohart and LS Greenberg (eds) *Empathy Reconsidered.* Washington, DC: American Psychological Association.

Warner, MS (1998) A Client-Centered Approach to therapeutic work with dissociated and fragile process. In L Greenberg, J Watson and G Lietaer (eds) *Handbook of Experiential Psychotherapy.* New York: The Guilford Press.

Warner, MS (2000) Client-Centered Therapy at the difficult edge: Work with fragile and dissociated process. In D Mearns and B Thorne (eds) *Person-Centered Therapy Today: New frontiers in theory and practice.* Thousand Oaks: Sage.

Warner, MS (2001) Empathy, relational depth and difficult client process. In S Haugh and T Merry (eds) *Rogers' Therapeutic Conditions: Evolution, theory and practice. Vol 2: Empathy.* Ross-on-Wye: PCCS Books.

Warner, MS (2002a) Psychological contact, meaningful process, and human nature: A reformulation of person-centered theory. In G Wyatt and P Sanders (eds) *Rogers' Therapeutic Conditions: Evolution, theory and practice. Vol 3: Contact and perception.* Ross-on-Wye: PCCS Books.

Warner, MS (2002b) Luke's dilemmas: A client-centered/experiential model of processing with a schizophrenic thought disorder. In J Watson, R Goldman and MS Warner (eds) *Client-Centered and Experiential Psychotherapy in the 21st Century: Advances in theory, research and practice.* Ross-on-Wye: PCCS Books.

CHAPTER 8

THE COMPLEMENTARITY BETWEEN CLIENT-CENTRED THERAPY AND PSYCHIATRY: THE THEORY AND THE PRACTICE

LISBETH SOMMERBECK

THE CRUCIAL DIFFERENCES BETWEEN CLIENT-CENTRED THERAPY AND PSYCHIATRY

The hermeneutic/phenomenological model of client-centred therapy stresses the therapist's empathic understanding of the client's world, and the therapist's unconditional positive regard for the client, as the primary therapeutic variables. This means that the client is treated as a unique individual whom the therapist wishes to get to know and understand. Since it is the uniqueness of the client that is in the foreground in this model, it also means that the therapist can in no way be an expert on what is best for the client, i.e. on what is the best conception of reality for the client, or on what is wrong with the client, on what are the best options for the client, or on what are the best courses of action for the client. (Throughout the chapter, this is what I mean by the phrase 'what is best for'.)

It is the other way round in the medical model of psychiatry. In this model the client is treated as a representative for a group of people who have been allocated a certain psychiatric diagnosis. It is from the psychiatrist's knowledge, according to research and other professional experience, of what is best for most people belonging to this diagnostic group, that the psychiatrist is an expert on what is best for an assumed representative of this group of people; i.e. the psychiatrist is an expert on what is best for the client, because it is the client as a representative for a group of people with the same psychiatric diagnosis that is in the foreground in this model. In this model the client is thus treated as a more or less close approximation to the average of a certain group of people.

Therefore, at a first glance, the hermeneutic/phenomenological model of Client-Centred Therapy and the medical model of psychiatry seem mutually contradictory and in conflict with each other. This makes itself particularly strongly felt in the following two areas:

1. The client-centred therapist strives to understand from the client's frame of reference, whereas the psychiatrist strives to explain from his/her own (theoretical) frame of reference and treats the client from this point of view. Psychiatry has many explanations—more or less well documented by research—for the diverse conditions

110

of patients: hereditary, bio-chemical, early environmental, etc. These factors are seen as causal aetiological factors that contribute, alone or in combination, to what is normally considered as discrete, specific disease entities. The client-centred therapist, on the other hand, is in no way concerned with explaining the condition and symptoms of the client. He or she is solely concerned with trying to understand the client from the client's frame of reference and checking the accuracy of this understanding with the client, thereby communicating his or her unconditional positive regard for the client as a unique individual. This is, according to client-centred theory, helpful to clients whether there exists a more or less well documented explanation for their ailment or not. Understanding people and explaining people are two very different things. It corresponds to the German philosopher Dilthey's (1894) distinction between the natural sciences as sciences that explain, and the humanities as sciences that understand.

2.   The question of whether a client is psychotic or not (one of the most crucial differential diagnostic questions in psychiatry) is made from the point of view of 'consensual reality', i.e. that which the majority in a given culture regards as reality. From the point of view of consensual reality, delusions and hallucinations (often prominent symptoms in psychosis) are not accurate perceptions of reality, but from the point of view of the delusional or hallucinating client they are real, and therefore they are real, too, for the client-centred therapist when he or she is trying to receive and accompany the client with acceptant empathic understanding. The client-centred therapist has to suspend his own sense of reality when in therapy sessions with these clients. Fundamentally, this is in no way different from work with clients who are not diagnosed as being psychotic, because the therapist will always strive to understand the client from the client's frame of reference no matter how unfamiliar the client's world may be to the therapist. However, the phenomenological field or psychological landscape of clients diagnosed with psychosis is often private and different from that of the therapist, and from that of 'consensual reality', to a more radical and extreme degree than is the case with most other clients. In the psychiatric setting, therefore, the client-centred therapist feels more acutely that he or she shuffles back and forth between the client's sense of reality, when in session, and the therapist's own sense of reality, which he or she probably shares to quite a large extent with most of his or her medical-model colleagues (consensual reality), when the session is finished. In session, for example, the client-centred therapist tries to empathically understand a client's experience of the threatening black-coated man in the corner of the office in just the same way that the therapist tries to empathically understand a client's experience of, say, the client's mother. When the session is finished, though, the therapist probably regards the black-coated man as an hallucination on a par with his or her medical-model colleagues and the therapist can likewise regard the client's perception of his or her mother as more or less realistic. However, the classical client-centred therapist's points of view and opinions, together with 'consensual reality', are utterly irrelevant in his or her therapeutic practice.

It is necessary for the client-centred therapist in the medical-model setting of a psychiatric hospital to find a way to encompass and reconcile within him/herself these seemingly conflicting viewpoints of (1) understanding as opposed to explaining and (2) psychotic reality as opposed to consensual reality. When the therapist cannot do this, he or she will tend to see the theories of Client-Centred Therapy and the medical model as being in conflict with each other or, in the extreme, as two camps at war with each other. With such a point of view, the therapist will most likely find him/herself in the midst of a fruitless 'who is right' discussion about the treatment of a given client with his or her medical-model colleagues, a discussion that will, more likely than not, end with the 'burn out' of the client-centred therapist and his or her retreat from the field of psychiatry where the medical model is, currently at least, the dominating model. Even worse, engaging in discussion with representatives of the medical model about what is best for one of the therapist's clients converts the therapist into just another expert on the client. Being an authority on what is best for one's clients in discussions with medical-model colleagues, and a non-authority on one's clients in therapy sessions is, at best, self-contradictory and, at worst, hypocritical.

THE THEORY OF COMPLEMENTARITY

To avoid this self-contradiction I have found the concept of complementarity exceedingly helpful in my work as a client-centred therapist in a psychiatric hospital and I will therefore explain it rather extensively as follows.

COMPLEMENTARITY IN PHYSICS

In physics, the concept or principle of complementarity is the standard way of thinking about some strange phenomena in very small-scale elementary particle physics. I will illustrate this, using the electron as an example. An electron cannot be studied directly; physicists use different kinds of experimental set-ups to study the nature of the electron. When they do that, the following strange phenomenon materialises: in one kind of experimental set-up the electron is seen to behave as a particle and in another kind of experimental set-up the electron is seen to behave as a wave. Logically, particle and wave are mutually exclusive categories, something cannot be both a particle and a wave, since the first is discrete (particles have precise location and delineation), and the second is continuous (waves do not have precise location and delineation). When physicists discovered this state of affairs in the 1920s and 1930s they were not happy about it. They therefore tried to find a 'hidden variable', (something in the electron yet to be discovered) that might sometimes appear as a particle and sometimes as a wave. As they were absolutely unsuccessful in this—the electron really *is* an elementary particle, it cannot be subdivided, no hidden variable exists—the Danish physicist Niels Bohr introduced the concept of complementarity to make some 'sense' of this particle/wave duality, as it is commonly called.

Bohr took the position that in choosing his experimental set-up the physicist chooses whether the electron shall be a particle or a wave. Alternatively, depending on the way he chooses to look at the electron, the physicist will decide upon the nature of the electron—wave or particle? However, he cannot, of course, see both at the same time. Bohr said that it is meaningless to ask what the electron 'really' is, out there, when nobody is looking at it: you have to look at it to know and then the nature of it depends on how you look at it, i.e. on your own viewpoint or frame of reference. When not being observed, the electron is said to be in a state of superposition of particle and wave.

COMPLEMENTARITY IN PSYCHIATRY

The earlier mentioned dualities, (understanding/explaining, private reality/consensual reality), can very helpfully be conceptualised as complementary viewpoints in analogy with the wave/particle duality: what one sees from one point of view cannot be seen from the other and vice versa, and what one chooses to see depends on one's purpose. In therapy sessions, the viewpoint of the client-centred therapist is, of course, that of understanding and private reality. In discussions with colleagues, it may be that of explanation and consensual reality. Person-centred personality theory, for example, explains psychological disturbance as the result of excessive exposure to conditional regard. The client-centred therapist, though, does not allow this explanation to get in the way of the client who explains his or her disturbance as genetically determined. Instead, the therapist empathises with the client's explanation of his or her disturbances. The client's personality theory is the therapist's personality theory for the duration of the session. On the general level, though, and when concerned with psychological disturbances, at large, (i.e. when taking the other perspective in the complementary duality) the person-centred therapist may very well disagree with the client.

In addition, the two viewpoints or dualities mentioned above could be said to be in a state of superposition when the therapist does not choose one or the other, i.e. when he or she is neither trying to understand the private reality of a given client in therapy nor concerned with potential explanations of the client's condition in, say, talks with medical-model colleagues.

One could also say that the client-centred therapist sees the uniqueness of the client whereas the psychiatrist sees the averageness, with respect to a certain diagnostic group, of the client. From the client-centred therapist's point of view it is the unique client that exists, not the average client. From the psychiatrist's point of view it is the average client that exists, not the unique client. The psychiatrist, for example, sees a more or less close approximation to his or her idea of 'the average schizophrenic' or 'the average depressive' and treats his/her patient accordingly. The psychiatrist's glasses are coloured (and they are supposed to be coloured) by the psychiatrist's knowledge of what is assumed to be typical for people diagnosed with one of the many different diagnoses of psychiatry. The client is a more or less close approximation to an average. The glasses of the client-centred therapist, in contrast, are not coloured (and they are supposed not to be coloured) by any previous knowledge of what may or may not be typical for this or that group of people. To the client-centred therapist the client is unique, the client is unlike any person seen before, the client is a person to be known, not a person already more or less known, and the client-centred therapist treats the client according to this view that is, fundamentally, diametrically opposite to the view of the psychiatrist. This is the complementarity divide between two mutually exclusive approaches and points of views that cannot be integrated, but can be, each in its own way, useful in their respective contexts. (This is not synonymous with being uncritical of the dominance of the medical-model view in psychiatry.)

The detailed meaning of the term 'complementarity', in this case, is, in analogy with the wave/particle duality from quantum physics, that (1) it is false to say that the client is both unique and average (because unique/average are logically self-contradictory terms), (2) it is false to say that the client is neither unique nor average (because one can choose a viewpoint where the client is unique, and one can choose a viewpoint where the client is average), (3) it is false to say, only, that the client is unique (because from another point of view the client is average), and (4) it is false to say, only, that the client is average (because from another point of view the client is unique). Thereby the logical possibilities for combinations with respect to the unique/average duality are exhausted and this is what characterises what one sees from viewpoints that stand in a complementary relationship to each other. Finally, as noted above, it belongs to the concept of complementarity that it is meaningless to ask what the client 'really' is, when he/she is not attended to, and that it is the person who attends to the client who decides whether the client shall be unique or average.

Other dual terms, like 'private reality' and 'public (consensual) reality' or 'the inside perspective' and 'the outside perspective' might replace 'unique' and 'average' and application of the principle of complementarity is not confined to the relationship between Client-Centred Therapy and the medical model of psychiatry.

THE PRACTICE OF COMPLEMENTARITY

Over the years, in the hospital where I work, I have explained the principle of complementarity and its foundation in physics, and it has been my experience that it has been very helpful in contributing to mutual respect between the practitioner of Client-Centred Therapy and the practitioner of the medical/psychiatric model. Being able to employ the principle of complementarity to understand their seemingly antithetical viewpoints with respect to individual clients is felt as a relief to the majority of professionals working in this setting, because the nagging question of who is right, whose viewpoint is the most truthful or real, is resolved in a meaningful way.

It must be remembered, however, that applying the principle of complementarity, in the way I have described above is exclusively a result of seeing an analogy between some phenomena of the world of quantum mechanics and some phenomena of the world of psychiatry. I postulate no true identity between these two classes of phenomena. Future research may point to ways of thinking about the many puzzling and seemingly antithetical phenomena of the client-centred model and the medical model that are more fruitful than thinking about them in terms of complementarity.

THERAPIST DUALITY

In accordance with the principle of complementarity, there is a duality to the client-centred therapist's practice in psychiatry; the therapist lives a sort of 'double life' when working in this medical-model context. From the moment a therapy client crosses the doorstep to his or her consultation room, the therapist sees the world from within the frame of reference of the client. When the therapy session is over, the therapist is back in a world where the dominating frame of reference is that of the medical model, and where the therapist may agree that the black-coated man that the client saw in the corner was an hallucination. Because of the seemingly antithetical elements of Client-Centred Therapy and the medical model, these two worlds cannot be integrated into one. The therapist has no other option than to go back and forth between these two very different worlds in the same way the physicist shuffles back and forth, as he or she chooses, between seeing the electron as a particle and seeing it as a wave, since there is no possibility of seeing them as both at the same time. There are, however, several situations, also between sessions, where the therapist must protect the position that he or she cannot be an expert on what is best for the client, because it is the uniqueness, not the averageness, of the client that exists for the therapist. This is not always easy, and in the following paragraphs, I'll describe some of the difficulties and some of the ways to overcome these difficulties, which have been fruitful in my own experience of 30 years' work in a psychiatric hospital. The main point is to simultaneously protect the Client-Centred Therapy process and respect other professionals' treatment of the client from the medical-model perspective. To do this it is first and foremost essential to avoid identifying with either the client or the medical-model setting of psychiatry, i.e. to avoid becoming an advocate, spokesperson, saviour or message deliverer of the client in relation to the medical-model setting and to avoid becoming an advocate, spokesperson, saviour or message deliverer of the medical-model setting in relation to the client. This has several practical consequences as follows.

PROTECTING THE THERAPY PROCESS

1. The therapist has to refuse to accommodate certain requests from the medical-model staff, which seem perfectly natural to them. The therapist says 'no' when he or she, for example, is asked to evaluate the client's condition in the next session with the client. Staff members may want this evaluation to assist them in making all sorts of decisions, and it is second nature for them, and part of their job, to make (diagnostic) evaluations when relating with clients; it is expected of them and they expect it of others. This is, of course, because they, from their medical-model perspective, attend to the averageness of the client. It can be difficult for non-informed staff members to understand and respect that the client-centred therapist,

who attends to the uniqueness of the client, can have no plans or intentions of any kind when he meets the client.

The therapist can also be asked to talk certain things over with the client or deliver a message, and, again, the client-centred therapist refuses to accommodate these requests in order not to have any agenda for the session with the client other than trying to empathically understand this unique client from this client's own frame of reference. Jerold Bozarth (1990: 63) puts it well when he writes that 'The therapist goes with the client—goes at the client's pace—goes with the client in his/her own ways of thinking, of experiencing, of processing. The therapist cannot be up to other things, have other intentions without violating the essence of client-centred therapy. To be up to other things—whatever they might be—is a "yes but" reaction to the essence of the approach.'

2. The therapist refuses to participate in meetings or conferences about one of his or her therapy clients if the therapist thinks this participation could have negative consequences for the therapeutic process with the client. The full psychiatric treatment of the hospitalised patient involves all sorts of meetings: ward meetings for all staff and patients in the ward, meetings with relatives of the patient (with or without the participation of the patient), meetings with staff from other institutors to coordinate treatment plans (again with or without the participation of the patient), etc. This is a delicate point and sometimes difficult for the therapist to decide on: will participation place the therapist in the role of an expert on what is best for the client, in the eyes of the client, or in the eyes of others and perhaps even in the eyes of the therapist him/herself, to the detriment of the therapy process? The rule of thumb is to refuse to participate if it is likely that participation will result in the therapist being regarded as an expert on the client.

    Normally I only meet with relatives and 'external' staff if they want my participation as a facilitator for themselves with their own process with the client. I refuse to meet with them if I am expected to tell them, as an expert, what is wrong with the client, and what the best way to 'put him/her right' is. If this is their expectation, I refer them to my client's psychiatrist. This is no different from my practice of consultation/supervision/facilitation with 'internal' staff members with respect to their own processes with patients, whether these are therapy clients of mine or not. The significant point, guiding the therapist's decisions on this issue, is that he or she shall not take on the role of expert, in any context whatsoever, on what is best for the client. At the same time, though, the therapist respects that medical-model representatives, from their perspective, naturally engage in processes with the therapist's clients where they behave as experts on what is best for the client.

3. The therapist must be careful with sharing information and opinions about his or her therapy clients in the regular staff meetings and conferences, which the therapist normally participates in as part of working in a psychiatric setting, particularly in a psychiatric hospital. The main point is not to say anything that others may

inadvertently and unbeknownst to themselves use—with the best of intentions—in their relationship with the client in ways that may harm the therapy process. It is useful to imagine what would happen if a staff member said to the client: 'I know from your therapist that …' I shudder at the thought of having the psychiatrist of a client of mine say to the client: 'Lisbeth said, at the ward staff meeting, that it would be better for you if we reduce and eventually stop your medication. She doesn't think you suffer from an illness but from excessive exposure to conditional regard so it will be an increasing understanding of this, in your psychotherapy, rather than medicine, that will help you' (or something to that effect). It is also useful to have as a rule of thumb that, when in doubt, it is better to say too little than too much. This is a delicate point, too; decisions on what to relate and what to keep back are not always easy to make as they depend on a multitude of factors specific to the given situation and the given moment. Most important among these, I think, is the relationship between the therapist and other staff: do they know and appreciate each other? Do they know, trust, and respect the professional characteristics of each other's work? To the degree that this is the case, to the same degree can the therapist, according to my experience, accommodate other staff members' requests for information from the therapy.

On the other hand, it is also the case that, in reality, very little information needs to be passed between the client-centred therapist and the representatives of the medical model for both parties to do their job. This is a consequence of the complementarity of their respective perspectives. The therapist has no use for knowledge from other frames of references than the client's own frame of reference, and he cannot offer representatives of the medical model the kind of information they need to help them make medical-model treatment decisions for and with the client. Therefore, at bottom, the sharing of information between the therapist and other staff members, which is needed for truly good reasons, is minimal.

4. The therapist does not try to control the way other staff members treat his or her therapy clients. The therapist offers the professionals in the medical model the same respect which he or she expects from them. The therapist is aware that the client is in hospital because psychotherapy alone—or, for that matter, psychopharmacological medication, or any other single treatment modality (physiotherapy, occupational rehabilitation, etc.), alone—has been deemed insufficient to help the client optimally. However, the therapist, being dedicated to the philosophy of client-centred theory, will probably often feel that the professionals of the medical model treat one of his or her clients with too little respect and understanding and the therapist can feel tempted to try to protect the client by trying to change the ways of other staff members with the client. Trying to do this is a mistake: first, it amounts to identification with the client; the client must, after all, find his or her own way of dealing with his or her world and protect him/herself in it, including the world of the medical model. (Would the therapist contact the client's mother, for example, to try to influence her to treat the client with more

respect and understanding?) Second, what seems disrespectful or insensitive to the therapist may not seem so to the client. Third, trying to change or control the ways of others is certainly not in line with the person-centred tradition. Fourth, acting on behalf of the client is, of course, synonymous with acting as an expert on what is best for the client, quite contrary to the essence of Client-Centred Therapy. Protecting the client and protecting the therapy process are two very different, often even mutually exclusive, endeavours.

The following example is meant to illustrate some of the points made in the preceding paragraphs. In order to protect client confidentiality and anonymity, I have made changes in the factual content of the original case material. I believe the example, as it stands, is beyond personal recognition. On the other hand, there is nothing unrealistic about it. The reality might just as well have been the reality of the example and the process, as such, is true to reality.

> *Marion is 30 years old, married, with a 5-year-old son. She has been admitted to hospital on her own initiative because of frequent psychotic episodes where she hears voices ordering her to stab, variously, her husband, her son, and herself to death. She is treated with medicine, which she feels helps her, and she has started in psychotherapy. She has also started going home for the weekends, but this occasions an upsurge of symptoms.*
>
> *In the therapy, she hesitatingly begins to express very negative feelings towards her husband. This is a change from the first sessions, where she mostly talked about her voices and her fear of giving in to them.*
>
> *In the ward, too, staff members have an impression of problems at home, because of the decline in her condition after weekends, because her husband never visits her, and because she tries to foreshorten her weekend-passes, telling her primary nurse that she is a burden on her husband when she is at home. He must take care to keep knives locked away from her, he must do all the cooking and other work in the kitchen, because it involves the use of knives, and he must not leave her alone.*
>
> *Her condition and treatment are discussed in the regular weekly staff meeting, and the following dialogue evolves between the chief psychiatrist of the ward (CP) and the therapist (T):*
>
> *CP: I really think we can't get further in the treatment of Marion without some sort of couples' therapy. As it is now, I can't imagine her out of hospital in the foreseeable future, and we have many patients on the waiting list. (Turning to T): What about you having some couple sessions with Marion and her husband?*
>
> *T: I'll gladly do that, if Marion wants me to.*
>
> *CP: OK, then you talk with her about that and we can see how it progresses.*
>
> *T: Oh, no, wait a minute. I'll not introduce this idea or any other to her, you know I only*

work with issues that she brings up, herself.

CP (smiling): Sorry, I forgot for a minute that you have this peculiarity. Then I'll propose it to her and suggest that she brings it up with you, if that is OK with you?

T: Sure, that's fine with me.

Two days later Marion (M) comes for her ordinary session and immediately brings up the subject of couple sessions.

M: CP said to me that it would be a good idea if I brought Douglas along to some talks with you.

T: Uhm, hmm ... (a short silence)

M: But I don't know ...

T: You are not sure it would be such a good idea?

M: No, ... I know I've told you that there are some things about Douglas that make me furious sometimes, but he also helps me a lot, and ... I don't know, ... I don't feel like sitting here telling him about these things, I am sure it would make him feel bad, and I'd understand that, I'd feel bad if he gave me a scolding in front of a stranger, too.

T: You feel sort of disloyal at the thought of bringing him here for a scolding, he doesn't deserve that because you also appreciate his helping you so much?

M: Yes, disloyal, and I'd also feel ashamed, as a coward, I should talk all these things over with him when we are by ourselves, it's just so difficult because he doesn't like to talk about that kind of thing.

Marion continues to discuss various aspects of her problems with her husband and decides that she will not bring her husband with her to a session. She prefers to try to find a way to have a talk with her husband at home about the way she experiences their relationship. Then she turns to the therapist:

M: Will you tell CP that I won't bring Douglas in, explain it to him?

T: For some reason you'd rather have me do it than do it yourself?

M: Yes, I'm afraid he'll be annoyed with me, because I won't bring Douglas in, but I'm sure he'd respect it if you told him.

T: Takes courage to say no to CP?

M: It sure does—I'm afraid he'll dismiss me from hospital soon, if I don't accept his proposal, so will you tell him?

T: You think that if I tell him, he won't dismiss you so soon?

M: Yes ... Oh, why should that make a difference ... It's just that sometimes it is a little difficult to talk with CP, he always seems to be in a hurry, a little impatient, and that makes me nervous. So I'd appreciate it, if you would talk with him?

T: You tend to feel nervous with CP, because you feel pressured when he seems to be in a hurry, and you'd prefer to avoid that by having me talk with him?

M: Yes, but ... Well, I ought to do it myself; I'll talk with him myself.

T: You feel an obligation to do it yourself?

M (Laughing): Yes, and I'm also a little annoyed with you, because I think you won't do it, but then I also just thought that this is the kind of situation I always try to avoid, saying no to others, and particularly to authorities, and it doesn't do me any good in the long run.

Marion spends the rest of the session coming to terms with her annoyance with me and preparing how best to tell CP about her decision not to have couples' sessions. She is transferred to day-patient status two weeks later and after a month or so as a day-patient she is dismissed from hospital altogether. She continues with the psychotherapy as an outpatient, and for a while, she also continues to see CP, concerning questions of medicine, until this aspect of her treatment is transferred to her GP. Her psychotic symptoms have almost disappeared, she has managed to engage her husband in talks about their relationship, and generally, things are going much better at home. Currently the most frequent theme in her therapy sessions is her fear of being alone.

Comments on the example

The dialogue from the staff conference is typical of the therapist's work to avoid getting into situations where he or she will be the expert on what is best for the client. The therapist avoids becoming an advocate, spokesperson, saviour or message deliverer of the medical model to his/her client. Such situations occur in countless variations and disguises.

When the chief psychiatrist mentions the possibility of couples' sessions during the staff conference, the therapist has a hunch, from sessions with the client, that the client will not like this idea. The therapist, though, sees no point in speaking about this hunch, because the therapist also wants to avoid acting as an advocate, spokesperson, saviour or message deliverer of the client vis à vis the professionals of the medical model. The therapist does not try to influence the psychiatrist, respecting that the psychiatrist will make the most constructive choice possible for him from his frame of reference, which, among other things, also includes balancing the needs, as experienced, of hospitalised patients with the needs of patients on the waiting list.

Hopefully, the example illustrates the 'double life' of the therapist in a medical-model setting like that of a psychiatric hospital, or the duality of the therapist's responsiveness in that setting, according to the principle of complementarity. Further, the client's process in the therapy hopefully illustrates how harmful it would have been to the therapy process if the therapist had either suggested couples' sessions to the client (on behalf of the medical model) or suggested to the psychiatrist that couples' sessions might not be beneficial (on behalf of the client).

The essence of the issues that have been discussed concerning the duality of the client-centred therapist's work in a medical-model setting, according to the principle of complementarity, can be summed up as follows:

- The therapy must progress in parallel, not integrated, with the medical-model treatments; those two worlds must be kept separate, not mixed together.
- In his/her relations with the client, the therapist must take care not to identify with, or become the advocate, spokesperson, saviour, or message deliverer of the medical model.
- In his/her relations with staff members, the therapist must take care not to identify with, or become the advocate, spokesperson, saviour, or message deliverer of the client.
- The therapist listens to the client's experiences of the medical-model representatives of psychiatry as acceptantly and respectfully as he or she listens to any other of the client's experiences.
- The therapist listens to the medical-model representatives' experiences of his/her clients as acceptantly and respectfully as he or she listens to any other of the staff members' experiences.

Dave Mearns (1994: 53–6) has stressed the importance of the therapist being 'beside' the client, not 'on the side of' the client. This is, to me, a very important point to stress, and when working in a psychiatric context it is equally important to be 'beside' the other professionals of that setting, but not 'on the side of' them. The concept of complementarity is helpful in this respect.

All this is much easier said than done. The therapist can sometimes feel quite split when he or she passes back and forth between the world of therapy sessions and the world of the medical model: there is so little of his/her experiences in one world that he or she can use or share in the other. The therapist can sometimes feel disloyal to clients, when he or she participates in 'medical-model talk' about a client with other staff members and does nothing to make them understand the client from the client's frame of reference. Likewise, the therapist can feel disloyal to his or her colleagues when listening with acceptant empathic understanding to a client's (negative) experiences of them in therapy sessions and does nothing to correct the client's impression in accordance with the therapist's own experiences of his or her colleagues. The concept of complementarity is useful to help the therapist to feel comfortable with this seeming 'split': both worlds can be considered true, but when in one you cannot see the other and vice versa.

PERSON-CENTRED CONTRIBUTIONS TO MEDICAL-MODEL STAFF IN PSYCHIATRY

As already stated, a consequence of conceptualising the hermeneutic/phenomenological model of Client-Centred Therapy and the medical model of psychiatry as standing in a complementary relation to each other is that the psychotherapy must proceed in parallel, not integrated, with the other medical-model treatments. This means that it can very legitimately be asked: what does the client-centred therapist actually have to say to medical-model representatives that might be important for both parties to do their job? In my experience the answer is: next to nothing. (See also point 4 above.) In spite of this I'd like to extend this chapter with a description of two ways in which the person-centred practitioner can contribute fruitfully to the work of the medical-model representatives in a psychiatric hospital and therefore, indirectly, to the patients, without transgressing the frame of the concept of complementarity, i.e. without running the risk of placing him/herself in the role of an expert on what is best for the individual client/patient.

First, the client-centred therapist can contribute fruitfully to the regular ward staff conferences by relating to the other participants of these conferences in a predominantly person-centred way. All sorts of decisions about treatment plans for patients are made in these conferences and therefore they are crucial for patients and staff alike.

As already mentioned, I have worked for 30 years in a psychiatric hospital, many of these without participating in ward staff meetings, and this was inconsequential as far as my therapeutic work was concerned. It was not inconsequential, however, for my personal feeling of well-being in my work. I came to feel more and more isolated and estranged from most of my colleagues: I might as well have had my consultation room far away from the hospital, as an occasional telephone contact was sufficient to exchange the necessary information between the staff members on the client's ward and myself. Therefore, for my own sake, I started to participate in the ward staff meetings of the two wards for which I did most of my work, with the intention of finding out whether I might have a contribution to make in this setting. It became apparent that this was the case, and in the following section I'll describe the contribution I, as a client-centred therapist, or more correctly in this context, a person-centred practitioner, could make to the ward staff meeting.

As a member of the staff meeting group, with no agenda of my own, I found that I could be helpful by facilitating the spontaneous tendencies towards a person-centred approach that already existed in the group, especially among the nurses. Although a holistic view of the patients in their uniqueness is a commonly accepted value of nursing, and although most nurses have an intuitive feeling that listening to their patients is part of good nursing, many feel that they are 'doing nothing' when they are 'just listening'. In addition, nurses often do not fully realise how important their relationship with their patients is: that their ability to create a good relationship with their patients is of primary therapeutic importance and not secondary to, for example, psychopharmacological treatment and psychotherapy or, even worse, irrelevant to the outcome of treatment. Nurses often welcome the great value which the client-centred therapist attaches to empathic listening and understanding and to the quality of the relationship with the patient, and can feel supported and strengthened by the therapist's interest in this aspect of their work. More specifically, I could be facilitative of the person-centred tendencies of the ward staff meeting group by my interest in translating a categorising and diagnosing language into a language of concrete and individualised characteristics of relationships. This could be the case, for example, if mention was made of a patient's narcissism. What does this mean in terms of nurses' daily relationships with the patient in the ward? Further, what does it mean that the client is 'unmotivated' or 'withdrawn' or 'psychotic', etc? Such questions underline the importance of the quality of staff members' relationships with patients and support staff members' tendency to deal with and talk about patients as unique human beings alongside their obligation to deal with and talk about them as representatives of a diagnostic group.

I could also be facilitative of the person-centred tendencies of the ward staff meeting group by my interest in the patients' points of view, i.e. by using appropriate occasions to ask: 'What does the patient him/herself want?' Does anybody know what the patient will feel and think about this? These thoughts that you have about the patient's problems: are they yours or are they the patient's?' Treatment plans with quite far reaching consequences for patients are sometimes discussed in staff meetings, and most nurses welcome the above kinds of question because they create a space for them to speak with the patient's voice, which they are most often very familiar with from their day-long contacts with patients in the ward. Nurses are most often the persons who know best what treatment plans are acceptable to patients, whether these plans are about changes in the psychopharmacological treatment of patients, changes in their social network, changes in their daily activities, or whatever. In addition, it is most often nurses who will discuss the treatment plans extensively with patients, so it is important to most of them that the plans are in reasonable accordance with patient wishes, and that they do not feel obliged to try, more or less subtly, to enforce treatment plans on patients.

Further, I could enhance the importance attached to empathic understanding, by using nurses' accounts and descriptions of patients to guess at one or several ways the patient might be understood empathically. This facilitates the nurses' spontaneous tendency to try to understand their patients empathically.

Finally, I could facilitate staff members' spontaneous feelings of compassion with their patients (an important aspect of unconditional positive regard), quite simply by listening with interest and acceptance to expressions of these feelings, and by expressing my own compassion for my clients openly. These attitudes are often regarded with a little suspicion in psychiatry because of the prizing of 'objectivity' in this discipline, although neither staff nor patients thrive well with this effort at pure 'objectivity'. It is often a relief for staff members to allow themselves to feel compassion for their patients. All too often, staff members in psychiatry lean over backwards in a somewhat distancing attitude in order not to risk being regarded as subjective or as identifying with clients. Rogers (1961: 52) wrote:

> We are afraid that if we let ourselves freely experience these positive feelings toward another we may be trapped by them ... So as a reaction, we tend to build up distance between ourselves and others—aloofness, a 'professional' attitude, an impersonal relationship ... It is a real achievement when we can learn, even in certain relationships or at certain times in those relationships, that it is safe to care, that it is safe to relate to the other as a person for whom we have positive feelings.

It is important that avoidance of identification with the patient is not confused with a distancing attitude that puts a taboo on feeling compassion for patients.

This role of mine, at ward staff meetings, has contributed to the wards becoming, in general, more 'person-centred' in the daily interactions between staff and patients. In addition, it has helped me out of my feelings of isolation and invisibility among all the other employees in the hospital. A precondition for this to happen is, of course, that the person in charge of the ward staff meeting, typically a psychiatrist, i.e. a representative of the medical model, is sufficiently broad-minded to allow space and time for it. To the degree that this is the case, ward staff meetings can develop into a very exciting and enriching dialogue between the medical model and the Person-Centred Approach.

I think most client-centred therapists working in a medical-model setting will recognise this feeling of their psychotherapeutic work being (and having to be) separated, isolated, and almost invisible from all the activity of the rest of the setting. Some therapists may prefer to live with this 'invisibility' of their therapeutic work. For others, though, 'living with it' may entail a risk of 'burn out' that has to be avoided by becoming visible in the setting, in some way or another, in spite of the 'invisibility' of their work with clients.

Second, the client-centred therapist can play an important role as 'helper for the helpers' and 'caretaker of the caretakers'.

Nurses working in psychiatric wards, and particularly in closed psychiatric wards, are exposed to unusually high levels of emotional intensity, and to unusually bewildering behaviours, during almost the whole of their working day. Episodes with outbursts of violence, whether directed towards others, towards the person, himself/herself, or towards material objects, are frequent, too. This is, of course, a constant strain and toll on nurses' own psychological resources, and the way they are exposed to, and must interfere with, different kinds and degrees of violence often has an impact on them that can best be described as traumatic.

It is important, therefore, that nurses themselves, as well as administrators, recognise that it is often not possible for nurses to process all these experiences on their own, during a normally very busy working day. First, they simply haven't got the time to take care of themselves, in the midst of taking care of the patients and all that that entails. Second, they will normally all be so 'filled up' with their own experiences that they are unable to listen to each other very well. Planned 'time out' and an external facilitator is most often necessary to counter the risk of 'burn out' among nurses, as well as the risk of frequent and large turnover of nurses, and the risk of nurses' behaviour rigidifying into defensive routine strategies with the patients.

The approach of the client-centred therapist, non-directive, non-diagnostic, and universally applicable as it is, is eminently suited to help psychiatric nurses 'survive' traumatic aspects of their work in a psychologically healthy way, i.e. to learn from their experiences, rather than being harmed by them.

The client-centred therapist, therefore, can also contribute fruitfully to the representatives of the medical model by facilitating group 'debriefing' sessions, and/ or doing individual 'crisis therapy' sessions with these people. This work is not much different from ordinary Client-Centred Therapy. The only difference, in my practice of it, is that I structure group sessions to make sure that everyone has time to talk and be listened to and understood, and I do not allow a short run of individual crisis sessions to turn into more long-term, personal therapy. This is partly because of my own time-schedule, partly because I do not wish to enter into a close, long-term therapy relationship with individuals whom I also meet every day as colleagues and, to a greater or lesser extent, friends. Apart from a few crisis sessions, I would doubt my ability to consistently 'keep out of the client's way', if the client was a near colleague and/or friend of mine.

A THIRD WORLD

However helpful the principle of complementarity may be to dissolve many potential dilemmas of the client-centred therapist working in a medical-model setting, it is of paramount importance that the therapist has access to a 'third world': a world of his or her own. There must be at least one person with whom the therapist can talk freely about all of his or her experiences, from the therapist's own frame, with absolutely no risk to either the therapist's relationship with clients or to the therapist's relationship with medical-model colleagues. This person would preferably be another client-centred therapist who is knowledgeable about, or working within, the medical-model setting. The therapist's need for somebody to pay attention to and to try to understand his/her experiences from his/her own frame of reference has to be met frequently to counter feelings of isolation with the concomitant risk of 'burn out'. The ideal solution is a small peer consultation or supervision group that meets regularly. If this need is adequately met, the above mentioned difficulties are more than compensated for by the richness, depth and diversity of experiences of the client-centred therapist working in the medical-model setting of, for example, a psychiatric hospital, however much of a struggle this work also sometimes is.

THE CRITIQUE OF PSYCHIATRY AND THE COMPLEMENTARITY OF CLIENT-CENTRED THERAPY AND THE MEDICAL MODEL

This chapter has dealt with one way for classical, non-directive client-centred therapists to work in psychiatric contexts with individual clients and individual representatives of the medical model without compromising the philosophy of Client-Centred Therapy. In order to avoid any misunderstanding, it is important for me to stress that using the principle of complementarity between Client-Centred Therapy and the medical model as a guideline for this work is *not* synonymous with an uncritical attitude towards, and acceptance of, the dominance of the medical-model perspective in today's psychiatry. The chapter has been concerned with work with the unique client and on this individual level the client-centred therapist is not an expert on what is best for his or her clients. This does not mean that the client-centred therapist cannot be an expert on what is best for 'the average client', or the group of users of psychiatry, at large. On this general level I am extremely critical of the dominance of the medical model in the psychiatric establishment, as such, and I voice this critique whenever the discussion is about 'the average user of psychiatry' and 'the average medical-model representative'. I do not, though, make the 'experts' mistake' (Sommerbeck, 2004) of confusing the perspective of the average and general with the perspective of the unique and individual. If I confuse these two complementary perspectives, by presenting myself to others (medical-model representatives, for example) as an expert on what is best for any individual client of mine, I would, at best, be self-contradictory, and, at worst, hypocritical. In either case, I would betray the essence of Client-Centred Therapy: the non-directive, non-expert, non-authoritarian empathic accompaniment of the client that maximally reduces the risk of conveying conditional regard to the client.

CONCLUSION

The chapter has been exclusively concerned with work on the level of individual and unique clients and medical-model representatives. Other chapters in this book (see for example Pete Sanders, Chapter 3, (Sanders, 2005)) and many other books and papers are concerned with the level of 'the average user of psychiatry' or the group of users of psychiatry and 'the average medical-model representative' or the psychiatric system. They express a critique of the dominance of the medical model in the psychiatric establishment with which I heartily agree. My own ambition with this chapter, has been to point to a way in which the non-directive, classical client-centred therapist can work in 'the lion's den' (Sanders, 2005) without compromising the therapist's non-authoritarian attitude towards the client or, to stay with this apt metaphor, towards 'the prey'. Perhaps the better choice would be to engage more directly in saving the prey from the lion, but that question belongs to another, albeit very interesting, discussion. Indirectly, though, Client-Centred Therapy does of course enable clients to better oppose any kind of authoritarianism according to their own organismic valuing process, including, at their discretion, the authoritarianism of psychiatry. That is the whole point of the therapy.

REFERENCES

Bozarth, J (1990) The Essence of Client-Centered Therapy. In G Lietaer, J Rombauts, and R Van Balen (eds) *Client-Centered and Experiential Psychotherapy in the Nineties.* Leuven: Leuven University Press.

Dilthey, W (1894) Ideen über eine beschreibende und zergliedernde Psychologie. In: *Gesammelte Schriften V*, p. 143 ff. Stuttgart: BG Teubner, (1957).

Mearns, D (1994) *Developing Person-Centred Counselling.* London: Sage Publications.

Rogers, CR (1961) *On Becoming a Person.* London: Constable and Company.

Sanders, P (2005) Principled and strategic opposition to the medicalisation of distress and all of its apparatus. Chapter 3 (pp. 21–41) this volume.

Sommerbeck, L (2004) Non-linear dynamic systems and the non-directive attitude in client-centred therapy. *Person-Centered and Experiential Psychotherapies, 3*, 291–9.

ADDITIONAL RECOMMENDED READING

About not being an expert on the client and the philosophy of client-centred therapy

Rogers, C (1951) *Client-Centered Therapy* (Ch. 2). Boston: Houghton Mifflin.

About client-centred therapy in psychiatry

Sommerbeck, L (2003) *The Client-Centred Therapist in Psychiatric Contexts: A therapists' guide to the psychiatric landscape and its inhabitants.* Ross-on-Wye: PCCS Books.

About the complementarity principle

Lindley, D (1996) *Where Does the Weirdness Go?* New York: Basic Books.

Polkinghorne, JC (1984) *The Quantum World.* Penguin Books.

CHAPTER 9

ASSESSMENT AND 'DIAGNOSIS' IN PERSON-CENTRED THERAPY

PAUL WILKINS

In this chapter, the meaning and relevance of assessment and psychodiagnosis across the family of person-centred approaches to therapy is explored and the differences between these concepts is explained. The continuing debate about 'assessment' is rehearsed (by, for example, reference to the symposium on psychodiagnosis first published in *Person-Centered Review* in 1989) and also presented in a contemporary framework by considering the work of (for example) continental Europeans often working closely in alliance with health-care professionals and the ideas relating to 'person-centred psychopathology' advanced by, among others, Elke Lambers, Gary Prouty and Margaret Warner. As a potential resolution to the debates and disagreements with respect to assessment in the person-centred tradition, a person-centred model for assessment drawing on classic client-centred principles is advanced.

THE PROBLEM OF ASSESSMENT AS DIAGNOSIS

'Assessment' has long been contentious in the context of Person-Centred Therapy. For some practitioners it immediately conjures up the ogre of 'diagnosis' which they believe an inappropriate adoption from medicine and therefore incompatible with person-centred theory and practice. Mearns (1997: 91) articulates this view:

> The whole question of client 'assessment' runs entirely counter to person-centred theory and fits those approaches to counselling which more closely align to the diagnostic 'medical model'. Within the person-centred domain the question of assessment is ridiculous: the assessor would have to make a judgement not only about the client but on the relational dimensions between the client and the counsellor.

It is assessment as a process of reaching a diagnosis and formulating a treatment plan to which Mearns objects. Such notions are antipathetic to Person-Centred Therapy because they arise from the frame of reference and 'expertise' of the therapist and may not reflect the experience and needs of the client.

Bozarth (1998: 127) agrees that 'psychological assessment as generally conceived is incongruent with the basic assumptions of client-centered theory' but (pp. 128–31) he also examines circumstances in which assessment may legitimately be part of Person-Centred Therapy. Bozarth (p. 128) lists three conditions suggesting the use of tests in Person-Centred Therapy. These are:

- The client may request to take tests.
- The policies of the setting may demand that tests be given to clients.
- Testing might take place as an 'objective' way for the client and counsellor to consider a decision for action that is affected by institutional or societal demands.

Whatever the reason, the 'critical factor' (p. 131) is that of honouring the client's self authority.

Writing about humanistic therapies in general, Stiles (2001: 609–10) reaches a different view from that exemplified by Mearns and Bozarth. He (p. 609) states:

> Placing people in categories is potentially dehumanizing ... Diagnoses may induce a false sense of security, a feeling that one knows more about another person than one actually does.

Broadly speaking, this accords with the classic client-centred position (Sanders 2000). *However*, Stiles goes on to argue that not only 'diagnostic categories need not be dehumanizing' but (p. 610) that:

> People who appear as depressed or as borderline or as schizophrenic may experience the world in distinctive ways that differ from their therapists' experience. Knowledge of a client's diagnosis, and the distinctive experiences it may entail, may thus help a therapist understand what the client is trying to say more quickly or more deeply.

Stiles (p. 610) also points out that 'delivering treatments that lack diagnosis-specific efficacy may be viewed by some people as unethical'. Stiles' arguments are reflected in the various person-centred approaches to psychopathology all of which necessarily involve assessment if not diagnosis.

The very fact that clients may have different needs raises problems. How and by whom are these needs to be recognised? Once recognised, how should they be met? Is it reasonable to suppose that all clients require sessions of the same length at the same frequency and would different clients benefit from therapists responding in different ways? (see Wilkins, 2003: 122–5). How and by whom is the nature of a 'contract' to be determined in Person-Centred Therapy? (see Worrall, 1997: 65–75). A consideration of all these things (and others) is essential to good practice and, arguably at least, this process of consideration is assessment. Among the various branches of the person-centred family of approaches to therapy, attitudes and solutions to these problems differ. This chapter is an exploration of these differences and culminates in a person-centred theory of assessment.

THE MULTIPLICITY OF VIEWS

EXPERIENTIAL PSYCHOTHERAPY AND CONTINENTAL EUROPE

Mearns and Bozarth draw on classic client-centred theory (Sanders, 2000) for their arguments. Other practitioners from the broader person-centred family take different views. For example, Rennie (1998: 35) who is influenced by the experiential tradition, writes of 'the need for person-centred assessment' (but is clear that it is problematic in as much as it shifts the locus of attention from the client to the counsellor) and Speierer (1990, 1996) has developed a 'differential incongruence' model of assessment. He (1996: 304) proposes that this provides, a 'theory of general psychopathology and specific psychic disorders' compatible with person-centred theory. This allows diagnosis (p. 306) and (p. 307) 'practically useful options' according to the nature of the client's incongruence. Also within the 'continental European' tradition, Eckert et al., (2003: 10–13) report client-centred therapy research in the German language region 'that has increasingly become more disorder specific'. Their references to this research (see also ibid: 5) make extensive use of diagnostic categories including 'depression', 'borderline personality disorders' and 'agoraphobia'. However, Berghofer (1996: 483–5) writing about the significance of diagnosing schizophrenia concludes (p. 484) that 'a diagnostic exploration of the schizophrenic patient hinders the establishment of an authentic relationship'. All this indicates differences within the family of person-centred therapies or at least that the position with respect to assessment within the approach is complex.

WITHIN THE UK

In the context of the UK, recent thought on assessment in Person-Centred Therapy distinguishes between that and 'psychodiagnosis'. For example, from within the approach, Tolan (2003: 135–6) takes the view that while diagnosing a client or (being informed of the diagnosis of the client by another) is not helpful (p. 135) 'some judgements must be made'. These centre on the likelihood of establishing a therapeutic relationship and are as much to do with the qualities of the therapist as those of the client. Milner and O'Byrne, writing about assessment in counselling as a whole, consider (2004: 120–34) the person-centred approach to counselling and conceptualise it as 'a growth map'. They (p. 129) state '[t]his approach is sceptical of diagnostic thinking and says it could be harmful'. Similarly to Tolan, Milner and O'Byrne (pp. 131–2) indicate that in Person-Centred Therapy, the usefulness of assessment is as a process by which therapists monitor their ability to sustain an effective therapeutic relationship. This too is the view of Wilkins and Gill (2003: 184–5) who offer a 'person-centred theory of assessment' based on Rogers' (1957: 96, 1959: 213) 'necessary and sufficient conditions' (see below).

RESISTANCE TO AND ACCEPTANCE OF THE 'MEDICAL MODEL'

Although this chapter is concerned with assessment in the person-centred tradition as a whole, in the UK context 'person-centred' is indicative of a distinctive approach to therapy. This approach is heavily influenced by the thought and work of Dave Mearns and Brian Thorne (particularly through the agency of their book of 1988 and its successors) but also by the fact that few of its practitioners have either previous psychological or medical training and by 'how far therapy in Britain has had its intrinsic assumptions defined by the psychodynamic lobby' (Dave Mearns, personal communication, 2003). These factors bring a particular attitude to assessment and diagnosis which is indicated in the research of Wilkins and Gill (2003: 180–4). For may person-centred practitioners in continental Europe, 'assessment' is not at all problematic. Here, the language of psychiatry and medicine seems to sit a lot more easily with person-centred practice than it does in either the UK or the USA. For example, in the Netherlands, Hans Swildens is both a psychiatrist and a client-centred psychotherapist who has promoted the adaptation of Client-Centred Therapy to more seriously disturbed clients. In his keynote address to the 2003 conference of the World Association for Person-Centered and Experiential Psychotherapy and Counseling (WAPCEPC), Swildens (2004: 4–18) makes free use of the languages of psychiatry, psychoanalysis, person-centred psychotherapy and process differentiation, moving easily between them. Implicit in his use of terms such as 'border-line', 'psychopathology' and 'self-pathology' is not only a role for assessment but for diagnosis. In Germany, Sachse considers his approach to be a development of person-centred psychotherapy and (Sachse, 2004: 27) unambiguously declares:

> Disorder specificity implies that *developing a diagnosis* is needed as part of CCT. Diagnosis ensures that therapists adopt the best possible client-centered approach! It makes it possible to identify at the earliest stage what different clients need and to what they will respond. Therapists can use this information to act in the best possible client-centered way. Rejecting diagnostics in CCT is highly unreasonable.

In making his statement, Sachse is moving a long way from what may be described as the classic client-centred position that diagnosis is unnecessary because there is only *one* treatment regardless of the nature of the client and the 'problem'; that is to respond in a manner consistent with the therapist conditions of empathy, unconditional positive regard and congruence.

While Sachse and Swildens may not be wholly representative of continental European thought on the matter of assessment and diagnosis in Person-Centred Therapy, it seems likely that their views are indicative of a prevailing 'cultural' difference with respect to the UK. Why else when I spoke of the problem of assessment in Person-Centred Therapy at the 2003 conference of the WAPCEPC was I met with puzzled looks by (for example) the German and Dutch members of my audience? It was not until Elke Lambers made a useful intervention explaining that what I saw as a fundamental problem with respect to client-centred theory was no problem at all to many continental

Europeans for whom assessment was an everyday part of practice that I recognised the difference in attitude and approach.

'DIAGNOSIS' AS A PROCESS

It would be mistaken to believe that all continental European person-centred practitioners are comfortable with schemes of assessment and diagnosis which in some way echo or mirror those of psychiatry. For example, the Austrian philosopher-scholar and person-centred therapist Peter Schmid (2004: 47) makes an argument for diagnosis as integral to Person-Centred Therapy. He is clear that he is not writing of a system based on client symptoms and the aetiology of mental ill-health but rather that 'diagnosis is the hard work of the client'. He states:

> [F]rom *a person-centered* point of view psychological diagnosis can only be a phenomenological process diagnosis, unfolded step by step through the joint process of experiencing and reflecting by both client and therapist. Just as therapy does, diagnosis needs both modes and requires both persons involved in the relationship, thus making it a *co-diagnosis process*. (original italics).

Although I understand that there are other meanings and a multiplicity of views (see above), this chapter is principally concerned with assessment as a process via which the suitability and viability of Person-Centred Therapy as a helpful intervention may be determined and which involves both therapist and client as assessors. In this sense, assessment is a process of negotiation and of addressing the questions arising from this negotiation. The emphasis is on the potential therapeutic relationship rather than on diagnosis. The main area where a different approach to assessment may be applied is that of 'deeper disturbance'. This is touched upon here and also in the chapter addressing person-centred theory and psychopathology. Also, my emphasis is, for the most part, on the situation in the UK—but I believe that the issues raised here are fundamental to client-centred theory.

PERSON-CENTRED ASSESSMENT IN CONTEXT

Perhaps there is an assumption on the part of person-centred therapists that therapists of other orientations for whom assessment is a necessity dictated by theory 'do' something to the client which is radically different from what happens in Person-Centred Therapy of any stripe. But the experience and research of Wilkins and Gill (2003: 180–4) indicates that, for example, practitioners of psychodynamic therapies do not differ fundamentally from person-centred practitioners in their attitudes to and practice with their clients in the early stages of therapy.

CRITICISMS FROM OTHER PERSPECTIVES

Just as we (person-centred therapists) make assumptions about therapists who draw on traditions different from our own, so sometimes they do with respect to us. It is not uncommon to find that the reluctance of person-centred therapists to 'assess' their clients is looked on with misgiving. To some it smacks of an irresponsible and slap-dash attitude which does clients a great disservice. For example, Wheeler (in Wheeler and McLeod 1995: 286) expresses a 'serious reservation' that person-centred theory (or rather its lacks) leads to a 'subsequent disregard for assessment'. To us, the absence of a rationale for assessment is rooted in theory and practice and our reasons are so obvious they do not need to be stated. To others, we demonstrate neglect and naïveté bordering on irresponsibility.

On the one hand, it may be sufficient to dismiss such criticisms as bogus because the fundamental premise of Client-Centred Therapy is different from that of other approaches but, on the other, this does nothing for mutual understanding. It is not that we have a disregard for assessment but that we have a different set of theories and procedures which take the place of the more conventional approaches (see Tudor and Merry, 2002: 115). However, Person-Centred Therapy is subject to criticism because (in some eyes) it is seen to have neither a theory of assessment nor are its practitioners adequately prepared by training courses to assess clients. For those who believe in the value of dialogue and understanding within the person-centred family and with practitioners of other approaches and disciplines, a clear statement of person-centred theory with respect to assessment is likely to be helpful.

REBUTTALS

It is mistaken to believe that there is total opposition to assessment and diagnosis amongst person-centred theorists and practitioners. Its usefulness has been recognised from the earliest days—although this usefulness is not of the conventionally perceived kind. For example, Rogers (1957: 101–2) while 'forced to the conclusion that diagnostic knowledge is not essential to psychotherapy' goes on to point out that the one useful function diagnosis seems to have is to make some therapists feel secure in the relationship with the client and thus (p. 102) 'the security they perceive in diagnostic information may be a basis for permitting them to be integrated in the relationship'. Berghofer (1996: 484) also draws attention to this factor as do Binder and Binder (1991: 34). Schmid (1992: 112) states that 'differential classification of suffering' is justified when it leads to higher empathy and congruence by the therapist. The argument made by these authors is that knowledge of how clients are likely to behave and to experience the world should not be understood as an explanation, still less as an instruction or prescription to the therapist but rather as an aid to understanding and consequent action.

THE CHALLENGE TO A CONVENTIONAL VIEW

Person-centred theory challenges the conventional view of assessment. As Tudor and Merry (2002: 5) indicate, there are person-centred theories 'which help to describe (rather than *prescribe* for) the client' and which are consistent with client autonomy and self-authority. It is incumbent upon person-centred therapists to clarify their theoretical and practical position with respect to assessment. We do have one, we can explain it—we do ourselves no favours by hiding our light under a bushel.

AN HISTORICAL PERSPECTIVE

THE DISREGARD FOR ASSESSMENT

Literature on assessment is relatively rare in the classic client-centred canon and is not much more prominent in the experiential and process-oriented literature. With the exception of Rogers (1951), a survey of major works of Rogers and his anthologisers indicates that assessment does not merit an entry in the indices. A consideration of assessment is similarly absent from Barrett-Lennard's (1998) comprehensive survey and from the widely read works of Mearns and Thorne (1988, 1999 and 2000). This is indicative of the perceived irrelevance of assessment to person-centred theory and practice. Rogers (1946: 421) remarked that 'diagnostic skill is not necessary for good therapy' and this is probably a view held by a majority of person-centred practitioners to this day and is understood by many to mean that assessment is unnecessary—even contra-indicated.

ROGERS' RATIONALE FOR DIAGNOSIS

In his early definitive work, Rogers (1951: 221–3) does refer to 'the client-centered rationale for diagnosis'. This rationale clearly puts the client and the client's experience at the heart of the process—in fact Rogers (p. 223) says it is really a rationale for psychotherapy without external diagnosis—that is not resulting from some assessment of the 'problem' by the therapist. Rogers' scheme is based on the following propositions:

- Behavior is caused, and the psychological cause of behaviour is a certain perception or a way of perceiving. The client is the only one who has the potentiality of knowing fully the dynamics of his perceptions and his behaviours.
- In order for behaviour to change, a change in perception must be experienced. Intellectual knowledge cannot substitute for this.
- The constructive forces which bring about altered perception, reorganisation and relearning, reside primarily in the client, and probably cannot come from outside.
- Therapy is basically the experiencing of inadequacies in old ways of perceiving, the experiencing of new and adequate perceptions, and the recognition of significant relationships between perceptions.
- In a very meaningful and accurate sense therapy is diagnosis, and this diagnosis is a process which goes on in the experience of the client, rather than in the intellect of the clinician.

Interestingly, Rogers' immediately (pp. 223–5) follows his rationale with 'certain objections to psychological diagnosis'. Patterson (1948, reprinted in 2000: 3–9) had previously considered the question 'is psychotherapy dependent upon diagnosis?' and reached the conclusion that it was not. He outlines a theory of behaviour, and examines the principles and practices of psychotherapy which leads him to state that (p. 8), given the motivation to change or grow:

> For therapeutic purposes all that is necessary is that the patient come for help and be in sufficient contact to be able to verbalize his behavior and attitudes and feelings.

THE 1989 SYMPOSIUM ON PSYCHODIAGNOSIS

Although, until recently, assessment has been largely neglected by person-centred theoreticians, some attention had been paid to 'diagnosis'—most notably in the form of a 'Symposium on Psychodiagnosis' published in *Person-Centered Review* in 1989. This symposium comprised a paper by Angelo Boy to which Julius Seeman, John Shlien, Constance Fischer and David Cain responded (see Cain, 2002: 385–414 for reprints of these papers). Although I take the view that 'psychodiagnosis' and 'assessment' are different processes with different ends and it is the conflation of these terms which causes some of the heated opposition to assessment, it is worth briefly considering this debate.

Boy (in Cain, 2002: 385–96) offers an historical perspective on psychodiagnosis, examines its purpose and tools and considers the relevance of the Diagnostic and Statistical Manual of the American Psychiatric Association, 3rd edition (*DSM-III*—the current version is the *DSM-IV*) to the practice of psychotherapy. Boy points out that the concept of psychodiagnosis emerges from the medical model and has at its heart the categorising of 'patient symptoms' which can then be summarised by a diagnostic label. He argues that it is pressure from the funders of psychotherapy that influences the use of psychodiagnosis and that psychiatry and psychoanalysis dictate its form.

Boy (pp. 387–8) is critical of the tools and methodology of psychodiagnosis pointing out, for example, that the cultural and social influences on the client are ignored and that its procedures fall short of the scientific standards of medicine per se and that, therefore, the objectivity claimed for it is spurious. Furthermore, traditional psychodiagnosis ignores the internal frame of reference of the client in spite of the fact that (p. 388) '[f]or nearly half a century Rogers … presented evidence that the only accurate and reliable viewpoint for understanding a client is from the client's internal frame of reference'.

Boy (p. 394) takes the view that the case for psychodiagnosis is unproved and that the (then) existing schemes for the classification of 'disorders' are questionable. From a person-centred perspective, he does not see an objection in principle to (p. 394) 'the development of a broad classification system for categorizing human behavior' but argues that this system must be rooted in very different criteria from those employed in, for example, the *DSM-III*. Boy refers to Rogers' (1951: 221–3) client-centred rationale for diagnosis as one which could be of value.

Seeman (in Cain, 2002: 397–9) responds to Boy outlining four aspects of psychodiagnosis:

- The value aspects of psychodiagnosis
- The technical validity of diagnostic tests
- The human judgements surrounding psychodiagnosis
- The positive function served by psychodiagnosis

Seeman broadly agrees with Boy regarding the value of psychodiagnosis suggesting that thinking *about* a person rather than *with* a person creates a split between client and therapist and establishes a (p. 397) 'one-up one-down hierarchy' inimical to Person-Centred Therapy. Seeman regards Boy's arguments as to the technical validity of psychodiagnosis as irrelevant because psychodiagnosis has no role in Person-Centred Therapy but he does see that psychological testing may sometimes offer other benefits. In considering the role of human judgement in diagnostic procedures, Seeman again agrees with Boy that there is a likelihood of error and strengthens this argument by reference to the literature. Finally, Seeman expresses limited support for psychodiagnosis. He believes that people are comprised of complex, interlocking subsystems, 'biochemical, physiological, perceptual, cognitive, interpersonal' (p. 398) and that therapists have access to some subsystems but not others. It may be that the stresses on the system as a whole are elsewhere in the hierarchy of subsystems than in those to which therapists have access. Seeman sees that, for example, neuropsychological testing may indicate the advisability of interventions other than psychotherapy. Seeman (p. 399) concludes with these words:

> [P]sychodiagnosis is irrelevant to the internal process of client-centered therapy [but] there are occasions when referral for psychodiagnosis is part of our ethical/professional responsibility.

Shlien (in Cain, 2002: 400–2) argues strongly against psychodiagnosis and while he broadly agrees with Boy, he clearly thinks Boy was too accommodating and conciliatory in his expressed views. Shlien (pp. 401–2) states that Rogers 'did not really' develop a rationale for diagnosis and that he was mistaken to use this description. Shlien concedes that psychodiagnosis makes some sense in some approaches to psychotherapy but sees it as having no role in Person-Centred Therapy. He writes (p. 402):

> [C]lient-centered therapy has only one treatment for *all* cases. That fact makes diagnosis entirely useless. If you have no specific treatment to relate to it, what possible purpose could there be to specific diagnosis? Nothing remains but the detrimental effects.
>
> Then, diagnosis is not good, not even neutral, but bad.

Fischer (in Cain, 2002: 403–7) accepts the long-standing criticisms of psychodiagnosis but (p. 403) argues that 'nevertheless all therapy should be planned in accordance with assessment of the client's circumstances'. She apparently has a different attitude to the first three contributors *but* we draw attention to Fischer's use of language. She refers to assessment, not psychodiagnosis and she writes of the client's circumstances, not the client per se still less some assumed psychopathological category to which the client may be assigned.

Fischer (p. 404) argues that assessment is necessary to the practice of psychotherapy. She gives examples from clinical practice and (p. 405) states ' in these cases, my familiarity with life patterns of disordered living allowed for planning that saved clients unnecessary anguish and effort'. Fischer is advocating 'life-oriented assessment'. She writes (ibid.):

> Life-oriented assessment addresses the person going about his or her life. Test scores, diagnostic categories, theoretical constructs, and other nomothetic devices are derived notions to be used as tools to understand the person's circumstances. The tools should not be confused with the results.

And (p. 407):

> In short, life-centered diagnostics serves the client's interests. It empowers the client by recognizing personal agency and by exploiting positive possibility. It respects the ambiguity and intersubjectivity that are inherent to human understanding. Emphasis on life context alerts clients and others involved in the assessment to the larger contexts of comportment, and to our responsibilities for grappling with systems as well as with individuals.

Then lastly Cain (in Cain, 2002: 408–14) responds to Boy. His first assumption is that what clients learn about themselves is more important than what a diagnostician learns in an assessment process. If the purpose of diagnosis is to facilitate the process of 'knowing the self' then, argues Cain (p. 408) it is compatible with person-centred theory and practice. He establishes his argument with reference to the advantages and disadvantages of three approaches to diagnosis: mechanical, prescriptive and collaborative. The first two of these are 'expert-centred' and thus of limited use in the context of Person-Centred Therapy while the latter is centred on the client and promotes self-knowledge. Cain (p. 413) characterises the collaborative approach to diagnosis. In summary, these characteristics are that collaborative practitioners:

- View their clients holistically, realising that psychological, biological and sociocultural aspects of the person are interrelated. Focus is on the whole experience of the client— that is as much on what is 'right' as what is 'wrong'.
- Take a phenomenological approach to their clients. Observation of immediate experience is of greater importance than explanation.
- Are more interested in enabling their clients to engage in an ongoing process of self-diagnosis rather than limiting themselves to understanding a problem in isolation.

Cain also states:

> A major strength of the collaborative approach is that it helps create in clients a new consciousness about the significant and crucial role they can play in determining the nature and quality of care afforded them. It enables them to realize that they are the best judge of their needs ... and that they can learn to take more charge of and influence the course of their lives ... (p. 413)

In summary, the 1989 symposium represents three main views of psychodiagnosis. Firstly that psychodiagnosis is irrelevant to Person-Centred Therapy and may actually be 'bad'. Secondly, there is a 'yes, but …' position in which the problems associated with psychodiagnosis are acknowledged but there is also an acceptance that diagnosis and assessment are realities in the world of psychotherapy and maybe person-centred practitioners must take this into account—and maybe too under some conditions, for some clients, some of the time, psychodiagnosis can be useful—this is also the view expressed by Bozarth (1998: 128–31, see above). Thirdly, there is the notion that if assessment focuses on the client and the client's self-knowledge then not only is it compatible with person-centred theory but also an advantage to the practice of Person-Centred Therapy.

THE CONTEMPORARY VIEW(S)

In terms of classic Client-Centred Therapy, the situation was and remains very much as stated by Shlien (above). Assessment (for which read 'diagnosis') is pointless because whatever and however the client presents, all that is required of therapists is that they adhere to the three therapist conditions of congruence, empathy and unconditional positive regard (conditions 3, 4, and 5 of Rogers' original six) and behave accordingly. Adherents of newer approaches in the person-centred family may take different views. For example, Lietaer (2001: 98–101) who is an experiential psychotherapist refers to the role of 'confrontation' in his approach and how this involves therapists in responding from their own frames of reference. He (p. 100) acknowledges 'the importance of timing' in making such interventions. This implies an assessment of the client's process and the client/therapist relationship.

Recently attempts have been made to frame person-centred theory and practice in terms of deeper disturbance or psychopathology (see Chapter 4). The very existence of 'person-centred psychopathology' suggests that, at least sometimes, it is helpful to know something about a person's way of being in the world and that responsible therapist behaviour must take account of it. For some practitioners, this means behaving differently with clients manifesting different 'symptoms' either by adding to classic client-centred therapist behaviours or by giving them a different emphasis. To decide on a particular approach for a particular client involves reaching some conclusions about the client from the therapist's frame of reference. This is diagnosis or something very close to it.

ASSESSMENT AND 'PSYCHOPATHOLOGY'

Although, at least from the perspective of classical Client-Centred Therapy and the British school of Person-Centred Therapy, there has been a general agreement that diagnosis and assessment have little if any relevance to Person-Centred Therapy, there is an increasing acceptance among person-centred practitioners that the concept of psychopathology has relevance (see Lambers, 1994: 105–20, Wilkins, 2003: 105–7).

There is an apparent contradiction here, for how is it possible to conclude that a client is 'psychopathological' without making an assessment and/or diagnosis? The argument seems to be that because criteria different from those of psychiatric/psychoanalytical models are used and these are consistent with person-centred theory, the process and ends are also different. But what are these criteria?

Tudor and Merry (2002: 115) recognise three strands in the Person-Centred Approach to understanding mental ill-health. These are Pre-Therapy (Prouty, 1990), expansions and developments of the concept of incongruence (see Speierer, 1990; Biermann-Ratjen, 1998) and identifying styles of processing (Warner, 2000). These and other person-centred theorists and practitioners who address 'psychopathology' base their ideas in person-centred theory.

Prouty (2001: 590–1) defines Pre-Therapy as:

> a theory and method that postulates psychological contact as the necessary pre-condition of a psychotherapeutic relationship for contact-impaired clients, such as clients with mental disability or chronic schizophrenia.

He takes the view that until the first of Rogers' necessary and sufficient conditions is met, there can be no effective person-centred therapy. Furthermore, there are groups of people who may, amongst other things, be distinguished as 'severely contact-impaired' (Van Werde, 1994: 121). For effective person-centred therapy to take place, absence of contact must be recognised and addressed. This clearly involves an assessment ('Are this client and I in psychological contact?') and a 'treatment': Pre-Therapy. Prouty and other pre-therapists also use a language of diagnosis. For example, in his list of people for whom Pre-Therapy has been 'documented and applied' Van Werde (1994: 121) refers to 'dual-diagnosed mentally retarded populations', 'acute psychosis', 'chronic schizophrenics' and 'people with multiple personality'. Prouty's method of Pre-Therapy also involves on-going assessment of a kind because part of the method is to repeat what seems to work.

Speierer (1990, 1996) and Biermann-Ratjen (1998) both base their approaches to 'illness' on incongruence. Speierer (1996: 299) states 'incongruence is the central construct of the client-centered illness concept.' Biermann-Ratjen (1998: 125) makes a similar statement:

> client-centred therapists regard different psychogenic illnesses as different ways of experiencing different kinds of incongruence, or as different signs of different efforts to defend oneself against self-experience which is incompatible with the self-concept and therefore seems inimical.

In both cases, it would seem that the therapist may be called upon to make a judgement as to the client's incongruence. Partly, this may be a matter of definition; the second of Rogers' conditions requires that the client is incongruent and that this incongruence manifests as anxiety or vulnerability. However, Speierer (1996: 300) makes a claim that 'neurotic disorders, personality disorders and psychotic disorders differ from each other due to differences in the presence or absence of conscious incongruence' and Biermann-Ratjen (1998: 126) considers that 'any symptom of psychogenic illness is the expression of experiencing incongruence'. In both cases, some judgement as to the nature and/or manifestation of the client's incongruence is made by the therapist. This is assessment. Speierer (1990) goes further and offers a scheme for diagnosis and differential treatment thus moving away from the classic client-centred position of 'one size fits all'.

Warner bases her ideas on the idea that while processing experience is a fundamental aspect of human nature, 'many clients do not find that processing experience in the context of a therapeutic relationship proceeds smoothly or naturally' (Warner, 2001: 181). Such clients Warner views as having 'difficult processes' and of these she has described three types: fragile process, dissociated process and psychotic process. Brief accounts of these can be found in Warner (2001: 182–3, see also Warner Chapter 7 this volume). In Warner's view, it is important that person-centred therapists recognise different difficult processes and to respond accordingly. She writes (2001: 184):

> While client-centered therapy works well, engaging in difficult process requires courage and endurance on the part of the client. To sustain this effort, clients typically need relatively high levels of psychological contact from their therapists, a willingness to meet them at 'relational depth' … While each client is unique, I think that some general sorts of understanding about difficult process can be helpful to developing and maintaining process-sensitive empathy.

Implicit in this is a requirement for assessment rather than diagnosis because people can and do shift in and out of difficult process and are not necessarily confined to one. The question to be asked is 'At this time, does my client appear to be experiencing a difficult process?' If so, the required response is to tailor attention and therapist responses appropriately. What is important here is that the emphasis is on the current client experience not on labelling the client once and for all as 'fragile', 'dissociated' or 'psychotic' and that the awareness of difficult process allows the therapist to respond in a way that can be received and understood by the client. Thus Warner offers a response to the issue raised by Stiles (2001: 610—see above) that knowledge of a client's distinctive experience leads to quicker, deeper understanding.

A PERSON-CENTRED THEORY OF ASSESSMENT

THE LEGITIMACY OF ASSESSMENT

Assessment, although probably not diagnosis in the clinical sense, does have a legitimate place in Person-Centred Therapy. The evidence above demonstrates how practitioners working with clients for whom establishing and maintaining a relationship incorporating the necessary and sufficient conditions is problematic take account of this and adapt accordingly. Also, it seems that 'assessment' may be part of the everyday experience of person-centred practitioners even though they resist the term (see Wilkins and Gill, 2003: 180). As a result of our research, we (Wilkins and Gill, 2003: 184) found that:

> When meeting a new client, ... person-centred therapists engage in a process concerned with establishing whether the therapist and client can and will build an effective therapeutic relationship (as defined by Rogers, 1957, 1959).

This process can legitimately be called 'assessment' but it does not of itself constitute diagnosis. Diagnosis is a possible product of assessment but it is not the only one nor is it a necessary one. Assessment may be thought of as a process by which therapists reach some conclusion as to the possibility or likelihood of effective working. In most models, diagnosis involves categorising the client according to a set of criteria arising from theory. Attempts to establish diagnostic categories in person-centred work centre on the client's experience and are framed in terms of contact, incongruence or experiencing. These are not universally accepted as 'client-centred'. However at least from a person-centred perspective, assessment (as suggested by Fischer, in Cain, 2000; Worrall, 1997; and the research of Wilkins and Gill, 2003) appears to be of the relationship/potential relationship not of the individual in the client role.

THE NECESSARY AND SUFFICIENT CONDITIONS AS CRITERIA FOR ASSESSMENT

It does not take much thought to realise that person-centred theory has contained a statement of an assessment process since at least 1957. This 'theory of assessment' centres on features of the relationship between client and therapist and not on the client alone. Rogers' (1957: 96, 1959: 213) necessary and sufficient conditions may be understood as a series of questions a responsible therapist must ask at the beginning of (and throughout) the therapeutic endeavour. Thus:

1. Are my potential client and I capable of establishing and maintaining contact? (For some, contact is assumed as an inevitable consequence of mutual presence, for others some other qualities are necessary).
2. Is my potential client in need of *and* able to make use of therapy? —i.e. is the potential client in a state of incongruence and vulnerable or anxious? (Wilkins and Bozarth (2001: ix) speculate that it may be possible to be incongruent and yet not vulnerable and anxious. This may be so when, for example, a potential client is referred by a third party without awareness of the nature of therapy. In this way condition 2 would not be met and therapy is contra-indicated.)
3. Can I be congruent in the relationship with the potential client?
4. Can I experience unconditional positive regard for this potential client?
5. Can I experience an empathic understanding of the potential client's internal frame of reference?

6. Will the potential client perceive at least to a minimal degree my unconditional positive regard and my empathy?

If the answer to one or more of these questions is 'No' and, the 'necessity' is not met by definition, therapeutic change will not occur. Making this judgement (which may very well be much more about the therapist's abilities and limitations than the client) is an assessment. It is easy to see how pre-therapy fits into this scheme for it is so evidently based on the need for contact. Warner's difficult process model, although based on classic client-centred ways of responding seems to revolve around making a judgement about the likelihood that the client will perceive the therapist's empathy and unconditional positive regard so it also fits. Perhaps the incongruence models are more problematic because the necessary and sufficient conditions do not include a consideration of a variety of manifestations of incongruence (apart from anxiety or vulnerability). However, in other ways person-centred theory does allow for different kinds of incongruence— the defence mechanisms of distortion and denial are an example.

THE SEVEN STAGES OF PROCESS

The seven stages of process (Rogers, 1961: 132–55) may also be understood as relating to assessment in as much as they indicate something about the client's likely way of being and so what is appropriate from the therapist. These stages represent (p. 132) 'a continuum of personality change' and although Merry (2002: 59) points out that there 'is a great deal of variation and individual differences in clients' processes' and Rogers (1961: 139) reminds us 'that a person is never wholly at one or another stage of the process'—or perhaps because of this—knowing something about a client's stage in the process continuum can inform the therapist and help in making appropriate ethical and professional decisions. Thus people in the early stages of process (1 and 2) are unlikely to enter into counselling or, if they do, not to stay. Those in stage 3, the point at which Rogers (1961: 136) believed many people who seek therapy to be at, are likely to commit to a counselling contract and (Merry, 2002: 60) 'need to be fully accepted as they present themselves before moving deeper into stage 4'. Rogers (1961: 139) expresses 'no doubt' that stages 4 and 5 'constitute much of psychotherapy as we know it' and (1961: 150) describes stage 6 as highly crucial. It is in this stage that irreversible constructive personality change is most likely to occur. Arguably, by stage 7 the need for the companionship of a therapist on the journey towards being fully functioning is over. Rogers (1961: 151) writes 'this stage occurs as much outside the therapeutic relationship as in it, and is often reported, rather than experienced in the therapeutic hour.' So, in the seven stages of process Person-Centred Therapy has not only a guide to when and for whom therapy is appropriate but an indication that different 'ways of being' by the therapist in the encounter suit different stages. Implicit in the scheme is that, for example, there are qualitative differences and differences of intent required of the therapist dealing with a client in stage 3 than one in stage 6. Reaching a judgement about all these things is assessment and requires appropriate action.

A PERSON-CENTRED RATIONALE FOR ASSESSMENT

Together, the necessary and sufficient conditions and the seven stages of process provide Person-Centred Therapy with an assessment rationale for deciding the likelihood of establishing a successful therapeutic endeavour, for monitoring its progress and, to a lesser extent, determining the nature of therapist behaviour. Not only is this scheme legitimate in terms of person-centred theory, it is essential to good practice. In short, there is an answer to the criticism that person-centred therapists have a disregard for assessment: there is a theoretical model for assessment, an associated language to describe and communicate processes in person-centred terms and the evidence from research and the literature reported here indicates that person-centred practitioners do conduct assessment.

CONCLUSION

Within the person-centred tradition, there are diverse views with respect to assessment. At the root of these lies differing attitudes to the legitimacy of diagnosis. The perceived problem of diagnosis is that it labels and fixes the client—the fear is that therapy becomes problem-driven rather than client-centred. On the other hand, diagnosis can be seen as helpful in that it allows the development of a mutual understanding between a variety of healthcare professionals and because it enables the therapist's understanding of the client's process. Both of these concepts are essential to a person-centred psychopathology. For example, Warner's concept of client process allows both correspondence to psychiatric ideas and the challenging of them and knowledge of, for example, 'fragile process' may also be helpful to the therapist working with a client experiencing it.

No person-centred scheme of psychopathology is possible without a process of assessment. However, assessment is not inimical to person-centred theory. The radical challenge of a person-centred scheme of assessment is that it sets aside the notion of the therapist as an expert, able to reach a definitive conclusion as to the nature of the client's difficulties and rather concentrates on the likelihood of establishing a relationship in which the six necessary and sufficient conditions will be met. It also highlights the potential shortcomings of the therapist.

REFERENCES

Barrett-Lennard, GT (1998) *Carl Rogers' Helping System: Journey and substance*. London: Sage.
Berghofer, G (1996) Dealing with schizophrenia—a person-centered approach providing care to long-term patients in a supported residential service in Vienna. In R Hutterer, G Pawlowsky, PF Schmid and R Stipsits (eds) *Client-Centered and Experiential Psychotherapy: A Paradigm in Motion*. Frankfurt-am-Main: Peter Lang.
Biermann-Ratjen, EM (1998) Incongruence and psychopathology. In B Thorne and E Lambers

(eds) *Person-Centred Therapy: A European perspective*. London: Sage.

Binder, U and Binder, J (1991) *Studien zu einer Störungsspezifischen Klienzentrierten Psychotherapie*. Eschborn: Dietmar Klotz.

Bozarth, JD (1998) *Person-Centered Therapy: A revolutionary paradigm*. Ross-on-Wye: PCCS Books.

Cain, DJ (ed) (2002) *Classics in the Person-Centered Approach*. Ross-on-Wye: PCCS Books.

Eckert, J, Höger, D and Schwab, R (2003) Developments and current state of the research in client-centered therapy in the German language region. *Person-Centered and Experiential Psychotherapies 2*, 3–18.

Lambers, E (1994) Psychopathology. In D Mearns *Developing Person-Centred Counselling*. London: Sage.

Lietaer, G (2001) Unconditional acceptance and positive regard. In JD Bozarth and P Wilkins (eds) *Rogers' Therapeutic Conditions: Evolution, theory and practice. Vol. 3: Unconditional Positive Regard*. Ross-on-Wye: PCCS Books.

Mearns, D (1997) *Person-Centred Counselling Training*. London: Sage.

Mearns, D and Thorne, B (1988) *Person-Centred Counselling in Action*. London: Sage.

Mearns, D and Thorne, B (1999) *Person-Centred Counselling in Action* (2nd ed) London: Sage.

Mearns, D, and Thorne, B (2000) *Person-Centred Therapy Today: New frontiers in theory and practice*. London: Sage.

Merry, T (2002) *Learning and Being in Person-Centred Counselling* (2nd ed). Ross-on-Wye: PCCS Books.

Milner, J and O'Byrne, P (2004) *Assessment in Counselling: Theory, process and decision-making*. Basingstoke: Palgrave Macmillan.

Patterson, CH (1948) Is Psychotherapy Dependent upon Diagnosis. *American Psychologist, 155–9*. Reprinted in CH Patterson (2000) *Understanding Psychotherapy: Fifty years of Client-Centred theory and practice*. Ross-on-Wye: PCCS Books.

Prouty, GF (1990) Pre-therapy: a theoretical evolution in person-centered/experiential psychotherapy of schizophrenia and retardation. In G Lietaer, J Rombauts and R Van Balen (eds) *Client-Centered and Experiential Psychotherapy in the Nineties*. Leuven: Leuven University Press.

Prouty, GF (2001) Humanistic therapy for people with schizophrenia. In DJ Cain and J Seeman (eds) *Humanistic Psychotherapies: Handbook of research and practice*. Washington DC: American Psychological Association.

Rennie, DL (1998) *Person-Centred Counselling: An experiential approach*. London: Sage.

Rogers, CR (1946) Significant aspects of client-centered therapy. *American Psychologist 1*, 415–22.

Rogers, CR (1951) *Client-Centered Therapy*. Boston: Houghton Mifflin.

Rogers, CR (1957) The necessary and sufficient conditions of therapeutic personality change. *Journal of Consulting Psychology 21*, 95–103.

Rogers, CR (1959) A theory of therapy, personality, and interpersonal relationships, as developed in the client-centered framework. In S Koch (ed) *Psychology: A study of a science, Vol. 3, Formulations of the person and the social context*. New York: McGraw Hill.

Rogers, CR (1961) *On Becoming a Person: A therapist's view of psychotherapy*. London: Constable.

Sachse, R (2004) From client-centered to clarification-oriented psychotherapy. *Person-Centered and Experiential Psychotherapies 3*, 19–35.

Sanders, P (2000) Mapping person-centred approaches to counselling and psychotherapy. *Person-*

Centred Practice 8, 62–74.

Schmid, PF (1992) Das Leiden. In P Frenzel, PF Schmid and M Winkler (eds) *Handbuch der Personzentrierten Psychotherapie*. Köln: Edition Humanistiche Psychologie.

Schmid, PF (2004) Back to the client: a phenomenological approach to the process of understanding and diagnosis. *Person-Centered and Experiential Psychotherapies 3*, 36–51.

Speierer, G-W (1990) Toward a specific illness concept of client-centered therapy. In G Lietaer, J Rombauts and R Van Balen (eds) *Client-Centered and Experiential Psychotherapy in the Nineties*. Leuven: Leuven University Press.

Speierer, G-W (1996) Client-centered therapy according to the Differential Incongruence Model (DIM). In R Hutterer, G Pawlowsky, PF Schmid and R Stipsits (eds) *Client-Centered and Experiential Psychotherapy: A paradigm in motion*. Frankfurt-am-Main: Peter Lang.

Stiles, WB (2001) Future directions in research on humanistic psychotherapy. In DJ Cain and J Seeman (eds) *Humanistic Psychotherapies: Handbook of research and practice*. Washington, DC: American Psychological Association.

Hutterer, R, Pawlowsky, G, Schmid, PF and Stipsits, R (eds) *Client-Centered and Experiential Psychotherapy: A paradigm in motion*. Frankfurt-am-Main: Peter Lang.

Swildens, H (2004) Self-pathology and postmodern humanity: Challenges for person-centered psychotherapy. *Person-Centred and Experiential Psychotherapies 3*, 4–18.

Tolan, J (2003) *Skills in Person-Centred Counselling and Psychotherapy*. London: Sage.

Tudor, K and Merry, T (2002) *A Dictionary of Person-Centred Psychology*. London: Whurr.

Van Werde, D (1994) An introduction to client-centred pre-therapy. In D Mearns *Developing Person-Centred Counselling*. London: Sage.

Warner, MS (2000) Person-Centred Therapy at the difficult edge: a developmentally based model of fragile and dissociated process. In D Mearns and B Thorne *Person-Centred Therapy Today: New frontiers in theory and practice*. London: Sage.

Warner, MS (2001) Empathy, relational depth and difficult client process. In S Haugh and T Merry (eds) *Rogers' Therapeutic Conditions: Evolution, theory and practice. Vol. 2: Empathy*. Ross-on-Wye: PCCS Books.

Wheeler, S and McLeod, J (1995) Person-centred and psychodynamic counselling: a dialogue. *Counselling 6*, 283–7.

Wilkins, P (2003) *Person-Centred Therapy in Focus*. London: Sage.

Wilkins, P and Bozarth, JD (2001) Unconditional regard in context. In JD Bozarth and P Wilkins (eds.) *Rogers' Therapeutic Conditions: Evolution, theory and practice Vol. 3: Unconditional Positive Regard*. Ross-on-Wye: PCCS Books.

Wilkins, P and Gill, M (2003) Assessment in person-centered therapy. *Person-Centered and Experiential Psychotherapies 2*, 172–87.

Worrall, M (1997) Contracting within the Person-Centred Approach. In C Sills (ed) *Contracts in Counselling*. London: Sage.

CHAPTER 10

THE CONCEPT OF EVIL
AS A KEY TO
THE THERAPIST'S USE OF THE SELF

RICHARD WORSLEY

Psychology from Sigmund Freud onwards has struggled to specify itself as a science, and hence 'respectable'. As such it has striven for an objectivity that at times has bracketed out the subject and the subjective. Counselling and psychotherapy have shown greater ambivalence: science or art? The Person-Centred Approach (PCA) has a strong investment in seeing counselling as encounter, as personal. To the psychologist, psychiatrist and some therapists brought up within the medical model or other models that strongly emphasise the objective and quantifiable, then to explore psychopathology from the category of personal reaction, and in particular the seemingly irrational, may feel like alien territory. I intend in this chapter to work from a debate about the nature of evil, towards a position that the therapist is bound to respond with her whole self to the client, and thus be open to the client's pathology in all of its range of meanings. Indeed, it is about openness to the client's self in all of its facets; the word psychopathology itself can be objectifying of people.

In this chapter, I will examine the use of the concept of evil in person-centred debate since 1980; I will use the concept as a sign of the impact of client psychopathology upon the therapist, making particular reference to David Parkin's anthropological view of the concept; from there, I will describe the underlying category error which characterises some uses of the term evil, and will describe some of the underlying interpersonal mechanisms; a brief case study of Ruth leads to the notion of renormalising the client's process; this I link to the work of Garry Prouty, Margaret Warner and Lisbeth Sommerbeck. The last of these in particular offers an eloquent plea to take seriously the impact of the client upon the therapist's internal world.

THE THEME AND CHALLENGE OF EVIL.

Concern for the theme of evil has hovered at the edge of the PCA over the years. Talk of evil is felt by many PCA practitioners to be riddled with difficulties. What or who is evil? Is the word evil useable of a person at all? How does this sit with unconditional positive regard? The PCA and the medical model seem at first sight to be in the same boat in abstaining from talk of evil. However, the existential therapist Rollo May challenged Carl Rogers, near the end of the latter's life, to reconsider evil and to acknowledge the tendency of person-centred therapists to miss a complete dimension of being human (May, 1982). The heart of the conflict between Rogers and May is Rogers' view that people are fundamentally constructive, however damaged they might be by their experience. By contrast, May puts forward the concept of the daimonic. This, he stresses, is not at all the same as the demonic, having nothing to do with dualism or non-human entities. Rather, May hypothesises that the constructive is very close to a destructive tendency in humans:

> The daimonic is the urge in every being to affirm itself, assert itself, perpetuate and increase itself ... [the reverse side] of the same affirmation is what empowers our creativity. (May, 1969: 123)

For May, the constructive tendency in people is an assertion of self which, differently expressed, can be destructive. As a corollary of this argument, May challenges Rogers to see that in the latter's extensive work with hospitalised schizophrenics—the Wisconsin project (Barrett-Lennard, 1998, pp. 68–9, 82–5, 267–73)— he and other person-centred therapists tended to miss this same destructive element in their clients.

Some eighteen years later, the theme returned in person-centred literature in the form of a debate between Dave Mearns and Brian Thorne (2000, chapter 3). They agree that therapy requires a category of thought which can be termed 'spiritual' or 'existential'. (It is far from clear to me that these two concepts necessarily serve the same function.) However, behind them is a concern with the nature of evil. Dave Mearns rejects the use of the word evil, certainly of any human being, for to do so would be to declare all possibility of hope exhausted. By contrast, Brian Thorne takes a Christian mystical approach to the issue:

> It is the experience that such a transformation is possible and that person-centred therapists can embody such attitudes and behaviour towards their clients which underpins and authenticates what is, in effect, an evolutionary view of humankind. What is more such an evolution takes place not by avoiding evil but by engaging with it and by disarming it through the power of relationship where spirit meets spirit, thus rendering evil both unnecessary and irrelevant. (Mearns and Thorne, 2000: 63)

Here, Brian Thorne accords a reality to evil which some would question. It is clear that he has taken up some aspects of May's challenge to Rogers. The question of evil is still important.

THE IMPACT OF EVIL

The word evil is used with increasing frequency in a secular society, not least by the tabloid press. I was struck by the need of the press to mark out as evil the two boys who had murdered the toddler, Jamie Bulger. The unimaginable had happened. It was two children who had murdered a third child. The impact of this as horror was patent. The underlying logic was frightening. Children must not murder children. (That is the role of adults?) When the unimaginable happens then the offenders are simply removed from the realm of normal humanity. They become 'evil'. This manoeuvre itself leaves a nasty taste in the mouth. Society, it seemed, needed victims who were offenders, onto whom we could project our shame at our failure to maintain the innocence and inviolability of any of these three boys. The rhetoric of evil discomforts.

I have a personal and theological interest in the question of evil—Worsley (1996). As such I have been asked from time to time to present a session on the theme with counselling diploma students. The driving force of the question that led to this session tended to be the impact of considering client psychopathology. In the same way that the Jamie Bulger case labelled the offenders as 'evil' in the popular imagination, these students' encounter with psychopathology threw up the same strange concept. Indeed I could resonate with their need to process something further. In 1987, I had a six-week encounter with a person labelled as a psychopath. I am still aware of the impact of him on me. I experienced a disturbance of my personal poise, and of my relationship with others— the latter stoked by an anxiety leading to aggression. I had met in this Other a version of humanity that I could scarce stomach.

Of course I can own in retrospect a certain naïvety in my response to him, yet perhaps this response is more real, more open to experience, than is the self-protecting denial of that shudder under the shelter of objectivisation and 'science'. How then is this shudder to be processed? How is evil to be seen?

AN ANTHROPOLOGICAL VIEW OF EVIL

It is not my intention to reduce the notion of evil to the status of a psychological misunderstanding. I am happy to leave other sorts of debate about evil to philosophy, ethics and theology. However, I contend that in using the word evil of some psychopathological phenomena a category error is being made. Yet, it is not an error to be erased. It requires our full attention. It speaks.

In 1985, David Parkin edited a volume entitled *The Anthropology of Evil*. He pointed out that the term evil was a difficult one for anthropologists. They preferred terms that were incontestable. He gave as an example the term 'witchcraft'. Once this is defined as a behaviour, it becomes a mere social artefact to be explored. By contrast, 'evil' is a contestable concept. Its meaning is far from clear. It is used in different cultures in radically different ways. Yet, it serves a key function that ought not to be ignored. In his introduction to the book, Parkin describes his conceptualisation of evil thus:

> The main suggestions ... are that evil refers to various ideas of imperfection and excess seen as destructive; but that these are contestable concepts which, when personified, allow mankind [sic] to engage them in dialogue and reflect on the boundaries of humanity. (Parkin, 1985: 23)

He points to the word 'evil' as representing a field of meanings that is particularly sensitive to cultural construction. This word is used—often through a process of personification—in order to assist us navigate our acts of living through crises of value and human identity.

The process of personification seems a powerful one. I am struck by the prevalence of the notion of Satan in religious thinking, in spite of severe theological problems with it. Yet Satan is but one personification. Any difficult being can come to personify evil. Those offenders who become the subjects of tabloid vilification are but one example. I suggest that there are times that this process focuses upon bearers of particular psychopathologies. It is no coincidence that mental illness used to fall under the category of possession, and, for a small number even in Western culture, still does. The schizophrenic, seen as evil because violent, even murderous, serves the same psychological function for society as does the possessed in earlier times.

How does the use of the marker 'evil' function? Parkin points to imperfection and excess. This is rather restrained language. Much in life we can experience as deeply troubling. Often this centres on difference. The schizophrenic is different from me, to such a degree that I cannot understand who she is for me. Of course, in coming to know myself at depth I come also to recognise those aspects of my own 'normal' experiencing which are tinged with the psychotic. This recognition then generates an existential anxiety, under the threat of meaninglessness or loss of self (Tillich, 1952: 41). This results in a splitting process in which the other, the object, takes on the quality 'evil' in order that the perceived self may remain safe. This process has been thoroughly described by Menzies' (1970) landmark study of the behaviour of nurses in the face of their anxiety over illness, helplessness, meaninglessness and death. The patient—and already the word patient is a distancing and subduing word to use of another person—ceases to be human or dynamic but becomes instead 'the liver in bed 10' or 'the pneumonia in bed 15' (Menzies, 1970: 12–13). No longer a person, but an organ or disease, the sick individual is less of a threat to the anxious carer. Where lies the sickness?

It would be remarkable if the psychologist, the psychiatrist, the psychotherapist or the counsellor were immune to this process. We are not. To be safe from the impact of anxiety, it must be faced, and not reduced to a pseudo-scientific commitment to objectivity. May and Thorne share at least this conviction. The ubiquitous concept of evil is a beginning point from which to take the subjective seriously.

Parkin argues that those things are labelled evil which embody a threat to our sense of our own being. It is in dealing with the experience of evil that the therapist can negotiate the truth about psychopathology. Before the question of hope can be dealt with, there must be a facing of the shudder, the sensation of encountering patterns that assail our own humanity.

Before moving on from the anthropological notion of evil, I want to acknowledge that some pathological structures evoke a question of evil in an ethical sense, and not just as a projection prompted by anxiety. I remember work with a woman, a deputy head teacher, whose mother carried a marked personality disorder. She was neither the person whom she had been, nor, in the face of the agony of fear that dominated her life, a fear of being found out by a brutal father, was the mother able to find respite in madness. For mother and daughter the suffering dragged over many years. The daughter strove to care, in the face of much adversity. Her heaviest burden turned out to be that she could not tell what the boundary was between her mother as ill and her mother as malign, manipulative, radically dishonest and wilfully treacherous. What sort of evil— projected or ethical? Even years of living with mother could not disentangle the two.

CATEGORY ERROR

The concept of evil has two significantly different denotations. The first is ontological. By this I mean that whatever is described as ontologically evil is in and of itself incapable of goodness, of being saved, to use Martin Buber's (1961: 200–5) category. Some strands of religious thought—but not my own—attribute ontological evil to non-human agency. Yet, it is deeply embedded within the PCA that human beings ought not to be described as evil. For many practitioners, this is a matter of absolute, principled faith in human nature, and is described by some as a spiritual commitment (Purton, 1998). In this, the PCA falls firmly within the more optimistic strand of Judaeo-Christian tradition that sees all creation as good. This chapter is not the place for further comment on the ontological meaning of evil.

The second, that expressed by Parkin (1985), is functional, and is crucial to our thinking about the impact of psychopathology. When something or someone is called evil, this is a naming. The focus is upon the need of the name-caller to separate herself off from the evil. (Such actions or propositions can also have an ontologically orientated truth-function, but that is simply a different matter.) Thus, when the killers of Jamie Bulger are called evil, something has to be exiled from human society, in order that society can maintain its humanity. But the question is, 'What?' If the killers are all that is to be disowned, then they are ontologically evil and thus beyond hope. This is not a convincing version. Those who kill whilst they are children can be rehabilitated. Hope is not lost. Therefore, what is to be driven out of society like a scapegoat is the force and horror of our inability as a society to protect our own. It is part of us that is projected into the two offenders. The name-calling of evil serves a function.

However, this function can be healthy or sick. (I suspect that these two terms form a continuum rather than a polarity.) If I describe the use of children for adult sexual pleasure as evil, I claim that this is a healthy use of the term. I note that it is absolutely and in principle unacceptable to have sex with children. In Parkin's terms, I deal with the murky issue of the paedophile's claim that sex with children is normal by exiling it from society. I exile the claim and the act, but not the person. I also note that I drive out into the desert like the scapegoat that part of me that could become addicted to the wholly unacceptable; and I struggle to recognise and accept that part of me is like that—open to corruption. However to call Jamie Bulger's killers evil, even if humanly understandable, is unhealthy because its sole function as name-calling is to disown and fail to take responsibility for that aspect of the murder which sits at all of our doors. A name-calling of evil can be used healthily or unhealthily. The unhealthy use is a category error. Child sexual abuse is evil because it is a behaviour and a belief-set that is to be excluded. The named is actually that which is to be exiled. With the boy-killers, it is not the named—the killers themselves—which are to be exiled as not-of-us. Rather they become the screen upon which we project unfaceable elements of ourselves. It is this radical misattribution that constitutes the category error. Yet, the emotions of revulsion and anger are similar: what we feel does not mark out the healthy from the unhealthy.

It is my contention that the experiencing of some psychopathology as evil is a similar category error. The error manifests itself in many ways. The tabloid name-calling of the violent psychotic is a valid enough plea for public safety and increased mental health resources, but is wholly inappropriate in that it is projected onto the person with schizophrenia. This same sort of misattribution happens in the demonisation of Islam in the face of terrorism. When the medical model objectifies the psychotic and reduces her to her symptoms and behaviours, ignoring her inward experiencing, this is also a category error. The same happens when counselling students feel 'freaked' by their contemplation of the possibility of working with certain psychopathologies, for they fail to see the people behind the symptoms and behaviour.

Mental health practitioners must therefore know themselves well enough to spot the category error within themselves. The more exotic feelings around the person-as-evil are clear enough signals of personal work to be done. The depersonalisation of the client in the name of professionalism, the use of *DSM-IV* in place of human encounter, is less easy to spot.

Within the literature of psychotherapy, a number of ways of conceptualising this category error exist. I will outline some of these very briefly, before moving on to explore the insights of the PCA into the re-personalisation of those who bear the traits often designated psychopathological.

CONCEPTUALISING THE CATEGORY ERROR

The counselling students who wanted to think about evil, having experienced the 'shudder' in the face of human psychopathological patterns, are following up a category error. Some forms of distortion within the human personality or functionality feel just like evil, as it might be conceived ethically, existentially or theologically. At least they are aware of the disturbance within: the category error is useful. By contrast, those who exile the disturbed person by objectifying him or her in the name of the medical model seem often blissfully unaware of their own disturbed experiencing, (Menzies, 1970).

I delight in the telling of a story that I found in Ronnie Laing's *Self and Others*. (Laing, 1961: 106). I delight in the confusion it creates. A nurse offers a cup of tea to a chronically ill, catatonic person. On taking the cup, the person said: 'This is the first time in my life anyone has ever given me a cup of tea.' Most hearers struggle to escape the 'madness' of this. Surely nobody has gone through life without being given a cup of tea? Of course the shift of frame of reference, of verbal emphasis, is crucial. The following concepts offer to me however provisionally and speculatively, ways of engaging with the category error:

1. I AND THOU

Martin Buber (1958) proposes that we engage with the world through the uttering of two primary words: I-Thou and I-It. Each precedes both ontologically and psychologically any notion of the separate self. We are created in relationship, but engage sometimes by seeing the other as radically like ourselves and at times in an object-like way. I-Thou relating is marked by intimacy and mutuality, and offers to the other a confirmation of their being by affirming not only that which is actual within them but also their very potentialities. However, I-Thou relating is always prone to fall back into I-It relating. Buber notes that the 'bad' person is 'lightly touched by the holy, primary word'. (Buber, 1958: 30). His way of thinking gives us the construct that, if the evil person declines to say 'Thou', the disturbed person can no longer find Thou. We are invited to a phenomenological description of the experience of, and an act of empathy towards, those who might be called mad.

2. EXISTENTIAL ANGST

Paul Tillich (1952) argues that in order to have the courage to exist, we necessarily have to affirm ourselves in the face of that which limits our very being. For Tillich, threat comes as either relative or absolute, in three pairs corresponding to the categories—being, the spiritual and the moral. His three pairs are fate and death; emptiness and meaninglessness; guilt and condemnation. The category error here is in mistaking the threat for the reality. Let us for a moment suppose that killing is evil in a moral or theological or ethical sense. In order for evil to be perpetrated, then the killing—or at least its serious contemplation—must take place. Yet, Tillich's point is that anxiety arises from the on-going awareness of our own finitude:

> The anxiety of death is the permanent horizon within which the anxiety of fate is at work. (Tillich, 1952: 43)

In other words, the anxiety over our own finitude echoes whenever we meet versions of that finitude in others. Guilt, meaninglessness and fate all lead us back to our mortality. The anxiety of the client leads us to our own existential angst, and thus it is only too natural to feel and experience others' disturbance as, in some incoherent but powerful way, evil. We find the shudder and know it.

3. PROJECTIVE IDENTIFICATION

Throughout her life Melanie Klein above any other developed the concept of projective identification as a description of one of the classic defences in which we all indulge. (Klein, 1946, for example.) Projection is simply the attributing of feelings or other experiencing to another, when it belongs to one's self. For instance, if I feel tired but cannot acknowledge that in the face of much work, I will tend to see tiredness in others, and react powerfully to it. Projective identification goes a step beyond this. The other experiences subliminal signalling which induces in them a required behaviour. In the face of some pathological patterns, this is a marked and difficult experience. In meeting in a pastoral context the person who I have most sincerely wanted to label as a psychopath, I felt an overwhelming sense of fear within seconds of our first exchange, as if being backed into a corner. The defensive structure of the other will evoke experiences in me. From time to time, these can be felt as invasive, threatening, malign. They are, however, mere defences! The category error is engaged. The psychopath is seen as evil.

4. THE SYSTEM IS MORE THAN THE SUM OF ITS CONTENTS

The life work of R. D. Laing was in challenging the medical model version of schizophrenia. In his 1964 book with A. Esterson, he explores through a number of interviews with families the possibility that schizophrenia is a manifestation in one member of a family of the dysfunction of the whole family unit. In other words, one individual has to become ill, like a scapegoat, to carry the dysfunction of the whole group. In some situations, the scapegoat is driven out into the desert of loneliness, meaninglessness and blame. They become 'evil'. It is easy for the therapist to collude with the system against the individual; once the phenomenon is uncovered, it is just as easy to reverse this splitting off, by blaming the family instead. Complex systemic interactions multiply the category error.

5. PARALLEL PROCESS

The everyday supervision of counsellors provides a more banal example of the category error. In the classic supervision text, Hawkins and Shohet observe:

> In the mode of paralleling, the processes at work currently in the relationship between client and therapist are uncovered through how they are reflected in the relationship between therapist and supervisor. (Hawkins and Shohet, 1989: 68)

The parallel process is a major way of exploring those elements of the counselling relationship that seem not to be available to the direct awareness of either the supervisor or the therapist in the first instance. Typically, I may note that the supervisee is behaving in an unusual manner: Is this how it is with the client? Yet, from time to time, the parallel process will manifest itself in my awareness of my own feelings: I really do not like this client of yours! Of course, these feelings can be just about bad supervision: I want to rescue my supervisee from a tight corner by demonising the client. However, on other occasions, the important and revealing question is: How does my feeling real distaste for your client echo with how they are with you? My internal process temporarily consigns the client to the category 'evil'—or a weaker form of that, such as difficult-to-accept, or aggressive, or manipulative or whatever. This is another version of the category error, but if I can be aware of it, it can put into the supervisory matrix useful information in the form of how the supervisee reacts to—owns or denies—my category error.

In short, there are a large number of theoretical concepts from different schools of therapy that can elucidate the category error by which certain structures or processes in the client are experienced—temporarily or otherwise—as evil. The whole point is that the therapist, in meeting the client at depth, needs to be aware of the impact of this category error. This is about personal development within the therapist, the developing of the need to contain and 'exorcise' the anxiety that is felt in the face of the client. The objectification of client-symptoms has exactly the opposite effect to the desired one. The aim is to renormalise the client within the therapist's awareness, and thus within her own awareness.

RUTH

Ruth was a primary school deputy head from a local village. We worked together for nearly two years. She was thirty-seven and single. Although very intelligent and an able and respected teacher, she experienced long-term depression and occasional self-harm and suicidal ideation. Her issues were from childhood—deeply depressed and non-communicative mother combined with some very painful bullying in secondary school. Yet, what seemed to haunt the early days of therapy, for me, was her self-presentation. On entering my workroom, she moved from being a crisply smart professional woman to being a six-year-old child. Her whole body language was that of late infancy. She twirled her hair, shuffled, yawned, squirmed in her seat, stretched out her hands, fiddled with her fingers and in every way undermined who she appeared to be.

More striking even than her behaviour was my embarrassed incongruence before it. It was the most powerful statement in the room, and yet I did not know how to get it back to her in a consumable form. One of us, perhaps both of us, had got me stuck. I was stuck with her stuckness at an early age. It was the very bizarreness of it that got in my way. It made me feel as if anything I might say to her that was honest would also be devastatingly hurtful.

In the end, the clue, the prod, the constructive moment came from her. She told me about doing an evening class in drama (which would be very helpful for her curriculum development work). She liked the drama teacher. She said that he teased her. There was a pregnant pause. Well, if he could, perhaps I could. If the therapist cannot be creative, then it must be up to the client. Ruth and I developed a whole dialogue about her experience of herself as 'odd'. Yes, in spite of the assumed behaviour of a competent professional, odd was how she felt—different, vulnerable, just not like anyone else. At last she had provided me with the elbowroom in which to empathise with this aspect of her—the little girl frozen before her mother's need and isolation. Her reaction, her self-concept was no longer 'odd', but rather just what she would have felt in the past, the distant past.

Ruth had managed to surround herself with a wall of others' incongruence. Her bizarre self-presentation expressed her self-experience. Others, like me, moved politely by on the other side and did not face up to what she screamed out. As the oddness-dialogue opened up, Ruth's whole way of being was normalised, not by her coming to conform straight away to more socially acceptable patterns, but by her seeing her current behaviour and emotional experience as normal. That is to say, she was not just different—as if ill—but rather she could work her way agonisingly towards acknowledging that in some aspects she had had an impossible life to live as a child. Emotional pressure at school could find no relief at home, where her prime carer was dominated by her own sense of neediness. There are many ways in which we might speak of the client becoming renormalised. It is a distortion to see this as a readjusting of the client. Rather it is a change of relationship between the client and her environment.

RENORMALISATION

Renormalisation occurs in three matrices: the internal world of the client; the flow of communication between the client and others; the radical encounter within the therapist of the phenomena that the client presents. However, these three matrices are not functionally distinct. Change happens in complex ways.

Pre-Therapy (Prouty et al., 2002) appears to address the communication process between the therapist and client in enabling psychological contact to happen. However, in so doing this renormalises the internal world of the client. The client experiences through the concrete reflections of the therapist her location, her rootedness in her surroundings. Her internal world changes. Instead of imprisonment in the self, the possibility opens up of exploring the leading of an impossible life—Shlien (1961) and Laing and Esterson (1964/1990).

Yet, these changes have a massive impact upon the therapist, who becomes increasingly able to enter the client's frame of reference, not least in coming to experience the client's way of processing with deeper empathy (Worsley, 2002). Margaret Warner (2002) describes her work with Luke, a young man with a diagnosis of schizophrenia, as the learning of a new language before it became possible to understand Luke as if from within. She noted the he tended to be both over-exact and quite imprecise in his use of language. For example, when someone observed that Catholicism was 'going to the dogs', Luke, a Catholic, spent quite a while in self-observation so as to note how and when he would begin to metamorphose into a dog. From this Warner develops her two key concepts of meta-facts and meta-causes.

> While meta-facts and meta-causes usually seem implausible as accounts of literal truth, they often work quite well as metaphors that serve as handles for his felt sense of the whole of his situation. (Warner, 2002: 463)

Why does Warner develop the notion of meta-facts and meta-causes? One feasible enough answer is that this contributes to her understanding of Luke's process. Yet, another version of this is to note that it gives Margaret Warner a handle on the therapeutic task of listening. In understanding Luke's process, she minimises the negative impact of that process upon her.

Lisbeth Sommerbeck (2003: 85) describes eloquently the effect of the psychotic client upon her. Because the client's talk is often fragmented and dissociated, then Sommerbeck notes that her literal empathic responses take on this quality too. She begins to experience the client's level of disturbance within her interventions. In working with manic clients she reports that she will often cry out: 'Wait a minute! Let me see if I understand you ... ' It is as if the client's chaotic process has to be seized in order to be rendered bearable, and only then comprehensible, to the therapist. (Sommerbeck points out that this sense of immersion in chaotic process can occur at times with non-psychotic clients too.)

The point of this brief summary of the complex process of renormalisation is that it is a false defence to see the process as only happening either within the client or within the communication process. The therapist too must face the impact of the client upon her, and seek to ameliorate its effects through ongoing personal development.

It is no wonder that the category error sometimes occurs that causes us to experience some pathological patterns as if evil—the shudder. It is at least better to use this series of defences than to drive the client out into the wilderness of the categories of the medical model misused. At the heart of work with challenging clients is the therapist's openness to facing who they are.

CONCLUSION

The rhetoric of evil is an important part of the internal discourse for the therapist concerning the impact upon her of the whole of the client, including those aspects often referred to as psychopathological. The medical model reduces the role of the helper in contact with the client to that of the expert who keeps herself safe by distancing and objectifying the client's extreme and disturbing distress. Yet, it is a most valuable insight of the Person-Centred Approach that what we term psychopathological in human beings is also the unique and undiagnosable response of a human being to her environment. When the therapist can remain open to the impact of the client upon her, she will be available to share in the journey towards renormalisation, and then integration and wholeness. To avoid the evil, however understandable, is to demonise the distressed person. The Other is forced to carry that which I cannot face. So much of the medicalisation of human distress is designed unconsciously to keep the medic safe, at the cost of the client's humanity.

REFERENCES

Barrett-Lennard, GT (1998) *Carl Rogers' Helping System: Journey and substance*. London: Sage.

Buber, M (1958) *I and Thou*. Edinburgh: C and C Clark.

Buber, M (1961) *Between Man and Man*. London: Collins.

DSM-IV (1994) *Diagnostic and Statistical Manual of Mental Disorders (fourth edition)*. Washington DC: American Psychiatric Association.

Hawkins, P and Shohet, R (1989) *Supervision in the Helping Professions*. Milton Keynes: Open University Press.

Klein, M (1946) Notes on some schizoid mechanisms. In H Segal (ed) (1988) *Envy and Gratitude: and other works 1946–1963 — Melanie Klein.* London: Virago.

Laing, RD (1961) *Self and Others:* Harmondsworth: Penguin.

Laing, RD and Esterson, A (1964/1990) *Sanity, Madness and the Family.* Harmondsworth: Penguin.

May, R (1969) *Love and Will.* New York: WW Norton.

May, R (1982) The problem of evil: An open letter to Carl Rogers. *Journal of Humanistic Psychology,* 22, 10–21.

Mearns, D and Thorne, B (2000) *Person-Centred Therapy Today: New frontiers in theory and practice.* London: Sage.

Menzies, IEP (1970) *The Functioning of Social Systems as a Defence Against Anxiety.* London: The Tavistock Institute.

Parkin, D (ed) (1985) *The Anthropology of Evil.* Oxford: Basil Blackwell.

Prouty, G, Van Werde, D and Pörtner, M (2002) *Pre-Therapy: Reaching contact-impaired clients.* Ross-on-Wye: PCCS Books.

Purton, C (1998) Unconditional positive regard and its spiritual implications. In B Thorne and E Lambers (1998) *Person-Centred Therapy: A European perspective* (pp. 23–37). London: Sage.

Shlien, JM (1961) A client-centered approach to schizophrenia: First approximation. In A Burton (ed) *Psychotherapy of the Psychoses.* New York: Basic. Reproduced in P Sanders (ed) (2003) *To Lead an Honorable Life: Invitations to think about client-centered therapy and the person-centered approach.* Ross-on-Wye: PCCS Books.

Sommerbeck, L (2003) *The Client-Centred Therapist in Psychiatric Contexts: A therapists' guide to the psychiatric landscape and its inhabitants.* Ross-on-Wye: PCCS Books.

Tillich, P (1952) *The Courage To Be.* New Haven: Yale University Press.

Ward, T and Mann, R (2004) Good lives and the rehabilitation of offenders: A positive approach to sex offender treatment. In P A Linley and S Joseph (eds) *Positive Psychology in Practice* (pp. 598–616). Hoboken, NJ: Wiley.

Warner, MS (2002) Luke's dilemma: a client-centered/experiential model of processing with a schizophrenic thought disorder. In JC Watson, RN Goldman and MS Warner (eds) *Client-Centered and Experiential Psychotherapy in the 21st Century: Advances in theory, research and practice* (pp. 459–72). Ross-on-Wye: PCCS Books.

Worsley, R (1996) *Human Freedom and the Logic of Evil: Prolegomenon to a Christian theology of evil.* Basingstoke: MacMillan.

Worsley, R (2002) *Process Work in Person-Centred Therapy: Phenomenological and existential perspectives.* Basingstoke: Palgrave.

Chapter 11

FACING PSYCHOTIC FUNCTIONING: PERSON-CENTRED CONTACT WORK IN RESIDENTIAL PSYCHIATRIC CARE

Dion Van Werde

In the early nineties, Professor Germain Lietaer (1990) pointed out a new trend in person-centred/experiential psychotherapy: there is now a greater differentiation between varied client populations and settings. Along these lines, and after several years of practice and refinement, I will give you some examples of our way of working with people suffering psychotic functioning.

I will start with introducing Prouty's Pre-Therapy, our major source of inspiration. Basically, Prouty defines contact as the antidote to psychotic alienation and formulates a way of restoring impaired contact functioning. I will describe how on our ward, this approach has been translated into a multidisciplinary contact-milieu to serve clients who are recovering from a psychotic breakdown and in the process of strengthening their contact-functioning.

Pre-Therapy was originally formulated in relation to severe contact-loss, and applied to different kinds of populations and in different settings (e.g. Prouty 1976, 1994; Prouty, Van Werde and Pörtner 2002, Krietemeyer and Prouty 2003; Coffeng 2001; Peters 1999; Pörtner 2000; Sommerbeck 2003; Van Werde 2002a, 2002b, 2004; Van Werde and Morton 1999). In this chapter, I want to highlight that a person-centred conceptualisation and practice proves to be possible in a residential setting and with clients who have a milder form of contact-loss, for instance those recovering from or fighting against the threat of psychotic breakdown. Mutatis mutandis, the ideas behind this practice can be transposed to work with other kinds of endangered contact-functioning.

PROUTY'S PRE-THERAPY

Dr Garry Prouty's work can be considered as a theoretical evolution in person-centred/experiential psychotherapy (Prouty 1994). Rogers (1957) had considered 'contact' as the first of the six necessary and sufficient conditions for constructive personality change. When starting his clinical work, Prouty however discovered that the clients he worked with in those days were not able to engage in a therapeutic relationship since contact in itself was problematic. Hence, a kind of pre-relationship activity was necessary before entering regular Rogerian psychotherapy. Clients Prouty worked with seemed unable to touch their experiences, if not being completely affectively frozen. This echoes with Eugene Gendlin's consideration of the concrete and bodily felt process of experiencing as the key issue in psychotherapy. Prouty consequently stated that pre-experiencing activity was needed to unfreeze frozen affective functioning so that people could access their inner life again. Pre-Therapy thus can be defined as pre-relationship and pre-experiencing activity.

In this respect, the notion of pre-expressive functioning (Prouty 1998) is highly important. It is an intuitive and heuristic concept derived from Prouty's personal experience, as well as from clinical and quantitative case studies of Pre-Therapy. It points to disorganised and incoherent experiencing as capable of being transformed into a meaningful pattern. In that respect, Prouty considers all symptomatic behaviour as a manifestation of relationship- and feeling-efforts, even though not yet on an expressive level. If the caregiver is able to work with these forms of functioning, the person might be able to develop into expressiveness and thus access relationship formation and experiential functioning. The use of the notion 'pre' indicates a highly therapeutic vision, since it underlines the teleological capacity of symptomatology: symptoms carry in themselves the key to understanding and meaning. If, for example, a man is standing in the corridor, face anxious, looking to the ceiling and addresses you when passing by with the words, 'Do you hear them?', this can be seen as somebody trying to relate by asking a question and trying to pre-experientially 'express' his fear by his facial expression, the tone of his voice and his physical closeness to you. Even when he is not conscious of how he looks and how he gives away his inner world by his appearance and behaviour, it is obvious that this man is trying to deal with the strange experiences he has and the consequent feelings he is suffering from. His contacting you is a significant moment in a possible process of disclosure of everything that is locked up in the alienating symptomatology of experiencing auditory hallucinations.

In Pre-Therapy, the therapist uses five kinds of reflections through which the client is invited to (re)contact reality, affect and other people. Contact reflections are extraordinarily literal and concrete reflections that aim to reach the severely withdrawn or regressed client. Through the technique of reflecting, the realities of world, self and others are offered in a non-directive yet very concrete, non-judgemental, non-evaluative and non-interpretative mode. The Pre-Therapy reflections are attuned to the low level of contact functioning of the client. The caregiver and reality are hereby allowed by the client to bridge into his or her idiosyncratic world. If the client permits himself to contact the reality that is mentioned in a reflection ('you are standing in the corridor', 'you look scared', 'you look into my eyes and ask whether I hear them'), this means that he has already come out of his idiosyncratic, sheltered position a little bit, and has let the world and the one who verbalises it come in. He has recognised that he is on the ward corridor, that he is addressing the nurse and that, in doing so, he has been showing and sharing some of his psychotic functioning for maybe the first time. This is individual Pre-Therapy. Basically, the client now can freely choose to stay in his reality or engage in a shared reality. This latter reality can be about outer and 'objective' realities such as people, places, events and things, or it can be about communication with others, but it can also be about contacting his own inner feelings. The five kinds of contact-reflections as defined by Prouty (1976) are:

1. SR: Situational Reflection, reflects the client's situation, environment or milieu. People, places, events and things are reflected to facilitate reality-contact, for example, 'a wooden chair', 'the sun is shining in', 'Bea is entering the room'.
2. FR: Facial Reflection, reflects pre-expressive feeling embodied in the face to facilitate affective contact, for instance, 'your eyes are wet', 'Céline smiles'.
3. BR: Body Reflection, reflects with words or through mimicking with his own body, the movements or positioning of the client. It helps clients to integrate body expression within the sense of self, for example, 'you are making a fist' or making and upholding a fist, just as the client does, or combining the two ways.
4. WWR: Word for Word Reflection, reflects single words, sentence fragments and other verbal disorganisation, to develop communicative contact. E.g. '(mumble), wood, (mumble), three, (mumble)', the therapist reflects 'wood, three', even if the meaning is not clear.
5. RR: Reiterative Reflection, repeats previous reflections that proved to make contact. It helps to re-contact the client.

Contact reflections (what the therapist does) facilitate the contact functions (client process) which result in the emergence of contact behaviours (which can be measured).

Once overall contact is (re)established, people can shift to more classical psychotherapy or enjoy the restored contact as it is and profit from the possibilities this holds. Prouty (personal communication) mentions a young woman with special needs who was granted permission to go to her mother at weekends again, after she—with the help of a Pre-Therapy treatment—became able to contact her feelings of anger and even express them, so preventing herself from unexpected explosions of feeling, causing repeated unreliable behaviour and management problems within this one-parent family.

PRE-THERAPY APPLIED IN A RESIDENTIAL WARD SETTING

Since we are working on a treatment ward in residential care for people with psychotic presentation, the question arose of how to translate Prouty's individual method into our setting and our specific client group. Within a rather traditional medical environment, we created the necessary space to formulate an explicit person-centred approach and apply Pre-Therapy whenever indicated. Of course, on our ward, the larger percentage of what happens and has to be done is quite similar to comparable wards anywhere else. Medication has to be distributed, people have to be motivated, beds have to be made, therapies offered, educational sessions given, visitors welcomed and so on. The Person-Centred Approach and the skill of working along the lines of Prouty's Pre-Therapy, however, bring about a different quality in the care given: the interactions, the overall atmosphere and the design of the therapy. We compare the impact of this with the impact of the leaven in the bread. A small adjunctive element can cause a big qualitative difference in the outcome. Seventy or more per cent of the work basically remains the same, whatever approach you follow, whatever therapeutic song you sing. The specifically person-centred element represents only thirty per cent or less of the whole work. It is that thirty per cent which makes the difference. In our situation, this means that staff need to be trained in Pre-Therapy and schooled in contact-facilitation. This is to say that a new vision can be integrated, which does not alter the everyday activities very much, and yet can have an enormous, determining impact on the essence and outlook of the care that is given.

The level of functioning of the clients on our ward can be situated at a grey-zone level. We use that term to describe a level in between 'up in the air' psychotic functioning versus well-rooted, so-called 'anchored' functioning. Typical of this level is that characteristics of pre-expressive as well as of expressive behaviour alternate rapidly or are even present simultaneously. A client described to me his weekend visit home in terms of '… so and so Mr Devil, and then I went to the shop to buy some stuff for dinner, Mr Devil, and my wife said, … ' He clearly every now and then mixed everyday reality with his idiosyncratic psychotic reality. Another client, asked a nurse, 'Are they coming to get me?' in a very slow monotone voice, and on the one hand talked about the reality of the schedule for leaving to go home, but at the same time, she was psychotically anxious about being taken away by God-knows-who to be killed. Each reality clouded the other and they were present together. It was thought that there was incest in that family, so the uncertainty about the hour of being picked up by her parents (father?) probably triggered the remembrance of the other reality of being suddenly visited or taken away, and as a result, this pushed her into a 'grey-zone' blend of asking a realistic question, but mixed with paranoid psychotic experiencing.

In general, both sides of this transition zone need to be dealt with, need a contact-offer. The people we work with are recovering from the most acute phase of contact-loss of their psychotic breakdown and are struggling to have their contact functioning restored. So they not only need our continuous support to overcome the still intimidating psychosis on the one hand, but can also profit from a contact strengthening offer to fortify their newly regained but still fragile anchorage in shared reality, so that they can build up their healthy functioning further.

First contact needs to be established and then more functional functioning becomes possible—participating in group activities, making arrangements for the coming weekend, getting together for coffee, dressing or clearing the table, emptying the dishwasher and so on.

I will highlight some applications of Pre-Therapy in facing psychosis as we do it on our ward. I also hope to spell out what it means to create a contact-milieu (see also Van Werde p. 61–120 in Prouty, Van Werde and Pörtner, 2002).

In our contact offer, we make a difference between spontaneous and informal use of Pre-Therapy reflections as described in this contribution, versus more structured contact work on the ward (ibid). Needless to say that looking at people through the spectacles of 'contact' has had an important influence on how we design and deliver our services.

161

It is not so easy to put across this kind of work to others. In general, when speaking about the praxis of Pre-Therapy, and especially when reflections are written down, they tend to look mechanical and a mere repetition of the client. Beautiful moments of delicate interaction, receptiveness of the existential situation, the required discipline and concentration, and the relatively distant playfulness combined with a sincere and close compassion are hard to transfer onto paper. The poetry and the art tend to get lost. Therefore we recommend combining the reading of texts such as this one with exposure to Pre-Therapy carried out by dedicated and experienced therapists, who have had feedback about their work by Prouty himself, who regularly present their work for peer supervision to the members of the Pre-Therapy International Network and annually attend the Network's meeting in order to stay up-to-date with what is happening with Pre-Therapy around the globe.

This chapter is attempting to illustrate the benefits to be had from understanding and knowing how to use Pre-Therapy and Pre-Therapy reflections, especially in dealing with people recovering from psychosis or people trying to avoid drifting away towards a full-blown psychosis again. I will call this 'contact work' rather than psychotherapy or Pre-Therapy. I will give some very practical examples about how this contact work can be an overarching concept in an individual session and how reflecting can be integrated in daily nurse-patient interactions.

UNDERSTANDING CONTACT WORK IN AN INDIVIDUAL CONSULTATION

Tina, is an ex-patient of our ward. She comes unexpectedly to my office for advice. She asks me a direct question: 'What can I do, so I don't become psychotic again?' Previous psychotic functioning seemed to be re-surfacing and is making her anxious. The same topics tend to flood her daily functioning: she is delusional about the media and suffers from feelings of guilt about things that had happened in the past. At the same time she seems relatively anchored: she can ask a question; understands that she had to wait half an hour before I could talk with her since I was busy with an other appointment; has contact with the growing threat of losing contact and so on. This functioning on these two levels simultaneously is typical of the population we serve.

She starts by telling me the story of her first psychosis again. She has been educated in media, is gifted at drawing, and has been very keen to work in audiovisual media. Once she was in love with a man who looked like a TV-newsreader (the anchorman). She starts sending him CDs, writing him letters and phoning him frequently. This behaviour increases. Finally, the man sues her for stalking. The lawsuit says that she must stop. Frightened by this verdict, she backs off. Later, she finds herself falling in love with a newsreader from a national network when she sees him reading an item about a matter of jurisdiction. She starts sending packages to the network with all kinds of graphics, CDs and messages. At work—she designs websites—she continuously feels spied upon by TV people and fears for her life. Her functioning becomes problematic. At her brother's one night, she says the newsreader on television asked a newspaper about what was on her mind. This is too much for her. She cannot bear it any longer and wants to find out what was going on. She decides to be admitted.

We continue to look at what is going on now. She tells how her past is coming back and about how this destabilises her. She feels, for example, confused about what the people who she sent the packages to a year ago have done with them. 'I don't know what they did with my mail. I have put everything of myself in it,' she says. 'It was full of very personal thoughts and hopes.' She also sees things on television that others can't see. 'Sometimes they look away from the camera. I frightened them.' She also feels guilty about the mail and is 'inclined to examine everything carefully'. Obviously, she is suffering from a mixture of realities which she lives in: the psychotic past, and the actual.

To complete the picture of how her life looks, we decide to make an inventory of the things that are not burdening her and that even give her joy and support. She sums them up: sleeping, to wake up in the morning, eating, going to the solarium, writing Christmas cards, decorating the Christmas tree, buying presents. She also likes housework such as doing the dishes and cleaning her room. Her job still gives her satisfaction as well. Sports such as swimming with others is still fine. When she doesn't quarrel with her friend, this contact is welcome too. She even makes plans for the future—looking for an internship, developing her CV, engaging in voluntary work—and this perspective helps her. Bringing all this together, we can recognise the so-called pre-expressive, grey-zone intermediate and anchored functioning. Respectively, they appeared as answers to the questions, 'Where do you come from and how has it been before?' 'What is threatening you?' 'What are your present doubts and fears?' 'What are your resources?' The conclusion that she formulates after having looked at her past and present contact functioning is that when talking about it, she clearly felt the difference between healthy and constructive versus difficult contents and actions. She states: 'I'd better stop letting myself be sucked into areas that can make me psychotic (again)', 'I'd better focus and direct myself to anchoring'. The conversation helped to strengthen her contact functioning and indirectly proved to be beneficial in reducing psychotic symptomatology. She got an overview and could decide herself which direction to go from there. She chose to invest in building up strength and to stay away from the quicksand of psychotic ideation. In contact terminology, we would say that the client herself realised that anchoring and contact-loss are directly and inversely related. Investing in building up strength prevented her from getting psychotic again.

NURSES BRIDGING INDIVIDUAL PROCESS AND WARD STRUCTURE

The following vignettes are taken from a video presentation the nursing staff made to illustrate how they are influenced by Pre-Therapy in their daily work, especially when working with clients functioning in the 'grey zone' between an anchored and an idiosyncratic/psychotic level. The art of making contact here requires the capacity to estimate and work on the same contact level as the client, and then slowly shift upwards towards congruent communication, once the contact is established and becoming more solid. Unlike the previous example, nurses live and deal with 'objective' or 'shared' reality all the time. In concrete terms, this means that besides reaching the client, they also have to take care of ward organisation, and especially help the client consent to and participate in it, even when afraid, or not understanding, withdrawn, bizarre, unmotivated. This requires a continuous building of bridges, particularly when the people are only just re-anchoring to the world that they were losing grip of, or that they were pulling themselves back from. So, the idea is to first make contact and then address surrounding reality together.

1. MAKING ARRANGEMENTS FOR THE COMING WEEKEND

The nurse enters the room of An—a patient—to call her for the coffee break, where she is expected. A bridge has to be built between ward life and the patient who sits alone in her room. On the one hand, An looks frozen, doesn't show feelings or comment on the things on her mind, doesn't react to a directly asked question and sits in her room like this for hours. On the other hand, going to the ward presupposes things like drinking coffee together, participating in the therapies on offer and responding to questions the nurses ask concerning, for instance, the arrangements made for the coming weekend. The nurse tries to bridge both sides of the given situation by making contact with An first, and then going over to the nurses' agenda about finding out when exactly An wants to leave the hospital for the weekend and when she will be back.

To do this, the nurse stays with the concrete. In the beginning it is in the format of mere Pre-Therapy reflecting. Later on, the level of functioning permits carefully asked questions. The nurse continuously estimates the level of contact functioning of the client and shifts her level up when this seems appropriate. This then takes the form of concrete questions or congruent remarks, but always centres on the here and now so as not to lose the client.

The reflections or first tentative questions can be about something that they see through the window (for example, SR:[1] 'Outside the room people are walking'; 'It's started raining again.'), about something that happened just before this encounter (RR: 'At noon, I came to get you and you were sitting in exactly the same position as you are sitting now.') or happened yesterday ('Did your son give you his little teddy bear that you are holding in your hand now, to bring with you to the hospital?'). Sometimes the client herself is addressed, be it her body position (BR: 'Your elbow is on the table.', 'You're sitting like you were at noon.'), the expression on her face (FR: 'You sigh … like you're thinking …'), or the words she starts to speak (WWR: 'Letting go hurts …', 'I can't let it go, mustn't ever let it go'). The Facial Reflection 'You sigh' opens the door to her contacting and expressing feeling. She thaws a little bit and makes eye contact. Her contact level improves and makes a question-answer interaction possible. They finally

---

1. See page 160 for key to abbreviations.

can talk about the arrangements made for the weekend. The client now is ready to leave her corner by the bed, and they can go for coffee in the living room together.

2. BIZARRE LAUGHING IN THE TELEVISION ROOM

Tine and Freya are watching television. Christophe (the nurse) comes over to sit with them for five minutes and asks if they would be willing to help him set the table for dinner later. Freya occasionally gives a sudden laugh without objective reason and mumbles words, spoken to herself. The nurse talks to Tine about the television programme she is watching and reflects to Freya when she is laughing and mumbling. By doing so, the situation seems contained. There is care for the structure on the one hand: Tine is talked to and the laughing is seen and dealt with by reflections. The empathic, accepting and non-judgemental non-interpretative contact offered to Freya on the other hand, can help her to get in touch with mounting affect, to realise where she is, how she is behaving and how it looks to her fellow patient and the nursing staff. Once she is in contact with all this, she can perhaps start mastering the situation and herself more.

When the nurse in the end asks for cooperation, Tine is willing to help and even Freya seems to understand that Tine is willing to help, thus coming out of her private world a little.

3. OVERCOMING CLOUDED DELUSIONAL FUNCTIONING

A middle-aged woman is recovering from a depression with psychotic features. She has a delusion of poverty: everything is gone, empty, broken or has ended. For a while she is convinced her husband has died, although this is not the case.

On another occasion, she sees the dishwasher full and stands motionless and frozen in front of it with three cups in her hand, not knowing what to do.

In this fragment, Jo, the nurse, contacts her by reflecting what she is doing (SR: 'You are laying the table'; BR and SR: 'You are standing here, with a little box and spoons in your hand '; WWR: 'You say: there aren't enough spoons in the box!') and how she looks (FR: 'You look puzzled', 'It is like you are asking a question'). This enables the woman to contact herself more, and consequently become more grounded, be it still fragile contact. Once this first contact is established, the nurse than turns to the reality of what has to be done. By asking cup by cup if a spoon is already there, the patient realises that every cup already has a spoon. So, the delusional thought of not having enough spoons for every cup diminishes by contacting and anchoring in reality step-by- step and cup-by-cup. Only in this way could the woman grasp the whole situation and could see and conclude that everything was OK. The nurse continues the contact-strengthening work and invites the woman to go to the kitchen with her to fetch sugar and milk to put on the table.

DISCUSSION

By constantly paying attention to the contact-level of the client, we discovered how complex therapeutic progress can be. We now hypothesise that distinction can be made between the level of contact with reality, contact with affect and contact with others (communicative contact). It is probable that, in a psychotherapeutic process, these three contact functions do not necessarily have an identical evolution. What is important for us at this point is the idea that maybe reality-, affective- and communicative-contact can be separately influenced. This is significant, in particular if we think of ward-settings where there are a lot of opportunities to have nurses focus on and work with reality and communication on a daily basis. Contact can be worked with. Theoretically, this also bridges the supposed gap often complained of in person-centred care, between following individual process ('being with') or working with the given reality ('doing with'). Within the borders of our specific setting, without losing the person-centred attitude, and by always taking the very concrete as the starting point for any action, the two inversely related realities are synthetically worked with. You reflect to restore, or you practice to strengthen the poor contact functioning.

We continuously try to steer the patients (and ourselves) away from a therapist-patient interaction that is characterised by interpreting, taking over, controlling, structuring, product-focusing, judging, authoritarianism; from an activity that is characterised by being repetitive, superficial, empty, dull, obligatory; from a level of functioning that is psychotic, inhibited, bizarre, isolated, non-accessible, insecure, covered-up and frozen; towards a functioning that is experiential, anchored, in-touch, shared, decided, active, creative, varied, concentrated, enjoyed and in process.

The treatment of choice is to look for contact and work with that part of a person that is (still or already) rooted and operative, however small that part may be. We ally ourselves with that part that can congruently deal with the situation or that still has some strength left. As a psychotherapist or contact-facilitator, we try to make contact, strengthen the anchorage and help the person to gradually master the situation again. The reasoning is that 'when contact increases, symptoms decrease'. We strive to communicate with patients and their families about how we think and what we do and why, to explain, for example, to clients why participating in all kinds of therapies is important. It helps them to strengthen their contact-functioning and thus indirectly reduces psychosis as well.

Sometimes it is hard to grasp the pattern of change in a patient. Maybe at a given moment, the patient suffers more chaos and is threatening to the ward structure; because old psychological patterns are challenged, then a process of problematic experiencing starts up again and, consequently, a new personal equilibrium has to be found. Working on the strengthening of the contact-functions however, does not mean that we lose sight of our responsibilities for managing the individual patient and the ward as a whole. Reality is presented and is worked with, even when this means confronting or temporarily restricting the patient. Pre-Therapy and contact work in general do help to bridge these two interests. As a matter of fact and as previously stated, when contact increases, symptoms decrease, and the patient as a consequence 'fits' the structure better.

Basic in all this thinking about the translation of the contact paradigm into establishing a person-centred milieu is that we try not to deny psychosis, nor hide it, nor patronise the client. In line with the thoughts of Garry Prouty, we see psychotic behaviour as pre-expressive behaviour. That means that we look at such behaviour as a way of the client expressing meanings that are there, but not yet fully in process, nor available to the person himself. Thinking in terms of 'contact' and using the Pre-Therapy reflections when indicated serves as an overall source of inspiration and a vehicle for concrete staff-patient interactions. Our interventions can be aimed at either restoring absent contact, or at strengthening the newly recovered but still fragile contact. It is interesting to note that these efforts can be made without neglecting the other tasks that have to be done on the ward. It also helps to make more appropriate observations from within a phenomenological attitude (meaning without immediate labelling, interpreting or judging patients and their behaviour). It becomes a natural way of looking at, thinking about, interacting and working with the patients. Bringing all this together in the multidisciplinary setting of a ward milieu can be considered as an advancement in the person-centred method and as an expansion of Pre-Therapy practice.

REFERENCES

Coffeng, T (2001) Contact in the therapy of trauma and dissociation. In G Wyatt and P Sanders (eds) *Rogers' Therapeutic Conditions: Evolution, theory and practice. Volume 4: Contact and Perception* (pp. 153–67). Ross-on-Wye: PCCS Books.

Krietemeyer, B and Prouty, G (2003) The art of psychological contact: The psychotherapy of a mentally retarded psychotic client. *Person-Centered and Experiential Psychotherapies, 2*, 151–61.

Lietaer, G (1990) The client-centered approach after the Wisconsin project: A personal view on its evolution. In G Lietaer, J Rombauts and R Van Balen (eds) *Client-Centered and Experiential Psychotherapy in the Nineties* (pp. 19–45). Leuven: Leuven University Press.

Peters, H (1999) Pre-Therapy: a client-centered experiential approach to mentally handicapped people. *Journal of Humanistic Psychology, 39*, 8–29.

Pörtner, M (2000) *Trust and Understanding: The Person-Centered Approach to everyday care for people with special needs.* Ross-on-Wye: PCCS Books.

Prouty, G (1976) Pre-Therapy—a method of treating pre-expressive psychotic and retarded patients. *Psychotherapy: Theory, research and practice, 13*, 290–95.

Prouty, G (1994) *Theoretical evolutions in person-centered/experiential therapy. Applications to schizophrenic and retarded psychoses.* New York: Praeger.

Prouty, G (1998) Pre-Therapy and the pre-expressive self. *Person-Centered Practice, 6*, 80–8.

Prouty, G, Van Werde, D and Pörtner, M (2002) *Pre-Therapy: Reaching contact-impaired clients.* Ross-on-Wye: PCCS Books.

Rogers, C (1957) The necessary and sufficient conditions of therapeutic personality change. *Journal of Consulting Psychology, 2*, 95–103.

Sommerbeck, L (2003) *The Client-Centred Therapist in Psychiatric Contexts: A therapists' guide to the psychiatric landscape and its inhabitants.* Ross-on-Wye: PCCS Books.

Van Werde, D (2002a) Prouty's Pre-Therapy and contact-work with a broad range of persons' pre-expressive functioning. In G Wyatt and P Sanders (eds) *Rogers' Therapeutic Conditions: Evolution, theory and practice. Volume 4: Contact and Perception* (pp. 168–81). Ross-on-Wye: PCCS Books.

Van Werde, D (2002b) The falling man: Pre-Therapy applied to somatic hallucinating. *Person-Centred Practice, 10,* 101–7.

Van Werde, D (2004) Cliëntgericht werken met psychotisch functioneren. In M Leijssen and N Stinckens (eds) *Wijsheid in Gesprekstherapie* (pp. 209–24). Leuven: Universitaire Pers Leuven.

Van Werde, D and Morton, I (1999) The relevance of Prouty's Pre-Therapy to dementia care. In I Morton (ed) *Person-Centred Approaches to Dementia Care* (pp. 139–66). Bicester, Oxon: Winslow Press.

CHAPTER 12

ANTISOCIAL PERSONALITY DISORDER AND THE PERSON-CENTERED APPROACH

LESLIE A. MCCULLOCH

The occurrence and publicity of crime and interpersonal violence has generated much discussion regarding antisocial behaviors. Public health models focused on prevention have emerged to help define the 'antisocial behavior' problem, identify causes, develop and test interventions, implement interventions, and measure intervention effectiveness (Potter and Mercy, 1997). However, integrating and implementing psychotherapy into these intervention programs has been problematic. In particular, the Person-Centered Approach (PCA) has been dismissed with those individuals diagnosed with antisocial personality disorder ASPD. This chapter: (1) examines definitions of ASPD, (2) reviews the etiology of ASPD, (3) outlines the history of treatment of individuals diagnosed with ASPD, and (4) presents the Person-Centered Approach as a psychotherapeutic approach that is appropriate and indicated to ASPD characteristics, etiology, and treatment.

ANTISOCIAL PERSONALITY DISORDER DEFINED

Defining ASPD is a complex task, made difficult by the ambiguous implications and inferences attached to the phrase 'antisocial behavior', and by the breadth of behaviors included in the definition of ASPD in present clinical use. Adding to the confusion are terms such as psychopathic personality, dissocial/dissocial personality disorder, criminal personality, moral defect, psychopathic inferiority, psychopathy, and sociopathy; these terms have all been historically attached to what we now refer to as ASPD (Mish, 1996; Thomas, 1997; First and Tasman, 2004).

According to the *DSM-IV-TR* (American Psychiatric Association, 2000) personality disorders are defined as enduring patterns of inner experience and behavior, deviating markedly from the expectations of the individual's culture, and manifesting in two or more of the following areas: (1) cognition, (2) affect, (3) interpersonal functioning, and (4) impulse control. These enduring patterns are '... inflexible and pervasive across a broad range of personal and social situations' and lead to '... clinically significant impairment in social, occupational, or other important areas of functioning' (p. 633).

Specific to antisocial personality disorder (ASPD), there is a pervasive pattern of disregard and violation of the rights of others since 15 years of age, as indicated by at least three of the following: (1) repeated unlawful behavior for which one could be arrested, (2) deceitfulness such as lying, 'conning', or using aliases, (3) lack of impulse control, (4) irritability and aggressiveness as indicated by physical altercations, (5) recklessness with respect to self or others, (6) irresponsibility (shown in inconsistent financial obligations and work behaviors), and (7) rationalizing and lack of remorse for having hurt others (American Psychiatric Association, 2000). Such behaviors prior to age 15 years and continuing up to age 18 years are labeled as conduct disorder (after age 18 years the conduct disorder diagnosis would change to ASPD); if no symptoms occurred before age 18 years, but did occur in adulthood, the diagnosis would be adult antisocial behavior (American Psychiatric Association).

Along with the symptoms of ASPD come features which include a distrust of all authority figures (including therapists) and an orientation of resistance towards help, from self or others (Beck and Freeman, 1990; Carson, Butcher and Mineka, 1996; Maxmen and Ward, 1995). These features are so marked that subjects with ASPD are considered by some to be untreatable with standard psychotherapies (Zanarini and Gunderson, 1997). For example, Maxmen and Ward state that no therapy has been found to be effective, since people with ASPD '… have no desire to change, consider insights excuses, have no concept of the future, resent all authority figures (including therapists), view the patient role as pitiful, detest being in a position of inferiority, deem therapy a joke and therapists as objects to be conned, threatened, seduced, or used' (1995: 406). Carson et al. (1996) agree, stating that treatments of ASPD have generally not proven to be effective due to factors inherent in the antisocial personality, such as the inability to trust and empathize. These factors make prognosis poor, since therapy is a collaborative effort, requiring cooperation between client and therapist (Beck and Freeman, 1990; Carson et al., 1996; Gladding, 1996; Scharf, 1996).

DIFFICULTIES IN DEFINING ASPD

Although no other definition has come into widespread, clinical, and/or standardized use, objections to the current *DSM-IV-TR* definition of ASPD exist (Cooke, 1998; Rutter, 1997a; Wootton, 1959; Sexton and Griffin, 1997). It has been noted that defining antisocial behavior as against (anti-) the societal (social) norms (Mish, 1996; Thomas, 1997) is inconsistent, changeable, and value-laden (Cooke, 1998; Rutter, 1997a). For example, by defining antisocial behavior according to societal criteria, changes in the law could easily redefine what is considered antisocial (Rutter, 1997a). Such inconsistency in legal standards might result in varying criminal justice interpretations and sentencing for identical behavior. Furthermore, certain acts of 'breaking the law' such as protesting gender or race discrimination are often thought to be acts of civil disobedience of great principle; these acts are considered by many to be far from antisocial (Wootton, 1959). Additionally, social norms vary according to culture, and what might be considered antisocial in one culture, may very well be an acceptable form of behavior in another (Rutter, 1997a; Wootton, 1959).

The American Psychiatric Association admits that concerns have arisen regarding the misdiagnosis of antisocial behavior when the 'antisocial' criteria in question may have been protective survival strategies (American Psychiatric Association, 2000). The American Psychiatric Association suggests that in '… assessing antisocial traits, it is helpful for the clinician to consider the social and economic context in which the behaviors occur' (2000: 647). These cultural issues are further confounded when considering the white, male, Eurocentric orientation of Western social sciences, including the *DSM-IV-TR* (Sue, Sue and Sue, 1990).

Another concern regarding the *DSM-IV-TR* set of ASPD criteria is the implication of heterogeneity among individuals with ASPD; that is, that all people experiencing a particular disorder fall into generalized patterns within the established criteria (Luske, 1990). In fact, individuals exhibiting widely varied degrees of antisocial behavior may meet all the *DSM-IV-TR* ASPD criteria. Consider the following example: the definition of antisocial personality disorder applies to a twenty-five-year-old individual who has been reckless, irresponsible, and involved in physical altercations since age fifteen; as well as to a twenty-five-year-old who has been serial-killing human beings for a decade. While both individuals share common characteristics, each is substantially and obviously different.

ASPD definitional disparities are also apparent when considering gender differences in diagnosis. Similar behaviors exhibited by both males and females will often result in the diagnosis of ASPD for males, and borderline or histrionic personality disorder for the females (Widiger and Corbett, 1997; Zanarini and Gunderson, 1997). Women with ASPD tend to meet the criteria with nonviolent behaviors such as forgery, fraud, or theft; men with ASPD tend to meet the criteria with violent behaviors such as rape, assault, or murder (Ruegg, Haynes and Frances, 1997). It has been theorized that ASPD is not sex-role compatible for females. Instead, females tend to resort to behaviors meeting Histrionic or Borderline Personality Disorder criteria, which are more congruent with traditional female sex roles (Robins, 1966; Sue et al., 1990; Widiger and Corbitt, 1997; Zanarini and Gunderson, 1997). This theory may account, in part, for higher reported ASPD prevalence rates in males, and higher reported histrionic and borderline prevalence rates in females. Theorists also suggest that some clinicians view women differently than men and these gender biases result in higher ASPD diagnostic rates for males, and higher borderline/histrionic diagnostic rates in females (Tardiff, 1984, 1992, 1996; Widiger and Corbitt, 1997). Regardless of the theory accepted as grounds for gender differences in diagnosis, it has been proposed that ASPD, Borderline, and Histrionic Personality Disorders represent gender variants of a common underlying disposition (Widiger and Corbitt, 1997).

In general, the *DSM-IV-TR* comprehensive conceptualization of ASPD poses at least the following three specific problems: (1) it does not account for individual differences or disorder extremes; (2) it may apply a false, inaccurate, and unhelpful generic label; and (3) it may dismiss an ASPD individual accurately conceptualized under the ASPD diagnosis (Sexton and Griffin, 1997). Overall, individuals diagnosed with ASPD would most likely be recommended en masse for *treatment* in the same way they were categorized en masse for *diagnosis*. Although the treatment of any degree of ASPD is difficult, effective treatment will include unique understandings, conceptualizations, and treatments which take into consideration the life-span experiences of each individual (Reid and Eddy,

1997; Rice and Harris, 1997). Such considerations are not facilitated within the constraints of the present *DSM-IV-TR* comprehensive ASPD definition.

Researchers and theorists have suggested changes in the conceptualization of ASPD. Hinshaw and Zupan state that the diversity of behaviors covered under *DSM-IV-TR* antisocial behavior criteria '... points to the importance of making theoretically and empirically meaningful distinctions related to specific subcategories of antisocial individuals and to subtypes of antisocial/aggressive behavior' (1997: 38). They suggest subcategories differing with respect to characteristic presenting features, developmental history, course and history, gender ratio, and prognosis. Hart and Hare (1997) suggest defining ASPD in terms of two constructs (psychopathy with affective and interpersonal markers and psychopathy with behavioral markers). Lahey and Loeber (1997) have suggested a life-span perspective on the interrelationships among attention-deficit/ hyperactivity disorder (ADHD), oppositional defiant disorder (ODD), conduct disorder (CD), adult antisocial behavior, and ASPD occur along a continuum impacted by multiple contextual factors including co-occurrence of ADHD. Although it has been noted that distinguishing criminal conduct from psychopathy is important legally, clinically, and scientifically (Hart and Hare, 1997), doing so can confound and thereby defeat the original purpose of separate constructs (Rutter, 1997a).

AETIOLOGY OF ASPD

ASPD is thought to have multiple etiological causes (American Psychiatric Association, 2000; Brain and Susman, 1997; Maxmen and Ward, 1995; Sue et al., 1990) involving a complex interaction of cognitive, emotional, social, and contextual factors (Brain and Susman, 1997; Hinshaw and Zupan, 1997). Certain factors, both genetic and environmental, are common to the development of ASPD. These include: (1) factors of the ASPD individual during prenatal development, infancy, early and middle childhood, adolescence, and young adulthood; (2) factors which are pervasive throughout the developmental life span, and are not specific to the development of the child; and (3) contextual factors which may directly or indirectly have an impact on the identified antisocial individual (Hinshaw and Zupan, 1997; Lahey and Loeber, 1997; Reid and Eddy, 1997).

DEVELOPMENTAL FACTORS ASSOCIATED WITH ASPD

Prenatal maternal smoking and substance abuse, poor maternal nutrition, and lack of prenatal care are linked to antisocial behavior (Maxmen and Ward, 1995; Reid and Eddy, 1997). Several long-term studies addressing these prenatal factors showed unusually high levels of effectiveness in reducing the development of antisocial behavior (Lally, Mangione and Honig, 1988; Olds, 1988; Zeigler, Taussig and Black, 1992). A study by Olds in 1988 showed that cessation of maternal smoking for just a few crucial months lowered chances of fetal central nervous system damage. Lowering the incidence of central nervous system damage reduced the incidence of infant temperament and cognitive problems after birth that affected the child and the family (Olds, 1988; Reid and Eddy, 1997).

Factors during infancy that may affect development of antisocial behavior include parents that are highly stressed, negative, abusive, and show low support of family members (Maxmen and Ward, 1995; Reid and Eddy, 1997). Infant temperament and health status are recursively linked to the above-mentioned characteristics of parents (i.e., when the infant 'fusses', the parents may become more stressed, negative, and abusive).

Factors during early childhood (2–5 years of age) found to be common to the development of antisocial behavior include coercive discipline by parents and other family members; modeling of these and other coercive behaviors by the child usually begins at this time (Hinshaw and Zupan, 1997; Lahey and Loeber, 1997; Reid and Eddy, 1997). Children at risk for continued antisocial behavior tend to begin a cycle of disobedience and withdrawal, as parent/caretakers exhibit low involvement, poor reinforcement, inconsistent discipline, and rejection of the child (Lahey and Loeber, 1997; Reid and Eddy, 1997). At this point, oppositional defiant disorder and attention deficit/hyperactivity disorder are often diagnosed (American Psychiatric Association, 2000; Lahey and Loeber, 1997; Pilkonis and Klein, 1997).

During middle childhood (6–11 years of age) parental low involvement, low supervision, and poor problem solving are common to the development of antisocial behavior (Hinshaw and Zupan, 1997; Lahey and Loeber, 1997). The child continues disobedience, aggressiveness, begins wandering, and takes no role in the family; poor social skills and fights with peers are typical (Reid and Eddy, 1997). The identified antisocial child typically exhibits deficiency in school entry skills, homework incompletion, inability or lack of desire to stay on-task, defiance, and aggressiveness (Reid and Eddy, 1997). Teachers may reject, retaliate, provide low support for positive behavior, and begin 'tracking' students into lower or special education classes (Hinshaw and Zupan, 1997; Lahey and Loeber, 1997; Reid and Eddy, 1997).

Characteristics during adolescence (12–18 years of age) common to the development of antisocial behavior include uninvolved, combative parents who do not discipline (Reid and Eddy, 1997). The child spends even less time at home than at previous stages of development: more time is spent with delinquent peer groups; and fighting, stealing and run-ins with the police increase (Hinshaw and Zupan, 1997; Lahey and Loeber, 1997; Reid and Eddy, 1997). The identified antisocial child will generally be failing academically; show social and cognitive deficits; and be truant, delinquent, and aggressive (Reid and Eddy, 1997). Bullying, fighting, substance use and early sexual activity are characteristic of the antisocial individual at this time (Hinshaw and Zupan, 1997; Lahey and Loeber, 1997; Reid and Eddy, 1997). If the child is still attending school, teachers have often given up on or suspended the child. During these years, and up until age eighteen, the diagnosis of oppositional defiant disorder is changed to conduct disorder (American Psychiatric Association, 2000; Reid and Eddy, 1997).

During young adulthood (18 years of age and older), the diagnosis will change from conduct disorder to antisocial personality disorder if the antisocial behaviors continue

(American Psychiatric Association, 2000; First and Tasman, 2004). The identified antisocial individual will typically have dropped out of school, become heavily involved in deviant peer groups, lawbreaking, substance use, and high-risk behaviors; pregnancy, sexually transmitted diseases, and depression are common (Reid and Eddy, 1997).

PERVASIVE FACTORS ASSOCIATED WITH ASPD

Certain pervasive factors may affect the identified antisocial individual at any time, or continuously, during the life span. For example, individuals exhibiting antisocial behavior generally have experienced considerable parental marital discord (Hinshaw and Zupan, 1997; Lahey and Loeber, 1997; Maxmen and Ward, 1995; Seligman, 1990). Witnessing the verbal and physical abuse which often accompanies such conflict in the home has shown to increase aggressive and violent acts in children (Shaw and Winslow, 1997; Widom, 1997). Family breakup is another pervasive factor in the development of antisocial behavior (Hinshaw and Zupan, 1997; Lahey and Loeber, 1997; Reid and Eddy, 1997). Family disruption may include early deaths, frequent moves, arrests and imprisonment; as well as parental desertion, separation, divorce, and custody fights (Maxmen and Ward, 1995; Seligman, 1990).

Parental alcoholism, particularly paternal alcoholism, is consistent with the development of antisocial behavior (American Psychiatric Association, 2000; Carson et al., 1996; Maxmen and Ward, 1995; Reid and Eddy, 1997; Sue et al., 1990). Alcohol and substance-related disorders are common among families with an antisocial member, the relationship between alcohol use and violence is well established in the literature, and the pattern of alcohol, substance abuse, and violence tends to continue in the ASPD individual (American Psychiatric Association, 2000).

Parental psychopathology is also a pervasive factor in the development of antisocial behavior. There is an increased prevalence of somatization disorder, substance-abuse disorders, and antisocial personality disorder among families with an antisocial member (American Psychiatric Association, 2000; Hinshaw and Zupan, 1997; Maxmen and Ward, 1995; Sue et al., 1990). Studies have indicated that the presence of an antisocial father or father figure, serves as a model for traditional sex-role training, inconsistent discipline, inadequate supervision, and/or family conflict (Reid and Eddy, 1997; Robins, 1966). It is theorized that boys then model the traditional-sex-role-congruent ASPD behaviors, accounting for higher ASPD prevalence rates in males; girls tend to resort to histrionic or borderline personality disorders, which are more congruent with traditional female sex roles (Carson et al., 1996; Reid and Eddy, 1997; Robins, 1966; Widiger and Corbitt, 1997; Sue et al., 1990).

CONTEXTUAL FACTORS ASSOCIATED WITH ASPD

Parental lack of affection, attachment, and discipline are typical of the antisocial individual's family, where emotional rejection, separation, or neglect allows little opportunity for experiencing attachment (Hinshaw and Zupan, 1997; Sue et al., 1990).

Attachment theories well established in the literature point to the ill effects on personality development in the absence of such early attachments (Rutter, 1997b). Benjamin (1993) outlines specific behaviors of parents toward their children and the respective antisocial consequences of those behaviors: (1) a harsh, neglectful parent who attacks or ignores increases the likelihood of rearing an individual who ignores, neglects, attacks and is pervasively detached and insensitive; (2) a sporadic, unmodulated, controlling, blaming parent increases the likelihood of rearing an individual who is fiercely protective and who easily blames and controls others; (3) an inept parent who inappropriately protects and ignores increases the likelihood of rearing an individual who abuses drugs, becomes a prostitute or commits a crime; and (4) parental dereliction of duty increases the likelihood of rearing an individual who controls without bonding.

Certain pervasive community factors originating from outside the family unit may severely affect the individual and lead to the development of ASPD. For example, the neighborhood environment plays a part in the development of antisocial behavior. Disorganized, high crime locations offering few employment, educational and leisure time opportunities are risk factors in the development of antisocial behavior (Hinshaw and Zupan, 1997). As mentioned earlier in this paper, witnessing and experiencing violence increases aggression and violent acts (Shaw and Winslow, 1997; Widom, 1997.

As can be see from this review of the etiology of ASPD, lack of affection, lack of attachment and lack of empathic relationships are common in the development of ASPD. The resulting ASPD characteristics of distrust and resistance appear early in the life of the ASPD individual and continue into adulthood.

THE HISTORY OF TREATMENT OF INDIVIDUALS DIAGNOSED WITH ASPD

The characteristic aggression, impulsivity, disregard for the rights of others and repeated unlawful behaviors of individuals diagnosed with ASPD often result in arrest, criminal prosecution and incarceration. As a result, the study of ASPD treatment has been a multidisciplinary pursuit involving the fields of criminal justice, criminology, law, penology, public health, sociology and anthropology as well as the mental health fields of counseling, psychology, psychiatry and social work.

This multidisciplinary perspective affects the terminology and treatment applied to individuals with ASPD. For example, the history and treatment of individuals with ASPD falls most commonly into the domain of offenders, inmates, prisoners, correctional facilities, jails and prisons rather than the domain of clients, patients, hospitals, clinics and private practice. Further, in the bulk of the literature on the treatment of ASPD the term 'treatment' does not refer to psychotherapy. Rather, the term 'treatment' has come to refer to correctional institution programming and vocational training, work release, probation, parole and incarceration. Additionally, the term 'counseling' often refers to casework management, social work and legal advisement, rather than mental health counseling intervention.

Panton pointed out in his 1979 study on treatment of first offender inmates that the few studies published on the psychotherapeutic treatment efforts '… within a prison context indicate that treatment intervention with receptive inmates may somewhat offset the impact of imprisonment as well as bring about changes in individual attitudes and social attributes' (p. 385). Unfortunately, correctional facility mental health clinicians generally perform lethality and mental health status assessments, not full-session psychotherapy; very little formal counseling occurs in prison (Schrink and Hamm, 1990). This is not to say that mental health clinicians would not like to work with the 'workable'. Prison professional staff '… find themselves spending a great percentage of their time working with individuals who characteristically do not respond appreciably to therapeutic intervention, while being forced, because of staff and time limitations to by-pass many inmates, who would be the most receptive to treatment, and who would profit most from its application' (Panton, 1979: 385). These unresponsive individuals '… are classified as chronic management problems. Despite the concentrated efforts of the professional staff, severely maladjusted prison inmates seldom respond to psychiatric and or psychotherapeutic intervention, but continue to be a disruptive influence within the correctional community' (Panton, 1979: 384).

Clearly, the study of ASPD has predominantly occurred within the realm of corrections, rather than that of psychotherapeutic intervention; very little psychotherapy is carried on in the prison setting. This distinction is relevant to this discussion since the bulk of the ASPD literature concerns itself with treatment other than psychotherapeutic counseling. The literature specific to psychotherapeutic treatment of individuals diagnosed with ASPD indicates three treatments of some limited success: cognitive therapy, behavioral interventions and drug interventions (Carson et al, 1996; Gladding, 1996; Scharf, 1996; Sue et al., 1990). As will be noted, ASPD distrust and resistance are isolated as common confounding factors in all three of these approaches.

COGNITIVE TREATMENT OF INDIVIDUALS DIAGNOSED WITH ASPD

Cognitive scientists have attempted to outline theoretical frameworks and psychotherapeutic treatments addressing the cognitive characteristics of ASPD (Beck and Freeman, 1990; Freeman and Leaf, 1989; Ross, Fabiano and Ross, 1991; Walters, 1990). For example, Freeman and Leaf (1989) developed their own cognitive theoretical framework for clinical focus and treatment, attempting to modify the impulsive, egocentric, illogical and rigid thinking of individuals diagnosed with ASPD. Walters (1990) theorized from his work with ASPD incarcerated felons that subjects with ASPD have eight cognitive characteristics corresponding to *DSM-IV-TR* ASPD criteria. He suggested that treating these cognitive features might be an effective approach to psychotherapy with ASPD subjects.

Beck and Freeman (1990) designed a cognitive treatment for ASPD that focused on improving moral and social behavior by changing self-serving cognitive dysfunctioning. Ross, Fabiano and Ross (1991) designed a program for teaching juvenile, adolescent, and adult offenders specific cognitive skills required for adequate social adjustment. They suggest that cognitive training '... has been found to be therapeutic in that it fosters improved interpersonal and social adjustment' (1991: 3).

Freeman, Davis and DiTomasso (1992) discussed cognitive therapy for individuals with personality disorders in general, and ASPD in particular. Treatment goals may include '... the development of empathy, reciprocity and respect for the rights of others' (p. 70). In a 1995 article, Nauth focused on the male antisocial personality and antisocial thinking from a cognitive perspective, examining power, control and respect.

The literature offers some research support for the efficacy of ASPD cognitive approaches. Kristiansson (1995) conducted a case study utilizing a cognitive training program with four ASPD subjects. One of Kristiansson's conclusions was that a structured program based on cognitive-behavior therapy combined with appropriate pharmacotherapy may be an effective treatment approach to ASPD.

A study by Woody, McLellan, Luborsky and O'Brien (1985) utilized a 24-week cognitive-behavioral intervention for treating male opiate addicts. Results of this study (n=110), which sampled a wide range of ages and pathologies, showed significant improvement for ASPD subjects in three problem areas.

The research literature specific to cognitive treatment of ASPD, like the ASPD treatment literature in general, indicates that cognitive interventions have some limited effectiveness (Holt, 1990). However, researchers and theorists conclude that distrust and resistance in ASPD subjects are present during, and interfere with, the efficacy of cognitive treatments (Beck and Freeman, 1990; Nauth, 1995; Sue et al., 1990). Beck and Freeman (1990) conclude that the cognitive approach is a collaborative effort, and since most clients being treated for ASPD are court mandated and/or are involuntary inmates, resistance is always problematic. Sue et al., (1990) agree, adding that traditional treatment approaches that require client cooperation have been shown to be ineffective with the distrust and resistance of psychopaths. It follows that addressing distrust and resistance in ASPD subjects should increase the efficacy of cognitive treatments.

BEHAVIORAL TREATMENT OF INDIVIDUALS DIAGNOSED WITH ASPD

Behavioral therapeutic interventions aimed at controlling ASPD behavior patterns have been conducted (Bandura, 1969; Van Evra, 1983). In 1986 Kellner reviewed the literature and concluded that behavior therapy can make a substantial difference in ASPD behavior patterns when treatment involved psychotherapeutic counseling, medication and behavior therapy.

Criticisms of behavior treatments include the reappearance of symptoms (antisocial behaviors) once the ASPD subjects return to their 'uncontrolled' environment (Bandura, 1969; Vaillant, 1975; Van Evra, 1983). For example, Bandura concluded that the controlled situation is necessary for treatment to succeed (1969), and Van Evra's findings with adolescents showed that once subjects leave their treatment programs, they are likely to revert to antisocial behaviors (1983). Vaillant (1975) also found that the successful treatment of ASPD can occur only in a setting where the subject's resistant behavior can be strictly controlled, such as correctional institutions and hospitals. Because ASPD subjects are typically uncooperative and resistant, treatment on an outpatient basis is doomed to fail (Carson et al., 1996; Vaillant, 1975). Fleming and Pretzer state that individuals with ASPD possess numerous strengths and capabilities which they can direct in more constructive ways personally and socially '... if only they could be induced to respond more adaptively to naturally occurring contingencies rather than being under-responsive to anticipation of negative contingencies and over-responsive to anticipation of positive contingencies' (1990: 128).

The literature specific to behavioral treatment, like the literature on cognitive treatment, substantiates the limited efficacy of behavioral ASPD treatments, which appear to work only, if at all, within the structured setting (Bandura, 1969; Carson et al., 1996; Vaillant, 1975). Further, the research on behavioral treatment concludes the same as the research on cognitive treatment of ASPD; distrust and resistance are problematic with behavioral ASPD treatments, and become even more problematic once the client leaves the structured setting, (Vaillant, 1975; Van Evra, 1983). Addressing distrust and resistance should increase the efficacy of behavioral treatments.

DRUG TREATMENT OF ASPD

Drug treatments of ASPD include tranquilizers, anti-anxiety drugs and stimulants. All have shown limited success in treating respective areas of the disorder, such as certain aggressive behaviors, hostility rates and cortical arousal (Markovitz, 2001; Carson et al., 1996; Sue et al., 1990). Research has linked aggressive, impulsive or detached behavior with dopamine, monoamine, acetylcholine, serotonin, norepinephrine, CSF homovanillac acid, and gamma-aminobutyric acid activity (Berman, Kavoussi and Coccaro, 1997). For example, Brown, Kent, Bryant, Gavedon, Campbell, Felthous, Barratt and Rose (1989) found that the serotonin uptake was linked to episodic aggression. In another study the relationship between personal detachment as a personality trait was examined in relation to dopamine D sub 2 receptor specific binding (Breier, Kestler, Adler, Elman, Weisenfeld, Malholtra and Pickar, 1998). A significant relationship was found between D sub 2 receptor specific binding and detachment scores supporting the conclusion that personal detachment is related to dopamine activity.

Despite these findings, '... no biologic factor has yet been shown to be either a necessary or a sufficient cause of aggressive behavior' (Berman, Kavoussi and Coccaro, 1997: 311). Furthermore, no drug treatment has made an impact on ASPD as a whole; drug treatment may diminish a particular ASPD symptom, but not allay the overall disorder (Berman, Kavoussi and Coccaro, 1997; Carson et al., 1996; Markovitz, 2001).

These findings are further confounded with research suggesting that environmental factors are suspect in influencing changes in neurotransmitter functioning (Berman, Kavoussi and Coccaro, 1997) and that hormones are thought to be 'causes, consequences, or mediators of transactions between individuals and their environments' (Brain and Susman, 1997: 321). For example, in a study of neurotransmitter-environment interactions (Rogeness and McClure, 1996), the relation between childhood neglect and effects on the norepinephrine system was researched (n=1,083). Results showed that those children with a history of neglect (with or without abuse) showed lower activity dopamine-hydroxylase levels. These data support the conclusion that the norepinephrine system is affected by neglect in a long-lasting or permanent manner (Rogeness and McClure, 1996).

Inability to treat ASPD as a whole and confounding environmental factors are not the only concerns with drug treatment. Drug treatment of ASPD is contra-indicated since clients: (1) often have a history of substance abuse, (2) are uncooperative and medication noncompliant, and (3) have a pattern of seeking external solutions, rather than internal answers. As a result, client suicide, prescription drug resale and/or abuse, and reinforcement of irresponsibility for actions and consequences are respective drug treatment concerns (Carson et al., 1996; Seligman, 1990; Sue et al., 1990).

Clearly, problems with drug treatment are multiple and complex, and lack of cooperation and treatment noncompliance, manifestations of the distrust and resistance characteristic of those diagnosed with ASPD, are problematic.

The difficulty in establishing trust to decrease resistance has been a constant barrier to effective cognitive, behavioral, and drug treatment of individuals diagnosed with ASPD. Significant distrust and resistance make prognosis poor, since therapy is a collaborative effort, requiring cooperation between the subject and the therapist (Carson et al., 1996; Charney, 1979; Gladding, 1996; Scharf, 1996; Sue et al., 1990). A psychotherapeutic approach that encourages the building of trust, thereby decreasing resistance, is indicated and appropriate in the treatment of ASPD; person-centered counseling is such an approach.

PERSON-CENTERED COUNSELING AS AN ASPD TREATMENT

THE PERSON-CENTERED APPROACH

Carl R. Rogers (1902–1987), considered the most influential of all American psychotherapists, proposed and advocated the Person-Centered Approach (PCA) over the course of his professional life (Kirschenbaum and Henderson, 1989). The PCA is an experiential, humanistic, affective psychotherapeutic approach with an optimistic and positive view of humanity, recognizing individual freedom, choice, and self-responsibility (Gladding, 1996; Scharf, 1996). The PCA has: (1) a phenomenological characteristic which supports the belief that humans have a unique capacity for reflective consciousness; (2) a theory of growth or actualization tendency which supports the belief that human beings can and do strive to grow; (3) a self-determination philosophy which supports the belief that humans are free, are influenced by history and context, but have a role in who they are; and (4) a desire to understand and respect each individual and their subjective experience of the world (Rice and Greenberg, 1992). The PCA recognizes the ability of humans to self-actualize, authentically exist, experience, and be in the world (Bozarth, 1998; Scharf, 1996).

The psychotherapist-client relationship is an integral component in person-centered counseling. Rogers stated that in '… the emotional warmth of the relationship with the therapist, the client begins to experience a feeling of safety as he finds that whatever attitude he expresses is understood in almost the same way that he perceives it, and is accepted. He is then able to explore …' (1951: 41). 'It is this absolute assurance that there will be no evaluation, no interpretation, no probing, no *personal* reaction by the psychotherapist, that gradually permits the client to experience the relationship as one in which all defenses can be dispensed with—a relationship in which the client feels, 'I can be the real me, no pretenses' (Rogers, 1951: 209).

In striving to be genuine, empathic, and respectful, person-centered therapists are not predictable and do not use particular techniques or methods. In general, person-centered engagement involves being with clients, attending to and reflecting client expressions, (Bozarth, 1998; Brodley, 1998, 1996; Kirschenbaum, 2003; McCulloch, 2003a; Rogers, 1986) and avoiding directiveness and interrogation (Kirschenbaum, 2003; McCulloch, 2003b; Rogers, 1951). The person-centered therapist: (1) tends to listen, rather than guide; (2) tends to clarify client feelings, thoughts, and behaviors; and (3) assumes the world of the client as much as is possible without losing self (Rogers, 1951).

Rogers stated that the individual has the ability for self-understanding and change (1951, 1980). Necessary and sufficient conditions for client change include client and therapist psychological contact, client incongruence, therapist genuineness, therapist unconditional positive regard, therapist empathy and client perception of empathy (Rogers, 1957, 1959). Under these six conditions, positive desired change will occur in clients (Rogers, 1957, 1959). Given the six conditions, growth is promoted (Rogers, 1980; Tausch, 1978) and clients become more open, more trusting, and more engaged (Rogers, 1961). As a consequence of their increased trust, individuals become more realistic, better at problem-solving, and less defensive (Grummon, 1972; Rogers, 1959; Scharf, 1996; Tausch, 1978).

Since the major confounds in the treatment of individuals diagnosed with ASPD have been distrust and resistance, the PCA seems indicated and appropriate. Patterson stated that 'so-called involuntary clients' (individuals diagnosed with ASPD are most often inmates or 'so-called involuntary clients') who are unmotivated for psychotherapy are resistant and distrustful clients who '… will not or cannot trust the therapist' (1990: 318). He further stated that although approaches other than person-centered suggest changing behavior by threat, coercion, argument, persuasion, confrontation, surgery or medication, lasting change does not follow such interventions and they are not likely to be successful. 'The only solution to the problem appears to be through persistent offering of the conditions [the six necessary and sufficient person-centered conditions]' (Patterson, 1990: 319).

THE PCA WITH DIVERSE POPULATIONS

Those diagnosed with ASPD come from a variety of social, economic, and cultural backgrounds, and the use of the PCA with individuals from culturally diverse backgrounds has been criticized. Questions have arisen regarding person-centered counseling with individuals who may wish immediate and directive advice, individuals from cultures where direction from authority is learned, and individuals from cultures which emphasize social or familial decision-making (Sue et al., 1990). These concerns do not appear based in an understanding of the PCA. Person-centered psychotherapists facilitate the goals of their clients as requested by their clients. Contrary to criticisms, the PCA assumes as a necessary component of counseling an understanding of the client, the client's world view, and the client's world (Rogers, 1951) and facilitates client counseling 'outcomes' as requested, desired, expressed, and/or determined by the client. As such, the PCA is culturally sensitive, appropriate, and thereby, effective, across diverse populations.

THE PCA FOR DEEPER ISSUES AND PSYCHOTHERAPEUTIC CHANGE

The PCA has been dismissed as inappropriate for deeper issues and/or psychotherapeutic change (Gladding, 1996; Maxmen and Ward, 1995). These claims are erroneous, since both theory and research exist supporting the PCA with individuals from a variety of populations exhibiting mild, moderate and severe psychiatric symptoms (McCulloch, 2002). A sampling of this literature includes the PCA with individuals exhibiting: symptoms of schizophrenia (Rogers, Gendlin, Kiesler and Truax, 1967; Sommerbeck, 2003), psychoses/near-psychoses (Sommerbeck, 2003), developmental disabilities (Demanchick, Cochran and Cochran, 2003), anxiety/depression (Tursi and McCulloch, 2004) and conduct disorder (Cochran and Cochran, 1999).

Psychotherapeutic change and successful outcome are significantly related to the building of a therapeutic relationship, recognized by many as the factor accounting for success in psychotherapy (Beutler, Machado and Neufeldt, 1994; Bozarth, 2002; Lambert and Bergin, 1994). The PCA is an approach based in the therapeutic relationship (Bozarth, 1998; Brodley, 1998, 1996; Rogers, 1951). According to Patterson,

> Some therapists may not believe that such an approach [the PCA] is effective. They do not have the patience or do not want to invest the time and effort to finally establish a relationship. So they abandon the necessary and sufficient conditions for psychotherapeutic change ... They are not likely to be successful in achieving lasting change. (1990: 320)

HISTORY AND RESEARCH OF PCA AND ASPD

Psychotherapy has been discouraged from use in ASPD treatment. First and Tasman (2004) note that ASPD is the most difficult personality disorder to treat, and that ASPD client tendencies 'to be manipulative, dishonest, exploitative, aggressive and irresponsible will often disrupt and sabotage treatment' (2004: 1249). They further note that friendliness, remorse and commitment to change by ASPD clients are insincere and unreliable. The PCA has been specifically discouraged from use in ASPD treatment. Seligman stated that '... person-centered and insight-oriented therapies are not indicated with these clients' (1990: 261), and Ruegg, Haynes and Frances stated that '... therapy with ASPD should not be based on the relationship with the therapist' (1997: 147).

Although these claims are not supported by research, they persist in published literature and as myths in the mental health profession. Contrary to these unsubstantiated claims, person-centered theory and research exists in the ASPD treatment literature.

In 1963 Smith, Berlin and Bassin published an article describing the problems experienced by a client-centered group therapist working in an experimental five-year program for offenders recently placed on probation. Among the conclusions was that 'the group will respond with surprising frequency to express positive sentiments toward a socially acceptable way of life' (p. 551).

In 1966 Truax, Wargo and Silber studied the effects of group person-centered counseling on female delinquents. Seventy residents in a home for delinquent children participated in this study, with 40 in the treatment group, and 30 in the control group. After receiving group therapy twice weekly, measures of changes in attitude or personality functioning were assessed on the Minnesota Counseling Inventory (MCI) Conformity Scale; on the MCI subscales of (a) family relationships, (b) social relationships, and (c) emotional stability; and on reductions in time spent institutionalized. Results showed significant reductions in delinquent behavior and duration of confinement.

In 1983 Whitely and Hosford noted that in '... addition to its use by professional psychologists and psychotherapists, client-centered approaches are also widely used by paraprofessional and correctional staff' (p. 29). This statement was in reference to the Carkhuff training program at the Federal Correctional Institution at Lompoc, California in 1970. The program offered training for the development of interpersonal relationship skills to 105 custodial staff members, 39 noncustodial staff members, and 49 inmates. Although this was a well-funded, comprehensive initiative within the correctional setting, it was not analyzed with respect to the effectiveness of person-centered counseling on individuals diagnosed with ASPD.

In 1988, Smith and Berlin discussed non-directive client-centered therapy in a case studies section of the group therapy chapter in their book on treating criminal offenders. However, more recent research has shown that non-directive counseling is more effective with highly reactive, highly resistant clients. Beutler, Engle, Mohr, Daldrup, Bergan, Meredith and Merry (1991) conducted a study comparing three types of therapy as treatment for 63 clients with major depressive disorder. Cognitive therapy (CT) and focused expressive psychotherapy (FEP) were administered for 20 weekly sessions by psychologists, each trained and experienced in the therapy they administered during this study. Supportive self-directed therapy (S/SD) was administered by telephone for 20 weeks by advanced graduate students who were pretrained and supervised. Variation among the client coping styles of externalization and resistance potential, assessed using Minnesota Multiphasic Personality Inventory (MMPI) scales, were used as a test of differential client-treatment interactions. Results showed that: (1) highly defensive, resistant clients improved most with supportive, self-directed counseling treatment, (2) authority-directed treatments proved less effective with resistant clients, and (3) directive interventions are contra-indicated with highly reactive clients.

A hybrid methodological study was conducted (McCulloch, 2000) in which four individuals diagnosed with ASPD received eight weekly person-centered counseling sessions. Participants were pre- and post-tested using the Personality Assessment Inventory (PAI) to clinically assess changes in criteria relevant to ASPD and monitor for deception. Data showed substantial desired changes in ASPD pathology for study participants.

Greenberg, Elliott, and Lietaer (2000) conducted a meta-analysis of 15 experiential-humanistic client-outcome predictor studies. Eleven of the studies analyzed were conducted between 1990 and 2000, three studies analyzed were conducted between 1981 and 1983, and one of the analyzed studies was from 1978. Greenberg et al. found that '... clients with high reactance (including high dominance, low submissiveness) [all ASPD criteria] appear to do better in client-centered or nondirective therapies' (2000: 517).

PCA AND ASPD DEFINITION

As noted earlier in this chapter, the *DSM-IV-TR* comprehensive conceptualization of ASPD poses at least the following three specific problems: (1) it does not account for individual differences or disorder extremes; (2) it may apply a false, inaccurate, and unhelpful generic label; and (3) it may dismiss an ASPD individual accurately conceptualized under the ASPD diagnosis.

From a PCA perspective, clients are accepted as individuals and diagnostic labels are not of psychotherapeutic concern. Rather, the unique understandings, experiences, desires, and conceptualizations of clients are the focus in therapy sessions. As a result, the definitional concerns noted above would be of little, if any, issue in a PCA psychotherapeutic experience.

PCA AND ASPD AETIOLOGY

Although no one factor has been shown to be causal in the etiology of ASPD, issues of rejection, abandonment, and lack of affection and empathic relationships have been isolated as common ASPD etiological factors. Person-centered counseling offers ASPD clients the empathy, genuineness and unconditional positive regard that may not have been extended to them historically. Person-centered counseling sessions provide the experience of empathic relationship, respect and genuineness. The atmosphere of caring facilitated by the PCA psychotherapist allows for the development of a place in which the ASPD diagnosed individual can be with another person (perhaps for the first time) in an empathic, genuine and respectful way. Clients are accepted as worthwhile, free from rejection and abandonment as persons. It might be said that within the PCA relationship, the possibility exists to fill the etiological gaps, to experience the look and feel of empathy, genuineness and respect; and to risk being with another in ways that may have been missing or overlooked developmentally.

TREATMENT HISTORY OF INDIVIDUALS DIAGNOSED WITH ASPD

Distrust and resistance have been isolated as common confounds in cognitive, behavioral and drug treatment approaches. As noted earlier in this chapter, providing an atmosphere that facilitates the PCA core conditions promotes client growth (Rogers, 1980; Tausch, 1978), openness, trust, engagement (Rogers, 1961), realism and problem-solving, while decreasing defensiveness (Grummon, 1972; Rogers, 1959; Scharf, 1996; Tausch, 1978). These characteristics, identified as lacking in individuals diagnosed with ASPD, are facilitated by the PCA. As early as 1954, Grummon and John found that defensiveness (a measure of distrust and resistance) decreased for individuals in person-centered psychotherapy. An overwhelming amount of literature supports the relationship building power of the PCA, indicated to effective ASPD treatment.

SUMMARY

Clearly, the PCA is indicated and appropriate with individuals diagnosed with ASPD. Theory and research on the definitions, characteristics, etiology, history and treatment support the PCA as appropriate and indicated for those individuals diagnosed with ASPD. Further, the consistent treatment confounds reported as problematic in all other treatment approaches, distrust and resistance, are *uniquely* addressed by the PCA.

It is not argued here that person-centered counseling alone is the recommended treatment for individuals exhibiting ASPD behavior. Effective treatment may likely include a range of multidisciplinary interventions within the context of the life of the individual. This chapter does argue that the PCA addresses the distrust and resistance characteristic of ASPD which have blocked effective therapeutic processes of other approaches; that the PCA is appropriate and indicated in the effective treatment of ASPD; and that the PCA is a critical, integral, and necessary component in the treatment of individuals diagnosed with ASPD.

REFERENCES

American Psychiatric Association (2000) *Diagnostic and Statistical Manual of Mental Disorders —text revision* (4th ed). Washington, DC: Author.

Bandura, A (1969) *Principles of Behavior Modification.* New York: Holt, Rinehart and Winston.

Beck, AT and Freeman, A (1990) *Cognitive Therapy of Personality Disorders.* New York: Guilford.

Benjamin, LS (1993) *Interpersonal Diagnosis and Treatment of Personality Disorders.* New York: The Guilford Press.

Berman, ME, Kavoussi, RJ and Coccaro, EF (1997) Neurotransmitter correlates of human aggression. In DM Stoff, J Breiling and JD Masur (eds) *Handbook of Antisocial Behavior* (pp. 305–13). New York: Wiley.

Beutler, LE, Engle, D, Mohr, D, Daldrup, RJ, Bergan, J, Meredith, K and Merry, W (1991) Predictors of differential response to cognitive, experiential, and self-directed psychotherapeutic procedures. *Journal of Consulting and Clinical Psychology, 59,* 333–40.

Beutler, LE, Machado, PPM and Neufeldt, SA (1994) Therapist variables. In AE Bergin and SL Garfield (eds) *Handbook of Psychotherapy and Behavior Change* (4th ed) (pp. 229–69). New York: Wiley.

Bozarth, JD (2002) Empirically supported treatments: Epitome of the 'specificity myth'. In JC Watson, RN Goldman, and MS Warner (eds) *Client-Centered and Experiential Psychotherapy in the 21st Century* (pp. 168–81). Ross-on-Wye, UK: PCCS Books.

Bozarth, JD (1998) *Person-Centered Therapy: A revolutionary paradigm.* Ross-on-Wye, UK: PCCS Books.

Brain, PF and Susman, EJ (1997) Hormonal aspects of aggression and violence. In DM Stoff, J Breiling and JD Masur (eds) *Handbook of Antisocial Behavior* (pp. 314–23). New York: Wiley.

Breier, A, Kestler, L, Adler, C, Elman, I, Wiesenfeld, N, Malholtra, A and Pickar, D (1998) Dopamine D sub 2 receptor density and personal detachment in healthy subjects. *The American Journal of Psychiatry, 155,* 1440–2.

Brodley, B (1996) Empathic understanding and feelings in client-centered therapy. *The Person-Centered Journal, 3,* 22–30 .

Brodley, B (1998) Criteria for making empathic responses in client-centered therapy. *The Person-Centered Journal, 5,* 20–8.

Brown, CS, Kent, TA, Bryant, SG, Gavedon, RM, Campbell, JL, Felthous, AR, Barratt, ES and Rose, RM (1989) Blood platelet uptake of serotonin in episodic aggression. *Psychiatry Research, 27,* 5–12.

Carson, RC, Butcher, JN and Mineka S (1996) *Abnormal Psychology and Modern Life.* New York: Harper Collins.

Charney, FL (1979) *The Psychopath: A comprehensive study of antisocial personality disorder.* New York: Brunner.

Cochran, JL and Cochran, NH (1999) Using the counseling relationship to facilitate change in students with conduct disorder. *Professional School Counseling, 2,* 395–403.

Cooke, DJ (1998) Psychopathy across cultures. In DJ Cooke, AE Forth and RD Hare (eds) *Psychopathy: Theory, research, and implications for society* (pp. 13–46). Dordrecht, The Netherlands: Kluwer Academic Publishers.

Demanchick, SP, Cochran, NH and Cochran, JL (2003) Person-centered play therapy for adults with developmental disabilities. *International Journal of Play Therapy, 12,* 47–65.

First, MB and Tasman, A (2004) *DSM-IV-TR Mental Disorders, Diagnosis, Etiology and Treatment.* West Sussex, England: John Wiley and Sons.

Fleming, B and Pretzer, JL (1990) Cognitive-behavioral approaches to personality disorders. In M Hersen, RM Eisler and PM Miller (eds) *Progress in Behavior Modification: Vol. 25.* (pp. 119–51). Newbury Park, Ca: Sage Publications.

Freeman, A, Davis, DD and DiTomasso, RA (1992) Cognitive therapy of personality disorders. In M Hersen, RM Eisler and PM Miller (eds) *Progress in Behavior Modification: Vol. 28.* (pp. 55–81). Sycamore, IL: Sycamore Publishing Company.

Freeman, A and Leaf, RC (1989) Cognitive therapy applied to personality disorders. In A Freeman, KM Simon, LE Beutler, and H Arkowitz (eds) *Comprehensive Handbook of Cognitive Therapy* (pp. 403–33). New York: Plenum Press.

Gladding, ST (1996) *Counseling: A comprehensive profession.* Englewood Cliffs, NJ: Merrill.

Greenberg, LS, Elliott, RK and Lietaer, G (2000) Research on experiential therapies. In AE Bergin and SL Garfield (eds) *Handbook of Psychotherapy Change* (4th ed) (pp. 509–39).

New York: Wiley.

Grummon, DL (1972) Client-centered therapy. In B Stefflre and WH Grant (eds) *Theories of Counseling* (2nd ed). New York: McGraw-Hill.

Grummon, DL and John, ES (1954) Changes over client-centered therapy evaluated on psychoanalytically based Thematic Apperception Test scales. In CR Rogers and RF Dymond (eds) *Psychotherapy and Personality Change*. Chicago: University of Chicago Press.

Hart, SD and Hare, RD (1997) Psychopathy: Assessment and association with criminal conduct. In DM Stoff, J Breiling and JD Maser (eds) *Handbook of Antisocial Behavior* (pp. 22–35). New York: Wiley.

Hinshaw, SP and Zupan, BA (1997) Assessment of antisocial behavior in children and adolescents. In DM Stoff, J Breiling and JD Maser (eds) *Handbook of Antisocial Behavior* (pp. 36–50). New York: Wiley.

Holt, DD (1990) Career and personal counseling of inmates. *Dissertation Abstracts International, 51,* 1500.

Kellner, R (1986) Personality disorders. *Psychotherapy and Psychosomatics, 46,* 58–66.

Kirschenbaum, H (2003) *Carl Rogers and the Person-Centered Approach* [Video Cassette Recording]. www.HowardKirschenbaum.com

Kirschenbaum, H and Henderson, VL (eds) (1989). *The Carl Rogers Reader*. Boston: Houghton Mifflin.

Kristiansson, M (1995) Incurable psychopaths. *Bulletin of the American Academy of Psychiatry and the Law, 23,* 555–62.

Lahey, BB and Loeber, R (1997) Attention-deficit/hyperactivity disorder, oppositional defiant disorder, conduct disorder, and adult antisocial behavior: A life span perspective. In DM Stoff, J Breiling, and JD Maser (eds) *Handbook of Antisocial Behavior* (pp. 51–9). New York: Wiley.

Lally, RJ, Mangione, PL and Honig, AS (1988) The Syracuse University family research program: Long range impact of an early intervention program with low-income children and their families. In D Powell (ed) *Parent Education as Early Childhood Intervention: Emerging directions in theory, research, and practice* (pp. 79–104). Norwood, NJ: Ablex.

Lambert, MJ and Bergin, AE (1994) The effectiveness of psychotherapy. In AE Bergin and SL Garfield (eds) *Handbook of Psychotherapy Change* (4th ed) (pp. 143–89). New York: Wiley.

Luske, B (1990) *Mirrors of Madness*. Hawthorne, NY: Aldine de Gruyter.

Markovitz, P (2001) Pharmacotherapy. In WJ Livesley (ed) *Handbook of Personality Disorders* (pp. 475–93). New York: Guilford Press.

Maxmen, JS and Ward, NG (1995) *Essential Psychopathology and Its Treatment*. New York: WW Norton and Company.

McCulloch, LA (October, 2000) *A Person-Centered Approach to Antisocial Personality Disorder* (Doctoral Dissertation, University of Rochester, 2000). Dissertation Abstracts International.

McCulloch, LA (2002) A person-centred approach to antisocial personality disorder. *Person-Centred Practice, 10,* 4–14.

McCulloch, LA (2003a) Conceptualizing Reflection. Unpublished manuscript. State University of New York College at Brockport.

McCulloch, LA (2003b) Increasing counseling effectiveness: No questions asked! Unpublished manuscript. State University of New York College at Brockport.

Mish, FC (ed) (1996) *Merriam Webster's Collegiate Dictionary* (10th ed). Springfield, MA: Merriam-Webster.

Nauth, LL (1995) Power and control in the male antisocial personality. *Journal of Rational-Emotive and Cognitive Behavior Therapy, 13*, 215–24.

Olds, DL (1988) The prenatal/early infancy project. In EL Cowan, RP Lorion and J Ramos-McKay (eds) *Fourteen Ounces of Prevention: A handbook for practitioners* (pp. 9–22). Washington, DC: American Psychological Association.

Panton, JH (1979) MMPI profiles associated with outcomes of intensive psychotherapeutic counseling with youthful first offender prison inmates. *Research Communications in Psychology, Psychiatry and Behavior, 4*, 383–95.

Patterson, CH (1990) Involuntary clients. *Person-Centered Review, 5*, 316–20. Reprinted in CH Patterson *Understanding Psychotherapy: Fifty years of person-centred theory and practice* (pp. 188–91). Ross-on-Wye: PCCS Books.

Pilkonis, PA and Klein, KR (1997) Commentary on the assessment and diagnosis of antisocial behavior and personality. In DM Stoff, J Breiling, and JD Maser (eds) *Handbook of Antisocial Behavior* (pp. 109–12). New York: Wiley.

Potter, LB and Mercy, JA (1997) Public health perspective on interpersonal violence among youths in the United States. In DM Stoff, J Breiling and JD Maser (eds) *Handbook of Antisocial Behavior* (pp. 3–11). New York: Wiley.

Reid, JB and Eddy, JM (1997) The prevention of antisocial behavior: Some considerations in the search for effective interventions. In DM Stoff, J Breiling and JD Maser (eds) *Handbook of Antisocial Behavior* (pp. 343–56). New York: Wiley.

Rice, LN and Greenberg, LS (1992) Humanistic approaches to psychotherapy. In DK Freedheim (ed) *History of Psychotherapy: A century of change* (pp. 197–224). Washington, DC: American Psychological Association.

Rice, ME and Harris, GT (1997) The treatment of adult offenders. In DM Stoff, J Breiling and JD Maser (eds) *Handbook of Antisocial Behavior* (pp. 425–35). New York: Wiley.

Robins, LN (1966) *Deviant Children Growing Up: A sociological and psychiatric study of sociopathic personality*. Baltimore: Williams and Wilkins.

Rogeness, GA and McClure, EB (1996) Development and neurotransmitter-environmental interactions. *Development and Psychopathology, 8*, 183–99.

Rogers, CR (1951) *Client-Centered Therapy*. Boston: Houghton Mifflin.

Rogers, CR (1957) The necessary and sufficient conditions of therapeutic personality change. *Journal of Consulting Psychology, 21*, 95–103.

Rogers, CR (1959) A theory of therapy, personality, and interpersonal relationships, as developed in the client-centered framework. In S Koch (ed) *Psychology: A study of a science Vol. III. Formulations of the person and the social context* (pp. 184–256). New York: McGraw-Hill.

Rogers, CR (1961) *On Becoming a Person*. Boston: Houghton Mifflin.

Rogers, CR (1980) *A Way of Being*. Boston: Houghton Mifflin.

Rogers, CR (1986) Reflection of feelings. *Person-Centered Review, 1* (4).

Rogers, CR, Gendlin, ET, Kiesler, DJ and Truax, CB (1967) *The Therapeutic Relationship and Its Impact: A study of psychotherapy with schizophrenics*. Madison, Milwaukee: The University of Wisconsin Press.

Ross, RR, Fabiano, EA and Ross, RD (1991) *Reasoning and Rehabilitation: A handbook for teaching cognitive skills*. Ottawa, Canada: Desktop Publishing.

Ruegg, RG, Haynes, C and Frances, A (1997) Assessment and management of antisocial personality disorder. In M Rosenbluth and ID Yalom (eds) *Treating Difficult Personality Disorders* (pp. 123–72). San Francisco: Jossey-Bass.

Rutter, M (1997a) Antisocial behavior: Developmental psychopathology perspectives. In DM Stoff, J Breiling and JD Maser (ed) *Handbook of Antisocial Behavior* (pp. 115–24). New York: Wiley.

Rutter, M (1997b) Clinical implications of attachment concepts: Retrospect and prospect. In L Atkinson and KJ Zucker (eds) *Attachment and Psychopathology* (pp. 17–46). New York: Guilford Press.

Scharf, RS (1996) *Theories of Psychotherapy and Counseling.* Boston: Brooks/Cole.

Schrink, J and Hamm, MS (1990) Misconceptions concerning correctional counseling. *Journal of Offender Counseling, 14,* 133–47.

Seligman, L (1990) *Selecting Effective Treatments.* San Francisco: Jossey-Bass.

Sexton, TL and Griffin, BL (1997) The social and political nature of psychological science: The challenges, potentials, and future of constructivist thinking. In TL Sexton and BL Griffin (eds) *Constructivist Thinking in Counseling Practice, Research and Training* (pp. 249–61). New York: Teachers College Press.

Shaw, DS and Winslow, EB (1997) Precursors and correlates to antisocial behavior from infancy to preschool. In DM Stoff, J Breiling and JD Maser (eds) *Handbook of Antisocial Behavior* (pp. 148–58). New York: Wiley.

Smith, AB and Berlin, L (1988) *Treating the Criminal Offender.* New York: Plenum Press.

Smith, AB, Berlin, L and Bassin, A (1963) Problems in client-centered group therapy with adult offenders. *American Journal of Orthopsychiatry, 33,* 550–3.

Sommerbeck, L (2003) *The Client-Centred Therapist in Psychiatric Contexts: A therapists' guide to the psychiatric landscape and its inhabitants.* Ross-on-Wye, UK: PCCS Books.

Sue, DW, Sue, D and Sue, S (1990) *Understanding Abnormal Behavior.* Boston: Houghton Mifflin.

Tardiff, K (1984) Characteristics of assaultive patients in private hospitals. *American Journal of Psychiatry, 141,* 1232–5.

Tardiff, K (1992) The current state of psychiatry in the treatment of violent patients. *Archives General Psychiatry, 49,* 493–9.

Tardiff, K (1996) *Assessment and Management of Violent Patients.* Washington, DC: American Psychiatric Press.

Tausch, R (1978) Facilitative dimensions in interpersonal relations: Verifying the theoretical assumptions of Carl Rogers. *College Student Journal, 12,* 2–11.

Thomas, CL (ed) (1997) *Taber's Cyclopedic Medical Dictionary.* Philadelphia: FA Davis.

Truax, CB, Wargo, DG and Silber, LD (1966) Effects of group psychotherapy with high accurate empathy and nonpossessive warmth upon female institutionalized delinquents. *Journal of Abnormal Psychology, 71,* 267–74.

Tursi, MT and McCulloch, LA (2004) A person-centered approach to individuals diagnosed with anxiety/depression. *The Person-Centered Journal, 11,* 71–5.

Vaillant, GE (1975) Sociopathy as a human process: A viewpoint. *Archives of General Psychiatry, 32,* 178–83.

Van Evra, JP (1983) *Psychological Disorders of Children and Adolescents.* Boston: Little-Brown.

Walters, GD (1990) *The Criminal Lifestyle: Patterns of serious criminal conduct.* Newbury Park: Sage.

Whitely, SM and Hosford, RE (1983) Counseling in prisons. *Counseling Psychologist, 11,* 27–34.

Widiger, TA and Corbitt, EM (1997) Comorbidity of antisocial personality disorder with other personality disorders. In DM Stoff, J Breiling and JD Maser (eds) *Handbook of Antisocial Behavior* (pp. 75–82). New York: Wiley.

Widom, CS (1997) Child abuse, neglect, and witnessing violence. In DM Stoff, J Breiling and JD Maser (eds) *Handbook of Antisocial Behavior* (pp. 159–70). New York: Wiley.

Woody, GE, McLellan, AT, Luborsky, L and O'Brien, CP (1985) Sociopathy and psychotherapy outcome. *Archives of general psychiatry, 42,* 1081–6.

Wootton, B (1959) *Social Science and Social Pathology.* London: George Allen and Unwin.

Zanarini, MC and Gunderson, JG (1997) Differential Diagnosis of antisocial and borderline personality disorders. In DM Stoff, J Breiling and JD Maser (eds) *Handbook of Antisocial Behavior* (pp. 83–91). New York: Wiley.

Ziegler, E, Taussig, C and Black, K (1992) Early childhood intervention: A promising preventative for juvenile delinquency. *American Psychologist, 47,* 997–1006.

CHAPTER 13

UNDERSTANDING POST-TRAUMATIC STRESS FROM THE PERSON-CENTRED PERSPECTIVE

STEPHEN JOSEPH

Since the term post-traumatic stress was first introduced there has been a huge research effort to understand the effects of trauma and how to help people cope. But more recently, researchers have also begun to note that sometimes in their struggle with adversity people are able to find new meaning, purpose in life, and are able to look back upon their tragedies and misfortunes as having provided a trigger towards a more enriched and fulfilled life, a phenomenon which has been labelled as post-traumatic growth.

In this chapter I will discuss how the Person-Centred Approach provides an understanding of growth processes, and encourages us as therapists to adopt a more positive psychological perspective to our understanding of how people adjust to stressful and traumatic events. I will also argue that person-centred theory provides an explanation not only for post-traumatic growth processes but also for the phenomena characteristic of the diagnostic category of post-traumatic stress disorder (PTSD: American Psychiatric Association, 1994).

Inspection of the major texts on PTSD does not reference person-centred theory or Client-Centred Therapy (CCT). This is not surprising given that client-centred therapists do not adopt the language of the medical model and do not make the assumption that specific conditions require specific treatments (see Bozarth, 1998; Bozarth and Motomasa, Chapter 19, this volume), and thus have not attempted to provide an understanding of PTSD. But although the fact that writers in the person-centred tradition have been largely silent on the subject of PTSD is not surprising, it has meant that CCT has become marginalised from mainstream psychological and psychiatric contexts which do adopt the medical model. Insofar as we want to be taken seriously within a culture in which the medical model is dominant, it is important that we are able to explain how person-centred theory provides a conceptual underpinning to client-centred therapy with traumatised people and to make it clear why we think CCT will be helpful.

POST-TRAUMATIC STRESS DISORDER (PTSD)

The term PTSD refers to a familiar constellation of psychological reactions often experienced by people in the aftermath of a traumatic event. PTSD can result following events that involve some form of confrontation with death and injury, such as major disasters, technological accidents, road traffic accidents, criminal victimisation, sexual assault, war experiences, disease and illness, and political violence (see Joseph, Williams and Yule, 1997). Typically, people with a diagnosis of PTSD are highly aroused and anxious and suffer from various intrusive and avoidance experiences. The person is likely to be experiencing highly distressing thoughts, images and dreams, while simultaneously trying to avoid anything that arouses recollections of what happened to them (American Psychiatric Association, 1994). PTSD consists of three symptom clusters: (a) re-experiencing symptoms (e.g., nightmares, flashbacks, intrusive thoughts and images); (b) avoidance and numbing symptoms (e.g., behavioural attempts to avoid reminders, feelings of estrangement); and (c) arousal symptoms (e.g., irritability, difficulty concentrating) (American Psychiatric Association, 1994). PTSD can only be diagnosed after one month from the time of the event. In practice, person-centred therapists may not use the term PTSD but it would not be unusual for them to work with people who have experienced trauma and tragedy and who may otherwise be diagnosed as suffering from PTSD.

For example, John was recently severely physically assaulted outside a nightclub. Although it is now two months later and John has made a good recovery physically, during the day his thoughts often turn uncontrollably to that evening, and at night he often has nightmares of the experience and wakes up feeling frightened. Another person, Jill, was driving to a late morning meeting at work when another car unexpectedly veered off the road and crashed into her sending her across the carriageway. Several other cars were then involved in a horrific accident in which one person died. Although Jill escaped with her life, she sustained severe injuries. Now, almost three years later she can't get back into a car, and is haunted by thoughts of that day and of how she may have avoided the accident. Although a careful driver, she blames herself for not paying enough attention that day. Another person, Ian, had a minor heart attack three months previously and although the doctors tell him his prognosis is good, he remains frightened that he will have another one. His thoughts keep turning to the attack itself, and his memory of the event, the shortness of breath, the tightness in his chest, the intense fear, the look of fear on his wife's face, and as he talks of the event he feels a sense of panic rising in him.

It is not unusual for people to seek therapy to help them cope with the experience of loss or the psychological aftermath of an accident or an illness. The experiences of John, Jill and Ian are typical of people who may meet the diagnostic requirements of PTSD. The point is simply to illustrate that PTSD is not some esoteric condition, but a term used by psychologists and psychiatrists to simply describe the set of reactions people often have to horrific and tragic events in their lives, e.g., trouble with upsetting thoughts and images that come to mind, and attempts to avoid the distress caused by these thoughts and images. These problems can become so severe and chronic that they cause significant upset in a person's life.

PTSD is unusual in the *Diagnostic and Statistical Manual* (American Psychiatric Association, 1994) in having a definable event as the trigger. Various theoretical models have been proposed to explain the constellation of reactions associated with the category of PTSD, mostly concerned in some way with the role of cognitive appraisal processes subsequent to the event (see e.g., Joseph, Williams and Yule, 1997). Psychologists and psychiatrists draw on these theories when working clinically, and it is not surprising that in their attempt to understand PTSD they would rarely turn to person-centred theory. Psychopathology in the Person-Centred Approach (PCA) is usually explained as what happens when the actualising tendency is thwarted by adverse social environmental conditions. But although thwarting of the actualising tendency can explain a variety of psychological problems, it is not immediately obvious how person-centred theory is able to provide an account of PTSD. Clearly, PTSD does not directly result from an internalisation of conditions of worth in childhood, but from exposure to a traumatic event.

However, I would argue that a more detailed exploration of person-centred theory is able to provide us with an adequate understanding of PTSD. This chapter is an adaptation of two previous articles in which I have explored this topic in different professional contexts (Joseph, 2003, 2004).

BREAKDOWN AND DISORGANISATION OF THE SELF-STRUCTURE

Although he was writing well before the introduction of the term PTSD, Carl Rogers provided a theory of therapy and personality which contains an account of threat-related psychological processes consistent with contemporary trauma theory, and which provides the conceptual underpinnings to the client-centred and experiential ways of working with traumatised people. In person-centred terminology, PTSD symptoms are simply another way of talking about what Rogers (1959) described as the breakdown and disorganisation of the self-structure.

SELF-STRUCTURE

Carl Rogers' most detailed theoretical paper was his 1959 paper in which he provides a theory of personality and therapy. The first important concept Rogers introduces in this paper is what he calls the self-structure. In the 1959 paper PTSD can be understood as representing the normal psychological manifestation of a process which is instigated when the self-structure comes under threat. Self-structure refers to:

> ... the organized, consistent conceptual gestalt composed of perceptions of the characteristics of the 'I' or 'me' and the perceptions of the relationships of the 'I' or 'me' to others and to various aspects of life, together with the values attached to these perceptions. (Rogers, 1959: 200)

Rogers (1959) goes on to discuss the process of breakdown and disorganisation of the self-structure. Experiences that are incongruent with the self-structure are, Rogers (1959) wrote, subceived as threatening and not allowed to be accurately symbolised in awareness. The denial to awareness of the experience is an attempt to keep the perception of the experience consistent with the self-structure. This is true, Rogers wrote, of every person to a greater or lesser extent. Only in Rogers' (1959) description of the fully functioning person is the self-structure congruent with experience and always in the process of changing with new experience.

THREAT TO SELF-STRUCTURE

Of course, the fully functioning person is an ideal, and at least some degree of incongruence between self and experience is usual, with wide individual differences existing between people in their degree of incongruence. This is the usual state of affairs; we maintain our self-structure with a process of defence, until we experience a threat that is overwhelmingly incongruent with our self-structure—at which time the process of breakdown and disorganisation of the self-structure described by Rogers (1959) is instigated. Rogers' writes:

> 1. If the individual has a large or significant degree of *incongruence between self and experience* and if a significant experience demonstrating this *incongruence* occurs suddenly, or with a high degree of obviousness, then the organism's process of *defense* is unable to operate successfully.
>
> 2. As a result *anxiety* is *experienced* as the *incongruence* is subceived. The degree of *anxiety* is dependent upon the extent of the *self-structure* which is *threatened*.
>
> 3. The process of *defense* being unsuccessful, the *experience* is *accurately symbolized in awareness*, and the gestalt of the *self-structure* is broken by this *experience* of the *incongruence in awareness*. A state of disorganization results.
>
> 4. In such a state of disorganization the organism behaves at times in ways which are openly consistent with experiences which have hitherto been distorted or denied to awareness. At other times the self may temporarily regain regnancy, and the organism may behave in ways consistent with it. (Rogers, 1959: 228–9)

Rogers (1959) theory is generic and the process of breakdown and disorganisation of the self-structure is usually considered within the context of more everyday events. What I would argue, however, is that the statement on breakdown and disorganisation of the self-structure applies equally well to traumatic events. Although Rogers was probably not thinking of traumatic events per se when he formulated his statement on the breakdown and disorganisation of the self-structure, and he was writing well before the term PTSD was introduced, it should be remembered that Rogers was experienced in working with Second World War veterans and was aware of the psychological impact of trauma (Rogers, 1942; Rogers and Wallen, 1946). Traumatic events most certainly present us with information that demonstrates incongruence between self and experience.

SHATTERED ASSUMPTIONS

The nature of traumatic events is that they will demonstrate incongruence to most people because there are common distortions in the self-structure. One aspect of self-structure in which there is high degree of discrepancy between self and experience is in the denial to awareness of existential experiences, for example, that we are fragile, that the future is uncertain, and that life is not fair. Although many people will say they know these to be truths, when it comes to how we actually lead our lives most of us go from day to day as if we were invulnerable, that tomorrow will certainly come as expected, and that there we will be rewarded for good deeds and punished for bad deeds. What traumatic events do is to abruptly and obviously present us with experience that leads to a breakdown of these aspects of self-structure. Trauma shows us the limits of the human condition and brings into questions our previous values and assumptions about ourselves and how we lead our lives.

To those familiar with the PTSD literature this is not saying anything novel. Rogers' description is simply consistent with the current social cognitive theories of post-traumatic stress. For example, one of the most influential theorists of recent years has been the social psychologist Janoff-Bulman (1989, 1992), who has discussed how the experience of trauma has a shattering effect on people's assumptive world. Janoff-Bulman (1989, 1992) described how individuals possess a schema of the self and the world. Janoff-Bulman suggests that there are common psychological experiences shared by victims who have experienced a wide range of traumatic situations. She proposed that post-traumatic stress following victimisation is largely due to the shattering of basic assumptions victims hold about themselves and the world.

Importantly, Rogers' description accounts for the phenomenology of PTSD. Certainly he does not use the term PTSD as he was writing well before this term was introduced, but his description of the process of breakdown and disorganisation shows how the phenomenology of PTSD arises. Rogers (1959) talks about the anxiety that is experienced as the incongruence is subceived. However, the hallmark signs of PTSD are the re-experiencing and avoidance phenomena, and any theory must be able to account for these. Rogers does account for the intrusive and avoidant features when he goes on to describe the disorganisation that results when the self-structure breaks down. He says that the person attempts, on the one hand, to accurately symbolise in awareness their experience (intrusion), and on the other, to deny their experiences and hold onto their pre-existing self-structure (avoidance). This account of the phases of intrusion and avoidance is similar to that of the information processing theory proposed by Horowitz (1986), a leading theorist in the field of trauma. Horowitz (1986) also describes how people work through their experiences in terms of a tension between intrusive and avoidant states.

Horowitz's (1986) information processing approach is based on the idea that individuals have mental models, or schemata, of the world and of themselves which they use to interpret incoming information. He also proposes that there is an inherent drive to make our mental models coherent with current information, which he refers to as the *completion tendency*. A traumatic event presents information that is incompatible with existing schemas. This incongruity gives rise to a stress response requiring reappraisal and revision of the schema. As traumatic events generally require massive schematic changes, complete integration and cognitive processing take some time to occur. During this time, active memory tends to repeat its representations of the traumatic event causing emotional distress. However, to prevent emotional exhaustion, there is a process of inhibition and facilitation that acts as a feedback system modulating the flow of information. The symptoms observed during stress responses, which Horowitz categorises as involving denials and intrusion, occur as a result of opposite actions of a control system that regulates the incoming information to tolerable doses. If inhibitory control is not strong enough, intrusive symptoms such as nightmares and flashbacks emerge. When inhibitory efforts are too strong in relation to active memory, symptoms indicative of the avoidance phase occur. Typically, avoidance and intrusion symptoms fluctuate in a way particular to the individual without causing flooding or exhaustion that would prevent adaptation. The person oscillates between the states of avoidance and intrusion until a relative equilibrium is reached when the person is said to have worked through the experience.

INDIVIDUAL DIFFERENCES IN VULNERABILITY

Contemporary theory in PTSD recognises that not everyone who experiences a traumatic event goes on to develop PTSD, and therefore any theory needs to be able to account for this observation. The above extract from Rogers' theoretical account is also able to account for individual differences. Rogers' theory provides a similar perspective to Horowitz (1986) who provides an account of cognitive processes involved in adaptation to trauma. Recovery from trauma is explained as resulting from cognitive assimilation of the traumatic memory or a revision of existing schemas to accommodate new information. Individual differences in trauma response are explained in Horowitz's (1986) theory in terms of the degree of disparity between the trauma and pre-existing expectations and beliefs, or in Rogers' terminology, the extent of incongruence between self and experience. The pivotal part of Rogers' description of breakdown is that the event demonstrates incongruence between self and experience. Here is the notion that it is how a person perceives the event that is important. It is in the nature of incongruence between self and experience that this will always be idiosyncratic to the person. We all have different experiences in life, and consequently an event which demonstrates incongruence to one person may not do so to another. In Rogers' theory, cognitive appraisal processes are central.

Also, Rogers suggests that the more obvious and sudden the threat, the greater the degree of anxiety that is engendered. Although as a description of the event characteristics that lead to difficulties in emotional processing, Rogers' use of the term 'obviousness' lacks the more fine-grained analysis provided by, for example, the behavioural psychologist Rachman (1980), it does capture the essence of the description necessary to understand which events might be most likely to lead to PTSD. Rachman listed other stimulus characteristics that would constitute obviousness, i.e., suddenness, intensity, and dangerousness. Of course, trauma theorists will have paid particular detail to event factors, individual difference factors, and so on (see Joseph, Williams and Yule 1997) that Rogers' generic theory from over forty years ago does not address, but what is important is that Rogers' theory provides us with sufficient understanding of trauma consistent with the big picture of contemporary trauma theory.

THE PROCESS OF REINTEGRATION

Rogers (1959) goes on to suggest that accurate symbolisation in awareness of experience was necessary for reintegration of self and experience to take place. Similarly, current thinking on the most effective ways of helping people with post-traumatic stress integrate their experiences emphasises therapies that use exposure (e.g., Foa and Kozak, 1986; Foa and Rothbaum, 1998). Certainly, the evidence shows that therapies that help the person to accurately symbolise their experiences, to use Rogers' terminology, are effective in helping people with PTSD. Person-centred theorists would therefore not disagree on the importance of exposure. Biermann-Ratjen (1998), for example, writes:

> As well as knowing that self-experience can only be integrated by accepting it, we also know nowadays that the best way of treating post-traumatic disorders is to help the traumatised person to remember the traumatic experience in the safety of a therapeutic relationship marked by empathic unconditionally [sic] positive regard. In this frame the experience which has been repeatedly driven out of consciousness can be retrieved piece by piece and reach awareness and the person can come to accept and understand his/her behaviour and feelings in reaction to the traumatic experience as a form of self-defence. (Biermann-Ratjen, 1998: 125)

What is key to the practice of psychotherapy is the way in which the therapist engages with the client in facilitating the process of exposure. The notion that the client should lead the process is not one confined to writers from the client-centred tradition however, and others have also commented on the importance of not pushing the client. In writing about exposure, Meichenbaum (1994) states:

> ... some clients may be reluctant to mentally 'relive' and 'reexperience' the trauma-related events in the course of treatment. Clients may resist doing so-called 'memory work' of traumatic events. There is a danger of the therapist 'pushing' his/her agenda of the way to conduct treatment without 'spelling out' the options for the client ... this therapeutic process needs to be collaborative with the clients being 'informed' and 'in-charge' throughout. (Meichenbaum, 1994: 303)

It is important to understand that the process of accurate symbolisation is what exposure therapies set out to achieve, but what person-centred theory adds is the idea that there is no need for the therapist to push the client because the client will be intrinsically motivated to increase congruence between self and experience, and to accurately symbolise their experiences in awareness when the right social environmental conditions are present. This is what makes Person-Centred Therapy different, the belief that the actualising tendency will—when the social environment is supportive—lead the person to accurately symbolise their experience. Thus there is no need to direct the client towards engaging in various cognitive-behavioural type exercises as the client will find their own best way to engage in retrieving, remembering and re-evaluating their experiences. Person-centred theory states that if the client is not engaging in this process it must be because the social environment is not supportive enough for them to feel unconditionally accepted and thus able to drop their defences and listen to their own inner voice.

GROWTH THROUGH ADVERSITY

As mentioned, one of the most important features of the person-centred conceptualisation of traumatic stress reactions is that it not only allows for a theoretical understanding of PTSD, but also of post-traumatic growth. As the client comes more to develop a self-structure that is congruent between self and experience, they should also become more fully functioning and able to be engage in organismic valuing. The nineteenth of Rogers' (1951) propositions sums this up:

> As the individual perceives and accepts into his self-structure more of his organic experiences, he finds that he is replacing his present value *system*— based so largely upon introjections which have been distortedly symbolized— with a continuing organismic valuing *process*. (Rogers, 1951: 522)

Thus, congruent reintegration of self with experience is not about the client returning to their pre-trauma levels of functioning, but about the client going beyond their previous levels of functioning, to become more fully functioning. As we have seen above, Rogers (1959) description of the fully functioning person is that of someone who, for example, is open to experience, perceives him or herself as the locus of evaluation, and has no conditions of worth. Such movement toward becoming fully functioning in traumatised clients might be described as post-traumatic growth (see Linley and Joseph, 2004; Tedeschi, Park and Calhoun, 1998). A more detailed account and integration of organismic theory within mainstream psychological approaches to trauma is available in Joseph and Linley (in press).

The focus on the fully functioning person is what makes the person-centred approach to understanding trauma very different from other social cognitive approaches. All psychological theories draw attention to the fact that the person must somehow integrate the new trauma-related information with pre-existing schemas, but what person-centred theory does is to draw the distinction between the two ways in which trauma-related experience can be accommodated. Those aspects of self-structure that have broken down can be rebuilt in the direction of the person's conditions of worth, or the self-structure can be rebuilt in the direction of the person's actualising tendency.

Person-centred theory offers a powerful explanatory framework for understanding both post-traumatic stress reactions and growth through adversity. Person-Centred Therapy is a way of working with people founded on the alternative paradigm that people have an innate tendency towards the actualisation of their potentialities.

THERAPY

The concept of the actualising tendency is unique to the person-centred way of working and has profound significance for therapeutic practice. What Client-Centred Therapy can offer to traumatised clients is an unconditionally accepting relationship in which the client does not feel pushed to move in any direction other than their own. As Kennedy-Moore and Watson (1999) write:

> In working with trauma survivors, it is essential to bear in mind that emotional expression rarely proceeds in an orderly fashion. Clients may express a little, then retreat from their feelings, then express a little more, then need to return to laying the groundwork for expression. Therapists need to be sensitive to these fluctuations and to let clients take the lead in determining how much they can handle and how fast. Forcing clients to express their feelings before they are ready to do so can lead to emotional flooding and can compound client's sense of victimisation. On the other hand, helping trauma survivors achieve a sense of mastery in their ability to articulate and manage their feelings can counter the sense of vulnerability and lack of control that traumatic events evoke. (Kennedy-Moore and Watson, 1999: 253)

The client-centred therapist in offering the core conditions to their client is able to offer a social environment that serves to slowly dissolve the conditions of worth, with the consequence that the self-structure is gradually broken down and the self reintegrated with experience to rebuild a new self-structure consistent with the actualising tendency. In working with traumatised clients, however, aspects of the self-structure have already been abruptly shattered. The task of the client-centred therapist is therefore to help the client rebuild their self-structure by reintegrating self with experience. As we have seen, person-centred theory suggests that as the client comes to develop a self-structure that is more congruent between self and experience they should also become more fully functioning, and that such movement toward becoming fully functioning in traumatised clients might be described in current terminology as post-traumatic growth (Linley and Joseph, 2004; Tedeschi, Park and Calhoun, 1998).

The danger from other therapeutic approaches is that they might inadvertently lead the client to integrate self and experience in line with conditions of worth as opposed to their intrinsic organismic valuing process. The person-centred therapist tries to go with the client at his or her own pace and direction, using their empathy and congruence to communicate their unconditional positive regard:

Client: I've just been feeling so horrible recently thinking about what could have happened, how close it all was, and if I had been one second slower it would have been so different, and God I feel scared, I just shiver when I think of that.

Therapist: It looks like you are shivering right now, telling me just how scared you feel when you think about how close you both were, it's still so real for you, and how life seems so on a knife edge, one second more and he would have been gone.

Client: That is it, there is nothing, today, tomorrow, a bus could come along, any second and that's it, goodbye, so what have we got, I feel so frightened I want to scream at people wake up it's not real …

Therapist: Wake up, this is it, life could end any second, and that's a terrifying thought …

Here, the therapist is trying to go with the client at their pace and direction. Person-centred theory says that this process will facilitate the client in becoming more congruent between self and experience. A more directive therapist however might thwart this process:

Client: I've just been feeling so horrible recently thinking about what could have happened, how close it all was, and if I had been one second slower it would have been so different, and God I feel scared, I just shiver when I think of that.

Therapist: It was a lucky escape, but what I suggest is we explore is the chances of this happening again. It's not unusual for people to have the feeling that something bad is going to happen again, after all it happened once, but actually the chances are minimal that this sort of accident is likely to happen to you again …

The above hypothetical example illustrates the essential difference, that is, trying to go with the client at their pace and direction or going with some other agenda. In the second case, the client might, for example, feel unheard by the therapist and hear the subtle message that a person should not express how they feel. By reassuring the client, even unintentionally, that the world is not a place where tragedy and suffering can strike us unexpectedly at any time the client is perhaps thwarted in their attempt to congruently integrate self and experience. Of course, therapy involves more subtle processes than illustrated in the rather pointed example used above. Unintentional messages from the therapist to the client are not always obvious, but they do happen. There is no doubt that a discussion about the likelihood of an event re-occurring may in some circumstances be useful, but the point here is that by not going with the client at their pace and direction the therapist does not necessarily provide the freedom for the client to integrate self and experience in the direction of their own actualising tendency, and thus to become more fully functioning in the longer term.

Experience of adversity tells us that the world is a place where tragedy and suffering can strike us unexpectedly at any time. One of the characteristics of the fully functioning person is that they trust in their own experiencing and develop values in accordance with that experience. The world is a place where unexpected events can happen at any time or place and the fully functioning person is aware of this and lives his or her life in light of this information.

CONCLUSION

Person-centred personality theory provides a framework to explain the development of growth through adversity, while simultaneously accounting for the phenomenology characteristic of PTSD. Having set out how person-centred theory is able to account for PTSD, empirical research now needs to be provided.

Empirical research on Client-Centred Therapy (CCT) for PTSD using well-controlled studies has not been conducted. We now need empirical evidence that Client-Centred Therapy not only helps to alleviate the so-called symptoms of PTSD, but that it also facilitates growth. This is what sets person-centred theory and CCT apart from other approaches, i.e., the theoretical stance that the client will be motivated by the actualising tendency to accurately symbolise their experience and with the right therapeutic conditions will be able to do so. The implication of this is that there is no need to direct the client to engage in exposure-based exercises because the theory holds that the traumatised client will be intrinsically motivated to do this for themselves in their own way and at their own pace when the therapist is providing the appropriate social-environmental conditions (Rogers, 1957).

However, the assumption that clients will be intrinsically motivated to accurately symbolise their experiences is one that many therapists from other traditions might question, and there is a need now for research to test out whether this is indeed the case.

In conclusion, the most significant feature of person-centred theory as it applies to understanding trauma is the fact that the theory not only accounts for the development of PTSD, but also for the development of growth through adversity.

REFERENCES

American Psychiatric Association (1980) *Diagnostic and Statistical Manual of Mental Disorders* (3rd ed). Washington, DC: American Psychiatric Press.

American Psychiatric Association (1994) *Diagnostic and Statistical Manual of Mental Disorders* (4th ed). Washington, DC: American Psychiatric Press.

Bozarth, JD (1998) *Person-Centered Therapy: A revolutionary paradigm*. Ross-on-Wye: PCCS Books.

Biermann-Ratjen, EM (1998) Incongruence and psychopathology. In B Thorne and E Lambers (eds) *Person-Centred Therapy: A European perspective* (pp. 106–18). London: Sage.

Foa, EB and Kozak, MJ (1986) Emotional processing of fear: Exposure to corrective information. *Psychological Bulletin, 99*, 20–35.

Foa, EB and Rothbaum, BO (1998) *Treating the Trauma of Rape: Cognitive behavioral therapy for PTSD*. New York: Guilford.

Horowitz, M (1986) *Stress Response Syndromes*. Northville, NJ: Jason Aronson.

Janoff-Bulman, R (1989) Assumptive worlds and the stress of traumatic events: Applications of the schema construct. *Social Cognition, 7*, 113–36.

Janoff-Bulman, R (1992) *Shattered Assumptions: Toward a new psychology of trauma*. New York: The Free Press.

Joseph, S (2003) Person-centred approach to understanding posttraumatic stress. *Person-Centred*

Practice, 11, 70–5.

Joseph, S (2004) Client-centred therapy, posttraumatic stress disorder and posttraumatic growth. Theory and practice. *Psychology and Psychotherapy: Theory, research, and practice, 77,* 101–20.

Joseph, S and Linley, PA (in press). Positive adjustment to threatening events: an organismic valuing theory of growth through adversity. *Review of General Psychology.*

Joseph, S, Williams, R and Yule, W (1997) *Understanding Post-Traumatic Stress: A psychosocial perspective on PTSD and treatment.* Wiley: Chichester.

Kennedy-Moore, E and Watson, JC (1999) *Expressing Emotion: Myths, realities, and therapeutic strategies.* New York: Guilford Press.

Linley, PA and Joseph, S (2004) Positive changes following trauma and adversity: A review. *Journal of Traumatic Stress, 17,* 11–21.

Meichenbaum, D (1994) *Treating Post-Traumatic Stress Disorder: A handbook and practice manual for therapy.* Chichester: Wiley.

Rachman, S (1980) Emotional processing. *Behaviour Research and Therapy, 18,* 51–60.

Rogers, CR (1942) *Counseling and Psychotherapy: Newer concepts in practice.* Boston: Houghton Mifflin.

Rogers, CR (1951) *Client-Centered Therapy: Its current practice, implications and theory.* Boston: Houghton Mifflin.

Rogers, CR (1957) The necessary and sufficient conditions of therapeutic personality change. *Journal of Consulting Psychology, 21,* 95–103.

Rogers, CR (1959) A theory of therapy, personality and interpersonal relationships, as developed in the client-centered framework. In S Koch (ed), *Psychology: A study of a science, Vol. 3: Formulations of the person and the social context* (pp. 184–256). New York: McGraw-Hill.

Rogers, CR and Wallen, JL (1946) *Counseling with Returned Servicemen.* New York: McGraw-Hill.

Tedeschi, RG, Park, CL and Calhoun, LG (eds) (1998) *Posttraumatic Growth: Positive changes in the aftermath of crisis.* Mahwah: Lawrence Erlbaum.

CHAPTER 14

WORKING WITH MATERNAL DEPRESSION: PERSON-CENTRED THERAPY AS PART OF A MULTIDISCIPLINARY APPROACH

ELAINE CATTERALL

My intention in this chapter is to write about postnatal depression by first referring to the psychiatric and psychotherapeutic evidence base to provide the reader with an overview of the current thinking and practice relating to this phenomenon. Against this clinical background, I will then consider postnatal depression from a person-centred theoretical perspective and what Person-Centred Therapy has to offer women experiencing maternal distress. The discussion would be incomplete though without including a brief review of Western social-cultural perspectives surrounding motherhood and postnatal depression, as I believe this will provide the therapeutic relationship with the necessary context in which to engage with this client group in a more meaningful way.

There is also an autobiographical element to this chapter, which inevitably brings in a subjective personal bias; however I make no apologies for this. At one time I may have considered such personal reference 'unprofessional' in a text of this kind, yet without it there would be a denial of the influence that phenomenological experience has on any of our work. Indeed, it is unlikely that I would be writing this chapter if I had not personally experienced postnatal depression. I make no pretence to original thought in what follows, but what I do hope to do is to bring together a range of ideas about postnatal depression that are already 'out there' and attempt to integrate them in a way that may not have previously been presented to mental health professionals, including person-centred therapists.

PERSONAL BACKGROUND

I have three daughters and my interest in postnatal depression started when I experienced severe psychological distress after my second daughter was born in 1992. The journey to recovery was a long and seemingly *ad hoc* affair, with family and friends at its core, but also involving primary care and psychiatric treatment interventions (including in-patient care), as well as privately arranged long-term psychotherapy, alternative therapies and invaluable support from other women through the voluntary support agencies. (See Appendix for details of UK-based organisations offering support for postnatal depression.)

Psychiatric opinion and interpretation did not provide a complete explanation of my experience of postnatal depression, nor did it alone 'cure' my depression. It was this discrepancy between internal experiencing and external, expert opinion that inspired me to want to know more, not only about myself but also about the label 'postnatal depression' and its relevance and meaning within society.

My subsequent involvement in voluntary support agencies, offering individual and group support to other new mothers, led to formal counselling training. It was at this point that I began to realise that much of what had helped my recovery and indeed what I was now trying to communicate to others, could be explained by person-centred theory. Now I work as a person-centred therapist with adolescents and adults, and some of this work includes clients seeking help for postnatal depression. More recently I have joined a small group of counsellors as a facilitator of psycho-educational support groups for women with young babies, specifically designed to explore the experience of motherhood. The countless conversations I have had with mothers experiencing postnatal depression in the last decade have all, in some way, informed and influenced the ideas set out within this chapter. For that I am eternally grateful.

MOTHERHOOD, POSTNATAL DEPRESSION AND PATHOLOGY: A MEDICAL, PSYCHOLOGICAL AND SOCIAL PERSPECTIVE

Historically in the West, newly delivered mothers were considered to be 'ill' and an enforced 'lying-in' period of three weeks usually followed delivery. The woman was considered to be in social and physical transition and remained in the house whilst the local women took over her chores. With the arrival of the industrial era in the mid-18th century this lying-in period started to reduce, especially for working-class women. Even so, the benefits of bed rest were still considered to be important even if women couldn't stick to it (Figes, 1998).

MATERNAL AND INFANT MORTALITY

Until the early part of the 20th century, childbirth was a leading cause of death, second to tuberculosis (Figes, 1998) and women would have known others within their families and communities who died or sustained serious injury during childbirth. Fear for their own life and that of their infant, as well as mourning for the loss of others are likely to have been the primary psychological focus for many women and thus any psychological changes associated with the transition to motherhood were likely to have been overshadowed. Except for the work of two French Doctors, J. E. D. Esquirol and Louis Marcé, in the 1850s, the notion of a specific mental illness associated with childbirth had not yet fully emerged.

INCREASING FOCUS ON CHILDCARE AND WELFARE

As obstetric and medical procedures improved maternal mortality and health during the early part of the twentieth century, the focus of care quickly shifted away from the mother to the infant, and women's health and welfare started to be overlooked in favour of the baby's health. Around this time, ideas from psychology and psychoanalysis relating to child development were also becoming increasingly influential. The work of the psychoanalysts Winnicott and Bowlby highlighted the importance of a good mother-infant relationship to ensure the emotional well-being of the child, and their ideas became widely known, becoming the accepted wisdom among doctors, teachers and social workers about good childcare practice. Despite findings of recent research criticising Bowlby's early work on attachment theory as being too simplistic and flawed methodologically (Holmes, 1993; Parker, 1995; Figes, 1998), there still remains a commonly held belief in society that babies and young children are best cared for solely by their mother.

Humanistic psychology and in particular, the ideas of Rogers, have also been assimilated into our child-centred culture. When I ask women what it means to them to be a 'good' mother, women often describe one aspect as being able to give 'unconditional love' and expect themselves to be able to do this, without having given much thought to the 'unconditional' aspect of this idea.

By implication therefore, it is 'mother's love' and 'mother's care' that produces a secure and emotionally stable child despite research that continues to demonstrate that influences on the development of the child are far more complicated than this, and that other significant relationships in the baby's life are just as important. For example, the importance of the father's relationship with the baby is being increasingly highlighted (e.g. Cox and Holden, 1994; Biddulph, 2003).

A CHANGE IN EMPHASIS FROM ILLNESS TO HEALTH

Western medical and childbirth experts have moved away from the earlier model of 'illness' and now define a newly delivered mother as 'healthy'. In the medical text, *The Fundamentals of Obstetrics and Gynaecology* (Llewellyn Jones, 1994), a new mother is considered to be 'a healthy, intelligent individual who has just achieved a memorable event' (Figes, 1998: 17). Whilst this is more in line with the anthropological view that becoming a mother is a natural experience (Kitszinger, 1992) and I agree with this from a biological viewpoint, it excludes those childbirth experiences where a woman's physical and mental state leave her feeling anything but healthy.

In her recent book critiquing the traditional explanations of postnatal depression, Paula Nicholson reminds us that, despite this notion of 'health', childbirth still remains a medical event in the UK and USA and that medical and surgical interventions are increasingly common during childbirth and delivery (Nicholson, 1998: 86). Ellie Lee also writes extensively on the increasing medicalisation of experiences relating to motherhood (Lee, 2003), and both authors point to the contradictions that exist within society about the experience of women becoming mothers. On the one hand, it is described as a natural, healthy and happy experience, but on the other, a medically 'monitored and managed' experience, making it almost impossible for a woman to follow any instinctive feelings that may emerge during this time. Within this context of 'health' it may be possible to see why the medical discourse relating to childbirth describes anything outside of this 'norm' as pathology and why a specific branch of psychiatry specialising in maternal mental illness, known as perinatal psychiatry has emerged.

POSTNATAL DEPRESSION AND CURRENT PSYCHIATRIC CLASSIFICATION

Before describing the psychiatric classification of postnatal depression, a brief description of the commonly used language and terminology within the field of maternal mental health is needed. *Postnatal depression* and the *baby blues* are the commonly used terms that many people will be familiar with (used by women and their families as well as by health professionals). *Postpartum, puerperium* and *puerperal* are the clinical terms used to refer to the period following childbirth (usually refering to the first four weeks). *Perinatal* is a recent addition to the psychiatric literature and describes the period from pregnancy to one-year postpartum, as it is now recognised that maternal distress is not exclusive to the postpartum period. It can start antenatally in some women (10 per cent of women experience antenatal anxiety and depression (Green and Murray, 1994)) and go beyond the first six weeks in others. Perinatal psychiatry specialises in the treatment of antenatal and postpartum mental disorders.

For ease of reference, I will use the term 'postnatal depression' within this chapter to refer to the range of psychological distress experienced by pregnant and newly delivered mothers. (Throughout the chapter, I use the terms 'new mother' and 'newly delivered mother' interchangeably. These terms are *not* restricted to first-time mothers.) I want to acknowledge at this point, that puerperal psychosis requires a separate discussion in terms of treatment and support, but there is not the space within this chapter to give it the attention it also deserves. However, my conversations and friendships with a handful of women who have experienced puerperal psychosis have also influenced the thinking behind this chapter.

PSYCHIATRIC CLASSIFICATION

In the 1960s, Professor Brice Pitt was one of the first British psychiatrists to describe depression following childbirth as atypical and different from depression experienced at other times (Pitt, 1968). By the 1980s, a group of American and British psychiatrists had formed the Marcé Society to counter the lack of information about postnatal mental illness. The society now has a broader membership and aims to advance the understanding, prevention and treatment of mental illness related to childbirth.

Three disorders are commonly described within the psychiatric literature: *postpartum blues, postpartum psychosis* and *postpartum depression*. Postpartum blues and postpartum psychosis are not used as formal diagnostic categories in the 4th edition of the *Diagnostic and Statistical Manual* of the American Psychiatric Association (*DSM-IV*, 1994), or the 10th edition of the *International Classification of Diseases* (*ICD-10*, WHO, 1992). Their relevance though, to medical professionals, is that each term conveys a sense of timing of onset and relative severity, being characterised as having a *postpartum onset* if the episode begins within four weeks of childbirth (O'Hara, 1997).

Postpartum or *baby blues* refers to the transient low mood, tearfulness and irritability that 50 to 80 per cent of women experience within the first few days following delivery. Neither the severity nor the duration of the blues passes the threshold for a psychiatric disorder and nor should it as this is widely regarded as a normal part of the transition into motherhood.

Postpartum or *puerperal psychosis* affects one to two women per 1000 births and 80 per cent of cases develop within 14 days after delivery. Postpartum psychosis is by definition, severe and may persist for a considerable period. It is usually classified as, for example, manic episode, depressive episode or brief psychotic episode. Despite reported symptom differences between puerperal and non-puerperal psychoses (e.g. puerperal psychosis has been described as 'being more bizarre or extreme pathologically, with greater perplexity or confusion, yet women recover more quickly and "completely"' (Cox, 1994: 4)), puerperal psychosis is increasingly being considered a variant of bipolar disorder (Oates, 1994; Brockington, 1996).

Based on studies using a *clinical* diagnosis for depression, *postpartum depression* affects 10 to 15 per cent of women (Cox and Holden, 1994). *DSM-IV* does not have a separate category but provides a general statement that a non-psychotic depressive episode can be classified as postpartum depression if it begins in the postpartum period; i.e. beginning within the first four weeks following the birth. *ICD-10* has taken this a step further and allocated a specific classification (F53) *for mental and behavioural disorders associated with the puerperium, not elsewhere classified* (*ICD-10*, WHO, 1992, cited in Cox, 1994: 4).

A *clinical diagnosis* usually requires that a woman be experiencing dysphoric (low) mood along with several other symptoms such as sleep, appetite, or psychomotor disturbance, fatigue, excessive guilt and suicidal thoughts. Typically, symptoms must be present for a minimum amount of time (at the very least, one week) and must result in some impairment in the woman's functioning (O'Hara, 1997).

PROBLEMS OF LABELLING

Despite its inclusion within the diagnostic criteria, many health professionals involved with perinatal mental health consider postnatal depression to be a 'relatively minor disturbance (in psychiatric terms), which tends to remit spontaneously within a few months' (Brockington, 2004; Cooper and Murray, 1997; O'Hara, 1997) and therefore does not warrant a separate classification. Indeed, a review of the research suggests that the symptoms and duration of postnatal depression are not noticeably different from depression occurring at other times (e.g. O'Hara, 1997; Brockington, 2004).

Other perinatal specialists meanwhile, argue that despite this clinical picture, women experience postnatal mental disorders as 'distressing and unexpected and not as a time of personal growth, or purposive suffering' (Holden, 1991, cited in Cox and Holden, 1994: 5). Cox states that many women regard postnatal depression as 'different' from depression at other times' (Cox, 1994: 5).

Of the women I've listened to, few have described their experience as a 'minor disturbance' that disappears after a few months. Whilst some find meaning in this experience, many do not. It is often shocking and frightening, with many women fearing they 'are going mad'. Women are therefore often relieved to be given the label 'postnatal depression' as it provides an explanation for their experience, but it can also feel stigmatising. Elliott points out that labelling can inhibit or delay the process of change that the 'depressed mood should be heralding' (Elliott, 1994: 223), (something I observed in peer support groups at times). A clinical label aligns the experience to a physical illness, often disconnecting the woman from any personal meanings and it can become something that is 'not a part of me' but something that is happening 'to me'. Something to get 'rid of', 'out of my control' and this disconnection or sense of helplessness is heard sometimes when women describe their experience as 'the illness' or 'when I had PND'.

The danger though, of dismissing the idea of postnatal depression as an illness is that it may deny the experiences of the small percentage of mothers who are severely depressed and describe feeling physically 'very ill' (often described in terms of overwhelming exhaustion and tiredness, not eating or sleeping) which is *in addition to* their psychological distress. For these women, 'the label may point the way out and bring in some badly needed care and attention' (Elliott, 1994: 223).

'POSTNATAL DEPRESSION'—AN OVERSIMPLIFICATION?

Professor Ian Brockington (2004) proposes that the traditional view of the *blues, postnatal depression* and *psychosis* is in fact an oversimplification and that the range of disorders that women experience in the perinatal period is much wider. Post-traumatic stress disorder, obsessions of child harm, serious disturbances in the mother-infant relationship, and a range of anxiety disorders are highlighted as separate disorders, each requiring specific psychological treatments (Brockington, 2004: 303).

What becomes clear from this debate is that the experience of maternal psychological distress is not a uniform experience and is too complex to fit neatly within a single clinical diagnosis of *postpartum depression*. Women do describe a wide range of symptoms that they associate with postnatal depression, which do not fit neatly into the clinical symptom list described earlier. Excessive and constant anxiety is commonly the main presenting symptom, rather than depressed mood (Dion, 2002), and is frequently accompanied by obsessional thoughts, often relating to fears about the infant's or mother's health. But are these 'separate disorders' as Brockington suggests, or all part of the same experience?

Traumatic experiences during pregnancy and birth do leave some women describing symptoms that warrant a diagnosis of PTSD associated with childbirth (Bailham and Joseph, 2003) and disturbances in the mother-infant relationship for example may exist *in the absence of* maternal depression (Cramer, 1997).

But is it any more helpful to these women to have their experiences delineated into a whole range of separate disorders that then require accurate diagnosis in order to receive the 'correct' treatment?

AETIOLOGY

The classification debate remains unresolved primarily because research has been unable to confirm a specific aetiology for postpartum depression. Hormonal factors have been thought to play an important aetiological role in postnatal depression because of the dramatic hormonal changes that occur in women in the first few days following delivery. Whilst there is growing evidence for a biological aetiology for puerperal psychosis that is similar to bipolar disorder (e.g. the neuroendocrine studies of Wieck et al., cited in Cox, 1994), O'Hara concludes in his comprehensive view of the research investigating the causal factors of postpartum depression, that hormonal factors 'may only be important for women who are otherwise vulnerable to affective disorder' (O'Hara, 1997: 16).

As well as biological factors, O'Hara reviewed studies investigating the relationship of postnatal depression to gynaecological and obstetric factors, stressful life events, marital relationship, mother's relationship with own parents, social support, personal and family psychopathology and psychological constructs. O'Hara concluded that whilst the evidence for specific social, psychological and biological factors remains ambiguous, there is:

> ... valid evidence that a woman's psychological adjustment before and during pregnancy is associated with the development of postpartum depression. Moreover, women who experience high levels of stress during pregnancy and after delivery, and women who lack a supportive partner, appear to be particularly vulnerable to developing postpartum depression. (O'Hara, 1997: 22)

It is now generally accepted that postnatal depression has a multifactorial causality, affecting women from all age groups and social classes (Cox and Holden, 1994), and whilst postpartum depression does not have a specific aetiology, Cox (1994), Riecher-Rossler and Hofecker-Fallahpour (2003) conclude that its use as a psychiatric diagnostic term should still be used to ensure that service providers are aware of the particular needs of this client group, which may otherwise be missed.

Even though the phenomenological experience of maternal psychological distress cannot be explained easily in terms of psychopathology, Riecher-Rossler and Hofecker-Fallahpour's recommendation implies that maternal distress needs to be pathologised in order to allocate resources to this client group. Whilst this attitude feels fundamentally wrong to me, I believe that it will remain the prominent discourse in societies that are dominated by the medical model (Lee, 2003 writes convincingly on this issue).

CURRENT APPROACHES TO TREATMENT AND SUPPORT

Postnatal depression is now usually recognised as a very distressing experience, occurring at a time when a woman is already highly vulnerable emotionally, and with an infant to care for who is, for the most part, totally dependent on her for meeting his/her needs. In addition to the woman's distress, there is growing evidence that postnatal depression impacts on the family, increasing the likelihood of adverse behavioural and development effects on the child (Cooper and Murray, 1997) and that the couple's relationship is likely to be under considerable strain. It is also recognised that fathers may experience depression after the arrival of a new baby (Watson and Foreman, 1994).

THE EDINBURGH POSTNATAL DEPRESSION SCREENING QUESTIONNAIRE AND THE ROLE OF THE HEALTH VISITOR

The above issues highlighted the importance of, and stimulated further research into, early detection and treatment of postnatal depression (Cox and Holden, 1994) and several studies have been influential in this area. Most notably, the development of a 10-item self-report mental health questionnaire known as the EPDS—Edinburgh Postnatal Depression Scale (Cox et al.,1987) and a controlled research trial to investigate the effectiveness of health visitor 'listening' visits (Holden et al., 1989).

Holden's study demonstrated a reduction in the duration and severity of depression in 69 per cent of those women receiving this type of support, highlighting the benefits of supportive relationships that offer a listening non-judgemental attitude. And, that such a relationship can be provided by health visitors (in particular), but also midwives, the voluntary sector and peer support groups (Holden et al., 1989; Seeley et al., 1996; Clement, 1995; Mauthner, 1997).

Based on Cox and Holden's work, the EPDS is now routinely offered to woman at about six weeks and three months following delivery, as part of a screening programme for postnatal depression. For woman scoring above 10 on the EPDS, four to eight health visitor 'listening' visits are recommended as common practice in terms of early intervention for postnatal depression. Growing evidence about the possible negative impact of maternal depression on the family has led to the development of a more comprehensive set of recommendations called the SIGN guidelines (*Scottish Intercollegiate Guidelines Network, No. 60*, 2002) which recommends further psychosocial interventions in addition to visits from health visitors.

HEALTH VISITOR LISTENING VISITS CONFUSED WITH PERSON-CENTRED THERAPY?

Some women do not find health visitor 'listening' visits sufficient in alleviating their depression (Alder and Truman, 2002). Shelagh Seeley, a health visitor involved in research and training related to postnatal depression, has recently started to include cognitive behavioural techniques in health visitor training programmes, as some health visitors report that non-directive counselling skills are not enough, and some women find it unhelpful to keep talking 'over and over' the same issues (Seeley, 2004, personal communication). It is worth noting that in some of the literature, the terms 'listening visits' and 'health visitor intervention' have become synonymous with non-directive or person-centred counselling (e.g. Watson and Foreman, 1994). By implication then, the experiences of some health visitors may suggest that person-centred counselling might not be the most helpful intervention for this client group.

The key issue here seems to be that Person-Centred Therapy has been reduced to a set of *skills* that can be used to facilitate listening and aid recovery. If we now consider person-centred theory (Rogers, 1957, 1959), Rogers proposed that it is the *quality* of the relationship that matters most. And it is this that determines the extent to which the relationship is an experience that 'releases or promotes development and growth' (Rogers and Stevens, 1967: 89). This would suggest therefore, that the six necessary and sufficient conditions for therapeutic change (Rogers, 1957) are not always present in the relationship between mother and health visitor. What may also be significant for some women is the short-term nature of listening visits, particularly for those women where their distress seems 'inexplicable', as these may only give the opportunity for a superficial exploration of the woman's experience.

Indeed, recent audits of the efficacy of the *EPDS* as a screening tool and of health visitor listening visits highlight resource implications in terms of health visitor training, time and numbers. In reality, it seems that this service is not reaching all women in the way that it was originally designed (Elliott and Leverton, 2000; Shakespeare, 2002; Rowley and Dixon, 2002).

Additionally, the dual role that health visitors have, in terms of looking after the care of the woman *and* the baby, can make it extremely difficult for some women to reveal their true thoughts and feelings if they fear that they will be thought of as an inadequate mother or that the baby may be taken away from them. This common fear may in part explain the findings of Whitton et al. (1996) that the help-seeking behaviour of this client group still remains relatively low.

SECONDARY TREATMENT INTERVENTIONS

If listening visits are not available or make little difference to the woman's mental health, antidepressants are still likely to be the next treatment option. Appleby et al. (1997) found that cognitive behavioural counselling and the antidepressant fluoxetine (Prozac) are equally effective in the treatment of postnatal depression so offering women an alternative to medication. This is an important choice for this client group because as Cooper and Murray (1997) point out, whilst antidepressants may be as effective as psychotherapy, in practice, medication is not usually the preferred choice of new mothers, especially for those breastfeeding. In fact Cooper and Murray go on to say, 'nondirective counselling is highly acceptable to women' (Cooper and Murray, 1997).

PSYCHOTHERAPY

Several other studies have evaluated the effectiveness of psychological therapies for postnatal depression. Although O'Hara (O'Hara et al., 2000) has highlighted design limitations of some studies, the overall conclusion is that individual and group work, as well as different therapeutic approaches (including person-centred, gestalt, psychodynamic, cognitive behavioural therapies and interpersonal therapy), are equally effective (Holden et al., 1989; Alder and Truman, 2002; Cooper and Murray, 1997;

O'Hara et al., 2000). Whether in practice women are routinely offered any form of psychotherapy as an alternative to medication is likely to be dependent on the allocation of local NHS Trust resources, despite the current SIGN recommendations for the management of postnatal depression (SIGN, 2002).

AN EXPLANATION OF POSTNATAL DEPRESSION FROM THE PERSON-CENTRED THEORETICAL PERSPECTIVE

Rogers' theory in relation to personality development (or self theory) and emotional disturbance requires an acceptance that from infancy the person develops a *self-concept* introjected with the values and judgements of significant others. The child accepts these external values as his own, in order to gain the positive approval of others that he so much requires to maintain his own sense of self-worth (Rogers, 1959; Mearns, 1994; Merry, 2004). It is the self-concept and associated conditions of worth that inform a person's way of being in the world and in future relationships with self and other. With respect to a woman becoming a mother (either for the first or subsequent time), I believe that her existing self-regard and self-concept will be challenged in a way not previously experienced, having to adapt to incorporate a new sense of self as a 'mother' and it is helpful to think of this occurring at three levels:

1. *At an intrapersonal or dialogical level.* The person-centred theoretical proposal of a *plural self*, described as 'configurations of self' by Mearns and Thorne (Mearns and Thorne, 2000; Mearns, 2002), is a useful way to conceptualise a woman's emerging identity as a mother and the processes and conflicts involved in integrating this 'part' or 'configuration', with other aspects of her self, including existing beliefs and attitudes about herself as a 'mother' that the woman may have held since childhood. I will revisit the relevance of configurations of self later in the chapter.
2. *At a societal level* with respect to how the mother sees herself fitting in with the cultural norms and expectations associated with motherhood. (I discuss the impact of society's expectations more fully in the section describing the cultural context for person-centred theory and therapy.)
3. *At an interpersonal level,* in terms of the mother's newly developing relationship with the baby and changing relationships with the significant people in her life.

With respect to the woman's relationship with her baby (particularly her firstborn), her existing self-concept will be confronted with a totally new set of experiences, quite unique from anything that has gone before, especially in terms of the woman's feelings and perceptions in relation to the unborn baby and then the newborn infant. The mother has to perceive and relate to the baby's needs primarily through non-language cues and empathic engagement (Warner, 1997). If the mother's sense of self-worth is low, and her internal locus of evaluation is fragile, she may be constantly preoccupied with her 'performance' as a 'good enough' mother and in the first instance

211

will only have feedback about her 'performance' from the baby's behaviour and levels of contentedness.

If the woman has always relied heavily on the values and judgements of others then she will be particularly vulnerable to any perceived negative value judgements; in this case taking the form of a crying or 'unhappy' baby. This is likely to fuel any beliefs she may have about being an inadequate mother and increase her self-preoccupation and anxieties about her abilities. A woman may then begin to lose her self-confidence.

DISSONANCE BETWEEN SELF-CONCEPT AS 'MOTHER' AND ACTUAL EXPERIENCE AS 'MOTHER'

Maternal distress may not however, specifically be about difficulties in the mother-infant relationship. In terms of her existing relationships, new conflicts may arise either for the woman personally if she is determined that the baby will not change her existing relationships or, in relationship with those around her (especially her partner, other children and close family) if they expect her to behave as she has always done. If this conflict between self-concept as a mother and the actual experience of mothering is too great, then psychological distress is likely to result. Mearns proposes that:

> if the threat (to the self-concept) has caused serious damage to the self-regard, disorder may result. The threat has invaded the person's fundamental existential process to create damage that can range from self-doubt to self-annihilation. (Mearns 2002: 24)

As a simple example, some women who experience postnatal depression describe themselves as previously being organised and able to 'cope', and therefore believe that as in other life situations they should be able to cope alone with a new baby. If the reality is that they feel out of control, or overwhelmed with the responsibility of mothering, or simply that they are exhausted and need sleep, to ask for help may threaten the existing self-concept, as they now perceive themselves as 'not coping'. From this theoretical perspective then, the development of maternal distress or postnatal depression may be explained.

INTEGRATING RECENT PSYCHOANALYTICAL AND PERSON-CENTRED THEORY TO UNDERSTAND THE PSYCHOLOGICAL JOURNEY INTO MOTHERHOOD

Psychoanalytical theory has always acknowledged the importance of the mother-infant relationship, firstly through the ideas of Freud and then more specifically following the work of psychoanalysts such as Winnicott and Bowlby. More recently Daniel Stern who is better known for his observational research of the psychological processes of the infant (1985) has proposed the theory of the *motherhood constellation*—a newly created psychic organisation or construct that new mothers pass through following the birth of a baby

(Stern, 1995). Stern's theory relates specifically to the woman's role as a mother and requires a different kind of therapeutic input that does not fit with a classical psychoanalytical approach.

From the person-centred theoretical perspective, what is perhaps most interesting about Stern's theory is that it highlights the importance of the *qualities* present in the counselling relationship. Stern states:

> While exploring this phenomenon, it has been eye-opening to me to realise that most mothers in therapy have known this all along ... they know full well that they have entered into a different psychic zone that has largely escaped psychiatry's official systematic theorising but is perfectly evident to them. And they have most often, when in psychodynamic-type therapies, tolerated the traditional psychodynamic interpretations without giving them too much weight, *in order to benefit from other aspects of the therapeutic relationship.* (1995: 198; my italics)

What excites me more however, about this idea of a distinct psychological 'motherhood' construct, is how it resonates with the recent advances in person-centred theory relating to the idea of a plural self (e.g. Rowan and Cooper, 1999). Mearns and Thorne have provided a working definition for self plurality, that they call configurations of self:

> A configuration is a hypothetical construct denoting a coherent pattern of feelings, thoughts and preferred behavioural responses symbolised or pre-symbolised by the person as reflective of a dimension of existence within the Self. (2000: 102)

From a person-centred perspective it may be possible to view Stern's psychoanalytical 'motherhood constellation' as a person-centred 'configuration of self as mother', but with the all-important distinction that the client will use her own language to describe her 'mother' configuration (or indeed, configurations).

From my own experience and listening to others, there do appear to be some common themes that weave through the narrative of postnatal depression that are similar to those described by Stern (1995: 173). Therefore, integrating Stern's theory of a specific psychic construct relating to motherhood with the attitudinal qualities offered within Person-Centred Therapy may be helpful to counsellors in furthering their understanding of motherhood and postnatal depression.

A CULTURAL CONTEXT FOR PERSON-CENTRED THEORY AND THERAPY

As described earlier, a woman's self-concept as a mother and her ability to adapt to emerging conflicts and distress can be described in terms of the *introjected* values and self-regard the woman experienced in childhood. However, I believe this does not adequately account for the wider influence of society's values and expectations on a woman's identity as a mother. Therefore a consideration of person-centred theory within the cultural context of motherhood is required.

Phenomenologically, the experience of pregnancy, childbirth and caring for a newborn baby is likely to trigger wide ranging emotions and sensations which may not necessarily fit idealised cultural images of motherhood that describe the experience as 'natural and instinctive' and where mothers 'bond' with their babies immediately. A woman can feel she has 'failed' as a mother if her experience does not match these cultural messages.

SOCIETAL EXPECTATIONS AND CONDITIONS OF WORTH

Within Western society at least (with the possible exception of ethnic minority communities where non-western cultural traditions are still upheld), when a woman is handed her baby, it seems that any (childlike) needs she may have must be forgotten. She is an adult now, a mother. Mothers are expected to 'get on with it', largely unaided and often with very little experience of newborn babies. Paradoxically, a new mother will be inundated with advice and opinions from almost everyone she meets. It seems that everyone (parent or not) has something to say on the subject of motherhood. It is such a fundamental part of our existence and yet it seems that most individuals only want to consider the brighter more idealised aspects of mothering. The negative aspects are too shadowy, too dark to contemplate and so remain hidden (Price, 1988; Littlewood and McHugh, 1997; Nicholson, 1998). If they do appear, it is often in a context that describes the negative impact on children of deficient mothering, leading to an attitude of blaming rather than acceptance; an attitude that Lee (2003) believes is a legacy of a child-centred culture that results in most parents feeling anxious and inadequate, rather than affirmed and supported.

CLIENT EXPECTATIONS OF SELF

Within a therapeutic context, to really hear and explore a new mother's vulnerability and negative feelings, without judgement and with empathic understanding may feel very unfamiliar to the woman and in stark contrast to the usual advice or sympathy she receives. In addition to this, the woman herself brings her own cultural prejudices and beliefs about motherhood to her experience. Therefore, to face those aspects within her self that feel unacceptable in societal, familial or individual terms, is likely to feel very threatening to her self-concept as a mother. Feminist authors often describe the negative thoughts and feelings around motherhood as being a 'big taboo' that rarely gets talked about in an honest, open way, even between mothers. The title of Kate Figes' book for example echoes this view, *Life after Birth. What even your friends won't tell you about motherhood.* Some feminist writing argues that it is the patriarchal nature of our society that maintains the myth of perfect motherhood and to challenge that view risks being branded a bad mother (Ussher, 1991; Choderow, 1978; Walker, 1990; Price, 1988; Nicholson, 1998; Figes, 1998).

SELF-THEORY AND SOCIETY

In countless conversations with new mothers I have had over the years, women know that the idea of perfect motherhood is a myth, and contrary to the feminist argument above, will talk about it and support each other in being less than perfect and even celebrate each other's successes, an aspect of mothers' groups that Stadlen also highlights (Stadlen, 2004b). However, this knowledge seems to make little difference in altering the distorted view of motherhood that exists in some parts of society and many women still feel guilty when they see their attempts at mothering as not matching society's expectations of what constitutes a 'good' mother. Self-theory may help to shed some light on this difficulty.

Mearns (1994) argues that to change a person's self-concept requires more than naïve attempts to change that person's attitude. The self-concept consists of cognitive, affective and behavioural components that tend to be consistent with each other. Therefore, trying to change one aspect of the self-concept in isolation is unlikely to be successful (Mearns, 1994). Mothers *knowing* that there is a discrepancy between the ideal and the reality of mothering may not be enough to make a lasting difference to their self-concept as mothers.

POSTNATAL DEPRESSION AND THE CORE CONDITIONS OF THERAPY

From the discussion so far, it seems that the attitudinal qualities that are at the core of a person-centred therapeutic relationship are highly pertinent to this client group, and I want to consider some aspects of these in more detail.

BEING AUTHENTIC

I propose that being in a state of *incongruence* becomes the inevitable starting point for many new mothers because of the many contradictions that are a part of the experience of motherhood. (I do not mean that this 'incongruence' equates directly to postnatal depression, only that it highlights the vulnerability of all new mothers in terms of the fragility of their self-valuing process at this time.) The importance therefore, of the therapist being able to be real and genuine and committed to the woman and her experience is vital, both in terms of the woman feeling understood and accepted and, also as a role model (especially for female therapists). For a woman to really get in touch with and express her own inner feelings and beliefs within a therapeutic relationship may then allow her to experience the value of authentic relating in terms of increased intimacy. This is then likely to be helpful in other relationships, especially the relationship with her baby (Raphael-Leff, 1991; Holden et al., 1989).

THE IMPORTANCE OF EMPATHY

At this point empathy deserves a special mention. As described earlier, being in relation is fundamental to the new baby's survival, and Jordan's work on the importance of *mutual empathy* in the therapeutic relationship is helpful in understanding the therapeutic significance (to the new mother) of developing empathy towards self, as a pre-requisite to increasing empathic attunement with others (i.e. the baby). Jordan describes this 'empathic expansion' as 'moving out of a certain kind of self-centredness into an understanding of the growth of the self and other, and of relational awareness' (Jordan, 1997: 344). In mutual empathy, Jordan states that 'one gets to experience oneself as affecting and being affected by another' (Jordan, 1997: 343). This includes both the client and the *therapist* (my italics).

Jordan's description of mutual empathy may not, at first glance fit within the boundaries of Rogers' 'as if' requirement of therapist empathy (Rogers, 1959); yet as a concept, mutual empathy is central to Buber's philosophy of the 'I-Thou' relationship (Buber, 1958) and resonates with Mearns description of working at relational depth, where the therapist is relating to the client at their deepest, existential level (Mearns, 2002).

Relating at this profound level is also significant with respect to lessening the experience of shame, often a prominent feature of postnatal depression. Jordan describes how 'in shame we lose the sense of empathic possibility ... when ashamed we have great difficulty trusting that another will accept the rejected aspects within ourselves. Fearing exposure, we contract and withdraw' (Jordan, 1997: 346). If the therapist offers 'acceptance' and reflective empathic understanding, but without ever experiencing the client at this deeper, relational level, those shameful aspects of the client's experiencing are less likely to be revealed.

There is not the space within this chapter to explore empathy more fully; however I think it is an important process to reflect on, not only in terms of its significance to the therapeutic relationship but also to its importance in the relationship between mother and baby.

CONDITIONAL ACCEPTANCE AND BLOCKS TO EMPATHY

Factors contributing to blocks in empathy in the therapeutic relationship have been described by several authors (e.g. Mearns and Thorne, 1988; Fairhurst, 1999). I will discuss Fairhurst's work briefly, as I feel her ideas relating to unconscious therapist prejudice are relevant to this client group. Fairhurst states that 'holding of *positive or negative beliefs* towards members of a group or 'types' of people *without prior experience* constitutes prejudice' (Fairhurst, 1999: 28; my italics). She describes the 'unconscious' aspect of prejudice as deriving from the introjected, learnt messages from significant others that signify conditional acceptance (Fairhurst, 1999). Good training, personal therapy and sound practice supervision, should all provide the person-centred therapist with an opportunity to allow personal prejudices into awareness.

I am not convinced however, that as therapists, our attitudes towards motherhood have been sufficiently explored and challenged in training, an issue that has also been highlighted recently by Stadlen (2004a). Whilst we may be aware of prejudices we have about certain 'types' of mothers, Fairhurst's statement, by definition, implies that 'motherhood' cannot be prejudiced against because we all have experience of this. Not necessarily in our work as therapists, but certainly in our roles as sons and daughters or as mothers, fathers and grandparents.

The concept of unconscious prejudice may help to explain why motherhood is rarely a topic for discussion in psychotherapy training outside of the traditional understandings provided by psychoanalytic theory and theories relating to child development. Therapists and indeed anyone working with new mothers need to devote some time to exploring their own attitudes and values towards women as mothers. Motherhood has a central role within society; it seems crucial therefore, that we become aware of how our own views and experiences of 'mother' and motherhood influence or interrupt the therapeutic process with a client experiencing postnatal depression. Questions we may ask ourselves are, for example:

What kind of mother did you have and how has that informed your views about the role of mothers?

How do you react to single, older, adolescent or lesbian mothers for instance? What about mothers with many children, or mothers' reactions to their screaming children? Mothers who work, mothers who stay at home?

If you are a parent how do your own parenting styles differ to those of your client's?

Psychological disturbance in children and adults is often linked back to poor parenting. Which child development theories inform your practice and how will this affect your ability to offer the core conditions to clients with postnatal depression, whilst at the same time sit with possible concerns somewhere within you, about the impact of the woman's distress on her baby?

MOTHERHOOD, DEPRESSION AND LOSS

Nicholson's (1998) important and key contribution to the theme of loss in relation to postnatal depression highlights how the accepted psychological concepts normally used to describe the relationship between depression and the process of loss and change in people's lives are not commonly applied to depressed feelings experienced by new mothers, and rarely described in the medical literature on childbirth. Nicholson argues that women are not permitted to grieve or mourn at this point in life. If they do they are pathologised.

> So strong is this taboo that women themselves frequently fail to admit their sense of loss in a conscious way. (Nicholson, 1998: 88)

Many new parents will have thought about the losses that accompany the arrival of a new baby. Losses relating to work, money, independence and leisure time for instance.

However, losses associated with status and identity change are often less tangible (and even more complex for adolescent mothers). It seems paradoxical to think about motherhood in terms of loss, when the main focus for everyone is the *gaining* of a baby and *becoming* a mother. Surely the happiness surrounding the baby's arrival more than compensates for any feelings of loss or sadness? A reluctance to dwell on this issue often occurs within the mothers' groups I facilitate because of the uncomfortable feelings it stirs up, even within an atmosphere of acceptance. The idea of grieving the loss of their old self is too far removed from and doesn't fit with images of motherhood as being 'happy' and fulfilling.

I did not experience a loss of my former or 'old self' when my first daughter was born. However, within days of my second daughter's birth I was overwhelmed and distressed by feelings of grief and loss. I felt as though 'someone had died' but this remained inexplicable to me and those around me, including other mothers and health professionals. My experiencing did not fit with my image of motherhood and so as I tried to push it away, other symptoms rushed in to fill its place and by six weeks, what started out as grief for many things lost (including my sense of self, but also the fantasies for me surrounding pregnancy, birth and being a 'mother of two') received a diagnosis of postnatal depression. A label that described my way of being in the world for the next two years. I wonder what this journey into self-disintegration would have been like if someone had really understood and accepted my reaction and feelings of loss and grief in those early weeks, and not tried to hurry me back on to the road of maternal 'happiness'.

Nicholson focuses particularly on loss relating to identity, but listening to the experiences of others, I feel that grief reactions can be just as acute around losses associated with the pregnancy or birth experiences, leaving a woman shocked, traumatised or disappointed. A client describing her second traumatic caesarean birth, recounted how she felt her feelings of panic, disappointment, sadness and anger about the birth were 'hurried' along by the midwives in hospital, with the well-meaning, but unhelpful encouragement to 'focus' on the baby and to put the birth behind her.

DO THE NEEDS OF WOMEN EXPERIENCING POSTNATAL DEPRESSION SET THEM APART FROM OTHER CLIENTS?

When Person-Centred Therapy is correctly framed within the classical proposition that it is *the relationship* between client and counsellor that is therapeutic 'aside from anything that may be said or done within it' (Merry, 2004), then I believe the experience of being accepted, valued and understood within the context of the 'six necessary and sufficient conditions' as first described by Rogers in 1957 will be therapeutic to women with postnatal depression. However, I propose that there are some special considerations relating to this time in a woman's life that may fall outside the scope of one-to-one Person-Centred Therapy.

THE NEED FOR REASSURANCE, THE NEED TO BELONG

Quoting from Mauthner's qualitative research into women's experiences of the types of support they found helpful in their recovery from postnatal depression:

> mothers experiencing postnatal depression also want ... reassurance that other mothers experience similar feelings and that they would get better. (Mauthner, 1997: 168)

Offering such reassurances may be seen as counter to trusting the client's own valuing process, by relating to the client outside of their frame of reference (Mearns and Thorne, 1988). Yet from my own experience and from talking to others, women do want reassuring that they are not going mad, not alone in their experience and that they will get better.

Watson and Foreman's (1994) work with postnatally depressed women acknowledges the role of support groups and group therapy in bringing together similar experiences, which often provides this sense of belonging. More recent studies have also demonstrated benefits of varying types of group therapy (e.g. Field, 1997).

LEARNING TO BE A MOTHER

A related theme to belonging and reassurance is the issue of instruction and learning which all new mothers need and are only likely to take from other women (preferably mothers) that they trust and respect (Raphael-Leff, 1991). Traditionally the extended female family network would have provided this. For many women in today's society this network has diminished, and midwives and health visitors provide instruction in the early days and weeks following the birth, with the woman's partner often being the woman's primary source of support and reassurance. (The support network for single mothers may be very different.)

Whilst a father's involvement is very important, it is different from that provided by other mothers. If the latter is not available, or the relationships are somehow deficient in practical or psychological terms (especially between mother and daughter) the mother may feel alone or abandoned with learning the job of mothering (Price, 1988). Therefore, the counsellor needs to be sensitive to this possible gap in the woman's experience and explore with her what other support and help might be available in addition to therapy. (Addresses are listed at the end of the chapter.)

MOTHERS NEED MOTHERING TOO?

A woman's primary need for nurture and support at this time is greatly heightened and may lead to strong feelings of dependency on those around her (Price, 1988; Raphael-Leff, 1991). This is therefore likely to impact on the therapeutic relationship as well. The ethical issue of dependency within therapy however, continues to be a topic for debate and within the humanistic philosophies, it goes against the psychology of separation and autonomy and the notion of self-sufficiency.

From a person-centred perspective, Mearns and Thorne (2000) do address the issue of client dependency, and embrace its importance, but also highlight the need for counsellor awareness about whose needs are being met. From my own perspective, both as the client and as a therapist, acknowledging and exploring the strong dependency needs that motherhood may evoke is clearly important. However, the dependency issue with this client group feels different, and the phrase that persistently returns to my mind is that 'mothers need mothering too'. By this I mean that when new mothers are cared for or 'mothered' by others, this allows them to focus on establishing a relationship with their new baby and their developing selves as mothers. The challenge to person-centred therapists therefore, is to find a respectful way to work with this need, so that the woman feels nurtured and supported but not disempowered.

AND BABY COMES TOO?

Compared to other clients, a new mother is in a unique relational situation. Her infant is primarily dependent on her and will take up much of her psychological and physical space. I am not sure that any special consideration would be given to the significance of this relationship by the person-centred therapist in terms of how it affects the woman's ability to be thinking and living as an autonomous person at this point in her life. The mother-infant relationship also raises practical issues in terms of what happens to the baby during sessions and how the woman feels about leaving the baby, opening up the whole question of where, when and how therapy sessions are set up.

Within the different psychotherapeutic models however, the person-centred therapist is well placed to acknowledge and consider ways of working creatively with such issues. For instance, a few clients have, on occasion, brought the baby to sessions, (at the young people's counselling service where I work and to private sessions). This has been for a variety of reasons ranging from cancelled childcare to fears about being separated from the baby.

Recently, a long-term client came to see me with her two-week-old second baby because she wanted the opportunity to share her difficult birth experience soon after the birth. Something this client felt she really needed to do. It also gave me the opportunity to genuinely celebrate with the client, the arrival of her second baby who had been so much a part of our sessions during her pregnancy. Far from being a distraction, a baby's presence has often stimulated discussion about the woman's relationship with and feelings towards the baby. This has allowed me to be more real by responding to what I see, rather than what I assume. I do acknowledge though that the baby can distract both client and therapist from more difficult aspects of the work and this possibility also needs to be explored within the therapy.

For me, Mauthner's conclusion from the in-depth interviews she conducted with postnatally depressed women summarises beautifully the important role that person-centred therapy could have in helping women with postnatal depression:

> Once their feelings had been identified, the women I interviewed wanted to be given permission to talk in-depth about their feelings, including ambivalent

and difficult feelings; they wanted to talk to a non-judgemental person who would spend time listening to them, take them seriously, and understand and accept them for who they were; they wanted recognition that there was a problem, and reassurance that other mothers experience similar feelings and that they would get better ... These were the essential types of support that mothers wanted and that helped them begin the recovery process. In a sense, the source of the support was less important ... (1997: 168)

PERSON-CENTRED THERAPY AS PART OF A MULTIDISCIPLINARY APPROACH

My intention within this chapter has been to provide the reader with a greater understanding of postnatal depression and some of the unique issues relating to this client group. Unlike many other clients seeking counselling, women experiencing postnatal depression are in most cases in contact with other health professionals, either directly because of the depression or indirectly through the contacts and check-ups associated with the welfare of the baby and any other children. Therefore it is prudent to be aware of the responsibilities of others involved in the woman's care and I hope the information provided in this chapter goes some way to highlight these.

If the woman seeks therapy privately, the therapist should still see their role as part of a team. Ethical practice and child protection legislation requires the therapist to take into account the best interests of the mother *and* the baby. If it becomes apparent in the first session that others are not aware of the woman's distress, the therapist needs to discuss with the client her feelings about the involvement of the GP or health visitor and consider what additional help the woman may need. As with general depression, assessment of suicidal ideation is also important. In addition to medical help, providing information about other sources of support (e.g. voluntary agencies, mothers' groups etc.) may also be appropriate, especially if the woman is feeling isolated from other mothers.

I know from my own experience that personal therapy alone would not have been enough. The help and support I received from a variety of sources, including family, medical and peer support, as well as group support and couples counselling were all important elements. In many ways, these other aspects provided the safety net and space for me to undertake personal counselling.

Whilst we can never know as person-centred therapists what a woman's experience of postnatal depression will be, I feel there is one aspect that is clear, and is an important part of the therapeutic relationship: *that the client's role as a mother can be affirmed by us as therapists as it is unlikely that the woman has received that affirmation sufficiently from anyone else.*

CONCLUSION

The clinical presentation of postnatal depression is considered to be the same as depression occurring at other times and a specific aetiology has not been found. Despite the clinical picture, many specialist workers and women themselves, consider that depression after having a baby is unarguably different in that its effects are experienced at a time when exceptional physical, psychological and emotional demands are being made on the mother. Research studies confirm that psychotherapeutic interventions, including Person-Centred Therapy, are particularly helpful to this client group. When the theoretical and therapeutic aspects of Person-Centred Therapy also take into account the unique relational situation of the mother and infant, as well as the social-cultural context of motherhood, then the person-centred therapist is well placed to provide a warm and caring therapeutic relationship as part of a multidisciplinary approach to the woman's care.

REFERENCES

American Psychiatric Association (1994) *Diagnostic and Statistical Manual of Mental Disorders* (4th ed). Washington, DC: American Psychiatric Press.

Alder, E and Truman, J (2002) Counselling for postnatal depression in the voluntary sector. *Psychology and Psychotherapy, 75,* 207–20.

Appleby, L, Warner, R, Whitton A and Faraghar, B (1997) A controlled study of fluoxetine and cognitive-behavioural counselling in the treatment of postnatal depression. *British Medical Journal, 314,* 932–6.

Bailham, D and Joseph, S (2003) Post-traumatic stress following childbirth: a review of the emerging literature and directions for research and practice. *Psychology, Health and Medicine, 8,* 159–68.

Biddulph, S (2003) *Raising Boys: Why boys are different and how to help them become happy and well-balanced men.* London: Thorsens.

Brockington, I (1996) *Motherhood and Mental Health.* Oxford University Press: Oxford.

Brockington, I (2004) Postpartum psychiatric disorders. *The Lancet, 363,* 303–10.

Buber, M (1958) *I and Thou.* (2nd ed) (RG Smith, trans). Edinburgh: T and T Clark.

Choderow, N (1978) *The Reproduction of Mothering. Psychoanalysis and sociology of gender.* Berkeley: University of California Press.

Clement S (1995) 'Listening visits' in pregnancy: a strategy for preventing postnatal depression? *Midwifery, 11,* 75–80.

Cooper, PJ and Murray, L (1997) The impact of psychological treatments of postpartum depression on maternal mood and infant development. In L Murray and PJ Cooper (eds) *Postpartum Depression and Child Development* (pp. 201–20). London, New York: Guilford Press.

Cox, JL (1994) Introduction and classification dilemmas. In JL Cox and JM Holden (eds) *Perinatal Psychiatry: Use and misuses of the Edinburgh Postnatal Depression Scale* (pp. 3–7). London: Gaskell.

Cox, JL and Holden, JM (eds) (1994) *Perinatal Psychiatry: Use and misuses of the Edinburgh Postnatal Depression Scale.* London: Gaskell.

Cox, JL, Holden, JM and Sagovsky, R (1987) Detection of postnatal depression. Development of the 10-item Edinburgh Postnatal Depression Scale. *British Journal of Psychiatry, 150*, 782–6.

Cramer, B (1997) Psychodynamic perspectives on the treatment of Postpartum Depression. In L Murray and PJ Cooper (eds) *Postpartum Depression and Child Development* (p. 237). London, New York: Guildford Press.

Dion, X (2002) Anxiety: a terrifying facet of postnatal depression. *Community Practitioner, 75*, 376–80.

Elliott, SA (1994) Uses and misuses of the Edinburgh Postnatal Depression Scale in primary care: a comparison of models developed in health visiting. In JL Cox and JM Holden (eds) *Perinatal Psychiatry: Use and misuses of the Edinburgh Postnatal Depression Scale* (pp. 221–32). London: Gaskell.

Elliott, SA and Leverton, TJ (2000) Is the EPDS a magic wand? 'Myths' and the evidence base. *Journal of Reproductive and Infant Psychology 18*, 298–307.

Fairhurst, I (1999) Empathy at the core of the therapeutic relationship: Contaminators of empathic understanding. In I Fairhurst (ed) *Women Writing in the Person-Centred Approach.* (pp. 19–36). Ross-on-Wye: PCCS Books.

Field, T (1997) The treatment of depressed mothers and their infants. In L Murray and PJ Cooper (eds) *Postpartum Depression and Child Development* (p. 221). New York, London: Guilford Press.

Figes, K (1998) *Life After Birth. What even your friends won't tell you about motherhood.* London: Viking, Penguin Books.

Green, MJ and Murray, D (1994) The use of the EPDS in research to explore the relationship between antenatal and postnatal dysphoria. In JL Cox and JM Holden (eds) *Perinatal Psychiatry: Use and misuses of the Edinburgh Postnatal Depression Scale* (pp. 180–98). London: Gaskell.

Holden, JM, Sagovsky, R and Cox, JL (1989) Counselling in a general practice setting: controlled study of health visitor intervention in treatment of postnatal depression. *British Medical Journal, 289*, 223–6.

Holmes, J (1993) *John Bowlby and Attachment Theory.* London: Routledge.

ICD-10 (1992) *International Classification of Diseases.* World Health Organization.

Jordan, JV (1997) Relational development through mutual empathy. In AC Bohart and LS Greenberg (eds) *Empathy Reconsidered. New directions in psychotherapy* (pp. 343–50). Washington DC: American Psychological Association.

Kitszinger, S (1992) *Ourselves as Mothers.* Canada: Doubleday, Transworld Publishers Ltd.

Lee, E (2003) *Abortion, Motherhood and Mental Health.* New York: Aldine de Gruyter.

Littlewood, J and McHugh, N (1997) *Maternal Distress and Postnatal Depression.* London: MacMillan Press Ltd.

Llewellyn Jones, D (1994) *Fundamentals of Obstetrics and Gynaecology* (6th ed). London: Mosby.

Mauthner, NS (1997) Postnatal depression: how can midwives help? *Midwifery, 13*, 163–71.

Mearns, D (1994) *Developing Person-Centred Counselling.* London: Sage.

Mearns, D (2002) Further theoretical propositions in regard to self theory within person-centred therapy. *Person-Centered and Experiential Psychotherapies, 1*, 14–27.

Mearns, D and Thorne, B (1988) *Person-Centred Counselling in Action.* London: Sage.

Mearns, D and Thorne, B (2000) *Person-Centred Therapy Today. New frontiers in theory and practice.* London: Sage.

Merry, T (2004) Classical client-centred therapy. In P Sanders (ed) *The Tribes of the Person-Centred*

Nation. (pp. 21–44). Ross-on-Wye: PCCS Books.

Murray, L (1992) The impact of postnatal depression on infant development. *Journal of Child Psychology and Psychiatry, 33,* 543–61.

Nicholson, P (1998) *Post-natal Depression. Psychology, science and the transition to motherhood.* London: Routledge.

O'Hara, M (1997) The nature of postpartum depressive disorders. In L Murray and PJ Cooper (eds) *Postpartum Depression and Child Development* (pp. 3–26). New York: Guilford Press.

O'Hara, M, Stuart, S, Gorman, L, Wenzel, A (2000) Efficacy of interpersonal psychotherapy for postnatal depression. *Archives of General Psychiatry, 57,* 1039–45.

Oates, M (1994) Postnatal mental illness: organisation and function of services. In JL Cox and JM Holden (eds) *Perinatal Psychiatry: Use and misuses of the Edinburgh Postnatal Depression Scale* (pp. 180–98). London: Gaskell.

Parker, R (1995) *Torn in Two. The experience of maternal ambivalence.* London: Virago Press.

Pitt, B (1968) 'Atypical' depression following childbirth. *British Journal of Psychiatry, 114,* 1325–35.

Price J (1988) *Motherhood. What it does to your mind.* London: Pandora.

Raphael-Leff, J (1991) *Psychological Processes of Childbearing.* Florida, USA: Chapman and Hall.

Riecher-Rossler, A and Hofecker-Fallahpour, M (2003) Postpartum depression: do we still need this diagnostic term? *Acta Psychiatr Scand Suppl. 418,* 51–6.

Rogers, CR (1957) The necessary and sufficient conditions of therapeutic personality change. *Journal of Consulting Psychology, 2,* 95–103.

Rogers, CR (1959) A theory of therapy, personality, and interpersonal relationships, as developed in the client-centred framework. In S Koch (ed) *Psychology: A study of a science, Vol. 3. Formulations of the person and the social contract.* New York: McGraw-Hill.

Rogers, CR and Stevens, B (1967) *Person to Person.* London: Souvenir Press Ltd.

Rowan, J and Cooper, M (eds) (1999) *The Plural Self. Multiplicity in everyday life.* London: Sage.

Rowley, C and Dixon, L (2002) The utility of the EPDS for health visiting practice. *Community Practitioner, 75,* 385–9.

Seeley S, Murray L and Cooper PJ (1996) The outcome for mothers and babies of health visitor intervention. *Health Visitor, 69,* 135–8.

Shakespeare, J (2002) Health visitor screening for PND using the EPDS: a process study. *Community Practitioner, 75,* 381–4.

SIGN Guideline Number 60 (2002) *Postnatal Depression and Puerperal Psychosis.* Edinburgh: Scottish Intercollegiate Guidelines Network.

Stadlen, N (2004a) Mothers at the cutting edge of science. *Counselling and Psychotherapy Journal, 15,* 5–7.

Stadlen, N (2004b) *What Mothers Do. Especially when it looks like nothing.* London: Piatkus.

Stern, DN (1985) *The Interpersonal World of the Infant: A view from psychoanalysis and developmental psychology.* New York: Basic Books.

Stern, DN (1995) *The Motherhood Constellation.* New York: Basic Books.

Ussher, J (1991) *Women's Madness. Misogyny or mental illness?* London: Wheatsheaf and Harvester.

Walker, M (1990) *Women in Therapy and Counselling: Out of the shadows.* Maidenhead, UK: Open University Press.

Warner, MS (1997) Does empathy cure? A theoretical consideration of empathy, processing, and personal narrative. In AC Bohart and LS Greenberg (eds) *Empathy Reconsidered. New directions in psychotherapy* (pp. 124–40). Washington DC: American Psychological Association.

Watson, M and Foreman, D (1994) Diminishing the impact of puerperal neuroses: towards an expressive psychotherapy useful in a community setting. In JL Cox and JM Holden (eds) *Perinatal Psychiatry: Use and misuses of the Edinburgh Postnatal Depression Scale*. London: Gaskell.

Whitton, A, Warner, R and Appleby, L (1996) The pathway to care in postnatal depression: women's attitudes to postnatal depression and its treatment. *British Journal of General Practice*, 46, 427.

APPENDIX

The Association for Postnatal Illness
145 Dawes Road, Fulham, London, SW6 7EB
Tel: 0207 386 0868
Email: info@apni.org
A national voluntary organisation with strong links to the medical profession, providing leaflets, information and one-to-one support to depressed mothers by other women who have recovered from PND.

The National Childbirth Trust
Alexandra House, Oldham Terrace, Acton, London. W3 6NH
Tel: 0870 770 3236 (Office and Administration: 9am to 5pm)
Fax: 0870 770 3237
Email: enquiries@national-childbirth-trust.co.uk
Offers support and information to all new parents on wide-ranging issues and experiences relating to pregnancy, childbirth and early parenting. Some local branches run PND support groups.

Meet-a-Mum Association
7 Southcourt Road, Linslade, Leighton Buzzard, Beds. LU7 2QF
Tel: 0845 120 6162
Email: meet_a_mum.assoc@btinternet.com
Website: www.mama.co.uk
A voluntary network of groups and individual contacts offering friendship and support to all mothers who are lonely, isolated or depressed.

Homestart UK
2 Salisbury Road, Leicester. LE1 7QR
Tel: 0116 2339955
Email: info@home-start.org.uk
Website: www.homestart.org.uk
A voluntary organisation that has local branches throughout the UK, offering regular home support, friendship and practical help to families (with pre-school children) under stress.

CHAPTER 15

LIVING WITH PAIN: MENTAL HEALTH AND THE LEGACY OF CHILDHOOD ABUSE

JAN HAWKINS

And must I then, indeed, Pain, live with you
All through my life?—sharing my fire, my bed,
Sharing—oh, worst of all things!—the same head?—
And, when I feed myself, feeding you, too?
Edna St Vincent Millay 1988: 159

The Person-Centred Approach (PCA) has much to offer in the understanding and recovery of those who have suffered abuse as children, and developed psychiatric illnesses as a result. This chapter seeks to encourage more collaboration between those who see the nature of human distress in pathological terms, and those who see it in more adaptive terms. The argument here is that the psychiatric system and the PCA could, when working together, make radical changes in people's lives. Where a person needs a period of respite and care within a therapeutic environment, real healing might occur where person-centred principles are embodied by all in the environment. The revolving-door difficulty so many people experience might be intercepted if the hospital situation became more relationship-based than medical and management-based. Here the focus is on those who come to the attention of therapists and/or psychiatric services, and therefore could have the opportunity for healing. Scientific research concludes that, whilst one third of abuse survivors do go on to abuse, two thirds do not (Langeland and Dijkstra, 1995). The only real hope we have of preventing intergenerational abuse is by offering reparative therapy to those who have suffered.

> Parents who had come to terms with their history of abuse ... who were able to admit what their parents had done, who had more detailed and coherent recollections of, and open anger about their abuse ... were more likely to refrain from abusing their own children ... (ibid: 7)

DIFFERENT SELVES

'If anyone were to see me when I am at my most distressed, they would send for the men in white coats, lock me up and throw away the key' (Maria's 'Reporter'). The 'Reporter' is one aspect of Maria, whose function is to tell what is happening. The Reporter does not have feelings, but is good at the facts. The Reporter has been the part of Maria who has attended most of her therapy, and has frequently mentioned this fear of being locked up. At other times Maria longed for the day when she could give up, crawl into a foetal position, and be left in a quiet, tiny, padded cell until death released her. There are many other selves within Maria, including the Teenager, the Youngest, the Tinies, the Performer. Her perceptions and fantasies of what a psychiatric system might be like have never been tested in reality. Maria is a survivor of multiple sexual abusers; she had a violently sadistic mother, and a history of abject emotional and physical deprivation. Yet she functions in the world, and has managed to endure her life and learned to overcome severe debilitating panic attacks, nightmares, agoraphobia, social phobia, numerous physical illnesses, bouts of unrelenting depression, and still be capable of feeling joy.

Maria has a sense of having achieved something by avoiding psychiatric institutions and sees her two brief spells of a few months on antidepressants as temporary failures. Maria has contact with what she identifies as her 'core self'—the part of her that was not damaged by the abuse, and she clings on to that, fearing any pharmaceutical intervention might threaten it. In person-centred terms this could be described as her 'directional organismic processes' (Rogers, 1963: 20–1) or 'organismic valuing process' (Mearns and Thorne, 1999: 9) the means by which the organism knows what it needs. She has reclaimed her organismic valuing process or (in her terms, 'self'), and knows how fragile other parts of her are. Her feeling is that she must, at all costs, keep her selves away from situations which might evoke memories of her abuse—any situation where another has power over her; any situation where chaos abounds; any situation where human distress is not heard or understood; any situation where only her 'madness' might be seen and her grounded, sane self might be missed. Her fantasy of psychiatric institutions includes all those threats. However desperate she has been, she has never let this be known to those who might try to fast-track her into the psychiatric system, for fear of losing herself completely.

Her survival has been possible due to her ability to dissociate (see below) by taking herself further away from where the pain is too great or too confusing and this ability may well have protected her from developing other more dangerous survival strategies, such as addictions or eating disorders, or other devastating psychiatric problems. But Maria feels that her recovery from her abuse may have been less costly in terms of her energies, had there been the possibility of a relationship with a therapist who understood what was happening for her much earlier. Had her brief brushes with general practitioners (GPs) and even briefer ones with psychiatrists been met with understanding and compassion—she might have recovered better, and sooner, she will never know. But she does know now that she always had the potential for healing. She knows this because she has a relationship with a therapist who is able to meet every one of her. A therapist who offers a real relationship, one that is steadfast, and safe. A therapist who never diagnoses or labels her, but seeks to truly understand how life and her inner lives are for her. Whatever distress she is feeling, and whatever the challenges posed by this relationship, hope lies in this relationship. Sadly it is still the case that the kind of relationship she needed to heal the damage earlier in her life is not readily available on the National Health Service (NHS). The psychiatric system, because it focuses on a medical model of human distress coupled with a psychoanalytically based history and practice, compounded by the duress of financial limitations, does not embrace the relationship-focused therapy approach.

INFANCY AND CONGRUENCY

Babies are capable of learning at least from their first breath, and will demonstrate preferences for sounds, tastes and sensations. The infant's cries need to be met with warmth and an empathic exploration to sense the source of expression: is the baby hungry? too hot? too cold? wet? uncomfortable? or lonely for a soothing voice? Where the infant is met with this empathic approach, she learns that she can trust her own instinctive needs. In a good enough environment, where the mother (usually, but not exclusively) is able to attune herself to the infant in this way, the infant will grow to trust that it is capable of letting its needs be known in the expectation that they will be met. In this sense the infant is born with the ability to be congruent (real or genuine). Children whose development is not distorted by the conditions of worth of others, or in other words those who do not have to find ways of being that fit in with others' needs or expectations, are equipped to recognise what is not safe or appropriate in the behaviour of others. These children are more likely to seek help and understanding if things happen to them that are confusing or frightening. They are more likely to have developed self-protective skills that may help them get away if they perceive danger.

The youngest of babies are capable too of being very angry when needs are not met—a very healthy sign, for anger is a signal that something is wrong (Averill, 1982). For infants who do not receive this empathic and accepting care-giving, learning takes a different direction. The infant quickly understands that their cries can bring a very angry or dangerous reaction—babies will take in the 'condition of worth' that says something like 'I am only acceptable if I am quiet'. If an infant's healthy anger and rage at not having his needs met are continually ignored or met with hostility, the child may lose touch altogether with that anger and rage, and slip into despair. It is easy to see how infants whose most basic organismic needs are not met with love, acceptance and empathic understanding will be vulnerable to learning that their needs are not only not important, but that their needs and feelings are in fact dangerous, and not to be trusted. Conditions of worth that teach a child that they are only acceptable if they meet an adult's needs create further vulnerability, such that the child has not learned how to protect herself, not learned how to defend himself. Children who are clearly not being protected and supervised, and who demonstrate a lack of ability to protect themselves are the targets of those who seek to abuse (Finkelhor, 1986).

> One of the first and most important aspects of the self-experience of the ordinary child is that he is loved by his parents. He perceives himself as loveable, worthy of love and his relationship to his parents is one of affection. He experiences all this with satisfaction. (Rogers, 1951: 499)

NEGLECT AND ABUSE AND THE IMPACT ON CHILDREN

For those children who have received no loving acceptance, no experience of having been protected from which s/he can learn the skills of self-protection, a self concept develops that includes the need and willingness to meet the other's needs without question. Where the child lives with the continual possibility of being required to do things that are confusing, humiliating, strangely and confusingly pleasurable, or brutal and painful, the sense of self includes the notion that 'I do not matter' and 'I am always at risk' and possibly also 'my very life depends on me figuring out what the other wants and doing it without question', moving further and further away from any sense of 'who *I* am', or 'what *I* want', to a position where contact with what satisfies the organism or core self is lost altogether. In situations where the child is repeatedly abused sexually and/or physically, they may learn to survive by dissociating, taking themselves further away from the core of themselves where the pain is too great or too confusing. For Maria (introduced above) each dissociated self stopped or 'died', and a new, even more compliant and need-less self emerged to take over, until the next self had to die. As an adult these selves each have their own memories, feelings, terrors and abilities. Finding her own, undamaged, core self, has been her life's work—who might she have been had she not been endlessly traumatised?

THE LONG-TERM EFFECTS OF CHILDHOOD ABUSE

Research consistently demonstrates that exposure to childhood sexual abuse (CSA) appears to increase the risk of psychiatric disorders by about two to four times those of people not exposed to CSA (for a review of studies, see Fergusson and Mullen, 1999). Increasing numbers of studies since the 1990s have shown evidence of an association between childhood sexual abuse and a wide range of problems as adults, including:

- depressive disorders (e.g. Fergusson et al., 1996; Mullen et al., 1993; Silverman, Reinherz and Giaconia, 1996)
- anxiety disorders (e.g. Fergusson et al., 1996; Mullen et al., 1993)
- antisocial behaviours (e.g. Fergusson et al., 1996; Scott, 1992)
- substance abuse disorders (e.g. Fergusson et al., 1996; Mullen et al., 1993; Scott, 1992)
- eating disorders (e.g. Miller and McCluskey-Fawcett, 1993; Romans et al., 1995; Wonderlich et al., 1997)
- suicidal and self damaging behaviours (e.g. Fergusson et al., 1996; Mullen et al., 1993; Peters and Range, 1995)
- post-traumatic stress disorders (Silverman et al., 1996) or Dissociative Disorders, including Dissociative Identity Disorder (Putnam et al., 1986)
- problems with sexual adjustment (e.g. Fergusson et al., 1997; Mullen et al., 1994).

Carmen et al., in 1984 found that 50 per cent of psychiatric inpatients report histories of physical or sexual abuse. One of the difficulties in extrapolating from studies is that researchers vary in what they consider to be abusive. For example, some studies focusing on childhood sexual abuse count only penetrative sex, whereas others include covert (non-touch) sexual abuse, and other forms of non-penetrative sex in order to measure the prevalence. From a person-centred perspective, the focus is on the experience of the person, rather than on any external judgement that something is or is not abuse.

It is helpful to have knowledge of the research as clients often have questions about the impact of abuse. It is striking how questions emerge such as 'does what happened to me count as abuse?' or 'it must have been me attracting them mustn't it?' Often these questions seem to be coming from someone far younger than the person in front of me. The tone or timbre of their voice and their appearance and posture may have changed too. The questions may arise in someone who, at other times, is utterly clear and sometimes very angry about what happened to them. What is in the forefront of my mind at these times is to meet the person empathically in that moment when the questions are being asked. I might share my sensing of the different quality of the question, occasionally going as far as saying 'how old are you feeling as you wonder if you attracted the abuse?' This question is put in the most tentative of terms—yet, what draws this question from me is the change in the energy between me and the client in the moment—a sense that the person has shifted gear, has shifted into another part of herself. Mearns and Thorne (2002) refer to 'configurations of self' to describe the different parts of self that many clients refer to. For those who have been abused, these parts of self may have deeper fissures between them. Certainly, in my own experience, having the different selves or parts of self recognised is deeply healing. For clients who want answers, and really need to know them, and feel empowered by knowing, their therapists' ability to point them in the direction of useful books or resources can be experienced as normalising ('I can't be that bonkers or you wouldn't know about this stuff!'), grounding and valuing ('I must be of some worth if my therapist is bothering to read about this stuff I'm dealing with').

GENDER CONSIDERATIONS

There is also recognition that men are not the only perpetrators of abuse. One deeply empathic person-centred therapist told his female client who was trying to talk about her experiences of abuse 'I feel guilty because I am a man'. This congruent response demonstrated that this particular male therapist had not given sufficient thought or exploration to his own attitudes towards abuse issues. The client internalised the guilt he was feeling as her own for 'making him feel that way' and was unable to continue in what had been a very positive therapeutic relationship. For practitioners of the person-centred approach, a central tenet is that the core conditions are both necessary and sufficient for growth to occur. As a person-centred practitioner, it is my responsibility to ensure that I am able to experience and embody the core attitudinal qualities, in particular of acceptance of and respect for the person, that I am able to meet the person in their world, to understand the world from their point of view, and to be as open as I can be to my own experiencing moment-to-moment and discern what I share of that experiencing. I can only do this if I give myself opportunities to look at my own attitudes, beliefs and experiences in particular areas, and if I am working with survivors of abuse, then I must do this groundwork in myself and continue to do it, if I am to truly be capable of embodying the qualities that allow psychological contact to be established and maintained with people whose experience of relationships has been so utterly damaging.

Male as (the only) perpetrator came from the feminist theory of why abuse happens. The feminists made society conscious of abuse, but unfortunately ignored the fact that it happens to little boys too, and that women also abuse (see e.g. Saradjian, 1996 and Elliott, 1993). Having said that, there is still—as far as research is able to demonstrate—a significantly higher number of women who were abused as children than men. Children are vulnerable whether boys or girls, and the potential is in all of us—men and women—to act out our own pain, frustrations and perhaps even warped thinking which has developed through our own experiences as children.

WHO IS RESPONSIBLE?

Studies demonstrating the prevalence of molestation of children were suppressed well into the 1970s. Whatever understanding there was explicitly or implicitly put the responsibility for abuse on the child—whether that was as a result of the seduction theory (Freud, 1898), the result of blaming a child's behaviour for their physical abuse, or whether it was blaming the individual for taking a 'victim' position and thereby 'allowing' themselves to be abused in whatever way—the responsibility and blame was there on the child. These ideas become part of the child's growing self-concept. Where an adult is unwilling or incapable of taking responsibility for their assaults, physical and verbal, on children, the child will pick it up and carry it through their lives. Along with the guilt they carry about things they 'did' that caused the treatment they got, there is the permeating shame about who they are, shame about existing—shame that goes to the very core of the being, and is very hard to lift.

Finkelhor's (1984) traumagenic theory is deeply empowering for survivors. The first to place responsibility solely and squarely on the perpetrator, he spelled out the prerequisite for abuse to occur: somebody has to want to do it. This challenges all previous ideas about what the child might be doing. It doesn't matter what a child is doing—and a pre-sexualised child (one who has been abused already) may behave in very provocative ways—any responsible adult would recognize the vulnerability. Only someone who wants to abuse will do so.

GROUPWORK EXPERIENCES

In groups I co-facilitated in the early nineties for women and men who had experienced abuse as children, many of the women had been told by various professionals to whom they had turned for help, that they had 'fantasised' their abuse, or that they were responsible for their abuse due to behaving in a seductive or provocative way. These were people who had managed to connect the difficulties they were experiencing as adults with what had happened to them as children—and people who wanted to heal. Yet they were being met with attitudes developed via the seduction theory and many had been told it would cause them more harm if they talked about what had happened to them as children. Within a group facilitated by two person-centred therapists, the individuals began to take more and more responsibility for caring for themselves and each other. The relief at being heard without interpretation, without labelling, and being met with acceptance, empathy and genuine responses from the facilitators created an environment where changes began happening.

THE SYMPTOMS OF ABUSE

Survivors of abuse rarely seek help for the legacy of that abuse. More commonly survivors will seek help initially from their GP for depression or anxiety and panic attacks. In the pressurised GP surgery, it is still very tempting to offer antidepressants. Sadly many individuals collecting such prescriptions collect another piece of evidence of their inadequacy. The tablets, though they can give some relief for symptoms, can often block a potential for healing. Other survivors might appear for treatment with an eating disorder, an alcohol problem, self harming, sexual dysfunction, difficulties concentrating and not being able to know who they are or a sense of unreality. These and other symptoms then become the pathology and survivors of abuse become trapped in the revolving door of mental health services because the symptoms are attended, not the cause. With the bombardment rate mental health professionals face, it is understandable that treatment modalities which offer apparently easily measurable outcomes very quickly become the order of the day. Many individuals who are given short-term therapies like Cognitive Behavioural Therapy (CBT), Solution Focused (SFT), or brief focal therapy, seem to improve, and then may return for further treatment later with either the same symptoms, or others. Statistically the results can look very attractive. But do we really know if patient 'X' appears in one set of statistics with positive measurable outcomes, only to reappear as patient 'Y' with positive measurable outcomes because of a new or repeated set of symptoms?

DISSOCIATION OR PSYCHOSIS?

Often too the creative survival skill of dissociation is perceived as psychosis, so that people experiencing terrifying flashbacks, or regressing to traumatic events are again traumatised by the treatment designed to help them. In extreme cases a survivor could, through a trigger event, dissociate, lose herself in the terrors of the past, and find him/herself involved with what will seem powerful people who are able to place him/her in a hospital ward with other people who may in fact be experiencing a loss of shared reality. This will only increase the terror, powerlessness and triggering problems s/he is already struggling with. Diagnoses of various pathologies can contribute to a continually developing negative self-concept that pushes the person further away from the healthy relationships they might otherwise find to show them they can be related to as healthy growing people.

> If I accept the other person as something fixed, already diagnosed and classified, already shaped by his past, then I am doing my part to confirm this limited hypothesis. If I accept him as a process of becoming, then I am doing what I can to confirm or make real his potentialities. (Rogers, 1967)

My sense is that the key word Rogers is referring to here is 'fixed'. Of course people who are traumatised as children are shaped by that—their sense of who they are and what they are worth is defined by their experiences. But they are not fixed, but in a process of becoming that can be mediated by their continued experiences. If these continued experiences label them, squeeze them into services that focus on the label, and stop seeing them as a person in the process of becoming, then the damage is continued.

THE EFFECTIVENESS OF THERAPIES

One of the problems facing anyone experiencing emotional distress of any kind is that there are continual arguments about which kind of therapy is the most effective. Because the NHS currently favours CBT and SFT, the implication is that those are the most effective treatments. In fact, research repeatedly demonstrates that no particular approach to therapy is more effective in terms of outcomes than any other. The evidence shows that therapeutic outcomes are related to the therapeutic alliance between therapist and client, and to qualities within the therapist. The therapeutic alliance is defined as a personal bond between therapist and client, and collaborative commitment to the mutual work and goals of therapy. The qualities of the therapist which promote such an alliance are: an ability to instill confidence and trust; dependability, benevolence, responsiveness; empathy; and responsive collaborative application of techniques (Ackerman and Hilsentroth, 2003). These findings support the assertion that the core attitudinal qualities of the Person-Centred Approach are both necessary and sufficient for growth to occur, though the word 'techniques' may jar with some person-centred therapists. Well over a hundred studies and meta-analyses find a significant, consistent relationship between the therapeutic alliance and successful outcome. This finding holds across all therapy approaches studied (Horvath and Bedi, 2002; Wampold, 2001; Martin, et al., 2000; Krupnick et al., 1996; Horvath and Symonds, 1991; Gaston, 1990). Castonguay et al., (1996) studied cognitive therapy with or without medication.

> Improvement was found to be predicted by ... the therapeutic alliance and the client's emotional involvement ... However ... therapists' focus on the impact of distorted cognitions on depressive symptoms correlated negatively with outcome ... Descriptive analyses [suggested] that therapists sometimes increased their adherence to cognitive rationales and techniques to correct

problems in the therapeutic alliance. Such increased focus, however, seems to worsen alliance strains, thereby interfering with therapeutic change. (ibid: 497)

Some therapists do damage, primarily through destructive relationship behaviors:
> ... the particular treatment that the therapist delivers does not affect outcomes ... Clearly, the person of the therapist is a critical factor in the success of therapy. (ibid: 202)

The 'deterioration effect' seems to result from:

- therapist's who have a 'take charge' attitude early in therapy
- 'cold', argumentative or irritable therapists
- insight or interpretations offered prematurely or general lack of empathy
- high concentrations of transference interpretations or negative countertransference
- 'aggressive stimulator' style: intrusive, confrontational, caring, self-revealing, charismatic, authoritarian
- high focus on the client-therapist relationship, combined with low empathy, genuineness, and warmth (Horvath and Bedi, 2002; Mohr, 1995)

These behaviours are damaging to any therapeutic relationship but they could also replicate those of abusing parents, providing a survivor with triggers that cause distress, and lead to the need for more engagement in their survival strategies—these (i.e. alcohol, drugs, eating disorders, self-harming, etc.) will only reinforce the trauma.

Antidepressants and antipsychotic drugs may be prescribed in an effort to relieve symptoms. Survivors may endure electroconvulsive therapy (ECT) where other treatments have failed—yet so often the underlying experience and legacy of childhood abuse has not even been mentioned. I have certainly seen clients who have been struggling to break their own cycle of psychiatric treatments, who have tried to speak about their abuse, but have been told categorically that it will be harmful to them if they talk about it. The layers of treatment can then act to further suppress the reality of what has caused the problem. The person's already fragile self-concept continues to collect conditions of worth as a 'good patient'. Though some psychiatrists hold to the view that talking about abuse issues will make matters worse, and that control of symptoms is the best treatment, '... the efficacy of psychotherapy has now been firmly established and is no longer a subject of debate' (Wampold, 2001: 59). Evidence further shows that 'Psychotherapy is successful in general, and the average treated client is better off than 80% of untreated subjects' (Lambert and Barley, 2002: 26). There is much evidence that demonstrates that relationship-based therapy provides the best chance of positive outcomes regardless of technique or orientation. The Person-Centred Approach with its focus on the relationship provides the survivor of abuse with something they may never have experienced.

Recently, for example, I was awestruck as I read the account of the relationship one of my trainees is currently forging with a woman who experienced sexual abuse from her father and her brother throughout most of her adolescence. My awe springs from the realisation of the healing that is being wrought in and through this relationship and almost as a matter of course in both the client and in the trainee therapist who is seeking to be with her in her pain ... (Thorne, 1998: 32)

The therapist's task is thus formidable for he or she has somehow to rekindle hope in the client's heart and that is impossible without the rediscovery of trust ... Psychological skills, therapeutic insights, sophisticated medication may all have their part to play in the process of healing but, as St Paul put it in another context, without love they are likely in the end to profit nothing. (ibid: 108)

DISEMPOWERMENT

Adults who were abused as children have been disempowered. Children in homes where there is persistent threat in the form of violence, sexual abuse, verbal denigration and assault—where there is chronic trauma—develop coping strategies that help them survive. These strategies can become so habitual that it is impossible as adults to let go of them when the threat has passed. Some children survive by becoming 'good girls/boys' who never complain, never make demands and attempt to anticipate the adults' every need, having received the idea that their existence depends on being 'good'. Some children survive by lashing out at others, involving themselves in crime—these children are the visible ones, though sadly their self-esteem is further damaged because of the negative attention they draw to themselves. Some children survive by squashing their feelings either by denying themselves food (what is anorexia saying? 'I have no needs'), or by developing a binge-vomit cycle (swinging between 'I have overwhelming needs', and 'I have no needs'), by overeating in vain attempts at comfort, by anaesthetizing themselves with alcohol or other drugs.

Some children develop a creative coping strategy of dissociation—often pathologised, but of all coping strategies the one that is the most invisible. Clients will describe their dissociative behaviours as, for example, 'leaving my body' ; 'hiding in the plug socket'; 'going numb'; 'it all goes black'; 'watching from the ceiling'; 'it happened to that child there, not me'; 'I wasn't real anymore, I dissolved'. Many and various descriptions show that the person had split away from the experience. All these coping strategies can be viewed as distress flares. It seems to me that these and other coping strategies are evidence of distress, but far from bringing in the rescue services, they serve to alienate people further from sources of comfort for their pain. Those people for whom dissociation has allowed their survival confuse others, including therapists, GPs and psychiatrists, by talking about very traumatic material in a totally flat voice. Divorced from the affect, the person is vulnerable to a whole variety of judgements, and also to the isolation and confusion of their traumatised inner world.

'Dissociated' process is a style of process in which aspects of the person's experience are separated into 'parts' ... allowing the person to alter perceptions, to alter physiological states and to hold contradictory beliefs without discomfort. Such parts seem to have been created in early childhood as a way to keep the person from being overwhelmed by experiences of incest or other abuse ... They may come into the person's consciousness as 'others' whose images and voices have an impact ... they may emerge as temporarily dominant personalities ... (Warner, 2000: 145)

SELF-HARM AND 'ATTENTION-SEEKING'

Survivors who self-harm to the point where they need the service of Accident and Emergency departments are often punished because of an attitude which assumes they are attention-seeking. Some clients report having been made to wait far longer than was the case of others with 'legitimate' injuries in casualty departments. They have been treated with contempt and rudeness and told that these self-inflicted injuries are a waste of NHS resources. I have met more than one survivor who was not given local anesthetic for stitches and told s/he did not deserve that since s/he caused the injury. People who self-harm are sometimes trying to get back into their body after having dissociated and feel completely unreal—the cutting makes them real again. Some do it to release some of the pent-up pain and frustration. Some do it to punish themselves. There are various reasons why people find self-harming to be the only option. Research suggests that most self-harming occurs in a dissociated state (e.g. Herman, 1992).

LONG-TERM DEPRESSION

Most authors consider there is a relationship between environmental factors (including life stress) and a genetic predisposition and possibly organic and/or biochemical disorders. For survivors of abuse, depression can be seen as resulting from persistent and total disempowerment. Where a child is not allowed to have their own needs, or not allowed to be angry about being hurt, not allowed to say no, not allowed to have 'no' attended to if they do say it, not allowed to have comfort for their confusion and pain, what alternative exists than depression? To add to this, as the child grows into an adult who only knows that others' needs are more important than their own, they can then be accused of staying in a 'victim position', and even worse, getting something out of that. The fact that the person has developed with no other experience than that of being the victim of others' violence and/or sexual attentions seems to be ignored. And the more that pain is denied, ignored, judged or appears in sublimated or distorted form, the more the person has to suppress to survive—and all this reinforces the depression.

ABUSE AND MENTAL HEALTH SERVICES

In mental health services the significance of abuse is often minimised and trivialised, and survivors are held responsible for their own trauma (Watson et al., 1996). Where diagnoses of 'borderline personality disorder', 'psychosis', and 'postnatal depression' are treated with familiar, but ineffectual and punitive treatment responses (Williams et al., 1998), the survivor has little chance of finding a new sense of worth that will play a part in healing from abuse. 'Given these difficulties it is unsurprising that with a few exceptions (e.g. Watson et al., 1996) most of the development in service provision for women survivors of abuse and violence has been in the independent and voluntary sector' (Williams, 1999: 34).

For women and men who were abused as children either within the home or outside it by strangers or family friends, there can be major difficulties and retraumatisation when they feel disempowered again by authority figures like doctors, nurses, social workers and any professional seeking, with the best will in the world, to help them. The very fact that psychiatric services tend to be clinical in appearance can act as a trigger to people who have been abused. Institutionalisation can very often reinforce feelings of powerlessness, failure and self-loathing. Men and women who have been abused are at risk for revictimisation because they have not developed self-defence systems, and can be triggered into feeling (and being) the age they were when abused as a child. In these dissociated states survivors will often revert to passive compliance, which may go some way towards explaining the evidence of sexual molestation within psychiatric units. Survivors, overwhelmed by responsibility and feelings they cannot comprehend, often yearn for the sanctuary of a place to be looked after. Their experience of asylum, however, is unlikely to meet these needs.

Children learn to protect themselves by being protected; they learn to defend themselves by being defended; they learn that they are worthy human beings because that is demonstrated to them. Adults with histories of chronic abuse were not protected, defended or shown they were worthy of love, comfort and support. So they simply do not learn the prerequisites for keeping safe in the world. Even when they do, they are at risk of being triggered to an earlier state.

WORKING TOGETHER

Survivors of childhood abuse need understanding; they need to be allowed to talk about what has happened. The damage was done within relationships; it makes sense that healing can only really take place within relationships. Survivors need to be able to choose their therapist, and be allowed to set the pace of therapy. It may take a long time to establish a healthy therapeutic alliance that will allow the survivor to do the work necessary to reclaim her/his life and move into positive and healthy ways of being in the world. At times of crisis, survivors need to know that there are safe places to go to for support and help, where there is an understanding of the legacy of abuse. These places of safety may provide residential care for a period. There are some therapeutic communities where re-parenting is offered; where people can bring what R. D. Laing (1965) referred to as the 'authentic state of madness'; where therapeutic support is available 24 hours a day. More are needed. Fears that people will become dependent on this are unfounded. Dependency may be a phase which occurs—but in healthy boundaried homes children do not usually get stuck in dependency—they move on and outgrow the safe home container—so do people who are allowed to work on their healing. And it is hard work involving commitment to taking responsibility for one's own actions and putting responsibility for abuse where it belongs—on the perpetrator of that abuse. It involves learning new skills for self care, communication skills and developing healthy boundaries. A place of safety needs to look like a place of safety—and needs to feel like a place of safety, or it will retraumatise and reinforce anxiety, fear and unhealthy ways of coping.

SANCTUARY AND SUPPORT DURING CRISES

Survivors who are healing from abuse may not need to be resident during their healing, but would benefit greatly from places where they can go alone or with their children when the struggle is too much. In these places there would be people who understand about the legacy of abuse and about the fears so many have about repeating that abuse on their children. Such places would not judge the survivor when they just need time out—when they need to talk—when they need someone to give some attention to the children because they can't do it. Such support would encourage survivors to take care of themselves, to receive care within the same nurturing environment where they can see their children being cared for. A couple of hours may be all that is needed. The companionship of other survivors who are working on their healing can make a very big difference. Group work and drop-in provision may provide a sense of home and care that men and women who have suffered childhood abuse may never have experienced. Such nurturing and acceptance are healing in themselves. Support workers for such provision would need to have a thorough understanding of the legacy of abuse, and the opportunity to experience in their own professional development, the core attitudinal qualities of the Person-Centred Approach. They would need to feel valued and supported if they are to offer those same qualities to clients. An emphasis on real relationships where empathy and acceptance are givens would offer real hope of healing.

> Abused people desperately require the corrective experience of an affirming, deeply committed, non-abusive relationship in which they can find healing and discover hope for living. So profound is the woundedness in some cases, however, that the offering of such a relationship may well uncover an ocean of pain or provoke in the client a fear of seduction. The therapist who is prepared to accompany such pain or fear and even face being falsely accused will need exceptional courage and absolute trust in his or her own integrity. (Thorne, 2002: 65–6)

Giving positive, hopeful reinforcement, including validating the truth of the experience, and that it was not the child's fault is like making a '*deposit in* [a survivor's] *psychic savings bank*' (Sanford, 1999: 129). Anyone supporting individuals who are healing from the legacy of abuse would benefit from being given the space and time to explore their own attitudes, feelings and needs so that they may develop within themselves the capacity to hear the truth behind the symptoms.

The repression of our suffering destroys our empathy for the suffering of others. (Miller, 1991: 10)

Women and men who have suffered abuse as children and have the courage to challenge their legacy need fearless companions, for they can feel like they are going mad. I have asserted elsewhere (Hawkins, 2002), healing from abuse is not going mad—it's going sane!

REFERENCES

Ackerman, SJ and Hilsentroth, MJ (2003) A review of therapist characteristics and techniques positively impacting the therapeutic alliance. *Clinical Psychology Review, 23*: 1–33.
Averill, JR (1982) *Anger and Aggression.* New York: Springer-Verlag.
Carmen, EH, Ricker, RP and Mills, T (1984) Victims of violence and psychiatric illness. *American Journal of Psychiatry, 141*, 378–83.
Castonguay, LG, Goldfried, MR, Wiser, S and Raue, PJ (1996) Predicting the effect of cognitive therapy for depression: A study of unique common factors. *Journal of Consulting and Clinical Psychology, 64*, 497–504.
Elliott, M (1993) *Female Sexual Abuse of Children: The ultimate taboo.* UK: Longman.
Fergusson, DM and Mullen, PE (1999) Childhood sexual abuse: an evidence based perspective. *Developmental Clinical Psychology and Psychiatry Vol 40.* London: Sage.
Fergusson, DM, Horwood, LJ and Lynskey, MT (1996) Childhood sexual abuse and psychiatric disorders in young adulthood. Part II: Psychiatric outcomes of sexual abuse. *Journal of the American Academy of Child and Adolescent Psychiatry, 35*, 1365–74.
Fergusson, DM, Horwood, LJ and Lynskey, MT (1997) Childhood sexual abuse, adolescent sexual behaviours and sexual revictimisation. *Child Abuse and Neglect, 21*, 789–803.
Finkelhor, D (1984) *Child Sexual Abuse: New theory and research.* New York: Free Press.
Finkelhor, D (1986) *A Sourcebook on Child Sexual Abuse.* Beverly Hills, CA: Sage.
Freud, S (1898) *Sexuality and the Aetiology of the Neuroses.* Standard Edition, 2 261 (37). London: Penguin Books.
Freud, S (1905) Three essays on the theory of sexuality. In A Richards (ed) (1977) *Sigmund Freud: On sexuality* (pp. 33–169). London: Penguin Books.
Gaston, L (1990) The concept of alliance and its role in psychotherapy: theoretical and empirical considerations. *Psychotherapy, 27*, 143–53.
Hawkins, J (2002) Paradoxical safety: Barriers to the actualising tendency, and beyond. *Person-Centred Practice, 10*, 21–6.
Herman, JL (1992) *Trauma and Recovery: From domestic abuse to political terror.* London: Pandora HarperCollins.
Horvath, AO and Bedi, RP (2002) The Alliance. In JC Norcross (ed) *Psychotherapy Relationships that Work* (pp. 37–69). New York: Oxford University Press.
Horvath, AO and Symonds, BE (1991) Relation between working alliance and outcome in psychotherapy: a meta-analysis. *Journal of Counselling Psychology, 38*, 139–49.

Krupnick, JL, Sotsky, SM, Simmens, A, Moyer, J, Elkin, I, Watkins, J and Pilkonis, PA (1996) The role of the alliance in psychotherapy and pharmacotherapy outcome: findings in the National Institute of Mental Health treatment of depression collaborative research program. *Journal of Consulting and Clinical Psychology, 6*, 532–9.

Laing, RD (1965) *The Divided Self.* London: Pelican Books.

Lambert, MJ and Barley, DE (2002) Research summary on the therapeutic relationship and psychiatric outcome. In JC Norcross (ed) *Psychotherapy Relationships that Work* (pp. 17–32). New York: Oxford University Press.

Langeland, W and Dijkstra, S (1995) Breaking the intergenerational transmission of child abuse: beyond the mother-child relationship. *Child Abuse Review, 4*, 4–13.

Lynskey, MT (1996) Childhood sexual abuse and psychiatric disorders in young adulthood. Part II. Psychiatric outcomes of sexual abuse. *Journal of the American Academy of Child and Adolescent Psychiatry, 35*, 1365–74.

Martin, DJ, Garske, JP and Davis, MK (2000) Relation of the therapeutic alliance with outcome and other variables: a meta-analytic review. *Journal of Consulting and Clinical Psychology, 68*, 438–50.

Mearns, D and Thorne, B (1999) *Person-Centred Counselling in Action* (2nd ed). London: Sage.

Mearns, D and Thorne, B (2000) *Person-Centred Therapy Today: New frontiers in theory and practice.* London: Sage.

Miller, A (1991) *Banished Knowledge.* London: Virago.

Miller, DAF and McCluskey-Fawcett, K (1993) The relationship between childhood sexual abuse and subsequent onset of bulimia nervosa. *Child Abuse and Neglect, 17*, 305–14.

Mohr, DC (1995) Negative outcomes in psychotherapy: a critical review. *Clinical Psychology: Science and Practice 2*, 1–27.

Mullen, PE, Martin, JL, Anderson, JC, Romans, SE and Herbison, GP (1993) Childhood sexual abuse and mental health in adult life. *British Journal of Psychiatry, 163*, 721–32.

Mullen, PE, Martin, JL, Anderson, JC, Romans, SE and Herbison, GP (1994) The effects of child sexual abuse on social, interpersonal and sexual function in adult life. *British Journal of Psychiatry, 165*, 35–47.

Peters, DK and Range, LM (1995) Childhood sexual abuse and current suicidality in college women and men. *Child Abuse and Neglect, 19*, 335–41.

Putnam, FW, Guroff, JJ, Silberman, EK, Barvan, L and Post, RM (1986) The clinical phenomenology of multiple personality disorder: review of 100 recent cases. *Journal of Clinical Psychiatry, 47*, 285–93.

Rogers, CR (1951) *Client-Centered Therapy.* London: Constable.

Rogers, CR (1963) The actualizing tendency in relation to 'motives' and to consciousness. In M Jones (ed) *Nebraska Symposium on Motivation.* (pp. 1–24). Lincoln, NE: University of Nebraska Press.

Rogers, CR (1967) *On Becoming a Person.* London: Constable.

Romans, SE, Martin, JL, Anderson, JC, O'Shea, ML and Mullen, PF (1995) Factors that mediate between child sexual abuse and adult psychological outcome. *Psychological Medicine, 25*, 127–42.

St Vincent Millay, E (1988) *Collected Sonnets* (p. 159). New York: Harper and Row.

Sanford, L (1999) *Strong at the Broken Places: Overcoming the trauma of childhood abuse.* London: Virago.

Saradjian, J (1996) *Women Who Sexually Abuse Children: From research to clinical practice.* UK: Wiley.

Scott, KD (1992) Childhood sexual abuse: impact on a community's mental health status. *Child Abuse and Neglect, 16,* 285–95.

Silverman, AB, Reinherz, HZ and Giaconia, RM (1996) The long term sequelae of child and adolescent abuse: a longitudinal study. *Child Abuse and Neglect, 20,* 709–23.

Solomon, A (2002) *The Noonday Demon: An anatomy of depression.* London: Vintage.

Thorne, B (1998) *Person-Centred Therapy and Christian Spirituality: The secular and the holy.* London: Whurr.

Thorne, B (2002) *Mystical Power of the Person-Centred Approach: Hope beyond despair.* London: Whurr.

Wampold, BE (2001) *The Great Psychotherapy Debate.* Mahwah, NJ: Lawrence Erlbaum Associates.

Warner, MS (2000) Person-centred therapy at the difficult edge: a developmentally based model of fragile and dissociated process. In D Mearns, and B Thorne (eds) *Person-Centred Therapy Today* (pp. 144–71). London: Sage.

Watson, G, Scott, C and Ragalsky, S (1996) Refusing to be marginalised: groupwork in mental health services for women survivors of childhood sexual abuse. *Journal of Community and Applied Social Psychology, 6,* 341–54.

Williams J (1999) Social inequalities and mental health. In C Newnes, G Holmes, and C Dunn (eds) *This is Madness: A critical look at psychiatry and the future of the mental health services.* Ross-on-Wye, UK: PCCS Books.

Williams, J, Liebling, H, Lovelock, C, Chipchase, H, and Herbert, Y (1998) Working with women in special hospitals. *Feminism and Psychology, 8,* 357–69.

Wonderlich, SA, Brewerton, TD, Jocic, Z, Dansky, BS and Abbott, DW (1997) Relationship of childhood sexual abuse and eating disorders. *Journal of the American Academy of Child and Adolescent Psychiatry, 36,* 1107–15.

CHAPTER 16

NINE CONSIDERATIONS CONCERNING PSYCHOTHERAPY AND CARE FOR PEOPLE 'WITH SPECIAL NEEDS'

MARLIS PÖRTNER

The following chapter will consider the question if psychotherapy—and in particular person-centred psychotherapy—for people 'with special needs' is useful or possible at all. First, I shall point out the variety of persons embraced by this term and describe how paradigms regarding them have changed over the last decades. I shall talk about my own experience (of more than 25 years) with person-centred psychotherapy for clients with special needs and highlight some specific aspects of this work, such as particular conditions, main issues in the therapeutic process, etc. I shall indicate two negative side effects of normalisation that—without belittling its invaluable merits and the unquestionable improvements it brings about—need to be looked out for. Furthermore the influence of the environment will be pointed out and the need for carers as well as for psychotherapists to find a disabled person's—verbal or non-verbal—language. Examples from the practice illustrate the complexity of working in this field.

It is concluded that a person-centred attitude is indispensable particularly with these clients and that psychodiagnostic knowledge is helpful as long as it is used to *understand* and not to label individuals. Cooperation and exchange between psychotherapists, carers and professionals of different backgrounds working in this field is considered useful and necessary.

1. WHO ARE 'PEOPLE WITH SPECIAL NEEDS'?

The use of 'politically correct' language sometimes makes it difficult to make clear who exactly we are talking about, especially when one term after another comes to be considered as disparaging and the 'correct' words to describe them are constantly changed. So 'retarded' was first replaced by 'mentally handicapped', then by 'mentally disabled', then by 'people "with" handicaps or disabilities'. For some time after that the correct way was to talk about 'special needs', whereas nowadays anything but 'learning disabilities' seems to be taboo. The trouble is that this term in no way covers the variety of persons we are talking about. Despite the undoubtedly respectable original intentions, this evolution has not only caused a regrettable impoverishment of language but also holds the danger that existing handicaps are not properly recognised and the persons concerned do not get the support they need. Moreover, to my surprise, I found that the scale of what is estimated 'correct' is in parts diametrically opposed to the original meaning of the words, e.g. 'retarded' (meaning 'slow') is much less judgemental and determinate than 'disabled' (meaning 'incapable', 'incapacitated') (Pörtner 2000: 2–3).

Not that the words themselves are derogatory: it is the attitude behind the words. And as long as the attitude towards mentally handicapped or disabled or retarded persons or people with special needs is disparaging, any word that is used, after a time, will become disparaging too. What we need is to accept and respect persons with mental disabilities as equal human beings. With such an attitude, I think there is no need to avoid words that indicate their existential condition. Therefore, depending on the context, I shall use the more neutral 'special needs' as well as other terms—thus taking into account that it is in no way a homogenous group we are dealing with, and that frequently we do not know much about how a person came to be labelled as 'special needs'.

The confusion about using the correct term is not just a language problem; it also reflects the difficulty of doing justice to the wide variety of individuals who live or work in communities and organisations for persons with disabilities. They are impaired in most different ways: learning disabilities, psychological disorders, genetic deficiencies, congenital or developmental brain defects, physical disabilities combined with not having been offered adequate opportunities for education—and sometimes we see persons who give the impression that their continued presence is more due to bad luck than to anything else. So, who are people with special needs?

2. CHANGING PARADIGMS

For many years persons with mental disabilities were not considered capable of further development and were kept either hidden in their families or—particularly those with severe behaviour disorders—in psychiatric hospitals. They were provided for in a very basic way but neither did they get proper treatment nor the necessary opportunities to learn and develop. It was commonly agreed that behaviour disorders of persons with mental disabilities were exclusively due to organic brain deficiencies and could neither be understood nor altered.

However, since the 1960/70s, it has gradually come to be understood that behaviour disorders might be caused by unfavourable circumstances. A movement developed to get persons with mental disabilities out of the hospitals and to normalise their life conditions. It was the beginning of an evolution that brought considerable improvements for people with special needs and created new prospects for growth and development. Mental disabilities were no longer seen 'as a disease but as one possible way to cope with the world'[1] (Hennicke and Rotthaus, 1993: 9) and as 'one possible mode of existence' (Hennicke and Rotthaus, 1993: 10). Deficiency-oriented views were replaced by growth-oriented concepts. A shift in thinking began 'from typology and classification towards

---

1. Original German quotations in this chapter have been translated by Marlis Pörtner.

243

individualization' that asked for a shift 'from a psychology from outside to a psychology from inside' (Eggert, 1993: 205). Even in a recent clinical textbook about mental handicaps we can find the following statement: 'We understand mental disability of a person as a complex condition that, influenced by manifold social factors, developed from medically defined disorders. Diagnosed pre-, peri- and postnatal deficiencies do not allow a statement about a person's mental disability, which is determined by the interaction between his/her potential abilities and the demands of his/her concrete environment' (Thimm, 1999: 10).

In this relatively new and in many aspects still little explored field, there is not such a clear dividing line between psychiatry/psychopathology on the one hand and humanistic approaches on the other. The borderline is much more between progressive and backward or uninformed views on both sides. There were unrecognised early pioneers among classic clinicians and there are to this day professionals of different backgrounds (educators, carers, psychologists, physicians, nurses) with alarmingly outdated or uneducated opinions about people with special needs. Often the humanistic approach is limited to fine ideals, which fail to be concretised in everyday practice. Moreover, there is a tendency of perverting humanistic intentions into the opposite by denying or not recognising existing handicaps thus depriving individuals of necessary support. And sometimes, in institutions, we find—dependent upon which person we come across—a confusingly inconsistent mix of it all, which certainly is not beneficial to the mental health and personal growth of those who have to live there.

The pioneers' assumption that the organism would react positively to favourable circumstances, and behaviour disorders would automatically disappear, proved to be wrong. Not all behaviour disorders disappeared just by normalising people's life conditions. Sometimes they became even more apparent because the new concepts allowed people's individuality to manifest itself more distinctly. It turned out that mental diseases were more frequent among mentally disabled people than among the average population (Gaedt, 1987; Lotz and Koch, 1994).

Despite the considerable improvements due to normalisation, these findings are not surprising, when we look at the biographies and life conditions of many people with special needs. The German psychologist Barbara Senckel explains quite plausibly why these persons are 'particularly vulnerable and wounded' (Senckel, 1998). She states that 'in addition to limitations due to disabilities', the reasons are traumatic experiences like 'fundamental lack of acceptance and esteem; repeated experiences of being abandoned and of separation; disparagement, neglect, isolation; heteronomy, pressure to conform; control, lack of self-determination (even where it would be possible) and no real prospects for the future' (Senckel, 1998: 37). In the biographies of people with mental disabilities again and again we come across such experiences that shape their behaviours in a way other people find strange and incomprehensible and that often are at the roots of psychological disorders.

In addition, Valerie Sinason, a British psychoanalyst and author, who for many years worked at the Tavistock Institute as a psychotherapist for mentally disabled persons, points to another aspect. She describes the 'handicapped smile' as a 'defence against trauma' (Sinason 1992: 136) and states: 'my own clinical work and that of colleagues has clarified instances where mental handicap is actually caused by abuse. Sometimes, trauma evokes handicap as a defence about the memory of physical and sexual abuse' (Sinason, 1992: 137). She refers to J. Oliver who confirms her opinion and, as a result of his research studies, speaks of 'VIMH = violence-induced mental handicap'. (Oliver, 1988, quoted in Sinason, 1992: 137). Moreover 'the environment in itself can be traumatogenic' (Sinason, 1992: 138) and she thinks that 'If knowing and seeing involve knowing and seeing terrible things, it is not surprising that not-knowing, becoming stupid, becomes a defence' (Sinason, 1992: 137). More than once during therapy sessions she observed a client, suddenly and for a varying length of time, express him or herself in an understandable and realistic way. Prouty refers to a similar experience with his disabled brother (Morton and Van Werde, 1999:146–7).

The Brisbane Study (Gunn et al., 1984/86) that follows the development of children with Down syndrome (trisomy-21) from birth to the age of five, is particularly interesting, because comparing a group of children with the same clearly defined genetic deficiency proves that the different ways that these children developed was much more determined by their environment than by the original deficiency. This was a real breakthrough as for years people with Down syndrome had been considered incapable of further development.

From all this it becomes clear that:

- the degree of mental disabilities and of the impact they have on a person cannot just be defined by psychopathological diagnostics, but is influenced as well by social factors;
- psychotherapy must be available for people with special needs;
- an environment that fosters mental health and personal growth is of crucial importance.

For all three aspects the Person-Centred Approach (PCA) offers valuable concepts and represents a helpful—and in my experience—necessary completion to psychopathological knowledge.

3. MY EXPERIENCE WITH THE PERSON-CENTRED APPROACH AND CLIENTS WITH SPECIAL NEEDS

It was by pure coincidence that I came to work with these clients. I didn't have any previous experience in this field when, more than twenty years ago, as a beginning psychotherapist and still in training for client-centred psychotherapy, I was asked to take a client with special needs. I was doubtful. Was there any point in psychotherapy for these people? Was it possible at all? This, at the time, was in no ways certain. It meant breaking new ground, not only for me, but also for my supervision group and our trainers. They shared my doubts, as we had learned that Rogers considered an average level of intelligence as a necessary condition for psychotherapy (Rogers, 1942). The general opinion at that time—with a few exceptions—regarded psychotherapy with mentally disabled persons as impossible. However, I decided to try—a decision I never regretted, as I owe to it most precious insights for my work as a psychotherapist.

The first experiences with two women with special needs (Pörtner, 1984, 1990) were crucial for my development as a client-centred psychotherapist as well as for my understanding of psychotherapy in general and of the PCA in particular. Since these beginnings I have always worked with (among other clients) more and less severely mentally disabled persons. The insights I owe them were meaningful for my whole therapeutic practice. With them I learned, even more than with other clients, that a therapist's work does not consist in 'doing', but in 'enabling', and that its most fundamental factor is to empathically and congruently enter the other person's world. No other clients have ever reacted as sensitively as those with special needs or given me such immediate and open feedback, when for a tiny moment I was not completely attentive or when I did not accurately understand them.

It was an important completion of my experience to not only do psychotherapy with individuals, but also to consult and supervise carers, staff and organizations. It highlighted the environment's crucial influence on the mental health and well-being of people with special needs and the significance of person-centred concepts for everyday care. I discovered that sometimes carers, who didn't know anything about the PCA, when everything else had failed, intuitively found solutions that to a large extent conformed to its principles. These experiences led me to develop a person-centred concept specifically designed for everyday care (Pörtner, 1996a, 1996b, 2000).

It was encouraging, in 1981, to meet Garry Prouty at a Gendlin workshop in Chicago and to realize I was not alone; there were other client-centred psychotherapists working with this group of clients. Later on, I got to know Isolde Badelt's pioneering work in Heidelberg (Badelt, 1984, 1990, 1994) and, with time, that of other colleagues in different countries, such as Hans Peters in Holland (Peters, 1992/2001). The circle slowly expanded. Yet, all in all, to this day there are still only a few practitioners who work in this field. This is highly regrettable, not only for the potential clients but also for the psychotherapists themselves, because entering the world of a person with a mental disability offers invaluable opportunities to expand the psychotherapist's horizons in ways that will benefit the whole of their therapeutic work.

4. WHY PERSON-CENTRED?

Since the 1980s, increasing attention has been paid to psychotherapy for people with special needs, at least at conferences and in literature. The question was: is psychotherapy with people suffering from mental disabilities possible and useful at all and how can it cope with their specific conditions and needs? Psychotherapists of different orientations have dealt with the issue and proposed their ideas (Lotz, Koch and Stahl, 1994; Lotz, Stahl and Irblich, 1996). Interestingly, the necessary conditions many of these authors describe correspond precisely with person-centred principles.

Sylvia Görres, an author of psychoanalytic orientation, writes on behalf of people with special needs: 'For them psychotherapy might be the first experience of a not valuating, non-judgmental relation with another person who takes them seriously' (Görres, 1996: 30). This corresponds exactly with what in client-centred psychotherapy is seen as an essential element of the therapeutic process. And her statement that 'people with mental disabilities are more helpless in the face of authoritarian power than we are, and not in a position to protect themselves against uncontrolled emotional infringements like, for example, in a negative transference' (Görres, 1996: 34), should be taken to heart not only by psychotherapists of any orientation, but by anybody who in some way or other has dealings with people with special needs. It remains a basic principle of the PCA which makes it explicit that empathy, acceptance, and a non-judgemental attitude are essential—also and especially—with persons suffering from mental disabilities, in psychotherapy as well as in everyday care. It is essential to be willing to enter their world, as unapproachable and incomprehensible as it may appear.

With good reason, some authors also express reservations against psychotherapy, claiming that people with special needs should be 'accepted, not treated' (Stahl, 1996: 20). Yet, from a person-centred viewpoint, psychotherapy and an accepting attitude are not contradictory. On the contrary, in client-centred psychotherapy, accepting human beings as they are is seen as a basic condition for facilitating personal growth. However, to accept a disabled person as she is does not imply that we do not believe her capable of further development. Both are needed, on the one hand accepting individuals as they are, and on the other hand, believing them capable of taking steps of growth. We have to be carefully aware of where such steps seem to emerge and empathically support them. Therefore my statement is: *we have to accept disabled persons as they are and not try to change them, but offer conditions that make changes possible.*

This, at the same time, describes a fundamental aspect of the PCA where psychotherapy is not seen as something to be 'done' with clients, but as opening a space where they may discover their own resources—resources that they previously could not access.

Another point in favour of the PCA: it is often hard to discern if a specific behaviour is due to mental disability or has to be seen as symptom of a psychological disease. For many symptoms 'it is not clear if they allow the same conclusions with a mentally disabled person as with one who is not disabled' (Senckel, 1998: 21). Traditional diagnostic categories therefore only partly apply. In this context it is an advantage of the PCA which does not primarily focus on diagnostics, but on trying *to understand the client's subjective world.* This is particularly important for people with special needs, as 'they have only a limited range of behaviours and reactions to express all kinds of states of mind' (Senckel, 1998: 21). The notion of a 'pre-expressive' level (Prouty, 1994; Prouty, Van Werde and Pörtner, 1998) where something struggles to express itself, allows a deeper understanding of ways to behave or express things which at first do not seem comprehensible.

The 'diagnostic eye' exclusively focused on deficiencies fixates a person with special needs on what she is not able to do, thus blurring the view of what she can do. Therefore the 'person-centred eye', focused on resources, is a helpful—and in my opinion

247

necessary—complement. Yet, on the other hand, we are of no help to a person with special needs if we are blind to the concrete limitations a specific handicap imposes on her. We then will ask too much of her and make her repeat once again the experience of failure. We must know about the nature of different disabilities, because ignorance of what people have to live with leads to inadequate support and inadequate care. This is a dark side of normalisation.

5. THE LIGHT AND DARK SIDE OF NORMALISATION

The principle of normalisation, calling for empowerment and self-advocacy, brought significant improvements in care and education of people with special needs. Their range of activity has considerably expanded and they are offered many more opportunities to participate in what is considered normal life. No longer do they live out of the public eye, but can be seen anywhere: on trains and buses, at the zoo, at the shopping mall, at the restaurant, at museums, on the beach. Compared to former times, their quality of life, without any doubt, has considerably improved.

Yet, there is also a dark side to normalisation (Pörtner, 2003: 62–71). To recognise it does in no way mean to condemn or give up on normalisation or to belittle its merits, but helps to clearly discriminate between where it really serves its purpose and where it risks turning into the opposite. Two tendencies are particularly pernicious:

• trying to adjust mentally disabled persons to 'the' normal
• ignoring existing handicaps

It is a misunderstanding that normalisation should, at all costs, try to adjust people with mental disabilities to what is considered 'normal'. Normalisation is not about creating 'normality' by hiding or denying handicaps. Normalisation means: it is as normal to be handicapped as it is normal to have blue or brown eyes, white or black skin, long or short legs or to need glasses. Normalisation is about accepting a broader range of modes of existence, including mental disabilities. Normalisation is about offering persons with special needs conditions that, according to their capabilities, facilitate their autonomy and personal growth and let them find *their* best way to cope with the world they have to live in.

It is certainly positive not to stigmatise individuals with the label 'handicapped' and to respond to them as normally as possible; however, it must not result in ignoring a person's disability and withholding from her the support she needs. Unfortunately this happens quite frequently, and the earlier mentioned impoverishment of language contributes to it. Even more harmful though, is widely-held black and white thinking that leads to either treat a person as 'disabled' and overlook her capabilities (thus impeding her potential development) or as 'normal' and overlook her disabilities (thus depriving her from adequate care). What we badly need is *differentiation*—its increasing lack is one of the most disastrous tendencies of our time, not only in care for mentally handicapped people, but in many other social and political issues as well.

We should not, from the perspective 'disabled', create differences where there are none, but we have to recognise and accept differences that really exist. To blur differences is just another way of discrimination. To only accept what is like us is not real integration. Integration is *not* about *making disabled persons equal* but about *accepting them as equal*. To respect the 'otherness' in other people is a basic principle of the person-centred attitude. Therefore knowledge about the nature of different handicaps and psychological disorders is necessary for psychotherapists as well as for carers, in order to better understand differences and be able to more adequately meet the needs of those who must live with such handicaps.

6. WHAT IS DIFFERENT IN COMPARISON TO 'NORMAL' PSYCHOTHERAPIES?

The therapist's basic attitude of empathy, acceptance and congruence is precisely the same as with any other client. However, concerning the circumstances as well as the main focus in the therapeutic process, there are some differences when working with disabled clients.

- As a rule, these clients do not see a psychotherapist on their own initiative . Others— who usually have quite concrete ideas about the effects psychotherapy should produce— decide that it is necessary for them.
- Language disorders, being non-verbal and bizarre behaviours are barriers to understanding that therapists have to overcome. Many people with special needs have only very poor or even no language available at all. The therapeutic relationship then develops on a very subtle non-verbal or pre-verbal level that therapists first have to discover.
- The setting may be very different from what psychotherapists are used to and from what would be desirable. Often there is no proper room to work in, and they have to make do with the entrance hall, the cafeteria or the living room and all the disturbances that implies.
- Persons with special needs only very rarely are in a position to consciously deal with, talk about or work on their problems.
- Cooperation and exchange with the carers in most cases is necessary.

For the therapist, it means to resolve not to let themselves be used to carry out the instructions of carers, yet to stay completely open to the concerns of the clients themselves. Only in this way is there a chance that trust will build up and a therapeutic relationship develop. Moreover, therapists must be flexible in terms of the setting and—this is perhaps the most difficult—lower their expectations with regard to what psychotherapy can achieve.

Phases where nothing seems to move are much more pronounced than in psychotherapy with other clients. All the more, the therapist has to be carefully aware of the *small, sometimes even tiny steps* that nevertheless do happen. Therefore it is helpful from time to time to look back. From a distance the—sometimes considerable—stretch of road that the client has covered despite the apparent standstill becomes visible. Also, what had seemed to turn in circles, on reflection might reveal itself as a spiral that imperceptibly but steadily is opening up. It is a matter of nuances: the client still may be overcome by rage about the behaviour of one of her roommates, but she now recovers more quickly; the client who used to frighten his group with his aggression might still get angry, but now for the most part expresses it verbally and only very rarely through physical attacks. Such changes *do count* even if they represent only small steps. The importance of small steps in client-centred psychotherapy as well as in everyday care for people with special needs has been emphasized and described in several publications. (Pörtner, 1994, 1996, 2000, 2003)

Mildly disabled persons too, frequently suffer from various kinds of language disorders which make empathic understanding difficult for the therapist. With them an old methodical element of client-centred psychotherapy proves to be helpful again: *to reflect what has been understood.* People who have difficulties in expressing themselves verbally experience again and again that others respond with 'mhm' or 'sure' without having understood anything of what they had tried to express. Such experiences increase the isolation of a person with special needs. Whereas to experience—perhaps for the first time—that somebody does not give up until she or he does really understand brings about deep release. (The person often expresses that by taking a deep breath.) I learned from one of my first clients with special needs how important this experience is. Despite my coming to understand her way of expressing herself quite well and no longer feeling it necessary to reflect everything, she stubbornly insisted on my repeating each sentence she said. Obviously she needed it to make sure that I had really understood (Pörtner, 1984, 1990).

Another difficulty is that clients who are verbal and seem quite able to express themselves, often do so in 'ready-made' stereotypes picked up from the 'normal people' they so much want to resemble. They are not used to talking about what they feel and experience and refer perhaps only to apparently 'banal' events of their daily life. The therapist has to be sensitively aware of the perhaps only very indirectly expressed *experiencing quality* in what on the surface seems to be banal or stereotyped. She needs patience and staying power to slowly and carefully help clients get more in contact with their experiencing, by again and again *reflecting the experiencing quality and emotional content* of what the person is expressing—another well-proven methodical element of client-centred psychotherapy.

It is even more difficult with people who do not speak at all or barely speak. An impressive example is the experience of the German psychologist Barbara Krietemeyer with a severely disabled non-verbal woman (Krietemeyer, 2000; Krietemeyer and Prouty, 2003) described in the chapter 'A hopeless case?' (Pörtner 2000: 105–13). Prouty's Pre-Therapy is an invaluable support in approaching persons 'without language' (Prouty, 1994, Prouty, Van Werde and Pörtner, 1998, 2002). Verbal or not, psychotherapists have to *find the 'language' of the other person*—and whenever they succeed, it will be a precious experience expanding their human understanding as well as their therapeutic competence.

The necessary cooperation and exchange with carers and at the same time—as with any other client—the obligation to strictly respect *confidentiality of the therapy session* is a delicate balance requiring subtlety, transparency and clear thinking on the part of the therapist. He may for example add to the carers' understanding by telling *his view* of where the client is at the moment, without giving away any of the contents the client had entrusted him with. A principle psychotherapists have to keep in mind: *Psychotherapy is never about remodelling disabled persons to the wishes of their carers.* So what is the purpose of psychotherapy for people with special needs if not to deliberately change undesirable behaviours, and particularly when it is not possible to systematically and consciously work on their problems?

7. MAIN ISSUES IN THE THERAPEUTIC PROCESS

There are two main issues in psychotherapy for people with special needs:

* changes in the self-concept
* development of contact functions

Facilitating changes in the self-concept is what psychotherapy basically is about. For most people with mental disabilities (and other clients as well) the crucial first step is to restore self-esteem and find *a more accepting and more positive attitude towards themselves,* in order that further changes become possible at all. This is particularly important for people with special needs. As they are constantly confronted with their incompetence and inadequacy, they usually find it hard to accept themselves. They suffer from 'being different' and judge themselves by what they think is 'normal'. Their self-esteem, in general, is very low—the unrealistic overestimation of some of them is just the other side of the same coin. To *develop more self-confidence* and on the other hand to *better recognise one's own limits*—these are issues psychotherapy can help with, and the person-centred attitude is a crucial factor. To be accepted by the therapist helps clients to accept themselves—including their inadequacies. This in itself represents a change. Awareness of life improves, and energies are set free that may open new prospects and facilitate further steps of growth.

Another essential aspect of psychotherapy with these clients is to *establish, restore and reinforce contact functions* as defined by Prouty as reality contact, emotional contact and communicative contact (Prouty, 1994; Prouty, Van Werde and Pörtner, 1998, 2002). In the majority of people with special needs, these contact functions are impaired or not sufficiently developed. Here Prouty's concept of Pre-Therapy, built on client-centred fundamentals, offers precious support. It is not only helpful in psychotherapy but can also be transferred to everyday situations. (Prouty 1994; Prouty, Van Werde and Pörtner 1998, 2002; Van Werde 1998) Dion Van Werde's work at the psychiatric hospital Sint-Camillus in Gent is exemplary in this respect and well transferable to organisations for people with special needs.

For them to be more able to accept themselves, to be more in contact with reality, with their own feeling and experiencing, as well as with other people, inevitably has consequences on their behaviours and expands their radius of action. Even so, we do not specifically aim at changing behaviours: it will happen when the self-concept changes and self-esteem improves. And it makes a crucial difference for a person to discover fallow resources in herself and take her own steps—even though perhaps not those the carers are expecting—rather than be pushed in a specific direction. This too is an essential element of the PCA, not restricted to people with special needs but particularly important for them.

Many persons with special needs are well able to verbalise changes in their self-concept, sometimes using amazingly expressive images. But above all, it shows in their behaviour: more self-assurance, more self-confidence, more trusting of their own ways and opinions—in daily life as well as in relation to the therapist.

8. THE CRUCIAL IMPORTANCE OF THE ENVIRONMENT

The most important happens outside the therapy session is a truism that psychotherapists can never keep in mind enough. The most exciting experiences during a therapy session will not be of much use for the clients if they cannot create new and different experiences with themselves and with others in their daily life. This is particularly true for people with special needs. They usually cannot, without support, transfer their experiences from the therapy session into daily life. They get stressed if there is too big a discrepancy between what is developing in psychotherapy and what is required or tolerated by their environment. The therapist and the carers must not work against each other, as it will always be the disabled person who has to suffer the consequences. That is the reason cooperation is necessary.

Carers should be in a position to understand when a psychological process is in the offing, in order that in daily routine it will not be impeded but be encouraged. Behaviours that might be seen as disturbing often are the first indications of a significant step of growth. If carers are sensitive to that, they will be able to respond more adequately. Much psychotherapy for people with special needs would not be necessary if some basic person-centred principles were followed in everyday care. A detailed concept of what this means concretely is to be found in *Trust and Understanding* (Pörtner, 2000).

It is essential for the mental health and quality of life of people with special needs that in daily life too, wherever possible, their autonomy is fostered and respected and they are offered choices, be it in even tiny issues that may appear of no importance to people who aren't disabled. For individuals whose lives are to a large extent determined by others, they mean a lot. It makes a crucial difference for a person not able to move, to choose where she wants the wheelchair to be put, rather than have it decided by the carer. To respect human dignity means to *ask* a person who is not able to use the toilet by herself if it is ok to take her to the toilet now. It matters for somebody, who cannot eat by himself, to be given a chance to open his mouth or to indicate in some other way that he is ready, before the spoon is put between his lips. With severely disabled persons, respect for human dignity and allowing self-advocacy is not about big words, but about these tiny issues that, because of their apparent triviality, much too often are neglected.

It matters for a person who does not speak that carers in her presence talk *with her and not about her*. Being asked means something to non-verbal persons too, as they will sense the attitude behind the words and realise that they are being taken seriously instead of just ignored. And with the very few who are not reachable by language at all, a question or the offer of an opportunity to decide about something themselves can be communicated non-verbally as well.

Not concentrating on deficiencies but being aware of and fostering resources as well as supporting every tiny step that a person succeeds in making, is at least as important in everyday care as in psychotherapy. It improves the quality of life not only for people with special needs, but for carers as well, as their work then becomes more interesting and satisfying. Just as in psychotherapy, focusing on resources does not mean that carers must ignore or deny existing handicaps and their possible impact on a person—on the contrary.

9. HOW CAN PERSON-CENTRED PRINCIPLES AND KNOWLEDGE OF PSYCHODIAGNOSTICS AND THE NATURE OF SPECIFIC HANDICAPS COMPLEMENT EACH OTHER?

In order to discover a person's resources, her disabilities have to be recognised. This is vital in order to be able to provide adequate care and foster individual potential instead of causing stress to disabled persons with unrealistic demands. In this respect knowledge of psychodiagnostics can be helpful—on condition that it serves *to understand,* and *not to label* a person. To know basic facts about different disabilities is useful—on condition that one is aware that these facts do not explain anything about how a person experiences and copes with their disability. Only from a person's individual way of experiencing can we learn how the handicap affects her and find the best way to offer her adequate support. What we always have to keep in mind: diagnostics are categories that help *us,* the observers, to get some orientation about and put in an order the multiple phenomena we come across. Diagnostics can *never* establish the reality of how this person is. This is only to be learned from the person herself. We have to carefully explore an individual's specific experience of and reaction to the disability, as well as her attempts to cope with it. For this, as I mentioned before, the 'diagnostic eye' is not sufficient, but needs to be complemented by the 'person-centred eye'. Both eyes together may help carers, as well as psychotherapists, to more clearly see the meaning of a person's strange behaviour and to discover—in their different ways and in relation to their different tasks—adequate ways to respond.

Yet, knowledge of diagnostics and psychopathology can also be treacherous if it entices carers (and sometimes also psychotherapists) to see symptoms everywhere and pathologise any behaviour or reaction that they have difficulty in understanding. The purpose of knowledge is not to set limits for disabled persons, but to *acknowledge* their limitations where they arise, and to help them find their own best ways to live and cope with these limitations. Knowledge must serve to *recognise* symptoms when they occur, but not to persistently look out for and attach them to disabled persons. The trouble is that if we are sufficiently determined, we will always find what we are looking for. We have to keep in mind that through our interactions and expectations we influence another person more than we may imagine. Interestingly, the considerable impact of interaction on development and behaviours of individuals has recently been affirmed by scientists doing research into brain functions (Koukkou and Lehman, 1998). The viewpoint we hold plays a powerful role in terms of self-fulfilling prophecy, on the personal, as well as on the scientific level.

So what we need is to keep knowledge in the background, in order to refer to it when reaching the limits of our empathic understanding. We also need to recognise the limits of our own professional background and enhance it by cooperating with other professionals. Educators, psychotherapists, physicians, psychiatrists, and carers—they all can learn from each other—on condition that they share the same basic attitude of accepting and respecting the individuality and 'otherness' in a person with special needs.

As we all well know, there is no formula in the mode of: 'if ... then'. In practice, the different points that have been described do not occur in isolation, but are interwoven, interdependent and in various combinations. To conclude my considerations, this complexity is illustrated by the following examples:

EXAMPLE 1: BRIAN

Brian, 20, suffers from a rare chromosome aberration. He recently moved from his parents' house to a supported-living unit. On one of his first Friday evenings there, the carers let him go to the pub, by himself and with more money in his pocket than he could handle. Brian could not cope with the situation; he did what he saw the other men doing there: drinking one beer after the other. He ended up totally drunk at the police station. When Brian's parents reproached the carers saying that they were irresponsible to let Brian get into a situation that he was not capable of handling adequately, the answer was: 'We are a learning unit, not a behaviour unit.' With justification the parents were upset: 'It is wrong to split a person up in this way. Intellect, feeling and environment are interconnected and come together as a whole which is expressed as behaviour. When carers only consider one aspect of the personality, they create a real problem.'

EXAMPLE 2: FRED

The fact that many persons with Down syndrome tend to suffer from fatigability is, unfortunately, not always sufficiently known to carers. Fred, 22, Down syndrome, during the psychotherapy session frequently has to fight against falling asleep. Yet, he refuses the therapist's suggestion to relax for a minute and close his eyes. 'No', he says resolutely. 'It's okay, I can pull myself together.' That's what he is always told, when the same happens to him at work or in his residential facility. The psychotherapist is perplexed to hear about Fred's schedule for this day: therapy session, a meeting with the staff, music lesson—all this after a full working day. Obviously the carers do not realise that they should consider Fred's fatigability when planning his schedule. Moreover, at work or during group activities, he should be allowed to relax for a few minutes when he is about to fall asleep. The staff should show him how to do that, instead of telling him to pull himself together. It would be to everybody's benefit, as Fred this way could certainly work more efficiently than when using all his energy to fight drowsiness. Hopefully the psychotherapist will find a good way to communicate with the staff about Fred's problem and to convince them to handle it more satisfactorily by helping him to adequately deal with instead of fighting it. In situations like this, it is important that the therapist does not come from a position of 'I know better' but shows empathy and understanding for the carers also.

EXAMPLE 3: KERSTIN

Kerstin, 35, lives in a supported-living apartment. She has learning disabilities (but there is no information about when and why this had first been diagnosed) and serious psychological disorders. She hears voices that persistently derogate her in a most painful way. About a year ago, she felt suicidal and, at her own wish, was hospitalised for some weeks at a psychiatric clinic. Since then she has medication and for that is seeing a psychiatrist every two or three months. She also has taken up seeing her former psychotherapist again every two weeks. She still hears voices but, due to medication, they are no longer as loud and persistent as they had been. This is a relief. But on the other hand, medication makes her very tired, passive, and even depressive sometimes. She is too intimidated to tell the psychiatrist about it, even though he asked her and seems really interested to know. In this situation it is helpful that the psychotherapist, with Kerstin's consent, communicates with the psychiatrist so that he can decide about changing either the medication or its dosage. After a while Kerstin feels better, if still somehow subdued. The voices are more persistent again, but as it seems to a tolerable extent.

Kerstin (at least up until now) is neither intellectually nor emotionally in a position to work on these voices and perhaps discover what they mean. But at least she is able to talk about how they belittle her and are sometimes more, sometimes less troublesome. The therapist encourages Kerstin to not just listen to the voices, but also to address them when they get too bad; for example, to try to contradict them or tell them to shut up. Though this will not stop the voices, it fosters the client's contact with herself and makes her discover that she has a little influence on them too. Sometimes they take it with humour. 'How are they behaving this week?' the therapist asks. The client smiles. 'More or less,' she says, 'but it is ok. Mostly I manage to just not listen.' It is a small, yet very important step for the client to be aware that she has some power over the voices, be it only to smile at them from time to time and not listen. She no longer feels entirely at their mercy but has gained a little more scope of action; this makes her feel a lot better.

EXAMPLE 4: THOMAS

Thomas, 40, lives in a supported-living facility and works in a sheltered workshop. His psychological disorders are obvious, but with him too, nothing is known about when and why he had originally been diagnosed as mentally handicapped. He seems rather intelligent, but has a speech defect (probably due to his operated-on harelip). It had been the carers' idea that Thomas should see a psychotherapist. They were worried about his psychological problems and sometimes extremely strange behaviour and felt it to be too much for them to deal with. The first time Thomas came to the psychotherapist, he just sat there, completely withdrawn and breathing heavily. He did not say anything and did not look at the therapist once. To the few questions she asked, he answered: 'I don't know.' However, to her surprise, he came back, and despite the next sessions being not much different from the first, gradually a therapeutic relationship began to develop. Thomas started to sometimes say something, never about himself, but perhaps about the weather or something he heard on the news. He often asked the therapist questions. With him she felt it more necessary to respond than is usual in a therapeutic setting. At that time it was, for Thomas, the only possible way to gradually establish contact and trust. Moreover, by the therapist telling him something about herself, a bridge was built over which he could be encouraged to talk about how he thought or felt as well. So very slowly and in tiny steps, he came more into contact with his own experience and feelings.

It soon became obvious that Thomas suffered from the so-called 'bipolar' disorder (formerly known as manic-depressive disorder). His depressive phases were so extreme, and he was suffering so much, that nothing could really reach him at that time. When it got too bad, he even skipped the therapy session. Nevertheless, he went to work, but in the evening and on the weekend locked himself up in his room and remained inaccessible to the carers.

With time he could, at least afterwards, tell the therapist a little about how he had felt and that he had been 'in a deep black hole'. More was not possible. The therapist could only be there, feel and bear the black hole with him. The manic phases were less extreme; he was just quite vivid and talked a lot. With time, the depressive phases seemed to become a little less severe. 'I was in a hole, but not that deep,' he said. Once, in a phase when he was talking a lot, he observed at the end of the session: 'Today I did not say anything about myself', and seemed to regret it. And another time, after having talked—very briefly—about something that bothered him, he said: 'This was a good conversation, don't you think so?' Obviously there was some progress.

Yet, even as the depressive phases became less pronounced, he still sometimes suffered terribly. He took it bravely, saying: 'I shall come through, I always have.' The therapist felt that medication might help him over the worst periods, and suggested that he should see a psychiatrist, who had experience with mentally disabled patients and was known for his subtly differentiated way to prescribe medication. But Thomas refused. He had once had a bad experience with a psychiatrist and medication, and has been determined ever since never see one again. So, unfortunately, he still suffers terribly from time to time, even though: 'The hole is not as dark and deep anymore.'

CONCLUSION

There is a need for psychotherapists willing and able to work with persons with special needs because many of them suffer from psychological disorders. The large variety of very different persons embraced by the term 'special needs' calls for a *subtly differentiated individual approach* in psychotherapy as well as in everyday care. Particularly with these clients a person-centred attitude is needed, as their strange and apparently inaccessible inner world can be approached only by empathically trying to understand their individual way of experiencing. The therapist has to be perceptive for *changes in the self-concept* and *development of the contact functions* along the therapeutic process and to take into account some conditions that are different than with 'normal' clients. Cooperation with carers is useful and necessary because psychotherapy will not work for the clients if it is not supported by their environment.

It is crucial that psychotherapists as well as carers do not stress a person with special needs (and themselves) by overly high expectations, yet at the same time remain open to surprises and the possibility that a person might develop more than, given her disability, she is credited for. It is necessary to be sensitively aware of, *to acknowledge and encourage even very small steps* that a disabled person succeeds in taking, in order to reinforce her self-confidence and possibly facilitate further steps.

Knowledge of psychopathology and the nature of different handicaps is useful, however with the purpose not to pathologise people with special needs or to define limits for them, but to be able to *recognise and understand existing* impairments and limitations of an individual and respond adequately. According to different tasks and professional backgrounds, the extent, level and main focus of knowledge will, of course, differ. For *all* professionals working in this field, it is important to be aware of their own specific limitations and be willing to turn to and cooperate with others when at their wit's end. Instead of competing and mistrusting each other, different disciplines could learn from and complement each other—not only for the clients' but also for their own benefit. Cooperation between different professionals in this field is necessary and helpful—on condition that there is common agreement *not to aim at remodelling* persons with special needs along concepts of what is 'normal', but at improving their well-being and quality of life and *enabling them to be themselves* and find *their* best way to cope with reality.

REFERENCES

Badelt, I (1984) Selbsterfahrungsgruppen geistig behinderter Erwachsener. In *Geistige Behinderung.* 23, 243–53.

Badelt, I (1990) Client-centered psychotherapy with mentally handicapped adults. In G Lietaer, J Rombauts and R Van Balen (eds) *Client-Centered and Experiential Psychotherapy in the Nineties* (pp. 671–81). Leuven: Leuven University Press.

Badelt, I (1994) Die klientenzentrierte Psychotherapie mit geistig behinderten Menschen. In W Lotz, U Koch, and B Stahl (eds) *Psychotherapeutische Behandlung geistig behinderter Menschen. Bedarf, Rahmenbedingungen, Konzepte.* (pp. 141–52). Bern: Hans Huber.

Eggert, D (1993) Veränderungen im Bild von der geistigen Behinderung in der Psychologie. In K Hennicke and W Rotthaus (eds) *Psychotherapie und Geistige Behinderung* (pp. 204–18). Dortmund: verlag modernes lernen.

Gaedt, Ch (ed) (1987) *Psychotherapie bei geistig Behinderten.* 2. Neuerkeröder Forum. Neuerkeröder Anstalten. Eigenverlag.

Görres, S (1996) Ethische Fragen in der Psychotherapie mit geistig behinderten Menschen. In W Lotz, B Stahl and D Irblich (eds) *Wege zur seelischen Gesundheit für Menschen mit geistiger Behinderung—Psychotherapie und Persönlichkeitsentwicklung* (pp. 29–39). Bern: Hans Huber.

Gunn, P, Berry, P and Andrews, RJ (1984/86) The development of Down Syndrome children from birth to five years. In JM Berg (ed) *Perspectives and Progress in Mental Retardation.* Baltimore: University Press.

Hennicke, K and Rotthaus, W (eds) (1993) *Psychotherapie und Geistige Behinderung.* Dortmund: verlag modernes lernen.

Irblich, D (1999) Gewalt und geistige Behinderung. In *Geistige Behinderung, 2,* 132–45.

Koukkou, M and Lehmann, D (1998) Ein systemtheoretisch orientiertes Modell der Funktionen des menschlichen Gehirns und die Ontogenese des Verhaltens. In M Koukkou, M Leuzinger-Bohleber and W Mertens (eds) *Erinnerung von Wirklichkeiten. Psychoanalyse und Neurowissenschaften im Dialog. Vol. 1* (pp. 287–415). Stuttgart: Verlag Internationale Psychoanalyse.

Krietemeyer, B (2000) Wege aus der inneren Isolation. In *Kerbe, 2,* 21–2.

Krietemeyer, B and Prouty, G (2003) The art of psychological contact: The psychotherapy of a retarded psychotic client. In *Person-Centered and Experiential Psychotherapies, 2,* 151–61.

Lotz, W and Koch, U (1994) Zum Vorkommen psychischer Störungen bei Personen mit geistiger Behinderung. In W Lotz, U Koch and B Stahl (eds) *Psychotherapeutische Behandlung geistig behinderter Menschen—Bedarf, Rahmenbedingungen, Konzepte* (13–39). Bern: Hans Huber.

Lotz, W, Koch, U and Stahl, B (eds) (1994) *Psychotherapeutische Behandlung geistig behinderter Menschen—Bedarf, Rahmenbedingungen, Konzepte.* Bern: Hans Huber.

Lotz, W, Stahl, B and Irblich, D (eds) (1996) *Wege zur seelischen Gesundheit für Menschen mit geistiger Behinderung—Psychotherapie und Persönlichkeitsentwicklung.* Bern: Hans Huber.

Morton, I (ed) (1999) *Person-Centred Approaches to Dementia Care.* Bicester, Oxon: Winslow Press.

Peters, H (1992) *Psychotherapie bij geestelijk gehandicapten.* Amsterdam/Lisse: Swets, Zeitlinger. German edition (2001) *Psychotherapeutische Zugänge zu Menschen mit geistiger Behinderung.* Stuttgart: Klett-Cotta.

Pörtner, M (1984) Gesprächstherapie mit geistig behinderten Klienten. In *Brennpunkt 18,* 6–23 und in *GwG-info 56,* 20–30.

Pörtner, M (1990) Client-centered therapy with mentally retarded persons: Catherine and Ruth. In G Lietaer, J Rombauts and R Van Balen (eds) *Client-Centered and Experiential Psychotherapy in the Nineties* (pp. 659–69). Leuven: Leuven University Press.

Pörtner, M (1994) *Praxis der Gesprächspsychotherapie. Interviews mit Therapeuten.* Stuttgart: Klett-Cotta.

Pörtner, M (1996) *Ernstnehmen, Zutrauen, Verstehen—Personzentrierte Haltung im Umgang mit geistig behinderten und pflegebedürftigen* Menschen, Stuttgart: Klett-Cotta. Dutch edition (1998) *Serieus nemen, vertrouwen, begrijpen.* Maarssen: Elsevier/De Tijdstroom. English edition (2000 see below). Danish edition (2003) *Den personcentrerede metode i arbejdet med sindslidende, undviklingshaemmende og demente mennesker.* Kopenhagen: Reitzels.

Pörtner, M (1996 a) Working with the Mentally Handicapped in a Person-Centered Way—Is it possible, is it appropriate and what does it mean in practice? In R Hutterer, G Pawlowsky, PF Schmid and R Stipsits (eds) *Client-Centered and Experiential Psychotherapy: A paradigm in motion* (pp. 513–27). Frankfurt am Main: Peter Lang, Europäischer Verlag der Wissenschaften.

Pörtner, M (2000) *Trust and Understanding: The Person-Centred Approach to everyday care for people with special needs.* Ross-on-Wye: PCCS Books.

Pörtner, M (2001) The Person-Centred Approach in working with people with special needs. In *Person-Centred Practice, 9,* 18–30.

Pörtner, M (2002a) Der Personzentrierte Ansatz in der Arbeit mit geistig behinderten Menschen. In W Keil and G Stumm (Hrsg) *Die vielen gesichter der personzentrierten psychotherapie.* Wien: Springer.

Pörtner, M (2002b) Psychotherapy for people with special needs: A challenge for client-centered psychotherapists. In JC Watson, RN Goldman and MS Warner (eds) *Client-Centered and Experiential Psychotherapy in the 21st Century: Advances in theory, research and practice.* Ross-on-Wye: PCCS Books.

Pörtner, M (2003) *Brücken bauen. Menschen mit geistiger Behinderung verstehen und begleiten.* Stuttgart: Klett-Cotta.

Pörtner, M (2005) *Alt sein ist anders. Personzentrierte Betreuung von alten Menschen.* Stuttgart: Klett-Cotta.

Prouty, G (1994) *Theoretical Evolutions in Person-Centered/Experiential Therapy—Applications to Schizophrenic and Retarded Psychoses.* Westport: Praeger.

Prouty, G (1998) Pre-Therapy and the pre-expressive self. In *Person Centred Practice, 6,* 80–8.

Prouty, G, Van Werde, D and Pörtner, M (1998) *Prä-Therapie.* Stuttgart: Klett-Cotta. English edition (2002) *Pre-Therapy: Reaching contact-impaired clients.* Ross-on-Wye: PCCS Books.

Rogers, CR (1942) *Counseling and Psychotherapy.* Boston: Houghton Mifflin.

Rotthaus, W (1993) *Menschenbild und psychische Krankheit des Geistigbehinderten aus systemischer Sicht.* In K Hennicke and W Rotthaus (Hrsg) (1993) *Psychotherapie und Geistige Behinderung* (pp. 195–203). Dortmund: verlag modernes lernen.

Senckel, B (1998) *Du bist ein weiter Baum—Entwicklungschancen für geistig behinderte Menschen durch Beziehung.* München: Beck.

Sinason, V (1992) *Mental Handicap and The Human Condition.* London: Free Association Books.

Stahl, B (1996) Zum Stand der Entwicklung in der Psychotherapie mit geistig behinderten Menschen. In W Lotz, B Stahl and D Irblich, (Hrsg) (1996) *Wege zur seelischen Gesundheit für Menschen mit geistiger Behinderung—Psychotherapie und Persönlichkeitsentwicklung* (pp. 14–28). Bern: Hans Huber.

Thimm, W (1999) Epidemologie und soziokulturelle Faktoren. In G Neuhäuser and H-C Steinhausen *Geistige Behinderung. Grundlagen. Klinische Syndrome. Behandlung und Rehabilitation.* 2. überarbeitete und erweiterte Auflage (pp. 9–25). Stuttgart: W Kohlhammer.

Van Werde, D (1998) Anchorage as a core concept in working with psychotic people. In B Thorne, D Mearns and E Lambers (eds) *Person-Centred Therapy: a European perspective.* London: Sage.

Van Werde, D and Morton, I (2002) The relevance of Prouty's Pre-Therapy in dementia care. In Morton, I (1999) *Person-Centred Approaches to Dementia Care* (pp. 139–76). Bicester, Oxon: Winslow Press.

CHAPTER 17

AUTISM AND ASPERGER SYNDROME: PERSON-CENTRED APPROACHES

JACKY KNIBBS AND HEATHER MORAN

The authors are both Consultant Clinical Psychologists working in National Health Trusts, one in South Warwickshire, one for the Coventry Primary Care Trust and have been responsible for initiating and developing local services for children, young people and their families where there may be a diagnosis of the autism spectrum. This chapter will consider the fundamental tenets of person-centred thinking in relation to autism and children. Whilst client-centred psychotherapists do not routinely take developmental histories, assess or diagnose clients, it will be argued here that these aspects of professional practice have a particularly important function with the autism spectrum. Having a framework for shared understanding and access to others with similar experiences may provide opportunities both for clients' growth and for the real fulfilment of congruence and unconditional positive regard for clients from therapists and surrounding systems.

This chapter will outline the current evidence supporting the biological bases of autism and describe the breadth of the autism spectrum. First-hand accounts of individuals with autism will be drawn upon to support the application of the medical model in identifying and diagnosing individuals. For appropriately informed advocacy, particularly within the educational system, assessment drawn from the clinical and research evidence base helps the systems around children to appreciate and convey the complexity of individuals' internal frames of reference. The person-centred perspective is central in recognising each individual's uniqueness, and in achieving true empathic understanding (Rogers, 1957). It also provides a model for considering the complex social conditions of worth and accompanying challenges for individuals with social learning difficulties. Whilst there is no 'cure' for autism, optimal recognition may contribute to preventing or ameliorating additional mental health difficulties, and help individuals to realise their social potential. The essential aim of our work is to achieve conditions where clients feel accepted and valued, listened to and understood, not judged or required to conform to inappropriate expectations.

AUTISM AND ASPERGER SYNDROME

AETIOLOGY

The autism spectrum is continuing to receive growing popular (Haddon, 2003; Hoopmann, 2001), clinical and research attention. Evidence relating to the aetiology of autism has shifted considerably over time, with Bruno Bettelheim's notion of refrigerator mothers (Bettelheim, 1967), now supplanted by neurodevelopmental findings. Strong evidence suggests that the autism spectrum is biological in origin, and not caused by parenting or other psycho-social environmental causes (Frith and Hill, 2003).

Some psychoanalytic authors (Tustin, 1988) argue for impoverishment in emotional nurturing (whether environmentally or constitutionally determined) as a precursor to the development of autism as a 'sensation-dominated' state of being. It is possible that in a minority of cases, extreme environmental events, e.g., significant early abuse impacts on the developing baby's brain to create or exacerbate the neurodevelopmental conditions for autism (Glaser, 2000; Rutter et al., 1999). Three typical potential biological causes have been identified (Attwood, 1998), namely unfavourable obstetric events, infections during pregnancy or early infancy that affect the brain, and genetic factors. Differences in the size and organisation of the brain, as well as how it works in individuals on the autism spectrum versus 'neurotypical' individuals have been found. There is increasing evidence from neuropsychological assessment and brain imaging techniques (Frith and Frith 2003; Brothers, 1997) implicating the frontal and temporal lobes in the processing of social and emotional information. There may be quite precise areas of unusual functioning in the frontal lobes that produce the pattern of behaviour and abilities associated with the autism spectrum (McKelvey et al., 1995; Happe et al., 1996; Frith, 2004; Volkmar et al., 2004). To date however no signature pattern, one that is universal and specific to the autism spectrum, has been found. This is not surprising given the very wide diversity of individuals so described. Early research involving the study of twin pairs demonstrated a genetic predisposition to autism: if one twin has autism the likelihood of the other twin having autism is far higher for identical (monozygotic) twins than for non-identical (dizygotic) twins (Folstein and Rutter, 1977). It has also been found that autism is fifty times more frequent in the siblings of people with autism (Smalley et al., 1988).The precise means of genetic transmission have not been identified (Pickles et al., 1995; Volkmar et al., 2004). What appears to be transmitted is not autism per se, but a certain distinctive style of thinking, relating and reacting to the world that brings with it limitations and strengths (Baron-Cohen, 2003; Dorris et al., 2004).

We think that this distinctive way of thinking is best understood through the lens of the medical model, and that person-centred approaches are not able to account for the aetiology of these core difficulties. But, what we argue is that the person with autism and Asperger's is subject to heightened conditions of worth which lead to a range of associated difficulties in living. This is where the person-centred perspective has an important contribution to make in helping the person to achieve self-acceptance, to value their differences, and to be able to develop their strengths.

ASSOCIATED PROBLEMS

There are also particular vulnerabilities associated with the autism spectrum (Berney, 2004). Individuals are at risk for a range of accompanying difficulties, some of which may be also neurodevelopmentally determined, e.g. epilepsy (Tuchman and Rapin, 2002), dyspraxia, and attention deficit hyperactivity disorder (Goldstein and Schwebach, 2004; Attwood, 1998; Tantam, 2003). Additionally, some problems may be exacerbated by the incongruence of individuals with their surroundings. High anxiety (Gillot et al., 2001; Kim et al., 2000), depression (Ghaziuddin et al., 1995; Ghaziuddin and Greden, 1998) and obsessive compulsive disorders (Baron-Cohen, 1989; Hollander et al., 2003) are common. David Andrews has a diagnosis of Asperger syndrome and writes:

> It is supremely important to value the Asperger autistic client and his or her experience and to realise that this experience will (in most cases) have been particularly nasty at some point. So when such client is showing signs of anxiety or depression, it is important that these problems not be attributed to 'the biochemistry of autism' or even to the autism itself. The problems come from how the client is experiencing society. (Andrews, 2004: 27)

A person-centred perspective is crucial in promoting advocacy, and in identifying and challenging the very significant stresses associated with social misunderstanding and inappropriate social conditions of worth.

DIFFABILITY RATHER THAN DISABILITY

Whilst the autism spectrum is now considered to be a much broader phenomenon (Wing, 2002; Volkmar et al., 2004), than when first described (Kanner, 1943; Asperger, 1944), the language associated with diagnosis within the medical and psychoananalytical models is essentially deficit driven (Baird et al., 2003; Alvarez, 1996). A triad of impairments is outlined as diagnostic criteria for autism in *ICD-10* (*International Classification of Diseases*, 10th revision) and the *Diagnostic and Statistical Manual of Mental Disorders*, fourth edition, (*DSM-IV*). These are qualitative impairments in social communication, social interaction and social imagination, with a restricted range of interests and often stereotyped repetitive behaviours and mannerisms (Baird et al., 2003). Asperger syndrome is used to describe those presenting with this pattern of development where there is not an accompanying clinically significant general cognitive or language disorder (Wing, 1981).

There is however an increasing range of first-hand accounts from individuals on the autism spectrum (Grandin, 1992, 1995; Holliday Willey, 1999; O'Neill, 1998a; Schneider, 1999) and accompanying pleas to be considered as different rather than impaired (Baron-Cohen, 2000). Wendy Lawson describes herself with a 'diffability' rather than disability (Lawson, 2001). Her references to the worlds of individuals with autism as being very distinct from that of the 'neuro-typical' population presumes an 'us and them' dichotomy which may not in itself be entirely helpful. Recent evidence of the broader phenotypes of the autism spectrum proposes that aspects and degrees of autism are experienced by large numbers of the population (Baron-Cohen, 2003; Dorris et al., 2004). Wendy Lawson's experience however is of being chronically misunderstood and misdiagnosed (she was treated with powerful anti-psychotics for 'schizophrenia' for 25 years and describes debilitating side effects). In the light of that, her strong sense of identity as someone essentially different may be better understood. In his book introducing a humanistic approach to autism, Stillman (2003) seeks to 'demystify the autistic experience'. He describes clearly the process of discovery of his own Asperger syndrome and his very particular, all-consuming enthusiasm as a child for the *Wizard of Oz*. He now acts as a consultant, helping to present an autism spectrum perspective. Although the generalisability of autobiographical accounts has to be considered carefully (Happe, 1991), these texts provide invaluable insights into others' diverse internal frames of reference (Jackson, 2002; Hale, 1998; Hall, 2001). Whilst there are times when receipt of a diagnosis is devastating for families and individuals, there are also many instances when it is described as a relief, and even life-enhancing and affirming. The thrust of most of these personal accounts is not to abandon diagnosis, but rather for much more widespread understanding of the complexity, interest and challenge of atypical worlds.

> I tried asking questions to find out if there was anything tangibly the matter with me. I had this vague, insistent idea all the time—that there was something wrong with me. But questions that to me were deeply serious were answered in amused voices: 'Oh, no, there's nothing wrong with you, dear.' (Gerland, 1997: 127)

Claire Sainsbury (2000) writes powerfully about her experiences, and argues for honesty:

> Because of our great difficulties in deciphering the social world by ourselves, we are particularly dependent on receiving accurate information from adults. Any child with Asperger's who is old enough to understand a simple verbal explanation of their condition is also old enough, if they don't get such an explanation, to notice that they are different from their 'normal' peers, and that they have difficulty doing things which seem to be easy for 'normal' children. Often they will infer that there must be something wrong with them. Many people with Asperger's concluded as children that they must be 'stupid', 'crazy', 'retarded', 'brain-damaged' or that what was wrong with them must be so awful that no-one would talk about it. A label is the key to self-understanding. A label lets a child know that their disability is not their fault; it lets them know that their problem has a name; and it lets them know that there are others out there like them. Accurate self-understanding is vital if a child is to take control and learn how to manage and work around their problems and make the best use of their strengths. Becoming aware of how one functions and of how others may perceive one's behaviour is essential if a child is to be able to begin to develop their own creative solutions of the problems they may come across, instead of being perpetually dependent on

others for help. Knowledge, as Francis Bacon pointed out, is power ... It is important not to give the impression that everything about Asperger syndrome is known, or that one knows the child better than they know themselves, but to recognize and help a child to articulate their own knowledge of how they function—to empower them to become experts on their own condition. (Sainsbury, 2000: 125–8)

Gunilla Gerland too makes a plea for a person-centred perspective in this process:

... you are not best helped if the people around you ... act as experts telling you that they know exactly what your condition is. What you need is guiding from them to come to your own truth, and to develop your personal approach to your condition. (Gerland, 2000)

As described in detail elsewhere, person-centred theory presents the core belief that the client is expert (Rogers, 1957; Joseph, 2003). Rogers emphasises that it is how the individual perceives reality that is important and that the best vantage point for understanding a person is that person. The perception of reality argument is a potent one here, given the awareness that it is precisely their unique and distinctive perceptions of reality that differentiate individuals on the autism spectrum (Jackson, 2002). Crucial to this is a preparedness from the therapist to be sensitive to and follow the clients' agenda. In children as young as three years, frequent observations are of children very strongly pursuing their own preferences with apparent disregard or avoidance of the wishes of those around them (Newson et al., 2003). The challenge for others is of finding ways to communicate effectively with a child who may have a particularly limited sense of how other people function. There is now overwhelming evidence that a core difficulty for individuals on the autism spectrum is related to the development of their theory of mind (Baron-Cohen, 1995). Here, there is a specific social and emotional learning difficulty; understanding the perspectives, emotions and worlds of others. From the age of around four years, children understand that other people have thoughts, knowledge, beliefs and desires that will influence their behaviour. Children on the autism spectrum appear to have some difficulties in conceptualising and appreciating the thoughts and feelings of another person. They may not realize that their comments could cause offence or embarrassment or that an apology would help to remedy a mistake (Attwood, 1998). This is often accompanied by problems for individuals in making sense of their own experiences and emotional states (Hill et al., 2004), and in seeking out ways of developing understanding. Temple Grandin (1992) explained:

I prefer factual, non-fictional reading materials. I have little interest in novels with complicated interpersonal relationships. When I do read novels, I prefer straightforward stories that occur in interesting places with lots of description. (p. 123)

There is also research and clinical evidence that individuals may have knowledge about other people's minds, but struggle to apply this knowledge effectively (Bowler, 1992). It is possible to appreciate at an intellectual level what a person may be thinking or feeling, but not recognise readily what behaviour is appropriate to the situation. This has been described as problems with a central drive for coherence—that is an ability to see the relevance of different types of knowledge to a particular problem (Frith and Happe, 1994; Hoy et al., 2004). Attwood (1998) cites an example of how, having taken the favourite toy of another child without permission, and then asked how they think the other child will feel, the child may give an appropriate answer, yet this consideration seemed not to be in their mind when they took the toy. Thus knowledge may be available but not recognised as relevant. This is where psycho-education, e.g. in the form of social stories which make social rules explicit, has been found to be helpful (Gray, 1998; Gray and White, 2002).

Where there are accompanying evident physical or learning difficulties, it may be recognised early on that children require different expectations and demands. However, particularly in high-functioning individuals who may be described as having Asperger syndrome, distinctive patterns of development are often misunderstood; Peacock et al., (1996) refer to the autism spectrum as the 'invisible handicap'. As a consequence, individuals may be exposed to a far greater extent than average to social conditions of worth. In social environments that demand compliance and cooperation, such as schools, youngsters with social learning difficulties are immediately significantly disadvantaged. At the same time, their behaviour is often misinterpreted as bloody-mindedness, or a consequence of poor parenting. In extreme cases, unusual or bizarre behaviours may be misattributed to child abuse, particularly where there are complex family circumstances.

Rogers (1957) outlines the six necessary and sufficient conditions of constructive personality change. Firstly that two persons (client and therapist) are in psychological contact, secondly that the client is 'in a state of incongruence, being vulnerable or anxious'. Conditions three and four are that the therapist is 'congruent or integrated in the relationship' and 'experiences unconditional regard for the client'.

Fifthly, the therapist 'experiences an empathic understanding of the client's internal frame of reference and endeavours to communicate this experience to the client'. Finally, 'the communication to the client of the therapist's empathic understanding and unconditional positive regard is to a minimal degree achieved' (p. 96).

The argument in this chapter is that by linking with the clinical, educational, research and advocacy worlds of those described as being on the autism spectrum, therapists in this field are much better equipped to experience empathic understanding; to appreciate and respond appropriately to the client's very individual internal frame of reference and to facilitate their potential for personal growth.

IDENTIFICATION

The initial challenge in work with children on the autism spectrum is identifying clearly those individuals for whom this is an appropriate description (Noland and Gabriels, 2004). Children may present in a range of different ways and to different services; one of the significant advances outlined in Lorna Wing's seminal paper (Wing, 1981) is the emphasis on the diversity of individuals and the importance of the concept of a spectrum of difference. A key question in person-centred thinking is whether it is in that individual's best interests to be identified, labeled, diagnosed. Parents often struggle with the dilemma of whether presenting their child to professionals or 'specialists' is creating more harm by targeting the child and highlighting difference. It is sometimes possible in very child-centred environments for children on the autism spectrum to thrive and for any differences to be acceptable and indeed applauded (Holliday Willey, 2001). Unfortunately, it is rare for both home and school together to be able to provide these optimal conditions. Children may respond well to high levels of structure and predictability at school, but struggle with the more emotionally-laden climate of home life—particularly when there are demanding younger siblings (Wood Rivers and Stoneman, 2003). Alternatively, home may provide a sanctuary and school a setting where children are overwhelmed (Carrington and Graham, 2001). Whilst a utopian position is clearly that the individuality of all is respected, the reality is that the social, communicative and behavioural characteristics of the autism spectrum often differentiate children and adults very explicitly. The argument here for working within a diagnostic model is that by early identification of vulnerable children, an understanding of their complex internal worlds may be promoted, along with the unconditional positive regard that grows from enhanced appreciation of other individual's positions and strengths.

ASSESSMENT

One of the key features of the autism spectrum is the complexity and diversity of individuals so described. It has been suggested that this is potentially the most severe of all child mental health presentations (Baron-Cohen, 2000). It could be argued that the concept of a broad spectrum is so over-inclusive to limit significantly the usefulness of it. The crucial task of assessment here is to reflect the individuality of clients. Evidence suggests that autism may include a range of complex and subtle neuropsychological presentations, (Manjiviona and Prior, 1999; Liss et al., 2001). Unusual sensory experiences are poorly researched, but feature largely in first-hand and anecdotal accounts of living with the autism spectrum (Grandin, 1992). For non-verbal individuals, or those who are unable to articulate their experiences, it is likely that aversive sensory stimulation is contributing to clients' distress which may then be translated into challenging behaviour (Clements and Zarkowska, 2000).

> Simply not knowing why, for example, certain noises upset you, can be frightening and frustrating in itself. (Sainsbury, 2000: 127)

> These situations where you suddenly realise you can't do something which is very easy to other people, and you have no idea why you can't do it, are very frustrating ... just to be able to explain to yourself why you can't do some things is very helpful. (Gerland, 2000)

A central requirement of practice from the person-centred perspective is to have an empathic understanding of the clients' unique frame of reference. It is argued here that to understand as fully as possible each client's unique presentation (Jacobsen, 2003), different sources of evidence should be accessed. Individual contact with children may be supplemented by parent, sibling, teacher and significant other accounts, and observations of children in different settings may yield a range of clues as to the very specific profile of each individual. Whilst this assumption of others' expertise may not sit comfortably with a traditional person-centred view, one important aspect of the autism spectrum is the challenge of effective communication. It may be possible to build an empathic understanding of the client's internal world by experience and trial and error, but this may be undervaluing the real complexity of some clients' developmental profiles (Ellis et al., 1994; McKelvey et al., 1995). Indeed, in more extreme instances of individuals for whom social contact is highly aversive, appropriate empathic perspective may be best achieved by less direct means initially than face-to-face client contact. Howlin (2000) and Le Couteur and Baird (2003) describe some of the assessment options currently available.

DIAGNOSIS

The diagnosis of autism is both much more widespread currently, and generally more acceptable. The latter is likely to be a result of high-profile media debate, a general demystifying of the condition, pioneering work of advocacy groups and the first-hand account literature which is beginning to celebrate autism. Berney (2004) provides a useful discussion of some of the issues to consider particularly for high-functioning individuals. The professional world abounds with confusing and unhelpful diagnostic terms—pervasive developmental disorders; semantic-pragmatic language disorder (Bishop, 1989); pathological demand avoidance syndrome (Newson et al., 2003); schizotypal personality disorder—to name but a few. Whilst some parents may be able to understand these more esoteric descriptions and their children may benefit from an enhanced understanding, many don't find them helpful. The crucial task is to find a shared language that promotes access to appropriate conditions, expectations and resources (Jackson, 2003). We have an additional responsibility to be open and clear with children and young people themselves, and the importance of using language that is comprehensible and acceptable is evident (Ives, 1999; Vermeulen, 2000). When diagnoses are explained to clients appropriately (Jones, 2001; Jackson, 2002), there are many accounts of how liberating this can be for the individuals concerned—as outlined by Sainsbury (2000) previously. Equally, some youngsters find this process highly aversive and their need for acceptance and struggles with difference are overwhelming. The following examples illustrate the range of difficulties that may be experienced and the potential impact of diagnosis for the child and family.

Claire was aged 16 at diagnosis. She was a bright young person who was failing badly in school in spite of her clear intellectual ability. She came from a somewhat alternative family with intellectual interests. Claire had a very intense interest in science and a love of philosophy and war games. At home, her interests were accepted and encouraged. However, she had been severely bullied in school because of her difference from teenage peers. Claire greeted the diagnosis with relief, explaining that she was very tired of trying to fit in with others her age, and that she was angry about the lack of acceptance of her right to be different. Within the family, the diagnosis was less acceptable because difference was not a problem. After diagnosis, Claire moved on to college to study for GCSEs and was provided with a package of support to help her organise and complete her academic work.

Robert was aged 12 at diagnosis. He had been diagnosed with dyslexia in primary school and his unusual behaviour was accommodated within a school which had many children with behavioural problems. Robert had been excluded from secondary school in his first term and had not been to school since then. He had become reclusive, barely leaving the house and finding it impossible to tolerate any visitors. Even family members were unwelcome if they called at the wrong time or on the wrong day. Robert's siblings had moulded around him, frustrated by his aggressive and intolerant behaviour, and embarrassed by his behaviour in public, but very aware that he could not manage without their support. An emphasis was placed upon understanding his behaviour in terms of a stress reaction and his family began to accept that the adjustments they had made instinctively were necessary for Robert, rather than an indication of their failure to help him socialise.

Craig was diagnosed at 9 years. He relied heavily on his younger sister to help him to socialise and look after him in the playground at school. When he moved into a different area of the school and she could no longer do this, Craig's social difficulties became much more evident. His family were accepting of the diagnosis, feeling that their son's intellectual ability far outstripped his social problem-solving skills. They were able to help him to develop more independence and tried to relieve his sister of some of the responsibility she had taken for him.

SYSTEMS AND SUPPORT

In her presentation of the fundamentals of person-centred planning, Mount (2000) emphasises the need to see people in the context of their local community. It could be argued that the necessary and sufficient conditions of constructive personality growth described by Rogers (1957) might be extended to encompass systems surrounding the child with autism as follows:

- The child is in psychological contact with siblings and parents at home and peers and adults at school.
- The child is in a state of incongruence being vulnerable or anxious.
- Home and school systems are congruent or integrated in the relationship.
- Siblings, parents, peers and teachers experience unconditional positive regard for the child.
- Individuals surrounding the child experience an empathic understanding of the

child's internal frame of reference and endeavour to communicate this experience to the child.

- The communication to the child of the above is to a minimal degree achieved.

Using this systemic extension of the client-centred position helps to focus on key areas for development. The experience of the individual with autism is very typically that of being misunderstood, of being alienated or marginalised. The titles of relevant accounts reflect this: *My World is Not Your World* (Hale, 1998); *Martian in the Playground* (Sainsbury, 2000); *Through the Eyes of Aliens* (O'Neill, 1998b), and accounts of bullying and peer difficulties are widespread (Little, 2001; Bauminger and Kasari, 2000). Appropriate psychoeducational interventions may be targeted at addressing these 'system deficits', by attempting to represent and describe reality for individuals with autism. This typically may involve advocacy within schools—aimed at peers and staff (Barron and Barron, 1992; Bozic et al., 2002; Jackson, 2002; Stillman, 2003; Lord, 1995). Stillman writes:

> In my work as a consultant, I'm certain that initially I bewilder and disappoint those who are under the impression that my purpose is to 'fix' the person. Nothing could be further than the truth. My presence is as an agent of transformation to shift the team's perceptions of the person in a kind and gentle manner. When this occurs truly, the person cannot help but to respond positively to the new ways in which others are demonstrating respect and interacting differently. This is when the seeds of change for all concerned may begin to bud and blossom. (Stillman, 2003: 9)

Families also often ask for help in supporting siblings (Pilowsky et al., 2004) where again information about the complex worlds and challenges for youngsters on the autism spectrum may be very helpful (Davies, 1994; Gorrod, 1997; Harris, 1996).

GROUPS

Psychoeducational groups for siblings help children to understand their siblings' differences and needs, using approaches based upon play, drama and relationships. Person-centred groups are also offered at a child and adolescent mental health service, for diagnosed children aged 10–16 years. Most of these youngsters are in mainstream school, yet few have friends and even fewer have mutually supportive friendships. Children are grouped by age (10–13 and 13–15) and group sizes are from five to eight youngsters. The aims of the groups are to reduce social isolation, to provide a place where the young person is accepted and welcomed. This is in stark contrast to the life experiences these young people often report. The group provides a regular meeting place for youngsters who know their diagnosis. There is a simple structure: sharing refreshments, taking turns to give news from the previous week, and playing a game. All the children and young people are listened to in turn, and their news is valued, whatever the topic. Often issues of family and school life are raised, but so are computer games, pets and special interests. The shared social events of refreshments and a game provides a connection between group members. It also provides an opportunity to develop social and relationship skills in a naturalistic setting.

In their final school year, young people transfer to a youth club for young adults (16–21 years) which is run by a voluntary agency. This group was designed by consulting young people with autism who were attending the groups at the Child and Adolescent Mental Health Service. Their parents and the professionals working with them were also consulted about the needs of these young adults. The group is open to young people with mental health needs but is suitable for young adults with autism because it provides a calm atmosphere with a high staffing ratio. This allows sufficient time to talk with young people who might take a long time to express themselves clearly. It is a place where young people can meet and feel accepted. It provides a place which is accessible to those who need support and encouragement to socialise, but who do want to mix with other people. One advantage of attending these groups is that young people have had an opportunity to ask questions about their diagnosis and what it means. Many myths and issues (e.g., will I die from it? will it change things at school?) have been addressed through group discussions. The questions raised have been used to develop a leaflet for young people to help them understand their diagnosis.

STRATEGIC THINKING

The most recent initiative in service developments for individuals with complex needs has at its very heart the experience and wishes of the individual. 'The active involvement of children and parents in decisions regarding their treatment, care and service planning is seen as key to service improvement' (Getting the Right Start. *National Service Framework for Children,* emerging findings, 2003: 29). 'A person-centred approach to planning means that planning should start with the individual (not with services) and take into account their wishes and aspirations.' (*Valuing People: A new strategy for learning disability in the 21ˢᵗ century,* 2001: 49).

Person-centred planning (Mount, 2000) is now gaining a strong following in the development of high quality services. Sanderson et al., (1997) describe five key features: the person is at the centre; family members and friends are partners in planning; the plan reflects what is important to the person, their capacities and what support they require; the plan results in actions that are about life, not just services, and reflect what is possible, not just what is available; and finally, the plan results in on-going listening, learning, and further action.

CONCLUSIONS

It is argued here that it is unhelpful to discard comprehensive assessment and diagnosis for individuals on the autism spectrum. Whilst the available diagnoses are crude and incorporate unhelpful medical terminology, and whilst it may be difficult at times to achieve consensus, there is potentially a significant advantage to individuals and families of being recognised and understood. A person-centred perspective instead rejects the language of deficit, and integrates an acknowledgement and where appropriate, celebration of difference. Whilst the distinctive personality profile of the autism spectrum is life-long and there are specific cognitive aspects which appear to have a genetic component, the vulnerabilities and associated difficulties that result as a consequence of the heightened social conditions of worth experienced by these individuals may be ameliorated by a person-centred approach. The considerably enhanced appreciation of clients' positions that follows clear and comprehensive understanding of their uniqueness, and the communication of this to individuals and those surrounding them, represents the best manifestation of empathy and unconditional positive regard and hence an optimal opportunity for clients to achieve self-acceptance and positive growth.

REFERENCES

Alvarez, A (1996) Addressing the element of deficit in children with autism: Psychotherapy which is both psychoanalytically and developmentally informed. *Clinical Psychology and Psychiatry 1*, 525–38.

American Psychiatric Association (1994) *Diagnostic and Statistical Manual of Mental Disorders* (4th edition). Washington DC: American Psychiatric Association.

Andrews, D (2004) Mental health issues in Asperger syndrome: Preventive mental health work in good autism practice. *Good Autism Practice, 3,* 22–8.

Asperger, H (1944) Die 'Autisticischen Psychopathen' im Kindesalter. *Archiv fur Psychiatrie und Nervenkrankheiten, 117,* 76–136.

Attwood, T (1998) *Asperger's Syndrome: A guide for parents and professionals.* London: Jessica Kingsley Publications.

Baird, G, Cass, H and Slonims, V (2003) Diagnosis of Autism. *British Medical Journal, 327,* 488–93.

Baron-Cohen, S (1989) Do autistic children have obsessions and compulsions? *British Journal of Clinical Psychology, 28,* 193–200.

Baron-Cohen, S (1995) *Mindblindness: An essay on autism and theory of mind.* London: MIT Press.

Baron-Cohen, S (2000) Is Asperger Syndrome/High Functioning Autism necessarily a disability? *Development and Psychopathology, 12,* 489–500.

Baron-Cohen, S (2003) *The Essential Difference: Men and women and the extreme male brain.* London: Allen Lane, Penguin Books.

Barron, J and Barron, S (1992) *There's a Boy in Here.* New York: Simon and Schuster.

Bauminger, N and Kasari, C (2000) Loneliness and friendship in high functioning children with autism. *Child Development 71,* 447–56.

Berney, T (2004) Asperger syndrome from childhood into adulthood. *Advances in Psychiatric Treatment, 10,* 341–51.

Bettelheim, B (1967) *The Empty Fortress.* New York: Free Press.

Bishop, DVM (1989) Autism, Asperger's syndrome and semantic-pragmatic disorder: Where are the boundaries? *British Journal of Disorders of Communication, 24,* 107–21.

Bolton, P, Pickles, A, Murphy, M and Rutter, M (1998) Autism, Affective and other Psychiatric Disorders: Patterns of familial aggregation, *Psychological Medicine, 28,* 385–95.

Bowler, DM (1992) 'Theory of Mind' in Asperger's syndrome. *Journal of Child Psychology and Psychiatry, 33,* 877–93.

Bozic, N, Croft, A and Mason-Williams, T (2002) A peer support project for an eight-year-old boy with an autistic spectrum disorder: an adaptation and extension of the Circle of Friends approach. *Good Autism Practice, 3,* 22.

Brothers, L (1997) *Friday's Footprint: How society shapes the human mind.* Oxford: OUP.

Carrington, S and Graham, L (2001) Perceptions of school by two teenage boys with Asperger syndrome and their mothers: a qualitative study. *Autism, 5,* 37–48.

Clements, J and Zarkowska, E (2000) *Behavioural Concerns and Autistic Spectrum Disorders.* London: Jessica Kingsley.

Davies J (1994) *Children with Autism* and *Able Autistic Children—Children with Asperger's Syndrome*: 2 booklets for brothers and sisters. Nottingham: Early Years Centre.

Department of Health (2001) *Valuing People: A new strategy for learning disability in the 21ˢᵗ century* (p. 49).

Department of Health (2003) Getting the Right Start. *National Service Framework for Children: Emerging findings* (p. 29).

Dorris, L, Espie, CAE, Knott, F and Salt, J (2004) Mind-reading difficulties in siblings of people with Asperger's syndrome: evidence for a genetic influence in the abnormal development of a specific cognitive domain. *Journal of Child Psychology and Psychiatry, 45,* 412–19.

Ellis, HD, Ellis, DM, Fraser, W and Deb, S (1994) A preliminary study of right hemisphere cognitive deficits and impaired social judgements among young people with Asperger syndrome. *European Child and Adolescent Psychiatry, 3,* 255–66.

Folstein, S and Rutter, M (1977) Infantile autism: A genetic study of 21 twin pairs. *Journal of Child Psychology and Psychiatry, 18,* 297–321.

Frith, U (2003) *Autism: Explaining the enigma.* Oxford: Blackwell.

Frith, U (2004) Emmanuel Miller Lecture: Confusions and controversies about Asperger syndrome. *Journal of Child Psychology and Psychiatry, 45,* 659–71.

Frith, U and Frith, CD (2003) Development and neurophysiology of mentalizing. *Philosophical Transactions of the Royal Society. London, B, 358,* 459–73.

Frith, U and Happe, F (1994) Autism: Beyond theory of mind. *Cognition, 50,* 115–32.

Frith, U and Hill, E (eds) (2003) *Autism: Mind and brain.* London: Royal Society.

Gerland, G (1997) *A Real Person: Life on the outside.* London: Souvenir Press.

Gerland, G (2000) Normality vs self-esteem: the road to increased independence and reflective thinking in children and young people with Asperger syndrome. Presented at Autism Europe Congress Glasgow, May 2000.

Ghaziuddin, M, Allesi, N and Greden, J (1995) Life events and depression in children with pervasive developmental disorders. *Journal of Autism and Developmental Disorders, 25,* 495–502.

Ghaziuddin, M and Greden, J (1998) Depression in children with Autism/Pervasive Developmental Disorders; A case-control family history study. *Journal of Autism and Developmental Disorders, 28,* 111–15.

Gillot, A, Furniss, F and Walter, A (2001) Anxiety in high functioning children with autism. *Autism, 5,* 277–86.

Glaser, D (2000) Child abuse and neglect and the brain—a review. *Journal of Child Psychology and Psychiatry, 41,* 97–116.

Goldstein, S and Schwebach, AJ (2004) The comorbidity of Pervasive Developmental Disorder and Attention Deficit Disorder: results of a retrospective chart review. *Journal of Autism and Developmental Disorders, 34,* 329–39.

Gorrod, L (1997) *My Brother is Different.* London: NAS.

Grandin, T (1992) An inside view of autism. In E Schopler, and GB Mesibov (eds) *High-Functioning Individuals with Autism.* (Ch. 6, pp. 105–26). New York: Plenum.

Grandin, T (1995) *Thinking in Pictures and Other Reports from My Life with Autism.* New York: Doubleday.

Gray, C (1998) Social stories and comic strip conversations with students with Asperger's Syndrome and High-Functioning Autism. In E Schopler and G Mesibov and LJ Kunce (eds) *Asperger's Syndrome or High-Functioning Autism?* New York: Plenum.

Gray, C and White, AL (eds) (2002) *My Social Stories Book.* London: Jessica Kingsley.

Haddon, M (2003) *The Curious Incident of the Dog in the Night-time.* London: Jonathon Cape.

Hale, A (1998) *My World is Not Your World.* New York: Archimedes.

Hall, K (2001) *Asperger's Syndrome, the Universe and Everything.* London: Jessica Kingsley.

Happe, F (1991) The autobiographical writings of three Asperger syndrome adults: problems of interpretation and implications for theory. In U Frith (ed) *Autism and Asperger Syndrome.* (Ch. 7, pp. 207–42). Cambridge: Cambridge Press.

Happe, F, Ehlers, S, Fletcher, P, Frith, U, Johansson, M, Gillberg, C, Dolan, R, Frackowiak, R and Frith, C (1996) 'Theory of mind' in the brain. Evidence from a PET-scan study of Asperger's syndrome. *Clinical Neuroscience and Neuropathology 8,* 197–201).

Harris, SL (1996) *Siblings of Children with Autism; A guide for families.* London: NAS.

Hill, E, Berthoz, S and Frith, U (2004) Brief Report: Cognitive processing of own emotions in individuals with Autistic Spectrum Disorder and in their relatives. *Journal of Autism and Developmental Disorders, 34,* 229–36.

Hollander, E, King, A, Delaney K, et al. (2003) Obsessive-compulsive behaviours in parents of multiplex autism families. *Psychiatry Research, 117,* 11–16.

Holliday Willey, L (1999) *Pretending to be Normal: Living with Asperger's.* London: Jessica Kingsley.

Holliday Willey, L (2001) *Asperger's Syndrome in the Family: Redefining normal.* London: Jessica Kingsley.

Hoopmann, K (2001) *The Bluebottle Mystery: An Asperger adventure.* London: Jessica Kingsley.

Howlin, P (2000) Assessment instruments for Asperger syndrome. *Child Psychology and Psychiatry Review, 5,* 120–9.

Hoy, JA, Hatton, C and Hare, DJ (2004) Weak central coherence: a cross-domain phenomenon specific to autism? *Autism, 8,* 267–81.

Ives, M (1999) *What is Asperger Syndrome and How will it Affect Me?* London: NAS.

Jackson, L (2002) *Freaks, Geeks and Asperger's Syndrome.* London: Jessica Kingsley.

Jackson, J (2003) *Multicoloured Mayhem. Parenting the many shades of adolescents and children with autism, Asperger syndrome and AD/HD.* London: Jessica Kingsley.

Jacobsen, P (2003) *Asperger Syndrome and Psychotherapy: Understanding Asperger perspectives.* London: Jessica Kingsley.

Jones, G (2001) Giving the diagnosis to the young person with Asperger Syndrome or High Functioning Autism: Issues and strategies. *Good Autism Practice, 2,* 65–74.

Joseph, S (2003) Why the client knows best. *The Psychologist, 16,* 304–7.

Kanner, L (1943) Autistic disturbances of affective contact. *Nervous Child, 2,* 217–50.

Kim, J, Szatmari, P, Bryson, S, Steiner, D and Wilson, F (2000) The prevalence of anxiety and mood problems among children with autism and Asperger Syndrome, *Autism, 4,* 117–32.

Lawson, W (2001) *Understanding and Working with the Spectrum of Autism: An insider's view.* London: Jessica Kingsley.

Le Couteur, A and Baird, G (2003) National Initiative for Autism: Screening and Assessment (NIASA); *National Autism Plan for Children.* London: National Autistic Society.

Liss, M, Fein, D, Allen, D, Dunn, M, Feinstein, C, Morris, R, Waterhouse, L and Rapin, I (2001) Executive functioning in high functioning children with autism. *Journal of Child Psychology and Psychiatry, 42,* 261–71.

Little, L (2001) Peer victimization of children with Asperger spectrum disorders. *Journal of the American Academy of Child and Adolescent Psychiatry, 40,* 995–6.

Lord, C (1995) Facilitating social inclusion. Examples from peer intervention programmes. In E Schopler and GB Mesibov (eds) *Learning and Cognition in Autism* (pp. 221–40). New York: Plenum Press.

Manjiviona, J and Prior, M (1999) Neuropsychological profiles of children with Asperger Syndrome and Autism. *Autism, 3,* 327–56.

McKelvey, JR, Lambert, R, Mottson, L and Shevell, MI (1995) Right hemisphere dysfunction in Asperger's Syndrome. *Journal of Child Neurology, 10,* 310–14.

Mount, B (2000) *Person-Centered Planning; Finding directions for change using Personal Futures Planning.* New York: Capacity Works.

Newson, E, Marechal, KL and David, C (2003) Pathological Demand Avoidance syndrome: A necessary distinction within the pervasive developmental disorders. *Archives of Disease in Childhood, 88,* 595–600.

Noland, RM and Gabriels, RL (2004) Screening and identifying children with Autism Spectrum Disorders in the public school system: the development of a Model Process. *Journal of Autism and Developmental Disorders, 34,* 265–78.

O'Neill, J (1998) Autism: isolation not desolation—A personal account. *Autism, 2,* 199–204.

O'Neill, J (1998) *Through the Eyes of Aliens.* London: Jessica Kingsley.

Ozonoff, S, Dawson, G and McPartland, J (2002) *A Parent's Guide to Asperger Syndrome and High-Fuctioning Autism.* New York: Guilford.

Peacock, G (1996) *Autism—The Invisible Children? Agenda for Action.* London: NAS.

Pickles, A, Bolton, P, Macdonald, H, Bailey, A, Le Couteur, A, Sim, CH and Rutter, M (1995) Latent-class analysis of recurrence risks for complex phenotypes with selection and measurement error: A twin and family history study of autism. *American Journal of Human Genetics, 57,* 717–26.

Pilowsky, T, Yirmiya, N, Doppelt, O, Gross-Tsur, V and Shalev RS (2004) Social and emotional adjustment of siblings of children with autism. *Journal of Child Psychology and Psychiatry, 45,* 855–65.

Rogers, CR (1957) The necessary and sufficient conditions of therapeutic personality change. *Journal of Consulting Psychology, 21,* 95–103.

Rutter, M, Anderson-Wood, L, Beckett, C, Bredenkamp, D, Castle, J, Groothues, C, Kreppner, J, Keaveney, L, Lord, C, O'Connor, TG and the ERA Study Team (1999) Quasi-autistic patterns following severe early global privation. *Journal of Child Psychology and Psychiatry, 40,* 537–50.

Sainsbury, C (2000) *Martian in the Playground.* Bristol: Lucky Duck Pubs.

Sanderson, H, Kennedy, J, Ritchie, P and Goodwin, G (1997) *People, Plans and Possibilities—*

Exploring Person-Centred planning. Edinburgh: SHS.

Schneider, E (1999) *Discovering My Autism.* London: Jessica Kingsley.

Smalley, SL, Asarnow, RF and Spence, A (1988) Autism and genetics: A decade of research. *Archives of General Psychiatry, 45,* 953–61.

Stillman, W (2003) *Demystifying the Autistic Experience. A humanistic introduction for parents, caregivers and educators.* London: Jessica Kingsley.

Tantam, D (2000) Psychological disorder in adolescents and adults with Asperger Syndrome, *Autism, 4,* 47–62.

Tantam, D (2003) The challenge of adolescents and adults with Asperger Syndrome, *Child and Adolescent Psychiatric Clinics of North America, 12,* 143–63.

Tuchman, R and Rapin, I (2002) Epilepsy in autism. *Lancet Neurology, 1,* 352–8.

Tustin, F (1988) What autism is and what it is not. In Rolene Szur and Sheila Miller (eds) *Extending Horizons.* London: Karnac.

Vermeulen, P (2000) *I am Special; Introducing children and young people to their Autistic Spectrum Disorder.* London: Jessica Kingsley.

Volkmar, FR, Lord, C, Bailey, A, Schultz, RT and Klin, A (2004) Autism and Pervasive Developmental Disorders, *Journal of Child Psychology and Psychiatry, 45,* 135–70.

Wing, L (1981) Asperger's Syndrome: A Clinical Account. *Psychological Medicine, 11,* 115–29.

Wing, L (2002) *The Autism Spectrum: A guide for parents and professionals.* London: Constable and Robinson.

Wood Rivers, J and Stoneman, Z (2003) Sibling relationships when a child has Autism: Marital stress and support in coping. *Journal of Autism and Developmental Disorders, 33,* 383–94.

CHAPTER 18

CLINICAL PSYCHOLOGY AND THE PERSON-CENTRED APPROACH: AN UNCOMFORTABLE FIT?

GILLIAN PROCTOR

In this chapter, I am exploring my unusual dual positions. I have worked within mental health services in the National Health Service (NHS) for the past eight years using the Person-Centred Approach (PCA) as a clinical psychologist. These dual positions, roles or approaches have many points of conflict in theory and practice. I aim to discuss how each of these approaches influences me and the drawbacks of each. I hope to clarify how I deal with the conflicts and integrate the two in theory and practice.

The main therapy model taught in clinical psychology training is Cognitive-Behaviour Therapy (CBT), although all courses must provide teaching about a variety of therapy models. Although a high proportion of clinical psychologists (CPs) describe themselves as integrative or eclectic therapists, there are very few who would claim to be person-centred. I ended up in this position, having struggled with the clinical psychology training, finding the position of expert inherent in the CBT approach ethically uncomfortable, and the psychodynamic approach no better (see Proctor, 2002a). During the period of my training, I then discovered the Person-Centred Approach from an introduction to counselling training, and was reassured that I could be a therapist in a way I found compatible with my personal ethics and politics. I completed the CP training, using classical Person-Ccentred Therapy (see Sanders, 2004 for an explanation of the various person-centred therapies) and have practiced this way exclusively in therapy ever since, devising my own further training in PCA through a combination of supervision, extensive reading, group experiences and conferences.

I will present a brief history and the current context of the profession of Clinical Psychology. I will then critique the idea of the 'scientist practitioner' and the psychologist as objective scientist, and how clinical psychology uses these ideas politically to ensure its status. I will use Foucault to examine the psychologist's role as an agent of social control, following Foucault's critique of psychiatry. I will then turn to the PCA, explaining its background in science and research and its subsequent development. I will elaborate the principles and ethics behind the PCA, and my critiques of the PCA. I will contrast the principles of the PCA with those used by clinical psychology and identify main areas of incompatibilities, in particular the idea of assessment, formulation and the 'expert' professional. I will then endeavour to describe how I bridge these two worlds, or more accurately, how I exist holding PCA principles and ethics within the world of clinical psychology. I will use the concept of the 'reflective practitioner' to identify some hope for the future of Clinical Psychology in taking on board many of the learnings from the PCA.

WHAT IS CLINICAL PSYCHOLOGY?

Marzillier and Hall (1992) describe the profession of Clinical Psychology and the main activities of clinical psychologists (CPs). They list the three main activities of CPs as:

1. *assessment* ('the use of psychological methods and principles to gain better understanding of psychological attributes and problems')
2. *treatment* ('the use of psychological procedures and principles to help others to bring about change')
3. *evaluation* ('the use of psychological principles to evaluate the effectiveness of treatments or other forms of intervention.') (p. 1)

They also list training, research and involvement in service policies as other possible activities of the clinical psychologist.

It is useful to examine the rhetoric of clinical psychology, the way CP is talked about within the profession, to explore how the profession has marketed itself. The focus of this rhetoric since the Manpower Advisory Group of the Department of health (MPAG) report (Mowbray, 1989) is on being a 'scientist practitioner'. Marzillier and Hall explain (p. 9) 'The clinical psychologist is first and foremost an "applied scientist" or "scientist-practitioner" who seeks to use scientific knowledge to a beneficial end.' According to Marzillier and Hall (1992), CPs are now involved in assessment and intervention with people with psychological problems, secondary consequences of medical problems and understanding and changing aspects of the healthcare system itself and the way care is delivered.

Another focus within CP is the CP's ability to 'formulate' problems'. This is often presented as the hallmark of the CP. Unlike diagnosis, formulation is a 'complex' understanding of the client's problems, putting together many factors, and is open to further clarification and adjustment as understanding with the client progresses. Here the CP is in her/his element, able to apply their complex understanding of a variety of theories to the uniqueness of a particular client's life and present hypotheses to the client of how their problems can be fitted within the theoretical frameworks of their psychological theories. Of course, if one theory does not quite fit, there is no worry— there are a plethora of other theories to choose from!

How did this profession come about with such a focus? It is useful to examine the history of the development of CP as a profession to contextualise the current modes of talking about the profession.

THE HISTORY OF THE PROFESSION OF CLINICAL PSYCHOLOGY

During World War II, clinical psychologists were used to recruit and select service personnel and, in 1948 when the NHS was formed, a few CPs worked in psychiatric hospitals (see Cheshire and Pilgrim, 2004 for a more detailed account of this history). From 1948 to 1960, CPs carried out psychometric tests. Lavender (2003) explains the role of Eysenck in determining the early direction of CP in the UK. Eysenck was involved in the development of the first CP course at the Institute of Psychiatry, and went to the US to look at how CP had developed there. He was clear that he believed CPs should have nothing to do with therapy (which was primarily psychoanalytic at the time) as he considered psychoanalysis to be 'pseudoscientific', and instead focused on the role of the CP to be scientist and researcher. However, Cheshire and Pilgrim (2004) argue that early professionalisation of psychology grew in tandem with early popularisation of psychology, both influencing each other and with professional psychology both trying to distinguish itself from popular psychology by appeals to its scientific base, and jumping on the back of lay psychology to appeal to a wider audience.

By the end of the 1960s, CPs had established themselves as practitioners using behaviour therapy. By the 1970s, pluralism or an eclectic approach to therapy was common in clinical psychology departments. In the 1980s, demand for CPs outstripped supply so the government commissioned a review of the special function of CPs. The MPAG report (Mowbray, 1989) resulted which suggested the way forward for CPs as consultants in psychological knowledge and skills to other professionals. The report claimed that only CPs among health professionals can offer level-3 skills, to offer unique complex psychological formulations and interventions in particular person-situation contexts. According to this report, CPs have 'an ability to form alternative hypotheses to help explain a given set of behaviours' and 'a variety of theoretical models for interpreting and understanding behaviour', and that their practice is 'determined by scientific method and systematic enquiry', and they have a 'sophisticated and eclectic grasp of treatment models'.

As is evident, the profession of CP has relied on the concept of science to argue for its status and expertise in healthcare, with a 'core orthodoxy of psychometrics and elaborated methodological behaviourism' (Cheshire and Pilgrim, 2004: 20). However, the idea of science and its objectivity has been problematised in most areas of academia in the last 30 years, by feminists, post-structuralists and social constructivists. Within each of these critiques, the value-base and subjectivity behind what has been presented as 'scientific fact' has been exposed and deconstructed.

FOUCAULT

The main foundations of post-structuralist critiques of science, and in particular of psychiatry and psychology are the critiques presented by Foucault. He provides a counter history of madness to that sanctioned by psychiatry.

THE HISTORY OF PSYCHIATRY

Foucault challenges the conventional conception of the history of madness, of the march of reason and progress to the final recognition of madness as mental illness and growth of knowledge of psychiatry. Instead, he contends that the conception of madness as mental illness is a result of the convergence of internment and medicine, not objective truth.

Foucault also focuses on the 'regimes of truth', 'the ensemble of rules according to which true and false are separated and specific effects of power attached to truth'. He identifies in our society the 'regimes of truth': that scientific discourses are truth, that there is a 'will to truth' and that truth is a battleground. He suggests that scientific discourses are but one way of talking about the world, but that the power attached to these discourses establishes science as 'fact'. Of course within this, what is defined as 'science' or 'fact' is determined by those in power to identify this. He emphasises that there have always been alternative discourses, or resisting discourses, but these are those ways of talking about the world that do not serve those with power.

THE CONTEXT OF THERAPY

Foucault's analyses of the human sciences, of the history of madness and of the history of sexuality all provide an analysis of the context in which therapy takes place (see Foucault, 1977a and b, 1979, 1980). He describes the idea of the 'confession' as a 'disciplinary technique', i.e. a tactic of social control, and questions the objectivity of 'madness' as a category entailing treatment. His analyses force us to investigate the way psychotherapy can be a context for surveillance and disciplinary techniques of the self, of normalisation. He describes the ways in which power can be observed in the practices within psychiatry and psychotherapy which normalise individuals, by defining expectations of 'sanity' or 'normality'.

CLINICAL PSYCHOLOGY AND SOCIAL CONTROL

Rose (1985), following Foucault, deconstructs the history of psychology. He notes that far from psychology developing a science of the 'normal' which was then applied to the pathological or 'abnormal', instead, psychological knowledge of the individual was constituted around the pole of abnormality. In fact, psychology specifically set itself up to deal with the problems posed for social apparatuses by dysfunctional conduct. From the origins of psychology, the pole of 'normal–abnormal' was set around social efficiency and need for social regulation. In other words, psychology only got off the ground as an accepted discipline when it abandoned its project of theories of cognitive function and succeeded in producing norms of regulating social behaviour. Pilgrim and Treacher (1992: 190) further explain the result of a Foucaultian analysis of the psy professions saying, 'during the twentieth century, with the decline of segregative control in institutions, coercive power has become less and less relevant. Within this analysis, psychological therapies, counselling and health education are examples par excellence, of a new type of moral regulation favoured by government and public.' Thus from its conception, psychology has gained its status as a form of regulation of social control, an agent of the state.

SCIENCE AS JUSTIFICATION

Pilgrim and Treacher (1992) examine further the historical context by looking at the origins of clinical psychology as a profession and the role of science within this. Following the same theme as Rose (1985) in terms of psychology as an agent of control, they point to the scientificism of psychology as a defence against accusations of performing the function of social control. They explain (p. 30) 'psychologists ... could play out a highly political role in terms of the management of the population, whilst at the same time disowning such a role by pointing to their "disinterested" scientific training and credentials'. They further contend that (p. 31) 'Scientificism as a justificatory ideology is still a dominant strand in the profession today.' This is demonstrated by the emphasis within the profession of being a 'scientist practitioner'.

This focus on science has many implications for the profession of CP. Pilgrim and Treacher (1992) point out that the conception of clinical psychologists being 'scientist practitioners' is neither accurate (with respect to the importance of research in clinical psychology) nor useful (in that it leaves moral and epistemological questions unanswered). Clinical psychology training was originally set up to train psychometricians, and although clinical psychologists now spend most of their time conducting therapy as opposed to psychometric assessment, the duration and philosophy of training has not changed substantially to reflect this. In particular, (p. 97) 'Above all else the *person* of the clinical psychologist never became a legitimate area of discussion within psychology.' Furthermore, they argue that the consequences of clinical psychology's fight for status based on elitism have been the insecurity of the profession in the NHS and the marginalisation of women, working-class people and black people within the profession.

This strategy of scientificism, in addition to removing the person of the CP from their training and their work, also serves the purpose of distracting from environmental causes of distress. Similarly to the medicalisation of distress, the psychologisation of distress firmly places the cause for psychological ill-health within the individual. This is reflected by the dominant model of CBT within CP, where the client's distorted thinking is blamed for their problems. Thus deprivation, abuse, oppression and the social and political context of distress can largely be ignored and the practice of CP can continue to try to mop up problems caused by a sick society, whilst preserving their status, power and the status quo of inequalities, which in turn perpetuates the creation of distressed people.

Furthermore, appeals to science serve to obscure how what counts as science or 'evidence' is decided. Evidence is chosen to serve the vested interests of those who seek to gain from particular ways of thinking being seen as fact or truth. For example, within mental health services today and the emphasis on 'evidence-based practice', the evidence that is focused on is research-funded and often conducted by pharmaceutical companies to 'prove' that their medication or even CBT is effective in improving mental health. The overwhelming results of research or evidence which suggest that the therapy relationship is the most important factor influencing change in therapy, or for environmental rather than biological or genetic causes of distress are rarely mentioned as 'useful' evidence. All research questions are determined by political agendas (harmful or benign) and which research is publicised the most and becomes the accepted 'evidence' is similarly politically determined.

A social constructionist perspective (e.g. McNamee, 2003) would see scientific discourse as one way of talking about the world and about mental health. However, CP has used the power given to science in our society to argue that the results of scientific research which serve the interest of the profession make CPs experts in such matters. Thus other ways of understanding 'mental health' such as spiritual understandings or reactions to and ways of coping with social and political inequalities are diminished under the guise of being 'unscientific'. The elitism which comes with the notion of science and who has access to understand scientific knowledge ensures the status of the profession. One consequence of the strategy of scientificism is to mystify therapy for the general public. Throughout its history CP has always been wary of sharing or disseminating psychological knowledge for fear of losing this expert status.

THE DEVELOPMENT OF THE PERSON-CENTRED APPROACH

I will now move on to explore the origins of the PCA in relation to science. Carl Rogers, the originator of the PCA, was a clinical psychologist. He was certainly, at least in the early days, a keen advocate of the scientific method. Rogers' theory of therapy was based on research into what seemed to help clients in therapy. His theory followed his experiences and experiments with how to help clients over many years. Indeed Rogers conducted his research within the unusual framework of scientist as open-minded explorer, rather than as someone trying to confirm a strongly held belief. Rather than start with a hypothesis and then investigate its validity, Rogers began with an open mind as to what could be helpful in therapy and was guided by the data he collected to form his hypothesis. He methodically examined hours and hours of recorded and transcribed therapy sessions to examine what the ingredients of effective therapy were. This was the first time that actual therapist-client interactions in therapy had been opened to the scrutiny of research. Instead of relying on therapists' recollections or interpretations of what therapy was about, he and his researchers looked directly as outside observers at what was said in therapy.

He used the transcripts of therapy sessions to systematically examine what therapists did that was helpful, and what was unhelpful. Initial findings identified that therapy progress was thwarted by therapists being directive, asking probing questions or interpreting. On the contrary, therapist interventions that lead to client insight and deepening or further exploration were those where the therapist 'simply recognizes and clarifies the feelings expressed' (Rogers, 1942, reprinted in Kirschenbaum and Henderson,

1989). From these direct observations of therapy, he developed his theory of therapy based on the six necessary and sufficient conditions (Rogers, 1959). Later, he used Q-sort methodology (where statements or characteristics are ranked and the results factor analysed) to investigate how clients' views of themselves and others changed during therapy (see Rogers and Dymond, 1954). Only from this data-generated hypothesis did Rogers then develop his theory of personality, a hypothesis to explain the therapy theory (see Proctor, 2004c to explain in detail the therapy theory and the personality theory).

CONTINUING RESEARCH

After the development of his theory of therapy, Rogers and many others spent much time continuing to research the effectiveness of PCT. Since the 1950s and continuing today, there has been much research evidence supporting the efficacy of Person-Centred or Client-Centred therapy for clients with many different types of difficulties, including psychotic experiences (see Barrett-Lennard, (1998) for a review of research). One of the most recent pieces of research in the UK's current climate of 'evidence-based practice' used a randomised controlled trial design to compare three treatments for people with depression or anxiety and depression in primary care. King et al. (2000) compared PCT, Cognitive Behaviour Therapy (CBT) and routine GP care. Unusual for such comparison studies, in this study the therapists providing PCT were qualified at a high level. The study found that both PCT and CBT obtained equally significantly better results than routine GP care at four months follow-up and clients reported higher levels of satisfaction with PCT than CBT.

In addition to specific research on the effectiveness of PCT, research to investigate the factors responsible for success in general in therapy have also added to the weight of scientific evidence for PCT. Forty years of psychotherapy research has consistently demonstrated the importance of the client's resources and the quality of the therapy relationship for effective and good therapy. Lambert (1992 cited in Lambert 2004) estimated that 40 per cent of outcome variance was accounted for by the client's external and internal resources and 30 per cent by the quality of the therapy relationship. Bozarth (1998, see also Bozarth and Motomasa, Chapter 9 this volume) discussed the implications of this research, concluding that the type of therapy or technique or training or credentials of the therapist are found to be irrelevant, and the most consistent relationship variables related to effectiveness are empathy, genuineness and unconditional positive regard. The results of this research are consistent with the philosophy and theory of Person-Centred Therapy (PCT), which relies directly on the client's resources and the therapy relationship. This consistency is unsurprising given the research-based way Rogers developed PCT.

One would imagine given the scientific research base of Person-Centred Therapy, that clinical psychologists would welcome such a rigorous approach with open arms. The fact that this is clearly not the case, and that the PCA is rarely taught on most CP courses, indicates that something other than how 'scientific' an approach is, is important for CP. I suggest that the value base of the PCA is inconsistent with the expert status and power sought by CPs.

Rogers himself was dubious about how science was used, and became more and more disillusioned with his profession of clinical psychology and its focus on status and elitism. In addition to believing in the importance of the scientific method, he always treated the ethics of what he was doing as a therapist as at least equally important as scientific claims to effectiveness. Indeed, it was his ethics which guided his scientific research and determined the questions he sought to answer using science. Whereas I would suggest that it is always the case that questions answered by research are determined by political or personal agendas, Rogers was unusual in how explicit he was about his value-base.

THE VALUE-BASE OF THE PERSON-CENTRED APPROACH

The fundamental ethical principle behind PCT, and specifically classical Client-Centred Therapy (see Sanders, 2004 for explanation of the various 'tribes' of Person-Centred Therapy) is the autonomy of the client, as opposed to the moral principle of beneficence (doing what's judged to be best for the client) employed by many other models of therapy. Grant (2004: 157) argues that the practice of PCT is consistent with the ethics of 'respect for the right of others to determine their own ways in life'. This trust in the client's process leads to the non-directive attitude. The *non-directive attitude* is a way for therapists to express their commitment to avoiding client disempowerment (Brodley, 1997).

Rogers explicitly set out to change the role of the therapist from that of an expert and to aim for a more egalitarian therapy relationship. This notion of the relationship followed from the implications of the therapy theory. It also reflects the theory of personality, which can be considered the philosophy underlying Person-Centred Therapy. Rogers contends that the premise of the actualising tendency challenges the need to control people, i.e., challenges:

> The view that the nature of the individual is such that he cannot be trusted—
> that he must be guided, instructed, rewarded, punished, and controlled by
> those that are higher in status. (1978: 8)

Rogers explains the implications of this philosophy and values system:

> The politics of the person-centered approach is a conscious renunciation and
> avoidance by the therapist of all control over, or decision-making for, the
> client. It is the facilitation of self-ownership by the client and the strategies
> by which this can be achieved; the placing of the locus of decision-making
> and the responsibility for the effects of these decisions. It is politically centered
> in the client. (1978: 14)

In this sense, PCT is a radical disruption of the dynamics of power in therapy. Rogers asserts that opposition to Person-Centred Therapy sprang 'primarily because it struck such an outrageous blow to the therapist's power' (Rogers, 1978: 16). Natiello (2001:

11) explains that 'Such a stand is in radical conflict with the prevailing paradigm of authoritarian power.' I argue that the aim for the PCT therapist is to reduce 'power-over' the client as far as possible and to maximise the 'power-from-within' of both client and therapist and the 'power-with' in the therapy relationship (Proctor, 2002a, 2002b). I suggest that this aim is contrary to the aim of the profession of CP which is to increase the power and status of the profession.

Throughout most of its history and development, the PCA has focused very clearly on its ethical base, at the expense of its scientific and research origins. In the last decade, PCA practitioners worldwide have realised the disadvantages of this focus in today's climate of evidence-based practice. In response, a World Association for Person-Centered and Experiential Psychotherapies (WAPCEPC) with an accompanying academic journal have been developed and calls for PCA practitioners to conduct research have increased. However, what has been more difficult to do is to challenge the claims of science and point out how ethical and value-based decisions are imbued in the scientific method from start to finish. Grant (2004) pursues this route to argue that ethical justification of any therapy is necessary, and these ethics determine what research, if any, is used to justify its effectiveness. In trying to play the game of science, a more secure position may be achieved for the PCA, but could this be at the expense of its ethical base?

Another question which I consider is the potential naïvety of the ethical position of the PCA. The PCA has been criticised for its claims to an 'equal' therapy relationship (for further examination see Proctor, 2002a) and I believe there is substance to these criticisms.

IS THE ETHICAL POSITION OF PCA NAÏVE?

Rogers clearly did a lot to challenge the position of the expert therapist with respect to power in the therapy relationship by his emphasis on a 'person-to-person' encounter and by demystifying the process of therapy. All the facilitative conditions work together to try to place the power with the client and minimise control by the therapist. However, I (Proctor, 2002a, b) have criticised person-centred theorists and therapists for the focus on the therapist as a person obscuring the power imbalance still present due to the roles of therapist and client. As Lowe (1999) emphasises, however transparent, therapy is still institutionalised within a particular mode of practice which carries with it the power and authority given to the person in the role of therapist and the stigma given to the person in the role of client. Larner (1999: 49) summarises this point saying 'Professional authority, power and social hierarchy in the therapeutic institution are real enough.'

Furthermore, other aspects of the dynamics of power in therapy can be ignored with the person-centred focus on 'equality' of the relationship or agency of the client. Often there are differences between the therapist and client in structural positions within society, with respect to, for example, age, gender, class, disability, sexuality and ethnicity. Additionally, by focusing on the therapist's provision of the facilitative attitudes, there is the danger that the client's perception of these is assumed, but due to the client's potential history of powerlessness or of expectations in relationships, they do not perceive the therapist's attitudes. Rogers emphasised the importance of the client's perception with the sixth of the necessary and sufficient conditions (Rogers, 1959) specifying that the client perceives the therapist's empathic understanding and unconditional positive regard at least to a minimal degree. However in practice the focus in training person-centred therapists is often on the therapist's attitudes and the other conditions are commonly assumed or taken for granted.

I argue that there is real radical potential in Person-Centred Therapy to emphasise the power and autonomy of the client, challenging the therapist as expert. The facilitative conditions give the maximum space possible for the 'power-from-within' or 'personal power' of the client to increase, and for the client to free themselves from normative prescriptions or conditions of worth which have limited their potential. If person-centred therapists can also be aware of the power within the roles of therapist and client in the institution of therapy and the material realities of inequalities in societal structural power (see Proctor, 2004b), I believe that Person-Centred Therapy can truly be a force for personal *and* social change.

INCOMPATIBILITIES

Clearly the main focus of CP and PCA are fundamentally different. Whilst CPs have been busy trying to prove and justify their status based on their expert credentials, PCA practitioners have been emphasising their lack of expert status with respect to their relationships with clients. Whilst CPs have been emphasising their ability to apply a variety of theoretical models to complex problems and achieve complex formulations, PC therapists have been keen to stress that it is the client's formulation of their problems that matters, and applying theoretical frameworks to understanding clients prevents empathy and change rather than promoting it.

How can these two conflicting paradigms co-exist? When working in forensic services for five years until December 2003, a system which exemplifies the idea of institutional power and coercion, I was expected to fulfill the traditional role of a CP (see Proctor, 2004a and Proctor, 2005, in press, for more details of my work in this context). As well as doing therapy (where it was possible to be purely a person-centred therapist with clients who chose to see me), I was also expected to conduct psychological assessments.

PERSON-CENTRED ASSESSMENT?

The idea of assessment is usually an anathema to a person-centred therapist, and particularly a classical client-centred therapist (see Sanders, 2004). As the therapist's aims are the same for all clients (to provide the core conditions of therapy), assessment has no use in determining intervention. Furthermore, the client is seen as the expert on their life and difficulties, the therapist's job being to understand as best they can what the client presents, always being alongside or one step behind the client, certainly not ahead. The idea of a therapist pronouncing or 'formulating' the client's difficulties, and talking about their client to other professionals, just does not fit with the attitudes and beliefs of the PCA. So how did I fulfil my role in conducting 'assessments' from a person-centred perspective?

When I was asked to conduct a psychological assessment of a client by a clinician from another discipline, what they were usually asking for was a deeper understanding of the client's thoughts and feelings and potential reasons for them coming to be in the position they were in. I was asked for a way to understand the client's difficulties from a psychological/phenomenological perspective as opposed to a medical or diagnostic perspective. Sometimes clients were coerced into seeing me for assessment; other times, clients wanted to talk to me. Often I was given much information and views from other clinicians involved in the client's care prior to meeting the client.

I shall illustrate this process with a hypothetical example. A client could be referred for assessment for other clinicians to gain greater insight into why he threatened his partner with a knife. The understanding the clinicians have so far is limited to 'drug-induced paranoia'. In talking to the client, different layers of explanation for his thinking, feeling and behaviour may become clear, although little is said about this incident. He may be happy for me to share my understanding of his story of why he took drugs with other clinicians, and how he is still not sure if his partner wants to kill him or not. He could express that he had found it useful for someone to try and understand his explorations with drugs and to want to tell his side of the story.

I see assessments as an opportunity to try to be helpful or therapeutic to the client. This is a very different start of a therapy relationship compared to usual conditions for PCT. In private therapy situations at least, a client usually chooses to see a PC therapist and has some idea in mind of why they would like to do this. In addition, the therapist rarely has access to other information about the client. However, for any therapist working within the mental health system, the client is rarely truly free to choose therapy. All sorts of pressures and implicit or explicit coercion can be used to persuade clients to see therapists and in any mental health setting, it is probably rare that a client decides completely autonomously that they would like to see a therapist. Of course this 'choice' to see a therapist is also probably much more complex than we like to think in private therapy settings; often others 'suggest' that clients come to therapy and a client is unlikely to be totally free from the influence of others.

My first job on meeting my client is to explain what I have been asked to do and why. If they have been obviously coerced to see me, I express my lack of involvement or agreement with that coercion, letting them know that I want them to decide if I can be of any help. I also explain what information I have already been given about them, but explain that I am more concerned with what they think about their situation than what anyone else thinks. I am clear from the outset that if they do decide they want to talk to me that I am required to write a report for the referrer towards the end of our time together and that I will tell them everything I will be writing and ask for their comments or corrections before I send it. I also explain the conditions of confidentiality in the meantime, which are that I will inform other staff if I am concerned about their or anyone else's safety. I usually suggest that we arrange to meet for a certain number of sessions (usually dictated by the time constraints of when my report is needed). I say that I am happy to answer any questions about what we are doing or about who I am. When I have answered any questions, I explain that it is up to them how they want to use the time with me, and my aim will be to try my best to understand them as a person without judging them.

I then meet with the client as planned and proceed as I would in PCT, trying to understand without judgement whatever the client talks to me about and following the direction of the client. Before the final or penultimate meeting, I write my report retelling my understanding of what the client has talked to me about, using the client's own words as much as possible. I return to the client and read to them what I have written, explaining my aim to tell their story and asking for their feedback on inaccuracies or anything I have omitted. I also include in this report information obtained from other sources and how that pertains to what the client has said. When I ask for the client's feedback, I also ask for their views about any inconsistencies between what they have said and what has been written elsewhere. As the referrers' particular interests are often around risk, I mention areas pertaining to risk that the client has not covered in our time talking which I think the referring clinicians may be interested in understanding further, and I ask if the client wants to say anything about these areas.

I usually add a short section at the end of the report entitled 'Opinion' where I suggest any possible factors that may contribute to an explanation of why the client may be in their current situation and also include the client's view about these factors. This section is clearly not from a person-centred framework, but following the CP remit for formulation and I do this to respond to what I believe the referrer is asking for. However, I am unclear whether this section is helpful for the referrer or more particularly for the client, especially if I continue with therapy with the client. Throughout my meetings with clients, for assessment or therapy, the message I try to communicate is one of respect and trusting the client as expert on their own life, so if I have included a section in the report from my 'expert' position, this message becomes ambivalent.

I then rewrite the report based on my client's feedback and ask them to check the final version during our last session. If it is possible for me to offer further therapy sessions to the client, I offer this if they would like it. We then discuss who the client would like the report to be sent to and if they want their own copy. Sometimes, we create abridged versions for certain professionals or clients contact me later to ask for reports to be sent to other people involved in their care.

My primary aim in conducting assessments requested by other professionals is to be open and honest about my constraints and requirements but to nevertheless try to provide as therapeutic an environment as possible for the client. Often, clients report that they have found their time with me helpful, even if they initially did not want to see me at all. I have not had a client who was unhappy for me to send my report and often, clients find the reports themselves very helpful, feeling that I have really understood their perspective, much more than it had previously been understood. Clients often seem to perceive my taking time to write from their perspective as a way of valuing them and they appreciate this. The referring clinicians also usually find my reports interesting and useful, providing a more in-depth explanation of their client's views and ideas. Often they are surprised how much a client has explained to me.

However, I am often unhappy about including a section containing my opinion and hypotheses. Sometimes when I have written a report from the client's perspective, clients have asked me to include what I think, as they are aware that my opinion would carry greater weight. I am usually asked for my opinion by other workers if I do not include this. However, adding this section seriously compromises the message I aim to give to my clients during our interactions: that they are the expert and that I trust them to find their own answers.

To illustrate this process again, I shall use another hypothetical example of a male client (the vast majority of clients in the forensic system are male). A client may have been asked to see me for assessment by other involved clinicians to gain an understanding of why he sexually abused his partner's children. In the assessment sessions, the client may initially be very careful about what he says, focusing on how he was abused as a child and his anger about this and not mentioning his abuse of children. Towards the end of our time together, I may suggest that the referring clinicians may be interested in his understanding of why he became an abuser, if he wants to talk about it. At this stage, he may talk more about this, whilst explaining his worries about doing this. He may then decide it would be useful for him to have a copy of my report detailing his life, as he may want to pursue legally the abuse that he experienced as a child. This assessment could become the start of a therapy relationship. This could be the first time the client has felt helped as opposed to policed by the professionals involved with him, although he is still well aware that I have to report to others about the risk he poses to others.

BRIDGING THE GAP

I now work in a primary care mental health team, where I work as a PC therapist and my role as a CP is used in other areas of the team and Trust functioning, such as research, evaluation, supervision and development. This is a much easier fit of my two hats. However, I believe there are welcome moves within the profession of CP towards some of the principles which attract me to the PCA.

The recent definition of the profession of CP by its professional body (The Division of Clinical Psychology, British Psychological Society, (DCP) 2001) fits within the ethos of 'scientific humanism' (Cheshire and Pilgrim, 2004: 105) thus showing signs of moving away slightly from the objective-scientist position. According to this statement, the philosophy of CP is as follows:

> The work of CPs is based on the fundamental acknowledgement that all people have the same human value and the right to be treated as unique individuals. CPs will treat all people—both clients and colleagues—with dignity and respect and work with them collaboratively as equal partners towards the achievement of mutually agreed goals. (DCP, 2001: 2)

However, the purpose of the profession of CP is defined as follows:

> Clinical psychology aims to reduce psychological distress and to enhance and promote psychological well-being by the systematic application of knowledge derived from psychological theory and data. (DCP, 2001: 2)

These statements demonstrate the mixed messages within CP, between clients as human subjects to apply psychological theory to (CP as scientist) and clients as unique autonomous individuals to be treated with respect (CP as humanist).

These dual strands of the profession of Clinical Psychology have been present since its inception. Stricker (1997) describes how in the USA, the 'scientist practitioner' model was set as the template for the profession following the Boulder conference in 1950. The discussion about the compatibility or otherwise of these two strands (the practitioner being the reflective clinically experientially-led part) has characterised the profession ever since. Whereas the 'scientist' was the focus for increasing the status of the profession in the 1990s, it seems that now in the UK at least, the 'practitioner' part is back in focus. At the same time, conceptions of 'science' have, at least in some circles, broadened to recognise experience as a form of knowing, in addition to purely 'objective' or experimental methods.

Lavender (2003: 15) suggests that within CP 'There is a growing recognition that there is a need to balance our longstanding position as scientist practitioners with an understanding and use of the processes of reflection.' The concept of the 'reflective practitioner' is now a marginal part of CP rhetoric, reducing the focus from scientist-expert, to person able to reflect on knowledge which has limitations. Stedmon et al. (2003: 30) suggest that 'whereas the scientific paradigm offers a method for discovering truths, the reflective position may be best construed as a metatheoretical framework for evaluating the status of these so-called truths.'

Indeed, the core themes of the reflective practitioner idea are now part of the accreditation criteria for training programmes in CP. Gillmer and Marckus (2003) present core themes generated by clinical psychology trainers about the idea of reflective practice. One of these was legitimising the personal in the professional and another was the recognition of the diversity of individual personal and professional development journeys. There has been an increasing focus on the socio-political context of distress and of self-care of CPs, bringing back the focus on CPs as people. Here parallels with training in the PCA become clearer.

Community psychology currently occupies a marginal position within CP with a focus on socio-political causes of distress, being community-led and collaborative interventions with socially excluded groups. Cheshire and Pilgrim (2004) argue that the current government commitment to social inclusion and increasing user involvement will lead to greater involvement of CPs in community psychology. However, they also warn that CPs are likely to become more responsible for social control under the proposals for reforms to the Mental Health Act, forcing a professional shift in the opposite direction.

SUMMARY AND CONCLUSION

I have presented my positions as clinical psychologist and practitioner of the PCA by describing the historical development of each and the methods that each approach uses to justify their existence. I have argued that CP has relied on justificatory claims to science which are dubious, and ignored issues of values and ethics that determine what research questions are asked and which methods used. I suggest that the motive behind this focus on science is the gaining and maintaining of status and power. Instead, I argue that the PCA has relied fundamentally on ethical justifications, and has been explicit about how its ethical position has determined the research undertaken to demonstrate effectiveness.

As CP responds to the challenges of the limitations and inconsistencies inherent in the scientist-expert model, PC practitioners are in an ideal position to offer an alternative view of 'knowledge', focusing on an ethical position of people being unique and self-determining. This position is based on Rogers' view of wisdom, which challenges the notion of expert knowledge which gives power, and believes in the knowledge and power that comes from congruence, that

> In such an individual, functioning in a unified way, we have the best possible base for wise action. It is a process base, not a static authority base. It is a trustworthiness that does not rest on 'scientific' knowledge. (Rogers, 1978: 250)

At the same time, the PCA has an opportunity to be clearer about its claims to science and its ethical focus on which scientific facts are most relevant. The PCA can also be accused of focusing exclusively on micro-relational causes and solutions of distress and thus ignoring overwhelming evidence for societal inequalities and deprivation and environmental causes of distress. Perhaps both CP and PCA could benefit from examining and widening their examination of relevant scientific evidence when discussing issues of effectiveness.

Newnes, Hagan and Cox (2000) suggest that a sign of a mature profession is its ability to examine what it does with a critical eye. Perhaps both CP and the PCA have suffered from having to defend what they do to outsiders which creates insecurity, making it difficult to be self-critical. Hopefully, both now have a firm and secure enough foundation to encourage practitioners to become mature by not only advocating what they do, but also maintaining a critical focus on taken-for-granted 'truths'.

REFERENCES

Barrett-Lennard, GT (1998) *Carl Rogers' Helping System: Journey and substance*. London: Sage.
Barrett-Lennard, GT (2002) Perceptual Variables of the Helping Relationship: A measuring system and its fruits. In G Wyatt and P Sanders (eds) *Rogers' Therapeutic Conditions: Evolution, theory and practice, Volume 4, Contact and Perception* (pp. 25–50) Ross-on-Wye: PCCS Books.

Bozarth, JD (1998) *Person-Centred Therapy: A revolutionary paradigm.* Ross-on-Wye, UK: PCCS Books.

Brodley, BT (1997) The non-directive attitude in client-centered therapy. *The Person-Centered Journal, 4,* 18–30.

Cheshire, K and Pilgrim, D (2004) *A Short Introduction to Clinical Psychology.* London: Sage.

Division of Clinical Psychology (2001) *The Core Purpose and Philosophy of the Profession.* Leicester: BPS.

Foucault, M (1977a) *Madness and Civilisation.* London: Tavistock.

Foucault, M (1977b) *Discipline and Punish.* London: Penguin Press.

Foucault, M (1979) *The History of Sexuality, Vol 1: An introduction.* London: Penguin Press.

Foucault, M (1980) *Power/Knowledge: Selected interviews and other writings 1972–1977.* Brighton: Harvester Press.

Gillmer, B and Marckus, R (2003) Personal professional development in clinical psychology training: surveying reflective practice. *Clinical Psychology, 27,* 20–3.

Grant, B (2004) The imperative of ethical justification in psychotherapy: The special case of client-centered therapy. *Person-Centered and Experiential Psychotherapies, 3,* 152–65.

King, M, Sibbald, B, Ward E, Bower, P, Lloyd, M, Gabbay, M and Byford, S (2000) Randomised controlled trial of non-directive counselling, cognitive behaviour therapy and usual general practitioner care in the management of depression as well as mixed anxiety and depression in primary care. *Health Technology Assessment, 4,* 19. Also published in the *British Medical Journal, 321,* (2000), 1383-8.

Kirschenbaum, H and Henderson, VL (1989) (eds) *The Carl Rogers Reader.* Boston: Houghton Mifflin.

Lambert, MJ (ed) (2004) *Handbook of Psychotherapy and Behavioural Change,* (5th ed). New York: Wiley.

Larner, G (1999) Derrida and the deconstruction of power as context and topic in therapy. In I Parker (ed) *Deconstructing Psychotherapy* (pp. 115–31). London: Sage.

Lavender, T (2003) Redressing the balance: the place, history and future of reflective practice in training. *Clinical Psychology, 27,* 11–15.

Lowe, R (1999) Between the 'No-longer and the 'Not-yet': postmodernism as a context for critical therapeutic work. In I Parker (ed) *Deconstructing Psychotherapy* (pp. 71–85). London: Sage.

McNamee, S (2003) Social construction as practical theory: Lessons for practice and reflection in psychotherapy. In G Larner and D Pare (eds) (pp. 9–21) *Collaborative Practice in Psychology and Therapy.* US/Canada: Haworth Press Inc.

Marzillier, J and Hall, J (1992) *What is Clinical Psychology?* (2nd ed). Oxford: Oxford University Press.

Mowbray, D (1989) *Review of Clinical Psychology Services.* Cheltenham: MAS.

Natiello, P (2001) *The Person-Centred Approach: A passionate presence.* Ross-on-Wye: PCCS books.

Newnes, C, Hagan, T and Cox, R (2000) Fostering critical reflection in psychological practice. *Clinical Psychology Forum, 139,* 21–4.

Pilgrim, D and Treacher, A (1992) *Clinical Psychology Observed.* London: Routledge.

Proctor, G (2002a) *The Dynamics of Power in Counselling and Psychotherapy: Ethics, politics and practice.* Ross-on-Wye: PCCS Books.

Proctor, G (2002b) Power in Person-Centred Therapy. In J Watson, R Goldman and M Warner (eds) *Client-Centered and Experiential Psychotherapy in the 21st Century: Advances in theory, research and practice* (pp. 79–88). Ross-on-Wye: PCCS Books.

Proctor, G (2004a) Responding to injustice: working with angry and violent clients in a person-centred way. In D Jones (ed) *Working with Dangerous People: The psychotherapy of violence* (pp. 99–116). Oxford: Radcliffe Medical Press.

Proctor, G (2004b) What can Person-Centred Therapy learn from feminism? In G Proctor and MB Napier (eds) *Encountering Feminism: Intersections of feminism and the person-centred approach* (pp. 129–40). Ross-on-Wye: PCCS Books.

Proctor, G (2004c) An introduction to the Person-Centred Approach. In G Proctor and MB Napier (eds) *Encountering Feminism: Intersections of feminism and the Person-Centred Approach* (pp. 26–38). Ross-on-Wye: PCCS Books.

Proctor, G (2005) Working in forensic services in a person-centered way. *Person-Centered and Experiential Psychotherapies,* 4(1): 20–30.

Rogers, CR (1942) The use of electrically recorded interviews in improving psychotherapeutic techniques. *American Journal of Orthopsychiatry 12,* 429–34.

Rogers, CR (1959) A theory of therapy, personality and interpersonal relationships as developed in the client-centered framework. In S Koch (ed) *Psychology: A study of a science, Vol. III: Formulations of the person and the social context* (pp. 184–256). New York and London: McGraw-Hill.

Rogers, CR (1978) *Carl Rogers on Personal Power.* Constable: London.

Rogers, CR and Dymond, R (eds) (1954) *Psychotherapy and Personality Change.* Chicago: University Press.

Rose, N (1985) *The Psychological Complex.* London: Routledge and Kegan Paul.

Sanders, P (ed) (2004) *The Tribes of the Person-Centred Nation: An introduction to the schools of therapy related to the Person-Centred Approach.* Ross-on-Wye: PCCS Books.

Stedmon, J, Mitchell, A, Johnstone, L and Scaife, S (2003) Making reflective practice real: Problems and solutions in the South West. *Clinical Psychology, 27,* 30–3.

Stricker, G (1997) Are science and practice commensurable? *American Psychologist, 52,* 442–8.

CHAPTER 19

SEARCHING FOR THE CORE:
THE INTERFACE OF CLIENT-CENTERED
PRINCIPLES WITH OTHER THERAPIES[1]

JEROLD D. BOZARTH AND NORIKO MOTOMASA

This chapter reviews: (1) Rogers' theory of client-centered psychotherapy, (2) the conclusions of research on the 'Necessary and Sufficient Conditions' postulated by Rogers (1957), (3) the conclusions of psychotherapy outcome research over the last decade, and (4) the utilization of the results of psychotherapy outcome research. This exploration is considered in relation to the interface of client-centered principles within the mental health treatment system, which operates from other views of psychotherapy. Vignettes of client-centered principles in therapeutic situations are presented.

Carl R. Rogers (1951) formally introduced a revolutionary theory of psychotherapy identified as Client-Centered Therapy. The theory was identified as Client-Centered Therapy (CCT) after first being labeled 'non-directive' therapy (Rogers, 1942). The theory was revolutionary for several reasons. First, the locus of control was centered with the constructive organismic direction of the client. Second, the client was considered the source of the healing process. It was within a special relationship with the therapist that the client's development could become congruent with the constructive organismic process. The activities central to most theories of therapy were reversed as Rogers' theory dismissed the importance of such activities as accurate diagnostic judgements and use of techniques to alter the client's attitudes and behavior. The relationship of power and control of the therapist was shifted to the power and control resting in the client (Rogers, 1977: 3). The therapist's task was to create the opportunity for the client to connect with the constructive direction of the organism.

The radical position of CCT is reviewed in relation to therapies that operate from other basic assumptions. Our examination suggests that the conditions of the therapeutic process postulated in Client-Centered Therapy are the basic therapeutic ingredients for effectiveness in all approaches of psychotherapy. Rogers (1957) proposed this commonality in an 'integration' paper that generated over three decades of psychotherapy outcome research. Analyses of psychotherapy outcome research during the 1990s conclude that 70 percent of successful therapy is predicated on the client-

---

1. Sections of this chapter were published under the title 'The Art of "Being" in Psychotherapy' in *The Humanistic Psychologist*, Special Triple Issue: The Art of Psychotherapy. *29*, 1–3, spring, summer, fall, 2001, 167–203. Reproduced with permission of the American Psychological Association, Division of Humanistic Psychology (Division 32).

therapist relationship and client resources (Duncan and Miller, 2000; Hubble, Duncan and Miller, 1999; Lambert, 1992).

CLIENT-CENTERED THERAPY

Rogers (1959) was the first investigator to apply quantitative empirical research to the field of psychotherapy. He presented the only formal theory of therapy that delineates a format for scientific inquiry research. His self-proclaimed *magnum opus* theory identified only six conditions that *are necessary and sufficient* for the therapeutic process. Three of these conditions are attitudes to be held by the therapist. Specifically, he states:

1. That two persons are in *contact*.
2. That the first person, whom we shall term the client, is in a state of *incongruence*, being vulnerable, or anxious.
3. That the second person, whom we shall term the therapist, is *congruent* in the *relationship*.
4. That the therapist is *experiencing unconditional positive regard* toward the client.
5. That the therapist is *experiencing* an *empathic* understanding of the client's *internal frame of reference*.
6. That the client *perceives*, at least to a minimal degree, conditions 4 and 5, the *unconditional positive regard* of the therapist for him, and the *empathic* understanding of the therapist. (Rogers, 1959: 213)

The three postulates (3, 4, and 5) that are 'therapist conditions' can be construed as theoretical and pragmatic instructions for therapists. Brief definitions of these conditions are:

Congruence: The symbolization of the therapist's own experience in the relationship must be accurate. The therapist '... should accurately "be himself" in the relationship, whatever the self of that moment may be' (p. 214). Synonymous terms are: 'integrated, whole, genuine' (p. 206).

Unconditional positive regard: The self-experiences of the client are perceived as worthy of positive regard without discrimination by the therapist. In general, acceptance and prizing are synonymous terminology (p. 208).

Empathy: 'The state of empathy, or being empathic, is to perceive the internal frame of reference of another with accuracy, and with the emotional components and meanings which pertain thereto, as if one were the other person, but without ever losing the "as if" condition' (p. 210).

The six conditions are the basic therapeutic assumptions that facilitate client change. The linear construction of the theory is that *if* these conditions exist, there will be certain process and outcome changes in clients. The changes include increased freedom to express feelings through verbal and other modal channels; greater unconditional positive self regard; one's self as the locus of evaluation; and the client experiencing himself less in terms of conditions of worth and more in terms of the organismic valuing process.

The outcome changes are predicated on the postulate that: 'The client is more *congruent*, more *open to his experience*, less *defensive*' (Rogers, 1959: 218). Hence, the client will be more psychologically adjusted, more objective and more realistic. The client is more apt to observe the locus of evaluation and locus of choice as residing in self. Process and outcome variables are interchangeable in that there are no intervening variables in the process conception of client-centered therapy (Rogers, 1959: 220).

The revolutionary difference between these assumptions and those of other theories has contributed to a chasm between client-centered and other therapeutic approaches. Ironically, Carl Rogers' (1957) abiding interest was that of discovering the common factors related to therapeutic effectiveness regardless of the therapy or type of helping relationship.

THE QUAGMIRE OF DIFFERENT ASSUMPTIONS

The search for effectiveness is affected by basic assumptions about psychotherapy. An article in the *New York Times* (Carey, 2004) reported the intense strain at the 2004 American Psychological Association convention between two directions of psychotherapy. One direction is predicated upon a particular view of scientific research requiring focus on problems and defined treatment procedures. The other direction focuses on the therapist's more general therapeutic involvement with clients.

One view believes that there is empirical evidence that supports the thesis of specific treatments for particular diagnoses. These treatments can be administered with the guidelines of manuals. The proponents of this view believe that there is 'Empirically Supported Treatment' (EST) (Task Force on Promotion and Dissemination of Psychological Procedures, 1995). Others (Bozarth, 1998, 2002; Duncan and Miller, 2000; Hubble, Duncan and Miller, 1999; Messer and Wampold, 2002; Norcross, 2000; Wampold, 2001) challenge the premises and the claims of these advocates. The latter view asserts that the research evidence supports the common factors of relationship and client resources as accounting for the major success variance in psychotherapy. This view is discussed later.

Differences about effectiveness of treatment for mental problems have existed since the advent of psychotherapy. The 1985 Phoenix Conference on the 'Evolution of Psychotherapy' dramatically illustrates this point (Zeig, 1987). In a report on the promotion of scientific psychotherapy, Joseph Wolpe described the conference '… as a babble of conflicting voices' (Wolpe, 1987). There is little evidence that there has been much change twenty years later. The advent of Empirically Supported Treatments (EST) and subsequent reactions have simply accelerated the babble.

The Phoenix conference exemplified two general assumptions about psychotherapy. One assumption is that humans are primarily reactive to external stimuli (e.g., Skinner) that reinforce behavior. The other assumption is that humans react to internal stimuli identified as inner motivations (e.g., Freud). The second assumption includes the conceptualization that humans are in the process of becoming.

Rogers delineated a more radical position within the second assumption; namely, he referred to the 'self-actualization process', a developmental process of the self that becomes congruent to the organismic 'actualizing tendency' when individuals experience unconditional positive self-regard and empathic understanding (Rogers, 1959).

Our conclusion is that the common factors embedded in the client/therapist relationship and the client's self-determination and own resources are the major contributors to therapeutic effectiveness. Client-centered principles have been integral parts of these factors and at the forefront in the exploration of common therapeutic factors.

THE NECESSARY AND SUFFICIENT CONDITIONS

Early in his career, Rogers indicated that his abiding interest was to find the common variables related to successful outcome for all therapies. He crystallized this search in the early 1950s, reported in 'Discussion' papers circulated at the Counseling Center of the University of Chicago. Rogers (1957, 1959) wrote two seminal articles emanating from these discussions. The first article published (Rogers, 1957) was dubbed the 'Integration Statement' (Bozarth, 1998; Stubbs and Bozarth, 1996) and also as 'Conditions Therapy Theory' by Barrett-Lennard (1998).

As early as 1974 Patterson wrote: 'The days of schools in counseling and psychotherapy are drawing to a close' (p. ix). In several books, Patterson (1974, 1984, 1985; Patterson and Hidore, 1997) identified the common factors identified by Rogers as the central assumptions for an eclectic psychotherapy. Patterson's (1984) review of the reviews of psychotherapy outcome research concluded that the conditions were the potent factors in the contribution to successful therapy. Nevertheless, different schools of psychotherapy increased throughout the decades of the 1980s and 1990s. Behaviorally-oriented schools of therapy perpetuating the view of the reactive human being have gained strong footholds in the mental health treatment system.

The research on the necessary and sufficient conditions dominated common factor psychotherapy outcome studies during the latter part of the 1950s into the 1980s (Bozarth, Zimring and Tausch, 2002). During this time there was substantial research supporting Rogers' postulates of the attitudinal conditions. Confirmation of the research support for over three decades of findings was dismissed by many researchers with the rationale that the conditions had been found to be 'necessary but not sufficient' and that more specificity was needed. The assumption that the research on the conditions was not supported was predicated upon fewer than a half dozen reviews. In addition, most of these reviews did not refute the research findings. Rather, they were calls for increased vigor of research designs (Bozarth et. al., 2002). Studies concerned with congruence, unconditional positive regard, and empathy diminished in the 1990s correlating negatively with the increased research emphasis on specificity. Later, overviews of the research and meta-analysis studies identified the greatest contributors to the effectiveness of psychotherapy as the common factors.

CONCLUSIONS OF PSYCHOTHERAPY RESEARCH OVER THE LAST DECADE

Rogers' 1957 paper was about the common factors of all therapies and helping relationships. Rogers' (1959) formal theory statement delineated his 'common factors' as the theoretical crux of the therapeutic process in Client-Centered Therapy. In short, the common factors posited for all therapies became the foundation of the therapeutic process in CCT.

It was the 1957 integration paper that had the most profound influence on the entire field of psychotherapy. There was a shift from research that studied the difference of effectiveness among different therapeutic approaches to that of examining the attitudinal conditions as related to the effectiveness of all therapies. Congruence, unconditional positive regard, and empathy were central ingredients in much of this research (Bozarth, Zimring and Tausch, 2002).

The power of more broadly defined common factors in psychotherapy became increasingly recognized over the decade of the 1990s. Lambert (1992) classified the variability of psychotherapy success to conclude that the contributions of common factors accounted for the major success variance. His estimates were not derived directly from meta-analytic techniques but, rather, characterized '... the research findings of a wide range of treatments, disorders, and ways of measuring client and therapist characteristics' (Lambert and Barley, 2001: 357). The percentages of a subset of more than 100 statistical analyses that predicted outcome were averaged by the size of the contribution that each predictor made to the outcome. The relative contributions of variables that impacted outcome were identified. These variables and the estimated percentage of success variance accounted for were: (1) Extratherapeutic change (40%); (2) Common factors (30%); (3) Expectancy (or placebo) (15%); and (4) Techniques (15%) (p. 97). Lambert's definitions are presented below:

EXTRATHERAPEUTIC CHANGE

Those factors that are a part of the client (such as ego strength and other homeostatic mechanisms) and part of the environment (such as fortuitous events, social support) that aid in recovery regardless of participation in therapy.

EXPECTANCY (PLACEBO EFFECTS)

That portion of improvements that results from the client's knowledge that he/she is being treated and from the differential credibility of specific treatment techniques and rationale.

TECHNIQUES

Those factors unique to specific therapies (such as biofeedback, hypnosis, or systematic desensitization).

COMMON FACTORS

Common factors refers to the host of variables that are found in a variety of therapies regardless of the therapist's theoretical orientation: such as empathy, warmth, acceptance, encouragement of risk taking, etc. (p. 97).

Others (Bozarth, 1998; Duncan and Miller, 2000; Hubble et. al., 1999; Norcross, 1997) also cite these variables and extend the terminology. For example, common factors and relationship are used interchangeably and extratherapeutic change is periodically referred to as client resources (referring to the inner and external resources of the client). As noted, Lambert derived his conclusion from logical classification of the research results rather than from statistical analyses. Later, meta-analysis demonstrated through statistical analyses that 70 percent of the success variance is accounted for by common rather than specific variance (Wampold, 2001).

Bozarth (1998) summarized major research reviews on psychotherapy outcome to conclude with the following statement:

1. Effective psychotherapy is primarily predicated upon (a) the relationship between the therapist and the client and (b) the inner and external resources of the client.

2. The type of therapy and technique is largely irrelevant in terms of successful outcome.

3. Training, credentials and experience of therapists are irrelevant to successful therapy.

4. Clients who receive psychotherapy improve more than clients who do not receive psychotherapy.

5. There is little evidence to support the position that there are specific treatments for particular disabilities.

6. The most consistent of the relationship variables related to effectiveness are the conditions of empathy, genuineness and unconditional positive regard. (Bozarth, 1998: 165)

Three decades later the research reviews reflected the major notions observed by Berenson and Carkhuff (1967) and the Strupp, Fox and Lessler (1969) survey. Namely, the core

298

of these notions was: '. . . the importance of the client's involvement in their own treatment and the minuscule influence of 'interventive' techniques' (Bozarth, 1998: 167).

There were two analyses of research that were especially revealing. First, Duncan and Moynihan (1994) summarized reviews of quantitative research studies and proposed a model of psychotherapy predicated upon the conclusions of the research. They suggested the intentional utilization of the client's frame of reference. Their conclusion suggested that successful therapy called for '. . . a function of the client's unique perceptions and experience and requires that therapists respond flexibly to clients needs, rather than from a particular theoretical frame of reference or behavioral set' (Duncan and Moynihan, 1994: 295).

The second study was a qualitative study of psychotherapy outcome research (Stubbs and Bozarth, 1994). A major finding was that a general conclusion of research literature was not consistent with the data. As noted previously, a general conclusion was that the common conditions postulated by Rogers were necessary but 'not sufficient'. This conclusion was, at best, an extrapolation of flawed logic that lacked even one direct study to support the assertion. Evolving temporal categories of effective psychotherapy suggested that:

> (1) the major thread running through the four plus decades of efficacy research was the relationship of the therapist/client and this thread included Rogers' attitudinal conditions of the therapist; and (2) that the research foundation for the 'specificity question' had '. . . abysmal research support and the precursor of the 'specificity' assumption is the unsupported theme of Rogers' conditions being necessary but not sufficient. (Bozarth, 1998: 168)

It became clear that the increased investigation of specificity was not based on the results of previous research. In fact, research demonstrated that client perceptions of the relationship are the most consistent predictor of improvement (Gurman, 1977; Lafferty, Beutler and Crago, 1989).

Wampold's (2001) meta-analysis brought forth continued revelation of efficacy of common factors over specificity. He examined the greater benefits of a 'contextual' over a 'medical' meta-model of psychotherapy. The medical model is characterized through specific problem-solving ingredients while the contextual model is characterized by the essence of therapy being embodied in the client-therapist relationship. It became clear that the therapist who is delivering treatment is more crucial than the specific procedure utilized. Other meta-analyses (Ahn and Wampold, 2001; Elliott, 1997; Grissom, 1996; Smith and Glass, 1977; Wampold et al., 1997) yielded comparable results.

Several articles and books identified the client as her own best generator of self-change. One review of research asked, 'What makes psychotherapy work?' and answered with, 'the active client' (Bohart and Tallman, 1996). They conclude that it is not only the client's frame of reference and more reliance on the client but also that '. . .we must truly understand that it is the whole person of the client who generates the processes and solutions that create change' (p. 26).

Another book summarizing research findings and clinical discoveries (Duncan, Hubble and Miller, 1997), resulted in their conclusion that '... clients' frame of reference, their worldview, as the determining "theory" for our work' (p. 206). Another is an edited book of reviews of psychotherapy research (Hubble, Duncan and Miller, 1999). The crux of this book is an emphasis on the common factors culled from reviews of research studies.

Bohart (2004) brings attention to clients who act: 'as active change agents who extract patterns of meaning from the therapy interaction, deduce implications, and use therapist empathy responses for purposes of self-support, validation, exploring experience, testing self-understanding, creating new meaning, and making connection with the therapist' (p. 104).

The major conclusion of psychotherapy outcome research is that the critical variables are the client/therapist relationship and extra-therapeutic variables (e.g., client resources). However, this is a contentious conclusion between the different views about human beings.

There is a great push by Task Force of Division 12, Clinical Psychology, of the American Psychological Association for the 'Empirically Supported Treatments' proposal. Their efforts are founded upon the assumption that there are specific treatments for particular dysfunction (Task Force on Promotion and Dissemination of Psychological Procedures, 1995). Others identify intrinsic flaws of the EST paradigm that ignore, among other things, the examination of four decades of psychotherapy outcome research (Ahn and Wampold, 2001; Bozarth, 2002; Duncan and Miller, 2000; Wampold, 2001).

The bulk of the studies that compare contrasting views of therapy reveal that they are equally successful (Lambert, 1992; Hubble, Duncan and Miller, 1999). As noted previously, the reason for such findings is that the common elements rather than differences among approaches account for the success. The above variables are more general than Rogers' postulates as indicated earlier by Lambert's (1992) definitions. Meta-analysis summaries (Ahn and Wampold, 2001; Wampold, 2001) have often identified the most familiar of the common factors to be the therapist-client alliance.

Horvath and Symonds (1991) found a correlation of .26 between alliance and outcome. Martin, Garske and Davis (2000) found a correlation of .22. These are medium-effect sizes accounting for 7 percent and 5 percent of the outcome variance. Messer and Wampold indicate that: 'Clearly, the relationship accounts for dramatically more variability in outcome than specific ingredients' (p. 23). When these two meta-analyses were combined with 10 more recent published research studies, the overall effect size of .21 was compared with the overall effect size of .39 of psychotherapy (Smith and Glass, 1977). Horvath (2001), assuming quasi-independence of the active ingredients of therapy, concludes that: '... a little over half of the beneficial effects of psychotherapy accounted for in previous meta-analyses are linked to the quality of the alliance' (p. 366). The differentiation of alliance from relationship is somewhat questionable from both a conceptual and empirical review. Much of the empirical evidence use therapeutic relationship and alliance synonymously. The conceptual base of alliance is from the authoritative stance of the therapist (e.g., Freud's early papers) and theoretically, if not functionally, at odds with the view of the client as her/his own best expert about her/his life.

The therapist's allegiance factor reflecting the therapist's belief that her therapy is efficacious (referring to effectiveness determined through true research designs (Seligman, 1995)) turns out to have a whopping effect. Wampold (2001) and Luborsky et al. (1999) suggest that 'almost 70% of the variability in effect sizes of treatment comparisons was due to allegiance' (Messer and Wampold, 2002: 23). In short, the therapist who believes strongly in her therapeutic approach is much more apt to have clients who improve regardless of the particular approach. Factors such as acceptance, empathy, and respect are generally embedded in the research findings that identify the relationship. Lambert (1992: 97) refers directly to these conditions in his operational definition of 'common factors' (later referred to as the 'relationship'). However, the specific variables of empathy and unconditional positive regard are often not explicitly included in the statistical analyses. Likewise, extratherapeutic variables are embedded within the client's utilization of her resources in Rogers' conceptualization. Rogers' assertion that the client's perception of the therapist's unconditional positive regard and empathic understanding facilitates change is seldom a central source of analyses in research designs during the 1990s. Nevertheless, the bottom line of outcome research over the last decade is that it is the client as the active participant that accounts for successful therapy. Certain therapists facilitate more improvement in clients regardless of the therapist's orientation of therapy. The fundamental premises in Client-Centered Therapy are embedded in the therapist/ client relationship and in focus on the client's frame of reference.

UTILIZATION OF THE RESULTS OF PSYCHOTHERAPY OUTCOME RESEARCH

Client-centered principles have been adopted in part by most therapies. These therapies, including behavioral, partially accept Rogers' (1957) 'necessary and sufficient' postulate. They accept the postulate as being necessary but do not consider it sufficient. Empathy and acceptance as necessary conditions have become common terminology for most therapies. However, these therapies believe that there must be something more that the therapist contributes. Generally, the idea of more therapist contribution refers to specific actions taken towards clients.

The Institute for the Study of Therapeutic Change (ISTC) group (www.talkingcure.com) insists that therapy that is change-focused, client-directed, and outcome-informed is based upon psychotherapy outcome research. This approach to therapy can help the non-medical helping professions establish an identity separate from the field of medicine and provide clients ethical and effective treatment. Hence, they are involved in a systematic program to focus on clients as the instruments of their own change. This group is spearheaded by the authors of *The Heroic Client* (Duncan and Miller, 2000). They transform the empirical 'facts' about successful therapy into practice dimensions. Their goals are to: (1) enhance the factors across theories that account for successful outcome; (2) use the client's theory of change to guide choice of techniques and integration of various therapy models; and (3) obtain

301

valid and reliable feedback regarding the client's experience of the process and outcome of treatment (Duncan and Miller, 2000).

The emphasis of the ISTC group is different from the CCT model. The major difference is that the group provides, or more precisely in their words, 'constructs with clients', intervention, whereas client-centered principles only instruct therapists to be congruent in their experiencing of unconditional positive regard toward the client, and empathic understanding of the client's frame of reference. ISTC advocates endorse selective listening, direct and pointed questions, and responses to certain contents of clients' stories, for the purpose of providing 'more effective' therapy that reflects on clients' theories of change. Their approach assumes appropriate intervention as determined by the therapist. However, it is only the client's theory of change that is considered the substantial contribution in Client-Centered Therapy. Nevertheless, the fundamental assumption about the client is the same; i.e., that the client is the real source of her own improvement. The ISTC group and CCT practitioners are in accordance about the major variables that are related to successful therapy; namely, the relationship and the client's unique resources.

CLIENT-CENTERED PRINCIPLES AND THE INTERFACE WITH OTHER THERAPEUTIC APPROACHES

There is striking correspondence with the core of client-centered principles and the crux of psychotherapy effectiveness. Correlation of success variance to the client-therapist relationship and the client's resources resonate with Rogers' basic postulates. However, nearly all therapies still focus on specific treatments and techniques even though they account for only 15 percent of the success variance. This percentage is comparable to the success variance of placebo effects. Messer and Wampold (2002) advise that: 'Because more variance is due to therapists than the nature of treatment, clients should seek the most competent therapist possible ... whose theoretical orientation is compatible with their own outlook, rather than choosing a therapist strictly by expertise ...' (p. 24).

The fact that the crux of successful therapy for all therapies is related to common factors has little effect on the position status of Client-Centered Therapy in most treatment programs. The mental health treatment system continues to focus on the concept of specific treatment for particular diagnoses or dysfunction. The client-centered assumption that it is only the *client's perception of the experiencing therapist* that facilitates constructive client change does not resonate well with specific treatment models.

This fact often requires client-centered therapists to adjust when working within systems that are neither sympathetic nor understanding of the Client-Centered Approach. Bozarth's (2001) delineation of his experience in mental health treatment and counseling centers suggest that such adjustment is possible.

Bozarth indicates that he learned Client-Centered Therapy from chronic long-term hospitalized patients in state mental institutions. This revelation took place before he was aware of Client-Centered Therapy or the writings of Carl Rogers. Bozarth was employed as a Psychiatric Rehabilitation Counselor in two state mental hospitals. One institution was a conventional state hospital that existed in the 1950s and the other a training center for psychiatrists that provided six-month treatment programs for a wide variety of patients during the early 1960s. Rehabilitation Programs focused on vocational development that involved very specific objectives of facilitating patients toward independent living and employment. Financial resources were available to assist clients with obtaining these objectives. Thus, the operational philosophy of the client-centered approach was at odds with the hospital operational assumptions of medical diagnosis and with the operational assumptions of specific agency goals (e.g., the goal of employment).

The following vignette offers one example of how the realities of institutional treatment goals and dedication to client-centered postulates were possible. The client, Howard, was in the conventional state hospital.

Howard had been in the hospital for over twenty years, diagnosed as schizophrenic, paranoid type. He spent several years in a special institution for the criminally insane because of brutal knife attacks on several people. When we first met, he said that he heard about me from other residents and had asked his physician to refer him. We met for two or three formal appointments during which time he talked mostly about his jobs in the hospital. He had a paper route delivering the local paper to hospital staff who lived on the grounds. As well, he did yard work for some of the staff. We also discussed some of the resources available through the rehabilitation program including support for vocational training. He said that he was interested in some kind of training but that staff had tried to help him get out of the hospital numerous times. It just never worked out. He then concluded that he was really too afraid to get out of the hospital and decided to not see me for any more appointments. He felt that he would not be able to function outside of the hospital.

Over the next year, we casually chatted in the coffee shop or under a shade tree about his girlfriends, his work activities, and sometimes about world events. Nearly a year after our initial contact, Howard asked for an appointment and immediately picked up on our conversation of the first formal meetings as though there had only been a few days lapse. He thought that he might be interested in going to 'barbers' school'. We talked weekly for several months ... Somewhere in that discussion, Howard decided to pursue training to become a barber. He was accepted for the program but had to wait six months to begin the next class. He decided during the interim to try to find work outside of the hospital. Hospital staff members were quite skeptical of his search for work since the industrial community was in a severe recession. I agreed with Howard's wish to meet before and after his job interviews. However, Howard missed most of those meetings and came by at the end of the week to report that he had three job offers. He decided to take the job where he would 'prep' hospital patients for surgery. Howard finally went to barbers' school and was a barber until retirement twenty years later. I was able to follow Howard's life to some extent because my mother was the Chief Medical Records Administrator for the state hospital and was also acquainted with Howard's daughter. It still strikes me as ironic that this 'knife wielding paranoid' and 'incarcerated psychotic' became a solid contributor to society through employment that involved the use of razors and scissors.

There were many variables that converged to help Howard return to society. If I was one of those helpful variables, what did I do that helped? One of my activities helped me examine this question. I kept copious notes of the sequential verbal responses of individuals recording them immediately after sessions. I would then try to determine the thematic 'I' statements of the individuals. Interestingly, I seldom included my responses except in a very general way. Howard's overall theme sequence was something like:

I'm curious about this rehabilitation program.
I'm pretty successful in the hospital at making a little money.
I have it made here. I have security and don't have to worry about a lot of things. I have girl friends. I have spending money. I have a certain kind of respect.
I don't think I could make it outside.
I wonder if I could make it?
I could give it a try. I could go to school while I am still in the hospital.
I am pretty sure I can do it but I have to get out right away or I might change my mind. I can't wait for the starting date of the school.
I am a successful man. I'm employed. I have contact with some of my family who disowned me years ago.

My sequential themes were along the following lines:

I am willing to meet with Howard to just listen to him.
I accept his fear of getting out of the hospital and will support him in his decision to not leave the hospital.
I will go with Howard in his decision to seek employment even though others think that he 'is crazy' to search.

In short, my way of being with Howard was to be involved, responsive, and willing to help him find ways to implement his decisions. I had no goals for him to get out of the hospital. I trusted his decisions at every level. I was willing to be with him on his terms. If I doubted his decisions, I would have shared this with him in depth as I did with many clients.

> I learned from Howard as well as others that clear improvements did not depend upon exploration of their internal experiences; they did not delve into self-exploration; and that they did not focus on their feelings in the ways that are usually considered important in therapy. (Bozarth, 2001: 175–8)

Client-centered principles were central to the client's pursuit of goals that were also institutional criteria for success. We chose this vignette as an example of the client-therapist relationship and the utilization of the client's resources that enabled the client to assimilate institutional/organizational resources into his personally developed vocational plan. The therapist's role was primarily that of listening to the client and facilitating the client with his development and implementation of concrete actions towards concrete goals.

Medically- and behaviorally-oriented organizations/agencies are often receptive to viable treatments that add to the overall benefit of their patients or clients. Primary health facilities in England that employ time-limited sessions for clients have accepted client-centered therapists on treatment teams (Bryant-Jefferies, 2003). Bryant-Jefferies offers detailed examples of client-centered sessions in a time-limited primary care setting. He presents fictional characterizations of some of his therapeutic relationships that describe specific struggles of client and therapist that are commonplace in the primary care setting in England. Experience with clients in the primary health facilities illustrates that a common ground between traditional problem-oriented approaches and client-centered principles can be reached.

Another scenario provides the way that a client-centered therapist worked with a client who came to a behaviorally-oriented counseling center seeking help with her four-year-old son.

> *Carolyn (C), a 33-year-old homemaker, came to the center asking for help with controlling the behaviors of her four-year-old son. She described the boy as disrupting the entire household with his behaviors. He had temper tantrums, would not listen to either his mother or father. As she described specific behaviors, the therapist thought about a behavioral analysis that might identify specific acts and reinforce more acceptable behavior from the boy. The center orientation was behavioral whereas the therapist was client-centered.*
>
> *C continuously discussed the boy's disruption of the family as she covered a myriad of themes. These themes included: (1) that her husband worked late and was seldom there to help her; (2) that her husband did not care about the behavior, but took the attitude that 'boys will be boys'. She indicated frequently that she did not receive emotional or practical support from her husband; (3) that she was dealing with everything alone. Her only friend was a neighbor who sometimes came over to try to talk to her son. He also cut their grass because her husband got home too late and worked weekends as well.*
>
> *When asked if she wanted to return, she somewhat reluctantly said that she could return in two weeks.*
>
> *When she returned, C did not mention her son at all nor did she raise issues about her son in future sessions. She briefly discussed her feeling of being alone and discontent with her life. Mainly, she talked about a sexual affair with her neighbor. But, again, she discontinued this discussion after this particular session. She focused more on her feelings of not being supported and being alone. She discontinued her therapy appointments after the eighth session. Three months later, she returned to say that things with her husband were going much better. They were going to church together and had bought a farm. She was instrumental in helping the farm to be a success. He was working forty hours a week rather than sixty hours on his construction job. C's son entered kindergarten and was 'pretty well' behaved.*

Stubbs and Bozarth (1996) report an experiment with student counselors using the scenario associated with C. The intention of the experiment was to explore the thesis that the personal embodiment of the conditions might transcend behavior and method.

A graduate student took the role of the client. The only information given to the 'client' was that of resisting discussion about the affair. Four graduate students followed models of therapy other than client-centered. The results were surprising in that the sessions went in a direction similar to the direction of the actual client. It is noted as follows:

> The actual client quit discussing the boy's behavior (never to be mentioned again) during the second session and discussed her affair. She then quit discussing the affair (never to be mentioned again) and talked about her feelings of being alone, discontent etc. This was the direction the role-play was going during the ten-minute integration model. (Stubbs and Bozarth, 1996: 30)

The student client thought that she might have been willing to discuss the client's affair with any of the therapists. Although the questions from the therapists were more focused on problems and resolution, the client believed that the questions kept her active and that she knew that the therapists were aware at some 'other level' that there was more than just the boy's disruptive behavior. One speculation was the following:

> This may be an example of the resiliency of individuals as clients but the point is that the client 'knew' at some level that the therapists 'knew', at least, vaguely that there was something else and that they were acceptant of her. (Stubbs and Bozarth, 1996: 30)

Most therapists, regardless of their theoretical orientation, are interested in the client's continued self-determination and self-authority. The data reveal little difference between success variance among those with different theoretical orientations. It also suggests that common factors might be perceived in different ways. Rogers' sixth condition is crucial; namely, that the client perceives the therapist's experiencing of unconditional positive regard and empathic understanding.

SUMMARY

The radical differences between the assumptions of Client-Centered Therapy and other therapies have a common ground. The conclusions of psychotherapy outcome research identify this common ground. Seventy percent of the success variance in psychotherapy is related to the client-therapist relationship (30%) and the client's own resources (extratherapeutic variables, 40%). CCT is more specific about the common variables in that the therapist's role in the relationship is defined as that of being congruent in experiencing unconditional positive regard towards the client and experiencing empathic understanding of the client's frame of reference.

It is the client's perception of the therapist's experiencing that facilitates the client's connection with her constructive organismic direction. It is the extent to which this connection exists that the individual is increasingly empowered to resolve her problems and dysfunctions. The therapist who acts with this therapeutic intent can work within the confines of organizational structures that operate from other theoretical foundations.

REFERENCES

Ahn, H and Wampold, BE (2001) Where oh where are the specific ingredients? A meta-analysis of component studies in counseling and psychotherapy. *Journal of Counseling Psychology, 48,* 251–7.

Barrett-Lennard, GT (1998) *Carl Rogers' Helping System: Journey and substance.* London: Sage.

Berenson, BG and Carkhuff, RR (eds) (1967) *Sources of Gain in Counseling and Psychotherapy.* New York: Holt, Rinehart and Winston.

Bohart, AC (2004) How do clients make empathy work? *Person-Centered and Experiential Psychotherapies, 3,* 102–16.

Bohart, AC and Tallman, AC (1996) The active client: Therapy as self help. *Journal of Humanistic Psychology, 36,* 7–30.

Bozarth, JD (1998) *Person-Centered Therapy: A revolutionary paradigm.* Ross-on-Wye, UK: PCCS Books.

Bozarth, JD (2001) The art of 'Being' in psychotherapy. *The Humanistic Psychologist, 29,* Special Triple Issue: The Art of Psychotherapy, 1–3, 167–203.

Bozarth, JD (2002) Empirically supported treatment: Epitome of the Specificity Myth. In JC Watson, RN Goldman and MS Warner (eds) *Client-Centered and Experiential Psychotherapy in the 21st Century: Advances in theory, research and practice* (pp. 168–81). Ross-On-Wye, UK: PCCS Books.

Bozarth, JD, Zimring, F and Tausch, R (2002) Client-Centered Therapy: Evolution of a revolution. In D Cain and J Seeman (eds) *Handbook of Humanistic Psychotherapy: Research and practice* (pp. 147–88). Washington, DC: American Psychological Association.

Bryant-Jeffries, R (2003) *Time-Limited Therapy in Primary Care: A person-centered dialogue.* Abingdon: Radcliffe Medical Press.

Carey, B (2004) For psychotherapies' claims, skeptics demand proof. *New York Times,* (August 10, section 1, p. 1, col. 1).

Duncan, BL and Miller, SD (2000) *The Heroic Client: Doing client-directed, outcome-informed therapy.* San Francisco: Jossey Bass.

Duncan, BL and Moynihan, D (1994) Applying outcome research: Intentional utilization of the client's frame of reference. *Psychotherapy, 31,* 294–301.

Duncan, BL, Hubble, MA and Miller, SD (1997) *Psychotherapy with 'Impossible' Cases: The efficient treatment of therapy veterans.* New York: WW Norton and Company.

Elliott, R (1997) Are client-centered/experiential therapies effective? A meta-analysis of outcome research. In U Esser, H Pabst and GW Speierer (eds) *The Power of the Person-Centered Approach* (pp. 155–38). Köln, Germany: GwG Verlag.

Grissom, RJ (1996) The magic number. 7 + - 2: Meta-meta-analysis of the probability of superior outcome in comparisons involving therapy, placebo, and control. *Journal of Consulting and Clinical Psychology, 64,* 973–82.

Gurman, AS (1977) The patient's perceptions of the therapeutic relationship. In AS Gurman and AM Razin (eds) *Effective Psychotherapy* (pp. 503–45). New York: Pergamon.

Horvath, AO (2001) The alliance. *Psychotherapy, 38,* 365–72.

Horvath, AO and Symonds, BD (1991) Relation between working alliance and outcome in psychotherapy: A meta-analysis. *Journal of Counseling Psychology, 38,* 139–49.

Hubble, MA, Duncan, BL and Miller, SD (1999) *The Heart and Soul of Change: What works in therapy.* Washington, DC: American Psychological Association.

Institute for the Study of Therapeutic Change (2004) Retrieved October 10, 2004 from http://www.talkingcure.com/

Lafferty, P, Beutler, LE and Crago, M (1989) Differences between more and less effective psychotherapists: A study of select therapist variables. *Journal of Consulting and Clinical Psychology, 57*, 76–80.

Lambert, MJ (1992) Implications of outcome research for psychotherapy integration. In JC Norcross and MR Goldfried (eds) *Handbook of Psychotherapy Integration* (pp. 94–129). New York: Basic.

Lambert, MJ and Barley, DE (2001) Research summary on the therapeutic relationship and psychotherapy outcome. *Psychotherapy, 38*, 357–61.

Luborsky, L, Diguer, L, Seligman, DA, Rosenthal, R, Krause, ED, Johnson, S, Halperin, G, Bishop, M, Berman, JS and Schweitzer, E (1999) The researchers own therapy allegiances: A 'wild card' in comparisons of treatment efficacy. *Clinical Psychology: Science and practice, 6*, 95–106.

Martin, DJ, Garske, JP and Davis, MK (2000) Relation of the therapeutic relation with outcome and other variables: A meta-analytic review. *Journal of Consulting and Clinical Psychology, 68*, 438–50.

Messer, SB and Wampold, BE (2002) Let's face facts: Common factors are more potent than specific therapy ingredients. *Clinical Psychology: Science and Practice, 9*, 21–8.

Norcross, JC (1997) Emerging breakthroughs in psychotherapy integration: Three predictions and one fantasy. *Psychotherapy, 34*, 86–90.

Norcross, JC (2000) Empirically supported therapeutic relationships: A Division 29 task force. *Psychotherapy Bulletin, 35*, 2–4.

Patterson, CH (1974) *Relationship Counseling and Psychotherapy: Theory and practice*. New York: Harper and Row.

Patterson, CH (1984) Empathy, warmth, and genuineness in psychotherapy: A review of reviews. *Psychotherapy, 21*, 431–8. Reprinted in CH Patterson, *Understanding Psychotherapy: Fifty years of person-centred theory and practice*. Ross-on-Wye: PCCS Books, pp. 161–74.

Patterson, CH (1985) *The Therapeutic Relationship: Foundations for an eclectic psychotherapy*. Monterey, CA: Brooks/Cole.

Patterson, CH and Hidore, S (1997) *Successful Psychotherapy: A caring loving relationship*. New Jersey: Jason Aronson Inc.

Rogers, CR (1942) *Counseling and Psychotherapy*. Boston: Houghton Mifflin.

Rogers, CR (1951) *Client-Centered Therapy: Its current practice, implications, and theory*. Boston: Houghton Mifflin.

Rogers, CR (1957) The necessary and sufficient conditions of therapeutic personality change. *Journal of Consulting Psychology, 21*, 95–103.

Rogers, CR (1959) A theory of therapy, personality, and interpersonal relationships as developed in the client-centered framework. In S Koch (ed) *Psychology: A study of science: Vol. 3 Formulation of the person and the social context* (pp. 184–256). New York: McGraw Hill.

Rogers, CR (1977) *Carl Rogers on Personal Power: Inner strength and its revolutionary impact*. New York: Delacorte.

Seligman, MEP (1995) The effectiveness of psychotherapy: The Consumer Report Study. *American Psychologist, 50*, 963–4.

Smith, ML and Glass, GV (1977) Meta-analysis of psychotherapy outcome studies. *American Psychologist, 32*, 752–60.

Strupp, HH, Fox, RE and Lessler, K (1969) *Patients View Their Psychotherapy*. Baltimore: The John Hopkins Press.

Stubbs, JP and Bozarth, JD (1994) The dodo bird revisited : A qualitative study of psychotherapy efficacy research. *Journal of Applied and Preventive* Psychology, 3, 109–20.

Stubbs, JP and Bozarth, JD (1996) The integrative statement of Carl Rogers. In R Hutterer, G Pawlowsky, PF Schmid and R Stipsits (eds) *Client-Centered and Experiential Psychotherapy: A paradigm in motion* (pp. 25–33). New York: Peter Lang.

Task Force on Promotion and Dissemination of Psychological Procedures (1995) Training in and dissemination of empirically validated psychological treatments. Report and recommendations. *The Clinical Psychologist, 48,* 3–23.

Wampold, BE (2001) *The Great Psychotherapy Debate: Models, methods, and findings*. Mahwah, NJ: Lawrence Erlbaum Associates.

Wampold, BE, Mondin, L, Moody, M, Moody, M, Stich, F, Benson, K and Ahn, H (1997) A meta-analysis of outcome studies comparing bonafide psychotherapies: Empirically, 'all must have prizes'. *Psychological Bulletin, 122,* 203–15.

Wolpe, J (1987) The promotion of scientific psychotherapy. In JK Zeig (ed) *The Evaluation of Psychotherapy* (pp. 133–42). New York: Brunner Mazel.

Zeig, JK (1987) *The Evaluation of Psychotherapy*. New York: Brunner Mazel.

CHAPTER 20

CLIENT-CENTERED VALUES LIMIT THE APPLICATION OF RESEARCH FINDINGS —AN ISSUE FOR DISCUSSION[1]

BARBARA T. BRODLEY

In this paper I discuss the view that the values of client-centered (CC) theory and practice should significantly limit the role of research findings in a CC therapist's efforts to develop the practice and theory. Values should probably place limits on the use of research findings by therapists from any orientation, but the issue is especially obvious in Client-Centered Therapy (CCT) because it is based explicitly on values. Early in his writings on CCT, Rogers (1951) asserted that the 'philosophical orientation of the counselor' is crucial in therapist development. He wrote that the therapist 'can be only as "nondirective" as he has achieved respect for others in his own personality organization' (p. 21). He was explicit about the underlying role of values.

> How do we look upon others? Do we see each person as having worth and dignity in his own right? If we do hold this point of view at the verbal level, to what extent is it operationally evident at the behavior level? Do we tend to treat individuals as persons of worth, or do we subtly devalue them by our attitudes and behavior? Is our philosophy one in which respect for the individual is uppermost? Do we respect his capacity and his right to self-direction, or do we basically believe that his life would be best guided by us? To what extent do we have a need and a desire to dominate others? Are we willing for the individual to select and choose his own values, or are our actions guided by the conviction (usually unspoken) that he would be happiest if he permitted us to select for him his values and standards and goals? The answers to questions of this sort appear to be important as basic determiners of the therapist's approach. (p. 20)

If one concurs with Rogers' view of the role of values, what should a CC therapist do with research findings that appear to suggest the efficacy of directive procedures or that omit or de-emphasize empathic understanding and acceptance of the client? A common response to such a question says 'since these techniques are effective ... they should be used' (Bergin, 1970: 271). My contrary contention is that, 'yes, one should mention

---

1. Revision of a paper presented at the Annual Meeting of the Association for the Development of the Person-Centered Approach, Cleveland, Ohio, August, 2002 and published in *Person-Centred Practice* (2003) *11*, 52–5.

these findings when discussing research, but ignore them in respect to theory and practice because research findings are not messages from a bank of truth.

The dominating context of this discussion is psychologists' and counselors' general belief that research findings are necessary to legitimize therapeutic practice and to improve theory. Rogers, himself, supported Thorndike's dictum that 'anything that exists, exists in some quantity that can be measured' (quoted in Gordon, Grummon, Rogers and Seeman, 1954: 13), and he fostered many empirical studies of CCT as well as pioneering the use of transcripts of sessions in psychotherapy research (Kirschenbaum and Henderson, 1989).

Some writers (Levant, 2004; McFall, 1996; Messer and Wampold, 2002; Peterson, 2004) qualify their general emphasis on empirical research by asserting that evidence-based practice should be integrated with clinical expertise. Some respond that it is true—so far, scientific procedures have not answered all the questions. But they argue that a wider range of questions and appropriate methods would keep therapy practice based on science and be best for clients (Beutler, 2004; Chambless, 2002; Rounsaville and Carroll, 2002).

Opinions vary about the role of not-strictly-scientific clinical expertise in modifying therapy. Still, all current writers on the subject appear to believe in and promote a scientific basis for therapy. None challenge the use of research for modifying practice, or assert the limiting role of values in incorporating research findings into therapy practice or theory.

Many of Rogers' descendents within the person-centered community use research findings to justify directive procedures and to change Rogers' theory. Outstanding examples are Gendlin (1969), Greenberg, Elliott and Lietaer (1998), Hendricks (2002) and Sachse and Elliott (2002). Rogers' own history as an innovative researcher and his encouragement of individualistic therapist development would seem, to some, to support letting the research chips fall where they may, even if it means abandoning non-directive CCT. Rogers' behavior as a therapist, however, belies that impression.

Indeed, Rogers was a pioneer in psychotherapy research (Cain, 2002), but the research he fostered on outcome, on the concomitants of change, and on the specific processes involved in change (Rogers and Dymond, 1954; Halkides, 1958; Rogers, 1959, 1961a, 1967) does not appear to have had much influence on his own therapy practice other than to give it support. His therapy sessions in the 1980s are little changed from those in the mid 1940s (Bozarth, 1990, 2002; Brodley, 1994; Cain, 1993).

Rogers recorded, transcribed, and studied his and his students' therapy behavior starting in 1940 (Rogers, 1942; Kirschenbaum, 1979). He critiqued his early therapy behavior in relation to his theory and on that basis made changes that are evident after 1942 (Brodley, 1994, 2004), but there is no evidence that any value-conflicting research findings available before his death influenced his therapy. He acknowledged that changes might be needed on the basis of research findings (Rogers, 1957, 1967) but he did not change his own behavior with his individual clients on those grounds.

An example of Rogers' fidelity to his values can be found in his response to a study of his own therapy. In the late 1950s Rogers listened to many of his therapy tapes and observed stages in clients' processes and manner of representing themselves as they improved (Rogers, 1961a). The pattern of therapeutic movement he observed in his clients was their response to his non-directive, congruent, offering of unconditional positive regard and empathic understanding to his clients—behavior consistent with his theory. For this good reason Rogers did not interpret his own process research findings as instructions for directive procedures.

Some other therapists originally in the CC milieu did use this and other research to adopt directive procedures. For example, reports by Tomlinson and Hart (1962), Gendlin, Beebe, Cassens, Klein and Oberlander (1968), Gendlin (1969), Klein, Mathieu-Coughlan and Kiesler (1969), Friedman (1982), and Mathieu-Coughlan and Klein (1984) showed their shift to an experiential process-directive therapy in part on the basis of Rogers' process findings.

A great deal of research shows the efficacy of Client-Centered Therapy. For example, Truax and Carkhuff (1967) reported research results from ten separate studies involving 850 clients. Those results 'overwhelmingly support' Rogers' hypothesis that therapist congruence, unconditional positive regard and empathic understanding result in constructive personality change (Friedman, 1982: 34). Rogers often reported such confirming studies and it appears that Rogers embraced research findings when they tended to support his values about persons and about therapy. However, he did not do this in a cavalier manner. In fact, Rogers (1961b) expressed a theoretical justification for the role of values in adopting scientific findings. He wrote:

> What I will do with the knowledge gained through scientific method ... is a matter of subjective choice dependent upon the values which have personal meaning for me (p. 223)

Rogers' client-centered therapy remained non-directive and empathic (Bozarth, 2002; Brodley, 1994; Merry, 1996; Van Belle, 1980) in respect to both content and process. After all the challenging research, his subsequent therapy remained consistent with his values.

Until the end of his life (early in 1987) Rogers continued to think that values determine what kind of therapy he would do, and that it is best to be aware of those values as one incorporates research findings. In a 1986 interview (Rogers and Russell, 2002) Rogers asserted, 'Whatever philosophical views I hold I clearly implement in practice' (p. 188) and said that client-centered therapy is 'an approach that simply lives a philosophy and puts its trust in the capacities of the client ...' (p. 259).

Rogers held to his description of CC therapy, written in 1946, for the rest of his career. He wrote:

> The therapist must ... give up the temptation to subtly guide the individual, and must concentrate on one purpose only; that of providing deep understanding and acceptance of the attitudes consciously held at this moment by the client ... (p. 421)

The obvious difference in Rogers' later-in-life therapy that I have observed from videos is that he manifests a less formal, less clinical, presence with his clients. He changed in his non-verbal, expressive behavior, but Rogers continued to exclusively communicate his non-directive, empathic intentions with clients with only rare exceptions to this purity (Brodley, 1996).

Rogers expressed his values in an interview late in his life (Baldwin, 1987), stating that the 'suitable goals' in the therapy interaction are for the therapist's self. He said,

> I want to be as present to this person as possible. I want to really listen to what is going on [in the client]. I want to be real in this relationship ... The goal has to be within myself, with the way I am ... 'Am I really with this person in this moment? Not where they were a little while ago, or where they are going to be ... ' This is the most important thing. (pp. 47–8)

Also, in 1986, a few months before his death, Rogers expressed his non-directive client-centered attitudes, commenting to an interviewer:

> When the situation is most difficult, that's when a client-centered approach is most needed and ... what is needed there is a deepening of the [therapeutic attitudes] and not trying something more technique-oriented. (Rogers and Russell, 2002: 258)

Research is useful. Outcome research can show some of the specific ways a therapy is helpful. It may also be useful for political or social purposes. For example, it may be used to justify a therapy to certification boards, or it may contribute to clients' decisions about who they would like to help them, by looking at the measures of benefits shown by research. Descriptive research using transcripts and tapes may help therapists evaluate the immediate effects of their behavior on clients or show how consistent or inconsistent their behavior is in relation to their theory.

Research results, however, should not be viewed as providing an objective truth (Rogers, 1961b) as grounds for modifying a practice—especially if the research results have implications that contradict the underlying values of the therapy. Psychotherapy research, itself—in its questions, in its methods, in the interpretation of results—and any move to apply results to a therapy—is influenced by the researcher's specific values and attitudes (Lietaer, 2002).

Consequently, one may legitimately argue that it is absurd to give credence to any research in respect to applying it to psychotherapy, given the proven role of the researcher's theoretical allegiance. Studies looking at theoretical allegiance are consistent in finding large effects (Messer and Wampold, 2002). There is as much as 69 percent of the variability in effect sizes of treatment comparisons attributable to researcher theoretical allegiance (Luborsky et al., 1999, 2002). Given such powerful researcher contamination of findings, it is hard to understand why therapists and others trust psychotherapy research results at all.

CONCLUSION

Psychotherapy should be viewed as fundamentally a practical art and recognized as an ethical activity (Schmid, 2002; Grant, 1985). Consequently, a therapist should place severe limits on his or her use of research in the theory and practice of therapy. Therapy, and the research applied to a therapy—both—always express the therapist's values and attitudes about persons whether the therapist is conscious of this or not. Conversely, therapists should be aware of how their operational values may be impacted if they adopt changes in their therapy on the basis of research findings.

REFERENCES

Baldwin, M (1987) Interview with Carl Rogers on the use of the self in therapy. In M Baldwin and V Satir (eds) *The Use of Self in Therapy* (pp. 45–52). New York: The Haworth Press.

Bergin, AE (1970) Some implications of psychotherapy research for therapeutic practice. In JT Hart and TM Tomlinson (eds) *New Directions in Client-Centered Therapy* (pp. 257–76). Boston: Houghton Mifflin.

Beutler, LE (2004) The empirically supported treatments movement: A scientist-practitioner's response. *Clinical Psychology: Science and practice, 11*, 225–9.

Bozarth, JD (1990) The essence of client-centered therapy. In G Lietaer, J Rombauts and R Van Balen (eds) *Client-Centered and Experiential Psychotherapy in the Nineties* (pp. 59–64). Leuven, Belgium: Leuven University Press.

Bozarth, JD (2002) The evolution of Carl Rogers as a therapist. In DJ Cain (ed) *Classics in the Person-Centered Approach* (pp. 43–7). Ross-on-Wye, UK: PCCS Books.

Brodley, BT (1994) Some observations of Carl Rogers' behavior in therapy interviews. *Person-Centered Journal, 1*, 37–48.

Brodley, BT (1996) Uncharacteristic directiveness: The case of Rogers and the 'anger and hurt' client. In BA Farber, DC Brink and PM Raskin (eds) *The Psychotherapy of Carl Rogers* (pp. 310–21). New York: Guilford Press.

Brodley, BT (2004, July) Rogers' responses to clients' questions in client-centered therapy: Some findings from a dissertation research by Claudia Kemp. Presented at the annual conference of the Association for the Development of the Person-Centered Approach. Anchorage, Alaska.

Cain, DJ (1993) The uncertain future of client-centered counseling. *Journal of Humanistic Education and Development, 31*, 133–9.

Cain, DJ (2002) Preface. In DJ Cain and J Seeman (eds) *Humanistic Psychotherapies Handbook of Research and Practice* (pp. *xix–xxvii*). Washington, DC: American Psychological Association.

Chambless, DL (2002) Beware the dodo bird: The dangers of overgeneralization. *Clinical Psychology: Science and practice, 9*, 13–16.

Friedman, N (1982) *Experiential Therapy and Focusing.* New York: Half Court Press.

Gendlin, ET (1969) Focusing. *Psychotherapy: Theory, research and practice, 6*, 4–15.

Gendlin, ET, Beebe, J, Cassens, J, Klein, M and Oberlander, M (1968) Focusing ability in psychotherapy, personality and creativity. In JM Shlien (ed) *Research in Psychotherapy.* Vol 3, (pp. 217–41). Washington, DC: American Psychological Association.

Gordon, T, Grummon, DL, Rogers, CR and Seeman, J (1954) Developing a program of research in psychotherapy. In CR Rogers and RF Dymond (eds) *Psychotherapy and Personality Change,* (pp. 12–34). Chicago: The University of Chicago Press.

Grant, B (1985) The moral nature of psychotherapy. *Counseling and Values, 29,* 141–50.

Greenberg, LS, Elliott, R and Lietaer, G (1998) *Handbook of Experiential Psychotherapy.* New York: Guilford Press.

Halkides, G (1958) An experimental study of four conditions necessary for therapeutic change. Unpublished doctoral dissertation, University of Chicago.

Hendricks, M (2002) Focusing-oriented/Experiential psychotherapy. In DJ Cain and J Seeman (eds), *Humanistic Psychotherapies Handbook of Research and Practice* (pp. 221–52). Washington, DC: American Psychological Association.

Kirschenbaum, H (1979) *On Becoming Carl Rogers.* A Delta Book. New York: Dell Publishing Company, Inc.

Kirschenbaum, H and Henderson, VL (eds) (1989) *The Carl Rogers Reader* (pp. *xi–xvi*). Boston: Houghton Mifflin.

Klein, MH, Mathieu-Coughlan, PL and Kiesler, DJ (1969) *The Experiencing Scale: A research and training manual.* Vol 1, University of Wisconsin.

Levant, RF (2004) The empirically validated treatments movement: A practitioner/educator perspective. *Clinical Psychology: Science and practice, 11,* 219–24.

Lietaer, G (2002, July) Paper presented on panel: Open discussion on person-centered research, at the Carl R Rogers Symposium, La Jolla, CA.

Luborsky, L, Diguer, L, Seligman, DA, Rosenthal, R, Johnson, S, Halperin, G, Bishop, M and Schweizer, E (1999) The researcher's own therapeutic allegiances: A 'wild card' in comparisons of treatment efficacy. *Clinical Psychology: Science and practice, 6,* 95–132.

Luborsky, L, Rosenthal, R, Diguer, L, Andrusyna, TP, Berman, JS, Levitt, JT, Seligman, DA and Krause, ED (2002) The dodo bird verdict is alive and well—Mostly. *Clinical Psychology: Science and practice, 9,* 2–12.

Mathieu-Coughlan, PL and Klein, MH (1984) Experiential psychotherapy: Key events in client-therapist interaction. In LN Rice and LS Greenburg (eds) *Patterns of Change* (pp. 213–48). New York: Guilford Press.

McFall, RM (1996) Manifesto for a science of clinical psychology. *The Clinical Psychologist, 44,* 75–88.

Merry, T (1996) An analysis of ten demonstration interviews by Carl Rogers: Implications for the training of client-centred counselors. In R Hutterer, G Pawlowsky, PF Schmid and R Stipsits (eds) *Client-Centered and Experiential Psychotherapy: A paradigm in motion* (pp. 273–84). Frankfort am Main: Peter Lang.

Messer, SB and Wampold, BE (2002) Let's face facts: Common factors are more potent than specific therapy ingredients. *Clinical Psychologist: Science and practice, 9,* 21–5.

Peterson, DR (2004) Science, scientism, and professional responsibility. *Clinical Psychology: Science and practice, 11,* 196–210.

Rogers, CR (1942) *Counseling and Psychotherapy.* Boston: Houghton Mifflin.

Rogers, CR (1946) Significant aspects of client-centered therapy. *American Psychologist, 1,* 415–22.

Rogers, CR (1951) *Client-Centered Therapy.* Boston: Houghton Mifflin.

Rogers, CR (1954) An overview of the research and some questions for the future. In CR Rogers and RF Dymond (eds) *Psychotherapy and Personality Change* (pp. 413–34). Chicago: The University of Chicago Press.

Rogers, CR (1957) The necessary and sufficient conditions of therapeutic personality change. *Journal of Consulting Psychology, 21*, 95–103.

Rogers, CR (1959) A theory of therapy, personality and interpersonal relationships as developed in the client-centered framework. In S Koch (ed) *Psychology: A study of a science. Vol. III. Formulations of the person and the social context* (pp. 184–256). New York: McGraw Hill.

Rogers, CR (1961a) A process conception of psychotherapy. *On Becoming a Person* (pp. 125–59). Boston: Houghton Mifflin.

Rogers, CR (1961b) Persons or science? A philosophical question. *On Becoming a Person* (pp. 199–224). Boston: Houghton Mifflin.

Rogers, CR (1967) *The Therapeutic Relationship and Its Impact: A study of psychotherapy with schizophrenics.* Westport, CT: Greenwood Press.

Rogers, CR and Dymond RF (eds) (1954) *Psychotherapy and Personality Change.* Chicago: The University of Chicago Press.

Rogers, CR and Russell, DE (2002) *Carl Rogers, the Quiet Revolutionary: An oral history.* Roseville, CA: Penmarin Books.

Rounsaville, BJ and Carroll, KM (2002) Commentary on dodo bird revisited: Why aren't we dodos yet? *Clinical Psychology: Science and practice, 9,* 17–20.

Sachse, R and Elliott, R (2002) Process-outcome research on humanistic therapy variables. In DJ Cain and J Seeman (eds) *Humanistic Psychotherapies Handbook of Research and Practice* (pp. 83–115). Washington, DC: American Psychological Association.

Schmid, PF (2002, July) The characteristics of a person-centered approach to therapy and counseling: Criteria for identity and coherence. Presentation given at the Carl R Rogers Centennial Celebration, La Jolla, CA.

Tomlinson, TM and Hart, JT (1962). A validation of the process scale. *Journal of Consulting Psychology, 26,* 74–8.

Truax, CB and Carkuff, RR (1967) *Toward Effective Counseling and Psychotherapy: Training and practice.* Chicago: Aldine Press.

Van Belle, H (1980) *Basic Intent and Therapeutic Approach of Carl R Rogers.* Toronto: Wedge Publishing Foundation.

CHAPTER 21

AN EVALUATION OF RESEARCH, CONCEPTS AND EXPERIENCES PERTAINING TO THE UNIVERSALITY OF CCT AND ITS APPLICATION IN PSYCHIATRIC SETTINGS

LISBETH SOMMERBECK

There exists a myth that Client-Centred Therapy (CCT) is unsuitable for clients diagnosed with severe psychopathology. In this chapter I identify five reasons for this myth and refute each of them, thereby demonstrating that the notion that CCT is only useful with less severe psychological disturbances is precisely what it is said to be: a myth. Let me start by listing the five reasons for the existence of this myth as I identify them:

1. The disappointing results of Rogers' own research with people diagnosed with schizophrenia (Rogers et al., 1967).
2. An erroneous notion that expression of empathic understanding of psychotic ideation is a collusion with or reinforcement of such ideation.
3. A confusion of 'non-directive' with 'unstructured'.
4. An erroneous notion that CCT is an in-depth exploratory approach.
5. A confusion of the theory of therapy with the theory of personality.

I will deal with each of these reasons in turn and in the final section I will give my reasons, based on 30 years of experience with psychotherapeutic work in a psychiatric hospital, for regarding CCT as being not only useful with clients diagnosed with serious psychiatric disturbances, but also for regarding CCT with its pre-therapeutic extension (Prouty, 1994) as being the only psychotherapeutic approach that is viable with those people whom other approaches regard as being 'beyond psychotherapeutic reach'.

1. THE DISAPPOINTING RESULTS OF THE WISCONSIN PROJECT

The material in this section is, mostly, edited excerpts of a previously published critique of the Wisconsin Project (Sommerbeck, 2002). Unless otherwise stated the quotations in this first major section are from Rogers et al.'s book about the Wisconsin Project (1967).

In 1967, Rogers and his co-workers published the book about the scientifically impeccably and ingeniously designed large-scale research project, which Rogers headed during his years as professor at the University of Wisconsin. The project investigated the effect of CCT on a group of 'normals', a group of 'acute schizophrenics', and a group of 'chronic schizophrenics', compared with matched and paired controls who did not receive CCT.

This book, as well as other commentaries on the Wisconsin Project, bears witness to Rogers' disappointment with the results of the project. Most revealing is, I think, the following statement by Rogers (quoted by Shlien, 1992: 1083–4):

> Our recent experience in psychotherapy with chronic and unmotivated schizophrenics raises the question whether we must modify our conception of this condition. Very tentatively it appears to me at the present time that, in dealing with the extremely immature or regressed individual, a conditional regard may be more effective in getting a relationship under way, than an unconditional positive regard.

In this quote Rogers is in effect saying that Client-Centred Therapy doesn't work with these people. It is precisely the unconditionality of unconditional positive regard that is normally recognised as the primary therapeutic agent in CCT (see, for example, Bozarth, 1998) and advocating conditional regard as being more effective with these people is synonymous with advocating an approach that is, in its very essence, different from CCT.

Here are a few more quotes that illustrate the disappointing results of the Wisconsin Project:

> In many respects the therapy group taken as a whole showed no better evidence of positive outcome than did the matched and paired control group. It had however a slightly better rate of release from the hospital, and this differential was maintained a year after the termination of therapy. The therapy group also showed a number of positive personality changes, which were not evidenced by the control group. The differences between the two groups, however, were not great. (Rogers, et al., 1967: 80)

The meaning of 'not great' is found on p. 282:

> ... it seemed probable that the discrepant ego strength scores for therapy and control groups accounted for their different hospitalization rates. While the therapy group continued to show a greater percentage of time out of the hospital, the difference was no longer statistically significant. Thus, when initial ego strength was controlled, the resultant findings became consistent with those for other outcome measures, indicating no differential improvement for the experimental and control groups. (ibid.)

Finally, Rogers accompanies the following quote with the explicit statement that the finding reported 'was disappointing' (p. 82):

> In general there was no differential amount of process movement over therapy in our schizophrenic group as a function of therapy. (ibid: 82)

Bearing these quotations in mind, I think it is no wonder that CCT came to be regarded by every one including client-centred therapists, as being unsuitable for people diagnosed with schizophrenia. However, a careful reading of the book about the project raises three important questions:

1. Was it really the diagnosis of schizophrenia that was the relevant variable accounting for the disappointing results?
2. Was the therapy offered really CCT?
3. Were the therapists experienced with people diagnosed with schizophrenia?

My answer to all three questions is 'no'. Reading the book about the project, it seems evident to me that the relevant variables accounting for the disappointing results were (1) lack of client motivation for therapy, (2) that the therapy offered frequently had nothing to do with CCT, and (3) that the therapists had no experience with people diagnosed with schizophrenia. In the following sections each of these three points will be illustrated by quotations.

THE RESEARCH SUBJECTS LACKED MOTIVATION FOR THERAPY

The following quotation should suffice to demonstrate the importance of the variable of motivation for the disappointing results of the Wisconsin Project:

> The experience of most of the therapists on the project had been primarily with outpatient clients who came voluntarily for help. They were faced with many difficult problems in establishing a relationship with the hospitalized schizophrenics and likewise with the normals, both of the groups being composed of individuals who were not seeking help. The problems of the therapist and the solutions to these problems were manifold: sometimes pathetic, sometimes amusing. How is a male therapist to deal with a female research client who dashes into the women's washroom when she sees him coming? ... The therapists came to realize that they were dealing with individuals who were unmotivated, often unreachable, largely without hope, lacking in any concept of therapy, and certainly lacking in any belief that a relationship could be helpful. (Rogers et al., 1967: 67–8)

It is important to note the reference to the normals who, like the schizophrenics, were a group composed of 'individuals who were not seeking help'. Like the schizophrenics these unmotivated normals didn't benefit from therapy:

> With our normal individuals, who were not motivated for therapy, there was even a trend toward a more superficial level of experiencing in second halves of the therapeutic hours. This finding in the normal individuals seems explainable on the basis of their tendency to execute a defensive retreat from therapeutic engagements. (ibid: 83)

It should be evident from the next to last quotation that the schizophrenics, surely, also executed 'a defensive retreat from therapeutic engagements' by, for example, hiding in the ladies room! I see absolutely no reason to believe that this defensive retreat is of less importance for therapy outcome in schizophrenics than it is in normals.

Although the pairs of control and research subjects were matched with respect to degree of disturbance, only one among more than 25 criteria for measuring degree of disturbance (ibid, p. 551–2) was directly correlated with the clients' motivation for therapy. This criterion was 'awareness of need for help'. Among so many criteria of disturbance, the criterion of 'awareness of need for help' was not allowed to weigh as heavily as it should have been allowed to. The researchers did become aware of this. In a footnote on p. 26, Rogers writes: 'With the wisdom of hindsight, we realize that motivation for help should probably have been another variable in our stratification, since this too has been judged to be related to therapeutic outcome. This factor was not, however, included in the design.'

To me, Rogers' laconic footnote has the flavor of a huge understatement. I think it is recognised by all psychotherapists, regardless of their orientation, that degree of motivation for therapy is a client variable that contributes much to the outcome of therapy and lack of motivation is certainly not confined to people diagnosed with schizophrenia. Lack of motivation is a client variable that is not correlated with any specific psychiatric diagnosis, and, as a matter of fact, not even with psychopathology, as the unmotivated normals of the Wisconsin Project demonstrated. Thus far, therefore, the Wisconsin Project has only demonstrated the rather self-evident fact that therapy with persons who are not motivated for therapy has disappointing results.

Furthermore, imposing therapy on anybody seems to me to be contrary to the focus on respect for client autonomy that characterises CCT. It is inherent to CCT that it cannot be forced on people. If it is, it is no longer CCT. This will, I hope, become evident in the next section.

THE THERAPEUTIC APPROACH WAS NOT NECESSARILY CLIENT-CENTRED

As a consequence, it seems, of feeling rather helpless with their unmotivated clients, the therapists in Wisconsin did a lot of things that were not at all client-centred. The following quotations illustrate this point:

> ... the therapists in our group found themselves trying out and developing many new and different modes of response behavior. The variety of specific behaviors among the therapists increased sharply. (ibid, p. 12)

The following are examples of the kind of response behaviour that was tried out and developed (Hart and Tomlinson, 1970):

> Patient did not wish to be seen after first two contacts. I told him 'that's okay with me' only to find that 'it isn't okay with me.' I called him back and asked him to come in ten times, then decide. Since we had already decided to play cards, since he refused to sit in silence, he then provided a cribbage

board. After five hours he indicated that he would like to come in as long as he is here. Now I have a cribbage partner who cheats, or tries to.

The patient refused right from the start to meet with me. To every mention of 'next time' and to every invitation to enter a room with me, he reacted with explicit anger and demands that I leave him alone. Over some weeks I accepted his feeling, anger, dislike of me: I *let* him leave; I had him brought by attendants; I argued with him; I was both honest and dishonest: I could not help but react negatively to his rejection and I felt he cut the ground from under my *right* to be with him. Because of these feelings in me I decided that he should not be further *coerced* to see me, since he would only discover a threatened and threatening person in me. (1970: 16–17; italics my own)

I find it evident that the approach of these therapists has nothing to do with CCT.

THE THERAPISTS WERE INEXPERIENCED WITH PEOPLE DIAGNOSED WITH SCHIZOPHRENIA

There are many passages in the book about the Wisconsin Project that illuminate the inexperience of the therapists with people diagnosed with schizophrenia:

For the majority of the therapists this was the first extensive work with hospitalized psychotics ... (Rogers et al., 1967: 8)

Our therapists were sometimes baffled by the lack of self-exploration among our schizophrenic clients, since they had come to think of self-exploration as characteristic of most psychotherapy. (ibid: 76)

... our therapists—competent and conscientious as they were—had over-optimistic and in some cases seriously invalid perceptions of the relationships in which they were involved. (ibid: 92)

Again, I think these quotations speak for themselves.

In the previous three sections I think there is ample evidence that the disappointing results of the Wisconsin Project had nothing to do with a failure of CCT to be of use to people diagnosed with schizophrenia. It had, rather, to do with the failure of a non-descript therapeutic approach, applied by inexperienced therapists, to be of use for people who were not motivated for therapy. There is, thus, no basis in the results of the Wisconsin Project for the existence of the myth that CCT is unsuitable for clients diagnosed with severe psychopathology.

2. THE ERRONEOUS NOTION THAT EMPATHY COLLUDES WITH OR REINFORCES PSYCHOTIC IDEATION

In the effort to follow the client's journey through his or her psychological landscape with consistent acceptant empathic understanding, the therapist must suspend his or her own conception of reality from start to finish of the session; the therapist puts his or her own conception of reality in parenthesis, and out of the way of the client for the duration of the session. Raskin (as quoted in Rogers, 1951: 25) expresses this beautifully:

> At this level, counselor participation becomes an active experiencing with the client of the feelings to which he gives expression, the counselor makes a maximum effort to get under the skin of the person to whom he is communicating, he tries to get within and to live the attitudes expressed ... to catch every nuance of their changing nature: in a word, to absorb himself completely in the attitude of the other. And in struggling to do this, *there is no room for any other type of counselor activity or attitude* ... [italics my own]

There is, thus, no room for the therapist's own conception of reality, however unfamiliar or mistaken the client's conception of reality may seem to the therapist. This is also the case with clients who present with so-called psychotic ideation, i.e. hallucinations and delusions, that do seem extremely unfamiliar to the therapist and quite at odds with the therapist's and others' more or less consensual conception of reality. With these clients the therapist's capacity to suspend his or her own conception of reality is put to the test and with these clients it is particularly important to remember that empathic understanding is neutral as far as confirmation or disconfirmation of the client's conception of reality is concerned. I've often seen empathic understanding confused with confirmation, even in psychotherapeutically well-informed circles. For example, the leader of the Danish Psychoanalytic Institute writes that 'empathic confirmation' is useful to strengthen the therapeutic alliance (Vitger, 1999: 200).

With a notion of empathic understanding as confirmative it is little wonder that empathic understanding is dismissed as useless and even harmful with clients who present with psychotic ideation. In the psychiatric circles I'm acquainted with, there is a widespread fear that one is colluding with or reinforcing psychotic ideation if one responds with expressions of empathic understanding of it. Instead of expressions of empathic understanding, 'reality correction' is the favoured approach, particularly among psychiatric nurses, to patients' expression of psychotic ideation. Sometimes psychiatric nurses seem to lean over backwards in fear of being misunderstood by the patient, as agreeing with or confirming the patient's, from their view, psychotic conception of reality. They often feel that they are not doing their job properly if they do not try to correct the patient's conception of reality by telling the patient, directly or indirectly, what the correct conception of reality is. They often relate to patients as if not doing 'reality correction' is synonymous with collusion with the patients' conception of reality. For people who regard 'reality correction' as a necessary element in the treatment of people diagnosed with psychosis, CCT is seen as inconsequential at best, and harmful at worst.

There is, naturally, no guarantee that a client does not experience a therapist's expression of empathic understanding as confirmative (or disconfirmative, for that matter) of the client's conception of reality. It is, though, contrary to the essence of Client-Centred Therapy to try to control client experiences in any way, including client experiences of the therapist. Client experiences of the therapist are received and followed with empathic understanding just like all other client experiences.

Contrary to this myth of collusion, it has been my experience, from my work in a psychiatric hospital, that it is 'reality correction' that is potentially harmful to clients diagnosed with psychosis, not expressions of empathic understanding—and that it is expressions of empathic understanding that are beneficial, not 'reality correction'. 'Reality correction' is, by its very nature, confrontational and patients with a diagnosis of psychosis feel, in general, threatened by confrontational approaches. Confronted with 'reality correction' they often tend to defend their conception of reality, thereby rigidifying and solidifying it and often expanding on it with more details and nuances, thereby developing their psychotic ideation further. In short, they can become more psychotic when confronted with 'reality correction'.

In contrast, expression of accurate empathic understanding, non-confrontational as it is, gives the client no reason to defend his or her perception of reality. This is precisely what makes it possible for the client to consider alternative points of view. The client feels that his or her perception of reality is understood and accepted, which leaves the client feeling free to explore it further. In this climate of safety and acceptance, the client will then most often, very tentatively and in very minor ways at first, start to question some inconsistencies that the client discovers in his or her psychological landscape; inconsistencies that are normally very different from and much more concrete than the inconsistencies other people have tried to point out to the client. The client will also start to speak with less fear and less psychotic distortions about his or her experiences with the significant persons in the client's life. This, of course, does not happen in dialogues that sometimes amount to a battle of whose conception of reality is the correct one. Ever so often, clients diagnosed with psychosis, have expressed to me that they feel our talks are little oases of safety and freedom to express themselves, contrasting our talks, implicitly or explicitly, with all the 'reality correction' they are exposed to in their talks with other people. This is not surprising from a client-centred point of view, since 'reality correction' is, basically, an expression of negative regard for the client's own perception of reality. These experiences of mine are thus in full accordance with the client-centred theory of therapy. Rogers writes (1951: 41):

> The therapist perceives the client's self as the client has known it, and accepts it; he perceives the contradictory aspects which have been denied to awareness and accepts those, too, as being part of the client; and both of these acceptances have in them the same warmth and respect. Thus it is that the client, experiencing in another an acceptance of both these aspects of himself, can take toward himself the same attitude.

Furthermore, it is in accordance with Rogers' concept of the fully functioning person (Rogers, 1959: 234–5) that it takes quite a high degree of openness to one's experiences to receive corrections of one's conception of reality non-defensively. Such openness to one's experiences is certainly not what normally characterises people diagnosed with psychosis; on the contrary.

The following excerpt of dialogue (factual content is changed so the client cannot be identified) is an example of a typical transition from expression of relatively more to relatively less psychotic ideation in the course of a client-centred therapy session where, of course, no effort at 'reality correction' is made. It illustrates that expressions of empathic understanding (and the contact reflections of Pre-Therapy that characterise the first part of the session) are in no way reinforcing of psychotic ideation; on the contrary. The excerpt is from the sixth session, and the therapist is the one who has taken, and still takes, the initiative to the contact between client and therapist (this is often the case in work with the most seriously disturbed patients in a psychiatric hospital). The therapist sees this patient in her room in the ward.

T: I thought that maybe ... if there was anything you might like to tell me today, about how you feel, and about your situation, how you look on it?

C (In a very matter of fact, 'there's no discussing it', way): I feel well.

T: You say you feel well, and you look very determinedly at me.

C: Yes, I feel well, and that's a fact.

(Pause, C looks down on her lap)

T: You say it's a fact you feel well, and now you look down and are quiet.

C: Yes, I feel well when I drink coffee, juice, and things like that, but water is no good— and I've stopped eating.

T: As long as you can drink something that tastes good you feel well, but you've lost your appetite?

C: Yes, and I also feel well because I'm now totally out of the church.

T: It's a relief to be finally out of it.

C: Yes, well, I'm not totally out of it, I still receive their newsletter, and I can't read it, it was a mistake that I joined the church, I'm confused about it—I have to tell them to stop sending the newsletter.

T: The church was really too much, and now you need to get that newsletter off your back, that'll be a relief?

C: Yes, that's it, I need to stop the newsletter and to have my mail delivered here, then I can feel fine—but I do feel fine here.

T: You like to be here, and if you had these things settled you could enjoy it better, be more at ease?

C: Yes, precisely, that would be nice.

(Pause, C moves her head around in abrupt jerks, staring at different spots)

T: You turn your head this way and that way and look around.

C (grinding her teeth): My father is a Satan.

T: You grind your teeth and say 'My father is a Satan'.

C: He has slaughtered my mother, he is the real Satan, and the Danes are his devils and devils' brood.

T: He is the real Satan, because he has slaughtered your mother, and the Danes are his devils and devils' brood.

C: Not all Danes, people here are nice to me, but he has slaughtered my mother and if he does it again, I'll slaughter him.

T: You feel you'll slaughter him if …

(C interrupts eagerly)

C: Yes, he has terrorised my mother all her life, psychological terror … her name is Maria, if Satan harmed Maria … Joseph would slaughter him, I'm Joseph.

T: You say 'I'm Joseph' and you feel like you think Joseph would feel if Satan harmed Maria, is that it?

C (nodding her head and smiling): Yes, and I'm not afraid of Satan, I'm not afraid of anything.

T: You smile at the thought that you are not afraid of Satan or …

C (interrupting): Yes, I'm not afraid, I'm glad of that, but why does he always have to be so rotten, last time he visited he brought some fruit from his back garden; it smelled real bad and then I took a bite and it tasted hellish … I threw it all away.

T: You think that everything he brings …

C (interrupting): Yes, why does he have to be so provocative?

T: Like 'Why the hell can't you buy me some good fruit that I like, instead of bringing me the rotten leftovers from your back garden?'

C: Yes, I think he never spreads anything but shit around him—I can't bear being near him.

The client spends the rest of the session exploring her relationship with her father in a way that seems much more coherent and less infiltrated with psychotic ideation than in the first part of the session. Note how the generalisation about Danes becomes modified, and how her conception of her father is modified: at first he is, literally, Satan; later he takes on more humane proportions and is 'merely' unbearably provocative. Also, 'slaughter' becomes 'psychological terror'. I feel convinced that if someone else had pointed these seeming inconsistencies in her conception of reality out to her, in the name of 'reality correction', she would have persevered more rigidly in them than ever. It was acceptant empathic following of her journey in her own psychological landscape that created the safety and space for her to consider alternatives in her conception of that landscape.

3. THE CONFUSION OF 'NON-DIRECTIVE' WITH 'UNSTRUCTURED'

It is common in psychiatric circles to believe that patients diagnosed with psychosis need 'structure'. What is meant by 'structure', though, is rarely defined. The practical implications of the conviction that psychotic patients need structure is normally that staff members in psychiatric hospitals try to make the patient follow a rather tightly scheduled daily routine, that 'limit-setting' is an important concept with these patients, and that an appropriate psychotherapeutic approach is assumed to be one that is goal directed and where the therapist structures the process by trying to keep the patient's focus on a certain issue or on several issues in an ordered sequence. In my experience some patients feel helped by this rather patronising approach, others don't, and this has nothing to do with whether they are diagnosed with a psychotic condition or not.

As a consequence of the belief that psychotic patients need 'structure' of the above-mentioned kind, the non-directive attitude of the client-centred therapist is thought of as being potentially harmful, as a passive 'laissez-faire' attitude that leaves the psychotic client helpless in his/her world of hallucinations and delusions.

What is ignored is that the most important aspect of the notion of 'structure' is the reliability of the social environment of a person. Patients diagnosed with psychosis are in my experience more vulnerable than people at large to 'surprises' in the way their significant others relate with them. In this sense I think it is true that patients diagnosed with psychosis 'need structure'. They seem to thrive better (and exhibit fewer psychotic symptoms) when they know rather precisely what they can expect of others and when expectations of theirs, that have once been established, are not disappointed or nullified at a later time. One could also say that they, more than most other people, seem to need others to relate consistently (or congruently) with them.

In this sense, CCT is probably the most structured approach of all psychotherapeutic approaches. Any client, including clients diagnosed with psychosis, quickly learns what they can expect from their client-centred therapist: the therapist's very best effort at acceptant empathic understanding, neither more nor less. This is the consistent attitude of the therapist all through the course of therapy; the client-centred therapist doesn't change attitude in sudden and surprising—and thereby, to the psychotic client, potentially provocative or over-stimulating—ways.

The client-centred therapist's non-directive attitude is, of course, precisely a consequence of the therapist's very active effort at following the client's process with acceptant empathic understanding. There is nothing 'passive' about it, no 'laissez-faire', no unstructured letting the client down, or leaving the client to his or her own devices, isolated and unaccompanied. It is truly unfortunate and sad that the therapist's non-directive attitude in CCT has been misunderstood in this way. It is particularly unfortunate and sad for patients diagnosed with psychosis, because the confusion between 'non-directive' and 'unstructured' is one of the reasons CCT has been dismissed as unsuitable for these people, when the truth is, in my experience, that it is eminently suitable for them (see Sommerbeck, 2003).

4. THE ERRONEOUS NOTION THAT CLIENT-CENTRED THERAPY IS AN IN-DEPTH EXPLORATORY APPROACH

In the rather wide psychiatric circles that I'm acquainted with from 30 years' work in a psychiatric hospital, there is almost no knowledge of CCT, and to the degree there is some slight knowledge, it contains many misunderstandings about CCT. Confusing the client-centred therapist's non-directive attitude with a passive 'laissez-faire' attitude is one of these misunderstandings. Another misunderstanding is that CCT is an in-depth exploratory approach on a par with psychodynamic therapy. Again, this is unfortunate and sad for patients diagnosed with psychosis. These patients are, in psychiatric circles, assumed not to benefit from an in-depth exploratory approach; on the contrary, they are assumed to be easily harmed by such an approach. The consequence of this misunderstanding is, therefore, that CCT is deemed unsuitable for these people.

In my experience it is true that people diagnosed with psychosis are easily harmed by an in-depth exploratory approach that, more or less subtly, directs the client to still deeper levels of experiencing, and to still closer contact with emotionally stimulating material. The therapist who is biased towards 'deep is better than shallow' and 'close is better than distant' and therefore more-or-less systematically aims in the direction of 'deeper' and 'closer' does pose a risk to psychotic clients who can easily be overwhelmed and over-stimulated by what is normally regarded as 'deep' and 'close'. People with a diagnosis of psychosis tend to respond to feeling overwhelmed and over-stimulated by displaying more rather than less so-called psychotic behaviours.

To the degree this bias ('deep' is better than 'shallow' and 'close' is better than 'distant') is shared by client-centred therapists, to that degree is it also true that they should not work with clients diagnosed with some kind of severe psychological disturbance. Unfortunately this bias does exist in the group of client-centred therapists, probably because most client-centred therapists work with less disturbed clients in private practices, university clinics, out-patient clinics, etc. They work, in short, mostly with clients who have never set foot in a psychiatric hospital and never will. With these clients, the bias that 'deep and close is better than shallow and distant' is probably inconsequential and it may even be helpful.

The existence of this bias among client-centred therapists is illustrated with the notion brought forth by some influential authors that 'additive empathy' (Mearns and Thorne, 1999: 45) or empathic understanding of 'edge of awareness experiences' (ibid: 52) is preferable to accurate empathy with what the client, in this moment, wants the therapist to understand about his or her psychological landscape. If I've understood Mearns and Thorne correctly, the client-centred therapist should, according to these authors, aim at additive empathy and empathy with edge of awareness experiences as opposed to 'ordinary' accurate empathic understanding of the client's inner frame of reference or psychological landscape. This preference is, apparently, supported by research: Rainer Sachse (1990: 300–2) has shown that clients typically react with a deepening of their level of experience when the therapist systematically strives for 'deep' empathic understanding responses and succeeds in this. However, the clients in this research were ambulatory clients, not in-patients in a psychiatric hospital. In-patients in a psychiatric hospital are, of course, more seriously psychologically disturbed, probably psychotic or in a so-called borderline condition, and they will typically react with withdrawal and/or intensification of psychotic symptoms to any effort to direct them to deeper levels of experiencing, whether it be by aiming systematically at 'additive empathy' or empathy with 'edge of awareness experiences' or by any other means. The tacit assumption that a deepening of the level of experiencing during the session is synonymous with therapeutic progress is not true for clients diagnosed with psychoses.

Therapist efforts at directing the client towards deeper levels of experiencing is, of course, an in-depth exploratory approach. But is it also Client-Centred Therapy? I think not, because the therapist who more or less subtly directs the client towards deeper levels of experiencing is, surely, process directive and this has, in my mind, nothing to do with CCT where the therapist is non-directive not only with respect to content but also with respect to process. Raskin (1988: 33) puts it beautifully when he differentiates between systematic and unsystematic therapist responses and says that therapists making systematic responses have '... a preconceived notion of how they wish to change the client and work at it in systematic fashion, in contrast to the person-centered therapist who starts out being open and remains open to an emerging process orchestrated by the client'. Rogers has the following to say (1959: 229–30) about in-depth exploratory approaches:

> In the freedom of therapy, as the individual expresses more and more of himself, he finds himself on the verge of voicing a feeling which is obviously and undeniably true, but which is flatly contradictory to the conception of himself which he has held ... Anxiety results, and if the situation is appropriate [a later section discloses that this means that the core conditions are dominant (this author's comment)], this anxiety is moderate, and the result is constructive. But if, through overzealous and effective interpretation by the therapist, or through some other means, the individual is brought face to face with more of his denied experiences than he can handle, disorganization ensues and a psychotic break occurs.

Aiming systematically at 'additive empathy' or empathy of 'edge of awareness experiences' is in my experience precisely such an overzealous and effective means that can easily bring clients diagnosed with psychotic or near-psychotic conditions face-to-face with more of their denied experiences than they can handle.

The usefulness of CCT to clients diagnosed with psychosis or other forms of severe psychopathology hinges, precisely, on the non-directive attitude of the therapist with respect to content as well as to direction of the process. Psychotic clients, and clients with a 'borderline' diagnosis, will often flatten their level of experiencing, as a sort of healthy recuperation, before they deepen it again. These clients can therefore talk about the latest fashion in shoes at one moment, only to talk about exceedingly painful experiences the next, and the therapist should follow the client in both directions with equal interest and respect. Alternatively stated, and with expressions borrowed from Godfrey Barrett-Lennard (personal communication, September, 2000), with near-psychotic and psychotic clients the focus of the therapist will be on 'the thinking' rather than on 'the thinker' more often than is the case with the ordinary, and less disturbed, client population of CCT. This is no surprise, when one considers how easily these clients are overwhelmed and over-stimulated and disposed to process their experiences, particularly their emotionally disturbing experiences, in psychotic ways.

The following example (factual content has, again, been changed for reasons of confidentiality) illustrates how the therapist follows the client up and down the levels of experiencing with no effort to direct the client to a deeper level of experiencing. The client is diagnosed with a borderline condition with paranoid features and was admitted to hospital after a suicide attempt that was his reaction to his first girlfriend, ever, breaking up their relationship. Formally he was a voluntary client, but a lot of pressure was put on him, from his father and his GP, to make him accept hospitalisation and it was also after a lot of persuasion from staff members that he started to see the therapist. In the session from which the excerpt is taken, he has been considering the possibility of writing a letter to his girlfriend, when he stops talking and looks down to the floor, his face turned a little away from the therapist. The therapist has no idea of what is going on in

329

his mind and remains silent. Finally, he looks up and evidently focuses his gaze on some photos on the wallboard in the therapist's office.

T: *You look at the photos.*

C: *Yes, is it your dog?*

T: *Yes.*

C: *It looks sweet.*

T: *It is very sweet.*

C: *It's a beagle, isn't it? (Seemingly, pleased that he knows).*

T: *Yes ... feel pleased to be able to recognise it?*

C: *Yes ... We used to have a basset; I did a lot of obedience training with him. Have you done that?*

T: *Oh, yes, if you don't do that with a beagle, it is just all over the place.*

C (*Laughing*): *Just like with a basset. (Falling silent again, and looking down on the floor. Then he looks at the therapist.)*

C: *Do you know what incest is?*

T: *I know what the word means, but I'm not quite sure if that is what you are asking me?*

C: *(Quickly looking away from the therapist and down to the floor again): Yes ... No, incest is many things, isn't it?*

T: *Yes. (The therapist feels that she has lost contact with Johnny again)*

(Client remains motionless and silent for a while; then he looks out of the window.)

T: *You look out of the window.*

C: *Yes, (looking at the therapist again) aren't you disturbed by all that noise from the birds? (A colony of crows in the big trees outside)*

T: *No, not really, I'm so used to them, I seldom notice.*

C: You know, I … I don't know … that question about incest … I don't know.

T: There is something about incest bothering you, and maybe it is too hard to talk about?

C: Yes. (Falls silent, seemingly thoughtful)

C (Very quickly and abruptly, almost spitting it out): It is about my father and maybe it was incest, I don't know, I don't want to talk about it.

T: You just want me to know that you are troubled by something your father has done that maybe was incest, and you don't want to go into any details about it?

C (With evident relief): Right, maybe later, I just wanted you to know that this is part of the picture, too.

T: It's a relief that I know there are such things bothering you, too, and that you are not obliged to tell me any details about it?

C: A huge relief and maybe we can talk more about it next time?

T: We sure can.

After a short silence, the client turned to other, much less emotionally provocative and more 'shallow' subjects. He didn't return to the issue of incest until three sessions later, when he associated to the topic after having told how he had had to give up his plan of watching television in the lounge, because the only seat left was next to a male nurse on a small sofa.

The approach of the therapist in this excerpt is non-directive both with respect to content and with respect to process. The therapist does not aim to deepen the client's level of experience by systematically responding with 'additive empathy' or empathy for 'edge of awareness experiences'. The client is in full charge of the direction of the process towards flattening or deepening his level of experience, and the therapist follows the client with equal interest and acceptance in talking about client experiences of dogs and birds as in talking about client experiences of incest. This therapist's approach is, clearly, not an in-depth exploratory approach and it is, therefore, not a potentially harmful approach with people diagnosed with severe psychopathology—on the contrary, as I have already stated.

5. THE CONFUSION OF THE THEORY OF THERAPY WITH THE THEORY OF PERSONALITY

Rogers explains psychopathology as the result of more or less excessive exposure to conditions of worth (see, for example, Rogers, 1959). Present-day psychiatry, on the contrary, favors biological explanations for, particularly, the more serious psychological disturbances, i.e. the disturbances of people diagnosed with a psychotic or near-psychotic (so-called ' borderline') condition. To the degree it is assumed that a conviction of the truth of Rogers' theory of personality, including his explanatory theory of psycho-pathology, is a necessary prerequisite for practicing CCT, to that degree is it also true that CCT cannot be considered useful with the patients of 'heavy psychiatry'. At least not when viewed from the point of view of 'heavy psychiatry'. And when viewed from the point of view of those client-centred therapists who regard Rogers' explanation of psychopathology as the infallible truth, there will be a battle of 'who is right' with representatives of the psychiatric establishment.

It is my contention, however, that one does not need to be convinced of the truth of Rogers' explanatory theory of psychopathology in order to practice CCT. One only has to be convinced that offering the core conditions to the client is the best one can do, as a psychotherapist, to facilitate actualisation of the client's most constructive potentials. The actualisation of these constructive potentials may have been blocked for a variety of reasons, or the potentials, as such, may have been diminished permanently for a variety of reasons. The reasons may be biological, psychological, cultural, or whatever, but this is of no real consequence to the actual practice of CCT.

In this connection it is important not to regard CCT as a curative treatment on a par with medical-model treatments. People with severe somatic illnesses or handicaps benefit from CCT in the sense that they find better ways to live with their illness or handicap; they do not benefit in the sense that they are cured of their illness or handicap. This is, to a certain degree, also the case with many clients diagnosed with a psychotic condition. CCT is useful to them, but not in the sense that they are cured of a presumed biological disposition to process stressful events in psychotic ways, but rather in the sense that they become better able to protect themselves against stress-factors that used to release a psychotic breakdown. With these clients, CCT can be regarded as a preventive, rather than curative, treatment.

There exists, in my experience, no theory that in a fully satisfying way explains the existence of the so-called psychotic conditions, particularly those of schizophrenia and manic-depression. It is not even certain that these conditions do exist as discrete illnesses. I do not believe that Rogers' explanatory theory of psychopathology (excessive exposure to conditions of worth) goes all the way to tell the full story of how psychological disturbances come about, although I think it goes a long way in that direction. I think that other factors play a role, too: socio-economic factors, educational factors and, of course, cultural factors that are important for the definition of what a given culture regards as psychopathological behaviour. Finally, I can't disregard what to me seems to be convincing evidence that biological factors play a role, too, although they, in my opinion, play a more peripheral role than they are given by biologically-oriented psychiatrists. Taken together, I think that the factors that determine what the psychiatry of Western societies regard as psychopathological behaviour are many and are complexly intertwined.

In spite of the predominance of interest in biological etiological factors in modern psychiatry, psychiatry also takes environmental factors into account in the so-called stress/vulnerability model. This model hypothesises that there exists in the individual a more or less pronounced disposition (hereditary and biological) to react with psychosis, or depression, when under psychological/environmental stress; i.e. when the conditions of the milieu of the person are too frustrating or burdening for the person to cope with. In this way, many psychiatrists today try to circumvent the 'nature/nurture' conflict by saying that it is a question of both; sometimes 'nature' is more pronounced than 'nurture', sometimes it is the other way around. This model corresponds quite well to my own experience that CCT with clients diagnosed with psychosis sometimes seems to result in a cure (more nurture than nature is probably involved); sometimes in better adaptation to an illness (more nature than nurture is probably involved). This, though, does not diminish my critical attitude to the predominance of the medical model in today's psychiatric establishment, as such. (See Chapter 8 for this author's discussion of the role of the critique of psychiatry in the client-centred therapist's daily work in the medical-model setting of a psychiatric hospital.)

Whatever theory of psychopathology and personality one adheres to is, as already stated, inconsequential as far as the practice of CCT is concerned. To the degree CCT helps clients process experiences in more constructive ways, it will also help clients process experiences in less psychotic ways, even if a disposition to respond with psychotic ideation under stress is more or less biologically determined. Furthermore, and also in the face of a biological disposition, Rogers' explanation of psychotic breakdown may well go a long way to explain why the individual client responds to one particular stressor, and not to others, with psychotic ideation. In CCT the client can find ways to handle individual 'risk-factors' so they become less risky. None of this is, fundamentally, different from the process with other clients: the positive changes that take place during a course of client-centred therapy make all clients less vulnerable to the psychological 'risk-factors' of their life, whether the risk is psychoses or something else.

Thus, confusing Rogers' theory of therapy with Rogers' theory of personality by regarding a conviction of the latter to be a prerequisite for practicing the former propagates the myth, at least in psychiatric circles, that CCT is not useful for clients diagnosed with conditions that are, in these circles, regarded as predominantly biologically determined, particularly the conditions diagnosed as schizophrenia and manic-depression. That it doesn't promote good communication between client-centred circles and psychiatric circles either, is another matter that is worth mentioning because it is probably an important reason that not more client-centred therapists are employed in psychiatry, although CCT is, in my experience, the only psychotherapeutic approach that can 'reach' the clients of 'heavy psychiatry'. I will give my reasons for this statement in the following and concluding section of this chapter.

6. REACHING THE UNREACHABLE

It is common practice in other schools of psychotherapy to regard people with the most severe psychological disturbances as being 'beyond psychotherapeutic reach'. The basic reason for this is that these therapeutic approaches normally demand some degree of cooperation from the potential client apart from this person allowing the therapist to make a 'perceived or subceived difference' (Rogers, 1959: 207) in his/her experiential field. At the very least, therapists of other approaches depend on experiencing a minimal degree of client ability to and interest in: (1) keeping a sustained focus of attention, (2) making him or herself understood by the therapist, (3) changing something about him or herself and (4) receiving and processing input/interventions from the therapist's frame. For various reasons, though, therapists will not have these experiences with many of the patients in the backyards of psychiatry. Floridly psychotic patients do rarely keep a sustained focus for any substantial length of time; withdrawn, so-called autistic, patients seem without any wish that others shall understand anything about them; people diagnosed with delusions of persecution apparently don't feel in need of help to change anything about themselves, they feel in need of having the relevant authorities put a halt to the persecution; people diagnosed with delusions of grandeur seem to think that it is everybody else who is in need of their help, not the other way around; people diagnosed with a psychotic depression seem so depleted of energy and hope that they can't contribute with anything in a therapeutic relationship; and, finally, people diagnosed with a manic psychosis feel happily elated without any worries they might wish a therapist's help with. And the groups mentioned are all either incapable of, or uninterested in, receiving input/interventions from the therapist's frame. Since these are people whose behaviour is often within the area of applicability of laws of use of force in psychiatry, they are frequently involuntarily admitted to hospital and involuntarily treated with medication. Offers of help from psychiatry that they are free to refuse, like, for example, psychotherapy, they normally do refuse.

Of course, this list is a crude generalisation. It is stereotypical and leaves out all the nuances and individual degrees of variation with respect to the stereotype. Yet, in these stereotypes lie the reasons these patients are normally considered 'beyond psychotherapeutic reach'. They are, however, not beyond reach of CCT, often in combination with Pre-Therapy (see, Pörtner, 2000; Prouty, Van Werde and Pörtner, 2002).

According to my experience, the reason for this is the non-directive attitude of the client-centred therapist and pre-therapist. This therapist makes no particular interventions in the hope that they will be helpful to the client. Of course, the therapist hopes that the relationship, in general, will benefit the client, but in a very basic sense he or she meets the client with an offer of interest rather than with an offer of help. The therapist tries to experience the client's momentary psychological landscape as the client experiences it; he or she has no wish to change the client in any way, only to get to know the client to the degree the client allows it. The patients described above are usually hypersensitive to other peoples' wishes to change them, and when they sense such wishes in another they typically react with resistance and withdrawal. They do not normally resist or withdraw, though, when they are approached with a sincere interest in their experiences and points of view. In this case they may put a limit to the contact because they have better things to do than being with the therapist, not because they are resistive or fearful of the contact, as such. And in many cases, they welcome the therapist's interest and some end up wishing the contact to continue because they feel helped by it and want further help. At this point the relationship has developed into an ordinary client-centred therapy relationship that is motivated by the client's wish for help as much, or more, than by the therapist's interest in the client.

A continuous effort at accurate empathic understanding is, by definition, post-dictive as opposed to pre-dictive and the non-directive attitude is a consequence of this. Empathic understanding follows or accompanies the client's moves, it does not anticipate them. I feel convinced this is the reason that CCT can reach the patients in the backyards of psychiatry where other psychotherapeutic approaches cannot. To these people, the client-centred therapist's attitude seems often to be experienced as an oasis in a desert of what they experience as more or less dissimulated, manipulative, over-protective, patronising, or coercive efforts to change them.

It is not the tendency of empathic understanding to stimulate self-exploration and clarification that is appreciated by these people. It is the unconditional interest and positive regard that is transmitted by the therapist's continuous effort at empathic understanding, devoid of any wish to change the client, which is appreciated by them. Only at a later point in the relationship will some of them, but far from all, come to appreciate the opportunity to clarify their psychological landscape that the empathic understanding of the therapist also offers them. As already mentioned, others will terminate the relationship with the therapist because they have found something more attractive to do. And of these, some will return with a request for renewed talks with the therapist at a later time. Client-centred therapists who want to relate with the patients in 'heavy psychiatry' must be flexible with regard to place, schedule, who takes the initiative in the contact, and the length of the relationship. They must also know about Pre-Therapy.

The therapists in the Wisconsin Project couldn't know of Pre-Therapy. Had they known, I feel convinced they would have been better able to remain more consistently in a non-directive empathic process with their clients and that the results of the research would have come closer to the positive results of Prouty's research (ibid: 44–6). The contact reflections of Pre-Therapy respond to these clients' expressiveness on the extraordinarily concrete level that is often appropriate with clients diagnosed with severe psychopathology. It is the addition of Pre-Therapy to my ordinary client-centred approach that has enabled me to relate with the patients in psychiatry who seem most 'out of contact' in a non-imposing, non-intruding, non-demanding, unconditionally acceptant way. The contact reflections of Pre-Therapy help me meet these patients where they are, in a way that, to me, feels truly person-centred. With most clients today, I fluctuate rather effortlessly between the ordinary empathic understanding responses of CCT and the contact reflections of Pre-Therapy depending on the variations I experience in the client's degree of being 'in contact' or 'out of contact'. (See also Sommerbeck, 2003: 68–84.)

CONCLUSION

It is, thus, not only a myth that CCT is not useful with clients diagnosed with severe psychopathology; it is the opposite of the truth. CCT is eminently suited for these clients and with the extension of Pre-Therapy, CCT can reach patients in the most remote corners in the backyards of psychiatry. The psychiatric nurses who participate in a training group in Pre-Therapy that I facilitate where I work, do not, as is normally the case, ask: 'Is this patient too disturbed to benefit from the approach?' On the contrary, they ask: 'Is this patient too *little* disturbed to benefit from the approach?' I feel touched by this because it is evidence to me that finally, there has been found an approach that makes it possible to reach the unreachable, an approach for those who are worst off, not another approach for those who are best off.

REFERENCES

Bozarth, JD (1998) *Person-Centered Therapy: A revolutionary paradigm*. Ross-on-Wye: PCCS Books.

Hart, JT and Tomlinson, TM (eds) (1970) *New Directions in Client-Centered Therapy*. Boston: Houghton Mifflin.

Mearns, D and Thorne, B (1999) *Person-Centred Counselling in Action*. London: Sage Publications.

Pörtner, M (2000) *Trust and Understanding: The person-centred approach to everyday care for people with special needs*. Ross-on-Wye, UK: PCCS Books.

Prouty, G (1994) *Theoretical Evolutions in Person-Centered/Experiential Therapy: Applications to Schizophrenic and Retarded Psychoses*. Westport: Praeger.

Prouty, G, Van Werde, D and Pörtner, M (2002) *Pre-Therapy: Reaching contact-impaired clients*. Ross-on-Wye: PCCS Books.

Raskin, N (1988) What do we mean by Person-Centred Therapy? Paper presented at the meeting of the Second Association for the Development of the Person-Centred Approach, New York.

Rogers, CR (1951) *Client-Centered Therapy*. Boston: Houghton Mifflin.

Rogers, CR (1959) A theory of therapy, personality, and interpersonal relationships as developed in the client-centered framework. In E Koch (ed) *Psychology: A study of a science, Vol. 3*. New York: McGraw-Hill.

Rogers, C, Gendlin, E, Kiesler, D and Truax, CB (1967) *The Therapeutic Relationship with Schizophrenics*. Wisconsin: The University of Wisconsin Press.

Sachse, R (1990) Concrete interventions are crucial: The influence of the therapists processing proposals on the client's intrapersonal exploration in Client-Centered Therapy. In G Lietaer, J Rombauts and R Van Balen (eds) *Client-Centered and Experiential Psychotherapy in the Nineties* (pp. 295–308). Leuven: Leuven University Press.

Shlien, JM (1992) Theory as Autobiography: The man and the movement. *Contemporary Psychology, 37*, No. 10. Reprinted in JM Shlien (2003) *To Lead an Honorable Life: Invitations to think about client-centered therapy and the person-centered approach* (pp. 212–16). Ross-on-Wye: PCCS Books.

Sommerbeck, L (2002) The Wisconsin Watershed—Or the universality of CCT. *The Person-Centered Journal, 9*, 140–57.

Sommerbeck, L (2003) *The Client-Centred Therapist in Psychiatric Contexts: A therapists' guide to the psychiatric landscape and its inhabitants*. Ross-on-Wye: PCCS Books.

Vitger, J (1999) Kurative Faktorer ved Psykoanalytiske Terapier. *Matrix, 3*, 200.

CHAPTER 22

SMALL-SCALE RESEARCH AS PERSONAL DEVELOPMENT FOR MENTAL HEALTH PROFESSIONALS[1]

RICHARD WORSLEY

Previously (Chapter 10, this volume) I argued that it is necessary for mental health workers to face within themselves the feelings and consequences, the undertow, of working with their clients' psychopathology. It is tempting to feign a sort of professional competence that seems to view objectively the client and their way of being. Clients have a real impact upon us. From time to time this impact will be major. Some psychopathological patterns are more difficult than others for any given individual to face. True professionalism involves developing the personal awareness to process these issues within us, lest they become stumbling blocks. In this chapter, I will demonstrate a model of small-scale, phenomenological research as a route to developing personal awareness. I will describe an encounter with a person who has known what it is to be anorexic; set out my initial responses to her; show how these develop and change within a two-hour encounter; in doing this, argue that even experienced therapists need to work upon their awareness of the impact of clients' presenting material upon them.

This chapter is a personal account of my encounter with Janet.[2] I had become aware that I felt discomfort at working with people with anorexia. This discomfort had a quality that suggested I needed to reflect in depth upon it. Janet, who has known anorexia for a number of years, was willing to engage with me in this reflection. I sought her permission to do this, with the aim of facing the demon of my own apprehension. Psychopathology is personal just because we who are person-centred practitioners encounter others, as best we can, from the depths of our being.

Mature, person-centred practitioners have had to develop a particular ability to be in tune with the phenomenal reality of their clients. We think phenomenologically, and strive to be aware of the impact of encounter upon us. Dave Mearns (1997: 151–2) has argued cogently that experientially-based research should be part of an extended period of counsellor development beyond the formal diploma training, in order to advance person-centred theory. Small-scale research can advance theory, but certainly can be a

---

1. This chapter was previously published in a slightly different version as 'Small is Beautiful: Small-scale phenomenological research for counsellor self-development'. *Person-Centered and Experiential Psychotherapies*, 2, 121–32. The chapter has thus been fully refereed in line with the policy of that journal.

2. Janet is not the co-researcher's real name. This article, in a previous version, has been seen by Janet and full and informed permission has been given for its use.

crucial element in the personal and professional development of the counsellor. It is part of the characteristic genius of the Person-Centred/Experiential Approach that its practitioners have, as an aspect of their daily experience of therapy, an immersion in phenomenological practice.

PERSONAL DEVELOPMENT AS RESEARCH

The present project is an exploration of unconditional positive regard, of the quality of my relating. Martin Buber's (1958) work, *I and Thou* is one of the foundation documents of the philosophical underpinning for being person-centred. Buber distinguishes between two primary categories of experiencing relationship. The I-It reduces the other to a mere object, a thing, that which can be used. By contrast the I-Thou acknowledges that the other is a self like the subject. Counsellors are committed in their daily work to the nurturing of the I-Thou relationship. I suggest that small-scale phenomenological research is truer to the I-Thou relationship. This is an ethical commitment, and one that is at the heart of person-centred thinking. To research through experiential learning is attractive to me just because it resonates with the core activity of therapy, to which I commit my professional life. This paper sees experiencing-as-learning as firmly rooted in the I-Thou relationship. How this sits within the family of phenomenological research methods will be briefly addressed below.

I suggest that, in small-scale work, researching through the familiar I-Thou relationship can release the practitioner into confident action learning. The researcher is a stakeholder in her own effort because its outcomes feed back to the daily practice of her art. When research focuses upon practitioner self-development, there is a deepening awareness of the very experience of learning, change and consequent improved practice. The remainder of this paper offers one such project by way of example.

A PERSONAL DILEMMA—A QUESTION IN ITS CONTEXT

Practice-based research begins with practice-based questions. I find that one practice issue comes round to haunt me. I struggle to accord unconditional positive regard to people with anorexia. I feel most uncertain that, in terms of others' bodies, small is beautiful. I need to learn and to grow.

In September 2002, I met Janet at a college reception. Grasping food and drink in our hands, I swiftly discovered something—but not much—of her life-journey, and of her consequent research into Christian pastoral care of those with eating disorders. I expressed my interest in what she was doing. I experienced myself as genuinely interested, but not at all willing to say what I felt about anorexia (which is to say, Janet herself). I felt incongruent, and that was painful.

Janet offered to talk further with me about her work. I contacted her to request two hours of her time, so that I could explore in that context the issues that face me. I felt aware that I might be using her—and indeed the language of co-researcher is about the possibility of exploitation. Her informed consent is crucial to me, but does not alleviate my anxiety that, in meeting Janet, I will meet difficult aspects of myself.

THE ETHICS OF PERSONAL ENCOUNTER

To encounter another human being is to take a risk, not least when that person is vulnerable. In fact, in my encounter with Janet, both of us were vulnerable, but in different ways. I was acutely aware of her vulnerabilities that had led her to become anorexic, but equally aware of my limited positive regard for her in the first instance. Both point to ethical issues. It would seem most unwise for one person who believes another person to be a problem for them, to blithely construct a meeting in which the co-researcher's vulnerability is open to the researcher's lack of positive regard.

It is simply not possible to work with a vulnerable co-researcher at random. In meeting Janet, I already knew that she had used her experience both for her own research and for subsequent teaching within faith communities. Her work with me was similar to other things she chose to do as part of her calling. Janet's strengths made it meaningful and safe to invite her to be a co-researcher. It was important to me throughout this, to discuss the whole project with one of my supervisors, who herself has a psychotherapy research qualification.

I contracted verbally with Janet to meet with me for two hours, and then to review what I wrote from that. Her background in research and teaching was evidence that the consent she offered was both informed and genuine. At the end of the encounter, and after the writing of the first draft of this paper, Janet knew that she had the right to withdraw totally from the project. On each occasion, I had consent from her, on the first, verbally, but on the second in written form. I have subsequently updated her on the review and redrafting process.

METHODOLOGY

In essence, my method of exploration, as a person-centred practitioner, is to reflect on who I am in the light of my fear of working with people with anorexia, and then to meet both Janet and her research experience in order to investigate/instigate change. I am exploring the darker side of me in a research environment, so that I may work safely with clients with anorexia, as I need to. I want to engage in meeting with Janet, and to record systematically my awarenesses both before and after that encounter. This record, reflection and narrative, will constitute the second half of this paper. Stated thus, my methodology feels simplicity itself. It is congruent with a person-centred way of being. My aim is to meet with Janet with as little encumbrance as possible. I do not want to record and analyse our meeting. I seek to explore its meaning as it is manifested in the Me who exists before and after it.

I construe the issue as being about unconditional positive regard. It is not that I fail to offer this to people with anorexia. Rather, it is that I see before me an anorexic rather than a Thou (Buber, 1958). In the face of anorexia, I abstain to some unacceptable degree from encounter, from the Other. While I affirm, with Purton (1998), that all human beings are of absolute worth, I opt in the face of anorexia not to live this out. I am failing to acknowledge the very being of those who happen to have anorexia. The philosophical basis of acceptant responding has been spelled out by Peter Schmid (2002), who draws our attention in particular to the thought of Emmanuel Levinas:

> In his main work *Totalité et Infini* Levinas (1961) points out that to exist means to be entangled in oneself, caught in the totality of one's own world. According to Levinas the first alienation of the human being is not being able to get rid of oneself. ... [T]he awakening from the totality of the being-caught-in-oneself does not happen through 'being independent'. Rather, the Other is the power which liberates the I from oneself. (Schmid, 2002: 53)

My seeing some people as primarily anorexic, rather than as Thou, is a caughtness-in-myself. Active learning is a seeking the Other. I am not initially aware of why I carry these feelings, but I make a first guess, in the light of Rogers' (1961) description of what it is to move towards full functionality in process terms, that I am mis-symbolising. The Other who will liberate the I from myself will likely cause me to resymbolise anorexia to a sufficient degree. I note Orbach's argument (1993: 3–11) that anorexia is a powerful metaphor for our times. In what sense is it a powerfully misconstrued meaning for me?

My initial intuition, then, had been that I needed to resymbolise my engaging with people with anorexia, so as to reconstrue the multiple meanings of this for me. Phenomenological research methodologies offer a range of possibilities. (Moustakas, 1994: 1–22). However, my conceptualisation of the research process had been naïve, based upon two tools that were familiar to me. I set out below these two procedures, and then a *post factum* critical reflection upon their use.

My first procedural tool was Moustakas' (1994: 84–101) procedure, based on Husserl's transcendental phenomenology. This procedure falls into four movements: bracketing (epoché), reduction, imaginative variation and synthesis. I had used it previously with a larger scale piece of work, but was aware of its limitations on the smaller scale. The aim is to reach a brief, phenomenological account of a particular experience, usually across a number of co-researchers. Thus the method might look for the commonalities amongst a number of bereaved people. It seeks to set out the structure and the texture of their experience. The four stages are as follows:

1. *Bracketing*. The researcher seeks to become aware of her own prejudices, by stating them as clearly as possible. Husserl believed that they could be removed by making them fully open to the researcher. This is rather optimistic. Limited awareness is as much as can be hoped for.
2. *Reduction*. The experience of a number of interviews, for example, can be reduced to a number of key themes. The researcher aims to describe each experience just as it is.

In practice, this involves the identifying of 'horizons'—the limits of core experience, and to remove duplication and irrelevancies.

3. *Imaginative variation*. The phenomenological truth is as much within the subject's grasp as within the 'out-there' world. Therefore, new understanding emerges as the researcher allows her imagination to experiment with the material derived from the reduction.

4. *Synthesis*. A complete account of the structure and texture of the experience is given. Husserl had seen this as a final truth. The more sceptical amongst us may well doubt that such a thing can be.

I abbreviated the Moustakas procedure by using time before my interview with Janet to reflect on my prejudices as a flow-of-consciousness exercise (bracketing) and then, after the interview itself, I reported to myself and recorded my immediate experience of recalling my encounter with Janet. In this, I combined the reduction with the imaginative variation—made possible by the smallness of scale of the project. I omitted the synthesis, partly because I doubt Husserl's claim that such a truth is available to us, but partly because my attention was focused upon my awareness of my own process and values. This shift of attention suggests that the Moustakas method is not a complete account of what I actually did. (See below.)

David Kolb's (1984) cycle of experiential learning formed the other conceptual tool. Kolb's cycle consists of a four-phase process, which can be entered at any point, and which can be repeated at will. The phases are:

- Concrete experience. What is happening?
- Reflective observation. What did happen?
- Abstract conceptualisation. What does it mean?
- Active experimentation. What shall I do (be) as a result?

(Kolb, as summarised by Dainow and Bailey, 1988: 6)

The project can be conceptualised as three circuits of the Kolb cycle of experiential learning:

1. Experience my formulation of the question from practice. Reflect upon the texture and structure of this formulation. Lay open—acknowledge and own, or bracket and remove—its theoretical preconceptions. Integrate the methodology as action within the project.

2. (the overall bracketing): Enter as deeply as possible into my experiencing of my fear of working with people with anorexia. Reflect upon the texture and structure of that experience. Theoretise the experience in terms of what it would be for me to meet the Other without undue mis-symbolisation. Integrate this bracketing-off into an encounter with Janet and her research.

3. Meet with Janet. Reflect upon the nature of that meeting for me. Theoretise this in terms of my resymbolisation of such encounters. Integrate this into practice by a summarising of my position as a starting point for any experience with an anorexic client.

341

LOCATING THE METHODOLOGY

The origin of this project was in life setting me a question about how I engaged as a therapist with people with anorexia. With some naïvety, I had allowed the question itself to dictate the methodology. I had used two tools with which I was familiar—Moustakas' procedure based on transcendental phenomenology, supplemented by Kolb's description of experiential learning. On reflection, I had done what I would do all over again, but it is only in the process of further reflection that I have located a more organised rationale for my way of working with Janet.

Formally, three approaches to phenomenological research are represented within what I did. Transcendental phenomenology is at the root of the process, in that I was already familiar with Moustakas' method. However, I altered this procedure in two ways. I put together the reduction with the imaginative variation. In part this was simply a matter of economy of scale. In such a limited project there is no good reason to rigidly separate these. However, this change, I now realise, shows a distrust within me for the rigidity of Husserl's conceptualisation of phenomenology. I was finally not interested in a methodologically pure statement of a phenomenological truth. I was interested in changing. I wanted to increase my positive regard for a particular client group.

I have come to recognise that my commitment was to a combination of heuristic and hermeneutical research. Moustakas (1990: 27) defines heuristic research in terms of six processes: initial engagement, immersion, incubation, illumination, explication and culmination. I find that what I did approximates to these. However, what I truly own is the underlying rationale:

> The deepest currents of meaning and knowledge take place within the individual through one's senses, perceptions, beliefs, and judgments. This requires a passionate, disciplined commitment to remain with the question intensely and continuously until it is illuminated or answered.
>
> (Moustakas, 1990: 15)

Although my conscious research procedure was derived from transcendental phenomenology, my dissatisfactions, which had caused me to modify the procedure, stemmed from a set of values largely in tune with heuristic principles.

I have also come to recognise that my belief, influenced by Rogers' process conception, that I was limiting my positive regard because I was mis-symbolising anorexia, also pushed me towards a hermeneutic turn. I was interested above all in the meaning of my experience and of Janet's for me. I wanted to change by finding new meaning within the metaphors of experience. I find myself resonating with the following passage of Paul Ricoeur's:

> The subject who interprets himself while interpreting signs is no longer the *cogito* ... he is a being who discovers exegesis of his own life, that he is placed in being before ... he possesses himself. In this way hermeneutics would discover a manner of existing which would remain from start to finish a *being-interpreted*. (Ricoeur, 1989: 11; original italics)

Ricoeur's perspective offers us the vision of a self that is continually in search of meaning through self-interpretation. When practitioner research has the courage to focus upon the being of the researcher-as-subject, there emerges a researcher who is nearer to the deeply human way of being required of a therapist.

BRACKETING

A week prior to meeting Janet, I reviewed my stance with my supervisor as an initial act of bracketing. Two days before our meeting, I spent half an hour making notes of my subjective flow of experience while focusing on the topic of this research. The following themes emerged. I have no sense that they connect or are ordered in any particular fashion, but rather that they represent a selection of significant symbolisations from a free-flowing reflection or meditation:

- A former tutor told me that people with anorexia cannot be counselled. I respect her opinions generally.
- Defiance is a key feeling. People with anorexia dare me to face their dying. They defy rescue.
- I become angry, helpless and vulnerable in the face of their defiance.
- They self harm. (But other forms of self-harm do not worry me as much.)
- Is it OK to let you die? Will you die? I do not know.
- It is so *visible*. Everyone will see my failure as a therapist. I feel shame.
- The thinness reminds me of terminal cancer. My partner used to be a hospice chaplain. The staff always ate well to avoid thinness.
- As a therapist I image myself as a provider. Am I rejected with the food? (Bulimia is OK?)
- All the while, frailty leaves *me* feeling attacked.
- My own (healthy and plump) body image becomes embarrassing—like drinking in front of an alcoholic.
- I cannot imagine the distress that leads to self-starvation.
- I work happily with addictions, but this seems like the very opposite. A not needing a thing. Why is that not OK?
- The anorexic body's image challenges my reality. I struggle for empathy. The schizophrenic's reality fascinates me, but not the anorexic's.
- As a person-centred practitioner can I trust the actualising tendency of a self-starving human being? It felt as if the destructive urge might put an end to her fulfilment of her potential. This would be a view wholly at odds with my normal feelings about clients.
- It feels like trauma. I need to give up any notion of cure. There is an existential reality. How do people live healthily with anorexia? (Is this a shift, or a head-defence?)
- Can I form an alliance if I do not trust?
- Will my interest in Janet harm her? Can I protect her? Is that my job? Can I trust her to look after herself?

343

These notes are all I have before meeting Janet to resymbolise. They echo with associations and possible interpretations. The act of bracketing has left me feeling warmer. This feels like a vague awareness that no amount of reflection will substitute for meeting.

MEETING

Janet and I met for two hours. We agreed boundaries around confidentiality and Janet's right to see and change the final text of this project, or to withdraw from it completely. The day after the meeting I made notes in another act of free-flowing reflection. I deliberately left a short time for the experience of meeting to settle, and for a meaning-constructing process to happen within me. I note that, unlike more objective research, the resultant forgetting and recalling seems important. I hypothesise that the settling down involves a forgetting of surface detail in order to become more aware of felt-meaning (Gendlin, 1997).

My first awareness on sitting down was of my being challenged by Janet as to what in me had this particular need to understand anorexia as if it were an alien territory. Far from feeling threatened—as I might, for I wondered this about me too—I felt a great sense of comfort. I knew at the time as well as on reflection two truths. Firstly, the firm, gentle congruence of the challenge told me that I was in the company of someone who could well look after herself. My anxiety that Janet might need protecting from my curiosity abated. From a practice perspective, I look now for those parts of the fragile client that need none of my protection. There is admittedly a major difference between Janet as a vigorous individual who happens to be in recovery from an eating disorder, and some clients who are, or seem to be, genuinely very fragile. Yet, being aware of, and simultaneously letting go of fragility seems as though it might be crucial to respect. Secondly, I noted that my underlying anxiety was well outside of Janet's frame of reference. My apprehension in the face of anorexia is not at all an obvious or universal construct. Anorexia can be part of ordinary living. In response to her challenge I talked of the tutor who had said that people with anorexia cannot be counselled, and dwelt on the impact this had on me. Yet, it felt defensive. Whatever the impact, there was more to it than that.

A second challenge came. How did I know that Janet had been anorexic? I resisted a fleck of defensiveness in me. I was completely perplexed. Had she not told me? Had I heard elsewhere? Was it not obvious? Why? On reflection, Janet shows no longer any signs how she might have been anorexic in the past. I have no answer to the literal question, but from it comes a sense of Janet's need to have control of her identity, a right to her personal boundaries. It would be easy to pathologise such a need. Is it any different from parallel needs in me? I suspect not.

All the while, I am aware now of my ambivalent feelings about what I was feeling. Was I listening to elements of control in Janet, or to my own fearful defendedness? I am reminded of the observation of Sheldon Cashdan (1988: 154–8) that the difference between therapeutic and personal counter-transference is not knowable with certainty.

There must be practised vigilance. I guess that my meeting with Janet will facilitate this in me in the years to come.

Before Janet and I had sat down together, she had expressed both an interest in counselling and a belief that person-centred work would be really valuable for people with anorexia. In conversation, this developed into an image about counselling being more difficult 'below the line'. The image is of a graph of the client's functionality. I needed to explore that in some depth. It spoke to a deep fear within me, about working beyond my competence and not knowing it—and perhaps of more than that. Janet clarified for me that when the body is weakest, special care must be taken to work in a way that avoids physical exhaustion. Within myself, I heard a distinct internal comment: So, it is not that 'below the line', psychological contact is absent (Rogers, 1957). It is sometimes the case that the question or fear only surfaces when the answer is in reach. At the level of practice I will be loathe to doubt psychological contact without due evidence.

I am aware of the nature of Janet's personal story and her telling of it. She affirmed that she had needed to face deep issues within herself. Neither of us needed to talk about these. I profoundly do not know what they are or were for her, save that there is an element around control. At the surface level, this is simply a question of respect between co-researchers. Underneath, I began to feel my ability to live with the unsaid of clients. Janet spoke of her experience of a directive and abusive GP, and her sense of the need for openness and non-directivity. This she had found in the eating disorders unit she had attended. My underlying feeling was of warm acceptance. This was a strong and irrational sensation.

On reflection, my growing sense of acceptance, the fading of my fear of the unknown, as I became more actively able to grant Janet her space, suggests to me that I have struggled with people with anorexia because their selves, their bodies, tend to be for me a metaphor of a largely irrational threat to my being with them. It is as if the therapy itself might starve. This too has been a strong and irrational sensation.

Talking about Janet's research could constitute for each of us a defence against the exploration we were committed to—a flight into the head. Yet, for me, even this aspect of our conversation was part of our I-Thou encounter.

The remainder of the conversation was a meandering between the personal—on both sides—and the research. From it five themes emerged for me. As I write I am aware of the selectiveness of this. Again, the learning is what emerges for me rather than an objective account. The first theme lives in the mental picture of Janet holding a chalice (cup) at the Eucharist. (Janet is training for the Christian ministry. At the heart of her being a priest will be her blessing and sharing with others bread and wine, symbolising the body and blood of Jesus Christ. Even to receive bread and wine has been a massive effort, a striving to confront fear at the very point where peace is hoped for.) It is tough for people with anorexia to share in a rite that requires even a minimal sign of eating. The road to recovery, if well negotiated and understood by the minister of that rite, can include a symbolising of gradual change. The chalice can be held without drinking. This is healing. To the extent that I have mis-symbolised within me elements of the experience of the person with anorexia, I also know that I can symbolise small and gradual elements of recovery, and thus of hope.

Secondly, Janet has made explicit for me a fact I thought I already knew. Anorexia is about protest, at least for her. I can empathise with protest. Thirdly, Janet's awareness that people with anorexia often feel guilt that their condition is seen by others as a *voluntary* illness feels to me the correlate of my judgementalism and fear of aggression, and hence of my own aggression. I can recognise a dynamic that is close to my own unwanted feelings.

Fourthly, I had become fascinated by the fact that addiction, which I deal with more easily, is about a substance. This substance competes with the therapist, but at least it is a clear opponent (Worsley, 2002: 150–6). In anorexia, there is no substance. As therapist I face nothing, as if a void. What is symbolised by me and within me are the feared existential voids. Lastly, I remember with great clarity my puzzlement that Janet said there was a time when she had forgotten how to eat. I explored this, and came gradually to see the texture and structure of her experience. My clients will need to introduce me to those aspects of their experience that, in spite of words, are a long way from me. I come to sense the excitement again of learning from the client, even the client who happens in part of herself to have anorexia.

CONCLUSIONS

The project of my meeting with Janet leads me to a number of personal conclusions. When I allow myself to be curious about who she really is, I move away from a sort of phobic quality in my previous attitude towards those with anorexia. In this I face my aggressive and fearful self, and can begin to empathise with the protest element in anorexia. I notice that anorexic guilt seems to correspond to the punitive element in me. I become prepared to meet others with a different configuration in place. The symbol of protest and the symbol of the Eucharist as a place of experimenting with gradual change each allows me to move towards a re-symbolisation of anorexia for me as a therapist, particularly as I can own and then move away from the non-rational fear that the therapy itself might starve and perish. I appreciate in the case of at least one human being the strong perception that non-directiveness is essential to her recovery. All these and other things yet to emerge are personal outcomes of this research. It is in the act of meeting that I found a new flexibility and responsiveness for my internal models of anorexia, and so become open again to the reality of non-directiveness and acceptance. Meeting opened for me the possibility of a new congruence between my beliefs about my therapeutic practice and my internal experience of encounter.

More generally, this piece of small-scale research illustrates the need for workers to be aware of the detailed impact of clients' presentation upon them; of their response to symptoms and diagnoses rather than persons; of the struggle at times to maintain unconditional positive regard for others in the face of one's own biases and projections. From a person-centred perspective, psychopathology is not an objective science but part of the journey of two individuals together. We meet not cases but others who, sometimes in spite of appearances, are distressingly like us.

REFERENCES

Buber, M (1958) *I and Thou*. Edinburgh: T and T Clark.

Cashdan, S (1988) *Object Relations Therapy: Using the relationship*. New York: WW Norton and Co.

Dainow, S and Bailey, C (1988) *Developing Skills with People*. London: Wiley.

Gendlin, E (1997) *Experiencing and the Creation of Meaning: A philosophical and psychological approach to the subjective*. Evanston, IL: Northwestern University Press.

Kolb, D (1984) *Experiential Learning*. Englewood Cliffs, NJ: Prentice Hall.

Levinas, E (1961) *Totalité et Infini: Essai sur l'extériorité*. Den Haag: Nijhoff.

Mearns, D (1997) *Person-Centred Counselling Training*. London: Sage.

Moustakas, C (1990) *Heuristic Research: Design, methodology and applications*. London: Sage.

Moustakas, C (1994) *Phenomenological Research Methods*. London: Sage.

Orbach, S (1993) *Hunger Strike*. Harmondsworth: Penguin.

Purton, C (1998) Unconditional positive regard and its spiritual implication. In B Thorne and E Lambers (eds) *Person-Centered Therapy: A European Perspective*. London: Sage.

Ricoeur, P (1989) *The Conflict of Interpretations: Essays on hermeneutics*. London: Continuum.

Rogers, CR (1957) The necessary and sufficient conditions of therapeutic personality change. *Journal of Consulting Psychology, 21*, 95–103.

Rogers, CR (1961) A process conception of psychotherapy. In CR Rogers *On Becoming a Person*. London: Constable.

Schmid, PF (2002) Acknowledgement: the art of responding. Dialogical and ethical perspectives on the challenge of unconditional relationships in therapy and beyond. In JD Bozarth and P Wilkins (eds) *Rogers' Therapeutic Conditions: Evolution, theory and practice. Volume 3: Unconditional Positive Regard*. Ross-on-Wye: PCCS Books.

Worsley, RJ (2001) *Process Work in Person-Centred Therapy: Phenomenological and existential perspectives*. Basingstoke: Palgrave.

CHAPTER 23

A POSITIVE PSYCHOLOGY OF MENTAL HEALTH: THE PERSON-CENTRED PERSPECTIVE

STEPHEN JOSEPH AND RICHARD WORSLEY

> The single most important contribution of positive psychology has been to provide a collective identity—a common voice and language for researchers and practitioners from all persuasions who share an interest in health as well as in sickness—in the fulfilment of potential as well as the amelioration of pathology. (Linley and Joseph, 2004a: 4)

For psychologists, the positive psychology movement represents new challenges and new ways of thinking. Positive psychologists are concerned with understanding what leads to well-being, fulfilment, joy, and what it is that makes life worth living, as well as the more traditional concerns of psychologists over what leads to unhappiness, distress, and human suffering. Positive psychology was launched in 1998 with Martin Seligman's presidential address to the American Psychological Association. This was followed in 2000 with the appearance of a special issue of the American Psychological Association journal *American Psychologist* devoted to the topic of positive psychology (see Seligman and Csikszentmihalyi, 2000), and in 2003 with a special issue of the British Psychological Society journal *The Psychologist* (see Linley, Joseph and Boniwell, 2003). Positive psychology is becoming deeply influential on both sides of the Atlantic and the world of psychology is changing fast. The aspiration of the positive psychology movement is that over time this new way of thinking should permeate all aspects of mainstream psychology so that ultimately the word 'positive' might simply fall away leaving the entire discipline transformed, so that all psychologists are positive psychologists.

All this will sound familiar to the person-centred psychologist, counsellor or psychotherapist who will feel uncannily at home in the world of positive psychology. Positive psychology aims to facilitate and not to direct; seeks optimal human functioning in terms of the organismic valuing process, and subjective as well as psychological well-being; rejects the medical model's aspiration to be value-neutral, but rather aims to promote 'the good life', 'good citizenship' and 'valued subjective experience'; expresses a professional interest in the whole range of human experiencing and not just dysfunction (Linley and Joseph, 2004a: 5–6). The person-centred practitioner might even think to themselves that there is nothing new here, but that these key commitments can be traced straight back to the writings of Carl Rogers.

Yet, in particular in the United States, person-centred thinking is very besieged and marginalised. Many positive psychologists will not recognise the origins of their central ideas, and the work of Carl Rogers now goes unnoticed. However, it should be clear from this book that person-centred theory offers an approach which is compatible with the goals of positive psychology.

META-THEORY

Perhaps the most important aspect of the positive psychology movement is that it has forced psychologists to stop and think about the fundamental meta-theoretical assumptions underlying their practice (see Linley and Joseph, 2004b). Martin Seligman has raised important questions about the fundamental assumptions of mainstream psychology:

> There has been a profound obstacle to a science and practice of positive traits and positive states: the belief that virtue and happiness are inauthentic, epiphenomenal, parasitic upon or reducible to the negative traits and states. This 'rotten-to-the-core' view pervades Western thought, and if there is any doctrine positive psychology seeks to overthrow it is this one. Its original manifestation is the doctrine of original sin. In secular form, Freud dragged this doctrine into 20th-century psychology where it remains fashionably entrenched in academia today. For Freud, all of civilization is just an elaborate defence against basic conflicts over infantile sexuality and aggression. (Seligman, 2003: 126)

Having discarded the 'rotten-to-the-core' view of human nature, positive psychologists are now casting around for new ways of conceptualising human nature. Carl Rogers, another past president of the American Psychological Association, also questioned the fundamental assumptions of mainstream psychology, proposing instead the view that human beings are organismically motivated toward developing to their full potential:

> I have little sympathy with the rather prevalent concept that man is basically irrational, and thus his impulses, if not controlled, would lead to destruction of others and self. Man's behavior is exquisitely rational, moving with subtle and ordered complexity toward the goals his organism is endeavoring to achieve. (Rogers, 1969: 29)

Rogers' person-centred theory offers a meta-theoretical perspective on human nature founded on the assumption that human beings have an inherent tendency toward growth, development, and optimal functioning (see Rogers, 1959). But these do not happen automatically. For people to actualise their inherent optimal nature they require the right social environment. Without the right social environment the inherent tendency towards growth can become thwarted and usurped leading instead to psychological distress and dysfunction. This assumption that human beings have an inherent tendency

349

toward growth, development and optimal functioning serves as the guiding principle for client-centred therapeutic practice, even when working with people who are deeply distressed (see Joseph, 2003; Mearns and Thorne, 1999; Worsley, 2002, for general reviews). Although not all positive psychologists yet recognise Rogers' legacy, many do. Sheldon and Elliot (1999), for example, wrote:

> ... along with Rogers (1961), we believe that individuals have innate developmental trends and propensities that may be given voice by an organismic valuing process occurring within them. The voice can be very difficult to hear, but the current research suggests that the ability to hear it is of crucial importance for the pursuit of happiness. (Sheldon and Elliott, 1999: 495)

The positive psychology movement can benefit from the ideas of person-centred theory. These ideas are again being picked up by the positive psychology movement in thinking about mental health and therapeutic practice (see Joseph and Linley, 2004; Joseph and Linley, 2005). Psychopathology and well-being are defined in relation to each other because both are a function of the extent to which self-actualisation is congruent with the actualising tendency (Ford, 1991). When there is greater congruence, greater well-being and more optimal functioning results. But when there is less congruence, greater psychopathology results (see Wilkins, Chapter 4, this volume). Thus, the Person-Centred Approach offers a genuinely positive psychological perspective on mental health because of its unified and holistic focus on both the negative and the positive aspects of human functioning (e.g., see Joseph, Chapter 13, this volume, for a discussion on how person-centred theory provides a theory of growth through adversity compatible with understanding post-traumatic stress).

Accompanying these shifts in meta-theoretical assumptions, many positive psychologists have also adopted a complementary critical psychology perspective, and are beginning to doubt the validity of the medical model for understanding psychopathology (see Maddux, 2002; Maddux, Snyder and Lopez, 2004). The idea that all psychological problems are best understood through the lens of the medical model and require specific treatments is an unfounded assumption (see Bozarth and Motomasa, Chapter 19, this volume). The dominance of the medical model is being seriously challenged from all quarters. It is likely that in the coming decade the discipline of psychology will come to contain a strong voice for the humanisation of professional practice:

> In contrast to the more mechanistic framing of [mental illness] in terms of abnormal brain chemistry or anatomical lesions, the new approach views the patient as a whole person troubled by apparently baffling problems, but also having the resources for ameliorating these problems. (Professor Aaron Beck in Bentall, 2004: xi)

EVIDENCE-BASED PRACTICE

In Britain, the work of Richard Bentall (2004) has deconstructed the categories of schizophrenia and bipolar disorder, seeing human distress as sitting upon a continuum, and as being best described as a series of multi-factorial conditions. This swingeing critique of the medical model comes from within clinical psychology, and is complemented by critical psychology and critical psychiatry (Newnes et al., 1999).

These critics, in turn, continue and augment a tradition of anti-psychiatry, in which the names of R. D. Laing and Thomas Szasz are perhaps the best-known representatives. The earlier work of Laing and Szasz was open to the criticism that it opposed the medical model fervently, but offered little in its place. By contrast this new generation has begun to implement practical and therapeutic work. Loren Mosher's Soteria communities in the United States, Finland and Switzerland, for example, have provided ample evidence of the effectiveness of the treatment of those diagnosed schizophrenic on a low-drug or no-drug regime (Read et al., 2004). In both the USA and Europe, the work of Garry Prouty in working with highly institutionalised psychotic people has motivated a whole way of thinking through person-centred approaches to psychosis and to contact (Prouty et al., 2002; Van Werde, Chapter 11, this volume).

In Britain, the situation is somewhat different, in that the boom in counselling and psychotherapy training since the early 1980s has seen a large, grass-roots growth in person-centred work. This training has mostly happened outside Higher Education in private institutions. Many of the courses in counselling and psychotherapy are excellent, but the fact that they have developed outside the university system has meant that research training aspects have been marginalised and as a consequence counselling and psychotherapy have struggled to compete with clinical psychology and psychiatry in status and the development of their evidence base. Although there has been considerable research within the person-centred tradition in the past (see Barrett-Lennard, 1998), person-centred theory has just not provided a concentrated focus for research over the last thirty years with the consequence that answers to the questions shaped in the current climate of evidence-based practice are not readily available.

As a result the British National Health Service has tended to privilege cognitive-behavioural therapy. The person-centred movement in Britain, in spite of its seeming numerical strength, thus feels threatened by two different phenomena. First, the increasing insistence upon an evidence base for therapy is felt to be an assault upon person-centred values. But why? Often this is because person-centred practitioners are not well trained in scientific research and seeing that empirical research is used by those working in the medical model, such research has become conflated in the minds of many with the medical model. But this is not necessary, the person-centred model makes clear scientifically testable hypotheses, i.e., that people will develop toward optimal functioning under certain social environmental conditions. There is no reason we should not test these predictions empirically. Sanders' chapter, Chapter 3, this volume, is an impassioned plea to fight our corner.

Second, the growth of a large, person-centred counselling movement at grass roots has fed the false belief held by many psychologists and psychiatrists that person-centred counselling is a good idea for the worried well, but that serious psychopathology should be left to the truly competent. There is, of course, a self-fulfilling prophecy to this. As the person-centred movement becomes marginalised from the National Health Service because of these false beliefs, training courses struggle to provide placements and supervision for trainees to work with clients with serious psychopathology. It thus becomes the case that person-centred practitioners are often ill-equipped to work with anyone but the worried well. But, this is not a reflection of the theory that underlies person-centred practice or the potential applicability of Client-Centred Therapy for helping people with serious psychopathology.

Person-centred practice can be its own worst enemy. We can no longer acquiesce in the idea that we are fit only to deal with those with life-event issues. The approach can provide the theory and practice for a large range of mental health services—individual work, group therapy, therapeutic communities, not to mention the philosophy underlying residential social work, as the chapters in this volume testify.

But to be taken seriously by funding bodies influenced by the ideas of evidence-based practice as they are framed through the lens of the medical model, we as person-centred practitioners and theorists can no longer be left saying that we do not have anything to do with psychopathology. We think that the person-centred movement can remain true to its principles and yet develop within itself and with other professionals a conversation about human distress which uses the terminology of other approaches but which challenges others to take on board the radical and revolutionary critique of the medical model which flows from person-centred theory, and also from positive psychology and the critical psychology and psychiatry movements. We do need to define our assessment procedures (e.g., Wilkins, Chapter 9, this volume). We do need to describe our own use of models of dysfunction (e.g., Warner, Chapter 7, this volume). Above all we need to engage with those professionals who inhabit the same spaces as we do (e.g., Sommerbeck, Chapter 8, this volume), winning their respect on the way through. Rather than remain isolated, person-centred practitioners can begin to see themselves as part of the wider enterprise of positive psychology (Joseph and Linley, 2004; Joseph and Linley, 2005).

Within this volume there are a number of accounts in theory, practice and research of this process of engagement and rapprochement. We need also to note the danger that besets the European arena, that so marked out the 2003 Egmond Conference of the World Association for Person-Centered and Experiential Psychotherapies. There are some practitioners who believe that differential diagnosis should and can lead to differential, technically orientated treatment plans, and thus even the manualisation of therapy. In this, critics say that they simply aspire to take on the medical model values and compete for resources with other technically orientated therapies. There is, however, a crucial debate to be had here. Many of the voices in this book would identify with classical, Client-Centred Therapy (Stephen Joseph being one), while others (Richard Worsley, for example) would place a greater emphasis on process-orientation, but still remain true to the core aspirations of the person-centred movement.

ONLY THE BEGINNING OF DIALOGUE AND DISCOURSE

'Positive Psychology' is an umbrella term that provides a home for those who seek to move away from the subordination of psychological theory and practice to medical-model, reductionist thinking. Its values and presuppositions are very close indeed to those of the person-centred movement. Yet, bizarrely, each discipline seems to exist in woeful ignorance of the other. Beyond mere ignorance, there is sometimes a real hostility and lack of professional respect between counsellors, psychologists and psychiatrists, based only in part upon the relation to the medical model, and often upon professional insecurity and consequent jealousy.

Dialogue begins at a personal level, and is based upon not only an empathic understanding of each others' initial frames of reference and ability to be honest about difference, but also an ability to learn from each other. This volume witnesses to the power of dialogue in changing and humanising institutions, the need to remain passionate but open about our values, and the need to unsettle ourselves enough to encounter others.

Each of the chapters in this volume speaks for itself, and needs no summary. We as editors have learned much in wrestling with the issues raised by the many distinguished authors who have contributed. However a number of issues have emerged which go beyond any individual contribution. The selection of these is personal, but does contribute to further debate.

The first issue is language. The inclusion of the term psychopathology in the title of the book was for some a matter of controversy. Perhaps person-centred people do not use such words. We certainly reject a range of meanings for this word. However, the inauguration of any dialogue involves the taking on board at some level of the language of other people and other schools. It is enough that we know that some psychologists and psychiatrists, not to mention counsellors from other approaches, regard the ability to talk intelligently about psychopathology as a mark of professional competence. They are not wholly wrong. Rather than keep our vocabulary in some strange way pure, the aim of dialogue is surely to engage within a semantic field so as to establish a respectful critique of each other's viewpoints. Thus, there is within the dialogues that happen in daily life in many settings a need to talk about psychopathology from the perspectives of Person-Centred Therapy and of Positive Psychology.

Language is just one iconic example of a larger question. How do we engage? Pete Sanders makes a powerful plea for principled opposition to the medical model. It would seem that others disagree. Lisbeth Sommerbeck uses the wave-particle duality to describe her daily relating to colleagues, some of whom are clearly working within the medical model. Margaret Warner, while not relying heavily upon a conventional language of psychopathology, generates her own set of concepts. Do these mimic medical model language in a way that is unhelpful? There is an important debate here—already begun between the three people mentioned. Connected to it is Dion Van Werde's observation that his ward is only thirty per cent person-centred, but that is enough to leaven the lump. The debate now begun will continue in print and at conferences where protagonists debate face-to-face. Such encounters sharpen our minds wonderfully.

353

Our commitment has been to a growing encounter and understanding between psychologists, psychiatrists and counsellors, and in particular between the person-centred counselling movement and the positive psychology movement. When and how will these encounters be carried on? We would encourage participation of the person-centred community at positive psychology events, and vice versa, in order to develop dialogue between the two movements.

Returning to the medical model, it is of practical and theoretical importance that nobody misunderstands what precisely is being objected to. There is no plea that talking therapies are omnicompetent (see, for example, Knibbs and Moran, Chapter 17, this volume, on the biological basis of phenomena which fall on the autism spectrum). The Person-Centred Approach is not opposed in principle to drug-therapy, nor as we have seen is it anti-scientific.

For too long the person-centred movement has been associated with an anti-scientific stance in some people's minds, but we stress that person-centred theory is not unscientific. Person-centred theory remains strongly grounded in the work of Rogers (1959). This was Rogers' most developed theoretical work and it provides empirically testable hypotheses. The person-centred model lends itself to science.

Indeed, person-centred practitioners may be surprised that there is already a wealth of scientific positive psychological research that is consistent with the person-centred model that they can turn to immediately in beginning to argue their corner. For example, the extensive work by Ryan, Deci, and their colleagues on self-determination theory will be of interest to person-centred practitioners and theorists (see, for example, Deci and Vansteenkiste, 2004; Ryan and Deci, 2000, 2002) as well as the work by Sheldon, Kasser and their colleagues on the organismic valuing process, goals and self-concordance (see for example Sheldon, Arndt, and Houser-Marko, 2003; Sheldon and Elliot, 1999; Sheldon and Kasser, 2001). The person-centred movement can benefit from the existing empirical research in positive psychology in making a case for itself as an evidence-based approach.

In objecting to the medical model, we set our faces against treating psychological problems as if they were physical illnesses when they are not. But sometimes peoples' problems in living may have their root in biology, we don't deny that. But distress, as Bentall (2004) argues magnificently, is not a disease. That is simply the wrong intellectual model with which to describe it—a position echoed by Sanders (Chapter 3 this volume). However, there will be organic components of distress, and for some people the use of medication may be most helpful. Our plea is not for a simplistic psychopathology, but for one that is trans-theoretical, and has the complexity to take into account both the interpersonal and the organic. We think that distress more often has an interpersonal aetiology and that the Client-Centred Approach is able to speak to a wider range of human suffering than many professionals in psychology and psychiatry recognise.

Behind this lies an issue in the philosophy of mind. The relationship between mind as subjective experience and brain-as-thing is transitive. A sound theory of psychopathology will do justice to all elements, and so will be as complex and sophisticated as the underlying mind-brain problem in philosophy.

Finally, there is a thread which can be felt within so many of the chapters. To work with people, and especially those who exhibit fragile process, is both moving and personally very demanding. It has long been part of the discipline of the counselling profession to monitor one's own functionality both through supervision and through continuing personal and professional development. Those professionals who work with human distress by objectifying and reducing it may characteristically fail to spot within themselves the need to pay attention to the personal impact of encounter. It has been Richard Worsley's experience that the resourcefulness of the Person-Centred Approach has unfolded to him gradually. Over time, he has discovered how to work with a variety of presenting issues, some of which are far more stressful than others. We hope that this volume encourages others on the same journey.

A question is raised for trainers. As the trainee counsellor becomes proficient in a new and challenging way of being with people, it will take time and growth before the full range of effectiveness of the approach becomes manifest. Yet, even in settings in which clients are assessed, it is not possible to protect trainees from the most demanding clients. How within training is this complex pattern of personal and professional development to be managed? Knowledge is useful in a limited way. Learning is a deeper and more experiential process than knowledge implies. Counsellors, psychologists and psychiatrists amongst others need to discover, slowly or swiftly, the way to be with challenging clients. Trainers and supervisors can support this process. They can trust the counsellor if she is given space to find non-judgemental support. In the end, no course can 'do' psychopathology technically, methodically, for the human spirit is more resourceful and unpredictable than that.

A WAY OF (WELL-)BEING OF DECEPTIVE SIMPLICITY

The medical model is defective in that it reduces human distress to mere illness. Yet, those experiences which attract the label of depression or eating disorder or psychosis, for example, are both more existentially painful and more laden with meaning than is a disease. The medical model at worst disables and fragments.

By contrast, the person-centred model, in its many aspects, and the work of positive psychology, are holistic. This way of thinking and being is rooted in biology. The faith I have in my self and in my organismic valuing process is rooted in my fleshiness. It is social because it sets the plural self within its systemic context, and recognises the powerful influence of the social environment as a facilitator or impediment to the actualisation tendency. It is psychological, in that it attributes to behaviour the capacity for meaning, without needing to deny organic malfunction in some aspects of distress. Above all it is humanising.

Acknowledgement: Grateful thanks to Alex Linley for his comments on this chapter.

REFERENCES

Barrett-Lennard, GT (1998) *Carl Rogers' Helping System: Journey and substance*. London: Sage.

Bentall, RP (2004) *Madness Explained: Psychosis and human nature*. Harmondsworth: Penguin.

Deci, EL and Vansteenkiste, M (2004) Self-determination theory and basic need satisfaction: Understanding human development in positive psychology. *Ricerchedi di psicologia: Special issue in positive psychology, 27*, 23–40.

Ford, JG (1991) Rogerian self-actualization: A clarification of meaning. *Journal of Humanistic Psychology, 31*, 101–11.

Joseph, S (2003) Client-centred psychotherapy: why the client knows best. *The Psychologist, 16*, 304–7.

Joseph, S and Linley, PA (2004) Positive therapy: a positive psychological theory of therapeutic practice. In PA Linley and S Joseph (eds) *Positive Psychology in Practice* (pp. 354–68). New York: John Wiley.

Joseph, S and Linley, PA (2005) Positive psychological approaches to therapy. *Counselling and Psychotherapy Research, 5*, 5–10.

Linley, PA and Joseph, S (2004a) Applied positive psychology: a new perspective for professional practice. In PA Linley and S Joseph (eds) *Positive Psychology in Practice* (pp. 3–12). New York: John Wiley.

Linley, PA and Joseph, S (2004b) Toward a theoretical foundation for positive psychology in practice. In PA Linley and S Joseph (eds) *Positive Psychology in Practice* (pp. 713–31). New York: John Wiley.

Linley, PA, Joseph, S and Boniwell, I (eds) (2003) In a positive light. *The Psychologist, 16*, 126. (Special Issue on Positive Psychology).

Maddux, JE (2002) Stopping the 'madness': Positive psychology and the deconstruction of the illness ideology and the DSM. In CR Snyder and SJ Lopez (eds) *Handbook of Positive Psychology* (pp. 13–25). New York: Oxford University Press.

Maddux, JE, Snyder, CR and Lopez, SJ (2004) Toward a positive clinical psychology: Deconstructing the illness ideology and constructing an ideology of human strengths and potential. In PA Linley and S Joseph (eds) *Positive Psychology in Practice* (pp. 320–34). New York: John Wiley.

Mearns, D and Thorne, B (1999) *Person-Centered Counselling in Action* (2nd ed). London: Sage.

Newnes, C, Holmes, G and Dunn, C (1999) *This is Madness: A critical look at psychiatry and the future of mental health services*. Ross-on-Wye: PCCS Books.

Prouty, G, Van Werde, D and Pörtner, M (2002) *Pre-Therapy: Reaching contact-impaired clients*. Ross-on-Wye: PCCS Books.

Read, J, Mosher, LR and Bentall, RP (2004) *Models of Madness: Psychological, social and biological approaches to schizophrenia*. Hove and New York: Brunner Routledge.

Rogers, CR (1959) A theory of therapy, personality, and interpersonal relationships as developed in the client-centered framework. In S Koch (ed) *Psychology: A study of a science, Vol. 3: Formulations of the person and the social context* (pp. 184–256). New York: McGraw-Hill.

Rogers, CR (1961) *On Becoming a Person*. Boston, MA: Houghton Mifflin.

Rogers, CR (1969) *Freedom to Learn*. Columbus, OH: Merrill.

Ryan, RM and Deci, EL (2000) Self-determination theory and the facilitation of intrinsic motivation, social development and well-being. *American Psychologist, 55*, 68–78.

Ryan, RM and Deci, EL (2002) An overview of self-determination theory: An organismic dialectical perspective. In EL Deci and RM Ryan (eds) *Handbook of Self-Determination Research* (pp. 3–33). Rochester, NY: University of Rochester Press.

Seligman, MEP (2003) Positive psychology: Fundamental assumptions. *The Psychologist, 16,* 126–7.

Seligman, MEP and Csikszentmihalyi, M (2000) Positive psychology: An introduction. *American Psychologist, 55,* 5–14.

Sheldon, KM and Elliot, AJ (1999) Goal striving, need satisfaction, and longitudinal well-being: The self-concordance model. *Journal of Personality and Social Psychology, 76,* 482–97.

Sheldon, KM and Kasser, T (2001) Goals, congruence, and positive well-being: New empirical support for humanistic theories. *Journal of Humanistic Psychology, 41,* 30–50.

Sheldon, KM, Arndt, J and Houser-Marko, L (2003) In search of the organismic valuing process: The human tendency to move towards beneficial goal choices. *Journal of Personality, 71,* 835–86.

Worsley, R (2001) *Process Work in Person-Centred Therapy.* Basingstoke: Palgrave.

CONTRIBUTORS

Jerold D. Bozarth, PhD, learned client-centered therapy from working with chronic psychotic, hospitalized clients. He has published over 300 articles and book chapters and three books, and has consulted with person-centered training programs in Austria, Brazil, Czech Republic, England, Portugal and Slovakia. He is Professor Emeritus of the University of Georgia and a member of the Golden Pantry Coffee Club.

Barbara Temaner Brodley, PhD, is an adjunct professor at the Illinois School of Professional Psychology (Argosy University) and has a private practice of client-centered therapy. She received her doctorate in clinical psychology at the University of Chicago where she was on the staff of the Counseling Center, founded by Carl Rogers. She has published many articles that express her interest in preserving recognition of non-directive Client-Centered Therapy as a continuing form of effective psychotherapy.

Elaine Catterall has worked as a counsellor since 1999 at a local youth counselling service. She is accredited with BACP and has a small private practice. She became actively involved in the voluntary support network for postnatal depression in 1995, offering individual and group support to women and their families as well as being involved in training and education awareness initiatives. More recently she has also worked as a facilitator of groups for new mothers exploring the experience of motherhood.

Catherine Clarke has a nursing background and is currently a practising podiatrist. She became intrigued with Prouty's Pre-Therapy on a PCA diploma course whilst pursuing her long-standing interest in psychology. Her fascination later turned into reality when she was able to help her psychotic son using Pre-Therapy. She is now committed to raising awareness of Prouty's work and her dream is to have Pre-Therapy and its values incorporated into Mental Health Services throughout the UK.

Mick Cooper is a Senior Lecturer in Counselling at the University of Strathclyde and a UKCP-registered psychotherapist, whose practice is informed by person-centred, existential, interpersonal and postmodern ideas. Mick has recently co-authored, with Dave Mearns, *Working at Relational Depth in Counselling and Psychotherapy* (Sage, 2005), is author of *Existential Therapies* (Sage, 2003) and has written several papers and chapters on person-centred, existential and self-pluralistic approaches to therapy. Mick lives in Glasgow with his partner and three daughters.

Jan Hawkins is a person-centred practitioner, supervisor and freelance trainer. In 1994 Jan created and co-facilitated a diploma course in Counselling Survivors of Childhood Abuse, the first initiative of its kind in Europe. For the past five years, through the Foundation for the Developing Person, Jan has continued to run accredited (Middlesex University) post-counselling training Diploma courses with a conviction that experiential learning is an imperative for developing empathy as well as skills (www.thefdp.demon.co.uk).

Stephen Joseph obtained his PhD from the Institute of Psychiatry, London, and later trained as a person-centred therapist at the Metanoia Institute, London. Stephen is currently at the University of Warwick, where he is a Reader in Psychology, with teaching duties on the clinical psychology programme. His research interests are in understanding how people cope with trauma and adversity and more broadly in the Person-Centred Approach and positive psychology applications. Stephen also has a part-time private psychotherapy practice specialising in Client-Centred Therapy and supervision.

Jacky Knibbs is a Consultant Clinical Psychologist. She helped set up the Child Mental Health (CAMHS) Team in South Warwickshire, and has a strong commitment to cross-agency collaborative working. Her current clinical work is mostly with youngsters (pre-school and school-aged children) with complex developmental presentations (e.g. Autism Spectrum). Other clinical interests include finding constructive ways forward with young people who, when they grow up, might be described as having 'personality disorders'.

Leslie A. McCulloch, PhD, is an assistant professor at the State University of New York College at Brockport. She has taught a variety of courses during her academic career including individual counseling, group counseling, advanced groups, testing, supervision, and internship. Dr McCulloch's clinical experience spans three decades and includes individual and group counseling in institutional, agency, and private practice settings. Dr McCulloch is a Nationally Certified Counselor, an Approved Clinical Supervisor, and an American Red Cross Disaster Mental Health Service provider.

Heather Moran is a Consultant Clinical Psychologist working in Coventry CAMHS. She is involved in the assessment and diagnosis of children with Autistic Spectrum Disorder. She also works as part of a multidisciplinary team to support young people and their families after a diagnosis. Her clinical interests include the psychological impact of early and ongoing traumatic life experiences and developing approaches to improve understanding of family relationships.

Noriko Motomasa, PsyD received her doctoral degree in clinical psychology with the minor in client-centered and experiential therapy at the Illinois School of Professional Psychology. She completed research on client-centered couple and family therapy with Dr Barbara T. Brodley as her chair. She received her clinical training at the Chicago

Counseling and Psychotherapy Center. She is currently in clinical practice and works as the archivist for the Chicago Counseling Center.

Marlis Pörtner, psychologist, trained as a person-centred psychotherapist in Switzerland and the US. Since 1983 she has worked in private practice, with people with special needs among her clients. In addition she is a consultant and trainer of staff members of social organisations in Switzerland, Germany and Austria. In her books, published in German and several other languages, she has developed specific person-centred concepts for different professional fields.

Gillian Proctor is a clinical psychologist working as part of North Bradford Primary Care Trust's mental health team. She is an honorary research fellow with the Centre for Citizenship and Community Mental Health at the University of Bradford. Her particular interests are power, ethics and oppression in relation to clinical practice, mental health systems, therapy and research. She has authored several articles on these subjects a book *The Dynamics of Power in Counselling and Psychotherapy: Ethics, politics and practice* (PCCS Books, 2002). She recently co-edited *Encountering Feminism: Intersections of feminism and the person-centred approach* (PCCS Books, 2004), and also co-edited a special issue of *Asylum* in 2004 on women and the diagnosis of Borderline Personality Disorder.

Lisbeth Sommerbeck, has an MSc from the University of Copenhagen and is accredited as a specialist in psychotherapy and supervision by the Danish Psychological Association. She was initiator of the founding of the Danish Carl Rogers Forum in 2002. Since 1974 she has been employed in Dianalund Psychiatric Hospital. Her special interest is in the application of the Person-Centred Approach with staff and inmates in the 'backyards' of psychiatry. She is author of articles on the non-directive attitude in Client-Centred Therapy and on the 'Wisconsin Project', as well as of a book on Client-Centred Therapy in psychiatric contexts.

Pete Sanders retired from practice after more than 25 years as a counsellor, trainer and supervisor. He is now a director of PCCS Books. He continues to have an interest in mental health issues and following the developing theory and practice of client-centred therapy.

Peter F. Schmid, Univ.Doz. HSProf. Mag. Dr., is Associate Professor at the University of Graz; faculty member of Saybrook Graduate School and Research Center; person-centered psychotherapist; founder of person-centered training in Austria; co-director of the Academy for Counseling and Psychotherapy ('Institute for Person-Centered Studies— IPS'), Vienna; Board Member of the PCE World Association (WAPCEPC) and the European Network (NEAPCEPC); author and co-author of 14 books and numerous publications about the foundations of PCT.

Margaret Warner, PhD, is a client-centered teacher and theorist who has written extensively about Client-Centered Therapy with clients with more serious psychological disorders and on client-centered theory as it relates to other disciplines in clinical psychology and the behavioral sciences. She trained in Client-Centered Therapy at the Chicago Counseling Center and has a doctorate in Behavioral Sciences from the University of Chicago, and is currently a Professor at the Illinois School of Professional Psychology. With other faculty at the Illinois School she is developing a Client-Centered and Experiential Minor and Certificate. She is also working with a group to develop a diversity-oriented person-centered training site called Nia II Inc.

Paul Wilkins says: I am a person-centred academic, therapist and supervisor with an interest in collaborative approaches to research and how the person-centred paradigm applies not only to psychotherapy but ways of being in relationship to the world. I once headed a local authority 'mental health' team and besides 'work', my interests include good food, walking, music and the wild places of the planet.

Richard Worsley says: I have worked for a number of years as a person-centred counsellor, supervisor and trainer. I am also an Anglican priest. I have particular interests in process in therapy, in spirituality, in philosophy and therapy, and in therapeutic groups. I work at the University of Warwick as a staff and student counsellor. In experiencing high-volume work with people with a wide range of presenting distress, I am even more convinced that people are unique, and process their experience in unique and creative ways.

Dion Van Werde is a psychologist with a postgraduate specialisation in Client-Centred/ Experiential Psychotherapy (Katholieke Universiteit Leuven). He is co-ordinator of the Pre-Therapy International Network, based at Psychiatrisch Ziekenhuis St-Camillus, Gent, Belgium, where he translated Prouty's Pre-Therapy into a ward model in residential care for people diagnosed as psychotic. He is a board member of the Belgian League for Schizophrenia and of the Netherlands–Flanders chapter of ISPS (the International Society for the Psychological Treatments of the Schizophrenias and other Psychoses).

INDEX

PCCS Books

www.pccs-books.co.uk

• browse by subject and author •

• pre-publication offers •

• discounts on all orders •

• free p&p in the UK •

• low cost shipping worldwide •